Bad Company
and Burnt Powder

"Bad Company," 24" × 36" oil on canvas (2011) by Donald M. Yena

Bad Company
and Burnt Powder

*Justice and Injustice in the
Old Southwest*

Bob Alexander
*Number 13 in the Frances B. Vick Series
University of North Texas Press
Denton, Texas*

Printed in the United States of America.

10 9 8 7 6 5 4 3 2 1

Permissions:
University of North Texas Press
1155 Union Circle #311336
Denton, TX 76203-5017

The paper used in this book meets the minimum requirements of the American National Standard for Permanence of Paper for Printed Library Materials, z39.48.1984. Binding materials have been chosen for durability.

Library of Congress Cataloging-in-Publication Data

Alexander, Bob (James R.), author.
    Bad company and burnt powder : justice and injustice in the Old Southwest / Bob Alexander. — Edition: First.
        pages cm — (Number 13 in the Frances B. Vick series)
    Summary: This book is a portrait of twelve lawmen or criminals or of famous events in the American Southwest in the late 1800s to the early 1900s. The events take place in Arizona Territory, Texas, or New Mexico Territory.—Adapted from the ECIP Data View Summary.
    Includes bibliographical references and index.
    ISBN 978-1-57441-566-7 (cloth : alk. paper) — ISBN 978-1-57441-580-3 (ebook)
    1. Southwestern States—History—19th century. 2. Southwestern States—History—20th century. 3. Crime—Southwestern States—History—19th century. 4. Crime—Southwestern States—History—20th century. 5. Law enforcement—Southwestern States—History—19th century. 6. Law enforcement—Southwestern States—History—20th century. 7. Frontier and pioneer life—Southwestern States. I. Title. II. Series: Frances B. Vick series ; no. 13.
    F786.A44 2014
    976.03—dc23
                                    2014015280

Bad Company and Burnt Powder: Justice and Injustice in the Old Southwest is Number 13 in the Frances B. Vick Series

The electronic edition of this book was made possible by the support of the Vick Family Foundation.

Contents

Preface and Acknowledgments

If hard truths be told about taming the Old West, it would not be the gunfighter or desperado or lawman earning the lion's share of credit—or notice. No, that crown would go to Mothers. True, history does bear witness that sometimes women did ear back hammers on long-barreled Colt's six-shooters or shouldered a Winchester, letting the bullets fly: Standing by their man or standing lonesome, afraid—and all alone. Carelessly challenging the innate ferocity of a lioness protecting her cubs or a pioneering mama defending her children in but a heartbeat could prove folly. Women can be warriors. Analytically speaking, however, the weight of the ladies' part in stabilizing the Wild West is not measured with episodic reexaminations of gunplay or the times they marched in front of the dugout dressed in men's clothing with a broom in hand—hoping it would look like a rifle to Indians lurking in the distance. Their shared donation to changing the face of America's West transcended those type goings-on.

Mothers wanted and expected—and demanded—stability and safeness for their children. There was no negotiating. Classrooms and churches were at the top of their grand scheme. Educated children had bright futures. Morals instilled at Sunday School were praiseworthy. Reading, writing, and arithmetic were important but teachers and preachers reinforced what kiddos were supposed to be taught at home: Good manners and good citizenship. Compromising on those principles was beyond the realm of argument. Such haggling would have simply been inappropriate and utterly worthless. God and grandma knew best! The town's flashy whores and leeching gamblers and unruly hard drinkers best know their assigned territory—and not dare cross a line. So, on the widespread blueprint of conquering hazard and hardship it was plucky women who really evened the score, then decimated their enemies of uncivilized behavior and unchecked self-indulgence. Women won the West.

That said: There is a downside. Most of the everyday drudgery women suffered wasn't newsworthy then or thrilling for today's marketplace. Childbirth was laborious and painful at anytime, and really could prove heavy-going if an unborn baby breached. Many were days a wife and mother spent bent over the washtub or burned her fingers removing cornbread from the woodstove. Many are the nights she lost sleep, bleary-eyed nursing a sick youngster—or husband. And sometimes it seemed if God had slapped her square across the brow, forevermore taking an innocent child from the comfort of her bosom and the reassurance of her undying love. With needle and thread and sore fingers she tirelessly mended and made clothing. She swept. She scrubbed. She settled squabbles. She scrimped pennies. She quieted her man's passionate fires while children slept—or pretended to. She socialized sporadically. And she changed dirty diapers relentlessly, day in and day out, from the crack of dawn until bedtime. Potty training while racing for an outhouse is chancy—not fun. To an outside world her day by day routine was mundane: Hardly worth writing about.

The workaday life of most Western men was not too newsy either. The vast majority of fellows were but ordinary persons, like barbers or blacksmiths or bakers or butchers or bankers— just regular hard-working folks. Off to a jobsite in the early morning—back to home most evenings. No high drama, no breathtaking thrills. If a regular guy steered clear of the barrooms and bordellos and the professional parasitical crowd there was little need to worry about embroilment in some idiotic gunplay. Those working men, too, were lynchpins in settling the American West, but just like their counterparts and soul-mates there wasn't much to capture the attention of journalists then—or historians later. It would take blood and thunder to do that.

Old West narratives—fiction and nonfiction—spin on an axis of conflict. Customarily the novelist's protagonist will reign supreme: Clearly dominating their adversaries by means of superior smarts and superior skills—most likely killing a few despicable desperadoes along the way. Needless to say these gallant heroes take life solely as last resort and only in self-defense. Such makes for a clean story.

Conversely, nonfiction researchers and writers and professorial thinkers have a differing take—theoretically just letting the chips fall where they may. But even those smart folks are wholly cognizant there is no real public appetite for a cold and bland menu of humdrum history. The wide-ranging readership—many discerning academics included—want true-life chronicles served steaming hot, liberally peppered with raw meat violence and basted with bloodshed. Sometimes an occasional scholar will deny it, but usually one only has to follow his/her storyline shortly before discovering the lynched freedman or the mercilessly gunned down *Tejano* or the Texas Ranger who shot first and asked questions later, or the Mexican bandit who breached the border with murder in his heart and blood on his hands. Injudiciously it seems, in certain quarters the real discord between an Anglo lawman and an Anglo badman is viewed with a jaundiced eye: It doesn't compute as bona fide history, worthwhile history; those asinine guys offing each other. But their stories are instructive too—valuably so. There really is a common thread. No matter the learned writer's earned credentials—in most cases—the bottom of their Old West story typically rests across the fulcrum of fighting—usually with guns. In and of itself that particular element does not make for a substandard corollary. True six-shooter struggles for superiority are a piece of legit history. Contemplatively probing those episodes absent preconception removes them from the stale category of just another titillating shoot-'em-up and onto the mountaintop of sober sociological reflection.

In this regard it is important to make note of a critical fact—and a fact it is. A career peace officer during the Wild West era—or even today—might have proficiently carried out 1000 safe arrests never seeing his/her name in newsprint. When things go right, there's zilch to write about. It is when conditions go haywire—usually in but a fractional second—that the journalists and tabloid scribblers start cranking the presses of awareness—and criticism and theoretical armchair second-guessing. One twenty-first century impact of the Old West heritage can readily be detected by noting an everyday saying in the jargon of today's lawmen. When retelling of a spine-tingling incident to fellow officers the comments are typically predicated with an alert: "Then, it turned Western."

Looking in on frontier-timeframe crime and criminals and law enforcers—even from afar—is constructive. Gauging a particular community's way of thinking vis-à-vis its remedies directed at curing society's evils is enlightening. It provides a window into an area's and era's outlook: What was tolerable and what was not. As mentioned in *Riding Lucifer's Line: Ranger Deaths along the Texas/Mexico Border* two distinct classifications of criminality come into play—way back when—and even today. For most of the world's societies specific acts are fundamentally immoral and consequently outlawed. Offenses such as murder and rape and robbery are near universally condemned. These crimes are *malum in se*, wrong in themselves. Other violations fall into the malleable category of *malum prohibitum*. These decrees are designed to prohibit or regulate certain types of behavior—but more often than not the state legislature's or city council's wisdom is subject to fervent and often bitter debate. As a rule these statutes are thought too churchy by one crowd and not near strict enough by the opposing faction. *Malum prohibitum* are the infractions prohibiting—in some form or fashion—such dubious deeds as gambling or drinking or barrooms staying open too late on Saturday and opening too soon on Sunday: Mix in prohibitions about prostitution and pornography and packing pistols in public, or a ban about making a right turn on red at the stoplight, etc. In plain talk: What's good for the goose in one burg may not be good for the gander in a neighboring town or across the state line. Time and place are relevant. Life and laws are not static—they change. It's a rich environment for sociological study, watching law enforcing transition from heady days of an Old West epoch to modern age professionalism.

From those days to this, the most powerful weapon in any lawman's toolkit is not his/her handgun or shotgun or any other implement made of metal or plastic or a combination thereof, those deadly utensils fully charged with bullets or buckshot or disabling perfume in a spray can. The most potent component is "Discretion"—a simple term often misunderstood in the context of policing. Discretion is not the actual decision, but the lawful handed-over authority to make *the* decision. Judgment—good or bad—is the lawman's actual implementation and execution of that decision. Communities—federal, state, and local—grant their peace keepers legal authority by legislative and/or administrative measures. They entrust specific parts of the decision-making process to the officer, the Discretion to act—or not act, to enforce a law with strictness or factor in any mitigating rationales. As a plain practical matter it boils down this way: A peace officer is awarded the Discretion to inquire, stop, detain, interview and/or interrogate, issue warnings or arrest someone—and he/she has the endorsed Discretion to choose just how to enforce which law and just how much force is reasonable or appropriate in proportion to the circumstances needed to accomplishment that end. How he/she exercises that Discretion is Judgment. Generally that is where the rub comes in. If that Judgment was/is flawed, oppressive, excessive, or just downright inappropriate there is a price to pay—sometimes a high price! Hardly ever questioned is a peace officer's officially designated authority—the Discretion—to make such fundamental decisions. Common—almost routine—are the queries and litigation and disciplinary actions resultant of how that Discretion was actually applied—the Judgment.

Carrying such a premise forward is not unfeasible for framing hard truths about nuanced fair and square dealing within the realm of private citizens choosing to be law abiding. A would-be criminal has the Discretion—a personal not legal choice—to break or not break the law. How and when he/she effects that option is Judgment. Behaving is good Judgment. Knowingly and willfully crossing legality's line is a case of poor Judgment. As would be resisting arrest and assaulting an officer—not smart—poor Judgment without a doubt. Ascertaining correct pictures of law enforcing and criminal justice issues, then, may best be capitalized on by studying not just good guys, but the bad ones as well.

Although generalized statements are ripe for dissection it's not unfitting at this juncture to make one. A handy conduit for watching—and learning from—that ever evolving law enforcing transition and the decisions those folks made is by peeking in on the real stories of real people. Admittedly, digressing from the strictures imposed by broad-spectrum overviews and focusing on specific episodes and personalities is not an all-inclusive methodology. Nor should it be. Wide-ranging abstract appraisals do contribute appreciably for an understanding of the American system of criminal justice: Particularly within a prescribed framework of the U.S. Constitution's Bill of Rights. On the other hand, distilling that awareness through the coils of down-to-earth story telling is meaningful, too. Much may be drawn by individualizing the focal point to an actual true-life scenario. Savoring the real stuff is palatable. And, candidly, for most folks it's the most appealing method of sprinkling history atop their diet of reading material. Aside from the intention of trying to tell—hopefully—attention-grabbing Wild West stories, an underlying theme of *Bad Company and Burnt Powder* is providing a platform for the reader to conceptualize: To earnestly and thoughtfully look past the busting of a cap and the mopping up of blood.

Deliberately this treatment is not one-sided with sagas spotlighting only lawmen or just desperadoes. Rather it is an amalgamation, a focused mixture. To be unconditionally candid, thematically *Bad Company and Burnt Powder* is a true bloodletting Old West nonfiction narrative, but its overall outlook is multi-dimensional, consciously so. Welding links in the storyline's chain with tales of good men and bad men and questionable men explicitly strengthens the honing of a better—or more practical—insight into the everyday lives of crime-fighters and criminals, as well as the sociological and geographical arenas they contested in. This is not a Texas Ranger book, although there are chapters about more than one Ranger. Likewise the compilation is not principally an Outlaw book, albeit several lawbreakers earned their special carve outs. Nor is it a volume solely focused on extralegal justice and vigilantes—or blood feuds—even though those elements are the core of particular chapters. Standing alone the unconnected sections chronicle exhilarating tales of the Old West, but there is sensible relevance to each—and with each a message broadening the familiarity of society's imposition of justice: Or miscarriages of justice. The dozen chapters herein, taken in the aggregate and thoughtfully dissected will open up—with any luck—the readers' awareness about enforcing and breaking laws during the generically dubbed Wild West era. Not just a few of those inflexible messaging implications reach into the twenty-first century with consequence.

Within these pages the reader will meet a nineteen-year-old Texas Ranger figuratively dying to shoot his gun. He even admits to hunting hard for adventure—just for the sake of adventure. On the one hand he is triumphant. He does get to shoot guns at people. On the other he soon realized what he thought was a bargain, in reality exacted a steep price. One he opted not to pay.

A career change was imminent. His enlightenment is educational: The message implicitly clear.

There is also the graphic tale of an entrepreneurial cowman—an old school cowman—who quite literally shut down illicit traffic in stolen livestock that had existed for years and years on the Llano Estacado. He was tough. He was salty. He had no truck with damned cow-thieves or sympathy for any mealy-mouthed politicians. He cleaned house, maybe not any too nicely, but unarguably successful he was—so said most Texans and so said a lauding correspondent for the faraway *New York Evening Post*. Was his methodology commendable or censurable?

For a time the bloodlines of a particular family dominated the doings in the southern stretch of a Central Texas county, one bordering the Brazos River. The geographical landscape was rich farmland—Plantation Country—and rich with insensitivity. From more than one camp tribal mentality prospered. Feuds and funerals flourished. Nightriders flaunted martial supremacy. Long overdue the acrimonious slate was at last wiped clean: A fresh beginning for peacefulness on the horizon. At what dear cost? A hardened set of five six-shooting brothers had been wiped out—fatally—wisps of blue smoke from the burnt powder enveloping their caskets. Did their tragic deaths move the barometer of a community's intolerance even one degree to the plus side? Or, was a man, a real man, regardless of the cost obliged to wheedle out revenge and settle the hash of supposed and/or bona fide foes with six-gun conclusiveness?

There is the story of a stalwart deputy sheriff and penal farm administrator foully murdered. Aside from the horrors of the killing the reader is proffered insight about America's functional and sometimes dysfunctional criminal justice system. A front row seat in the standing-room only courtroom is helpful in harvesting the yield of a zealous—maybe overzealous—district attorney. Were his trial tactics fair? Was the district judge impartial? Or, did public sympathy for the deceased cloud what he allowed jurors to know? Was a deal made with the Devil—or perhaps the defendant's brother? Did strategic shenanigans backfire? Was justice served?

Then there is the tale of a fugitive—an accomplished fugitive, an unbeaten fugitive. Since the offender's name was known, coupled with the fact there were witnesses to the murder of a Texas peace officer, one would think the case closed quickly: Society throwing the book—the law book—at him. Would he be salted away in prison to never see the light of day or would the merciless yahoo be hanged by the neck till dead, dead, dead? Texas Rangers couldn't find him. County sheriffs wouldn't hold him. Slipping through bounty hunter's hands he hit Owlhoot Trail.

On the High Plains he would prove bad company for an undomesticated brute beating his wife. How could a much wanted man bounce throughout Texas, Arkansas, Indian Territory, Colorado, New Mexico Territory and—even distant California? Was he more or less hiding in plain sight? Did compatible cow country cohorts, thumbing their noses at law-dogs wittingly cover his scent? Was the justice system broken, in shambles? Or, did he have friends in high places—say, a well respected and connected brother-in-law? Could it have been both?

Another fellow on the dodge wasn't so lucky. He wasn't too polite and he wasn't too likeable. His alleged Texas crimes were many, his courtroom convictions real. His crafty jailbreak, well, if not spectacular, it was successful. His shooting at a Lone Star sheriff was a misfire. The scribbling in a daily diary—detailing his flight from Texas flatlands through the Rocky Mountain Country and into the state of Wyoming was weird for a bad guy, but a luminous gem for latter day Old West chroniclers fortunate enough to peruse its pages. But it is a story with an ending fitting for a flitting jailbird. Conditions on that southern Wyoming borderline changed ever so quickly and, truly, the state of affairs turned "Western." Two peas in a pod had met. Both were familiar with jailhouses—from behind bars looking out. On this day though, one sported a badge and carried a Colt's .41 six-shooter. The other had a gun or two, but not Mr. Right or Lady Luck at his side. There is a hard truth: Second place is a loser—during a gunfight.

An altogether different man, a gentleman, made his mark in Texas history not as a loser—not even in gunfights—but a winner, physically, and in eyes of the public as well. In the beginnings he was a horseback lawman. He survived shootouts with desperate fence cutters and inebriated idiots. Quite rewardingly he chased murderous and/or thieving outlaws—and caught them: Now and again even red-handed. Traveling vast distances he tracked and recovered stolen livestock, returning same to appreciative owners.

The seizure of a vial of nitroglycerin and the arrests of two night-time safe burglars was a humdinger—a real newsmaker. He was a transitional peace officer, sitting tall in the saddle or tall behind a sputtering Ford's steering wheel. Sandwiched between law enforcing gigs he was a first-rate rancher, as well as a wheeling and dealing big time banker. His worthy name, through the good times and the bad times, stayed unsullied—the electorate proudly putting him in office as their county sheriff—more than once. On behalf of unrehabilitated criminals he fought for hard prison time. For those deserving a second chance, he fought hard for clemency. Fairplay was his motto, a tenet worth adhering to. By any standard he was a lawman worth emulating, professionally and personally.

Another real frontier character held dear his personal sense of justice and evenhandedness. The prohibiting Biblical scriptures and the persnickety wordiness in law books was subject to interpretation—his interpretation. God may not have passed him by, but it seems Father Time had. For this hardened creature of the Old Southwest, living life within the confines of a pliable civility was critical: Living close to civilization wasn't. He was made of grit, he tolerated naught.

A political rival miscalculated, paying the highest of prices: Forfeiting votes, as well as his life. On his frontier, preparedness was the watchword. His worn leather saddle-pockets were weighted equally, the Good Book in one, a good big Colt's .45 in the other. Thus fixed he could sermonize or shoot. Or vice versa! Outlaws or officers alike were invited to sip boiling Arbuckles or drag cathead biscuits through gravy at his table: Remoteness extorted neutrality. There was God's law and man's law. Complying with the former and winking at the latter was not necessarily sinful. His vast ranch-land holdings not only took in the Diamondbacks and Sidewinders slithering on the secret side of Rattlesnake Hill, but moreover the whiskey still, too. In a desolate country inhabited by bronco Apaches and desert desperadoes—and little law—be it a shindig or funeral or sitting on the front porch, a taste of sour mash was not unseemly—even for a preacher. Perhaps foremost in his mind—even more exalted than the Almighty which he worshiped in his own way—was his family. Woe it would be for the haughty U.S. Army general that insulted his wife. Outfoxed would be hard-charging lawmen looking for his son, the one on the lam for mortally gunning down lawmen during an unwarranted Wild West extravaganza of too much booze and too many bullets. Were he given a second go, the capability of looking up at Heaven from beneath that pile of rocks covering his bones, would he have asked for forgiveness or for a chance to change anything? *¿Quién sabe?*

Do tough times always call for tough measures? Herein is the condensed biographical profile of a tenacious Texas Ranger. He was a gutsy Ranger, of that there's no doubt! He would stand his ground—not giving an inch. In a fight he was a tiger. When circumstances may have called for thoughtful mediation he was ever energetic, but sometimes cocky, ham-fisted, and mean. Were honesty and loyalty and pluck the only vital attributes of a good lawman, a good Ranger? Was such a volatile fellow's slot on the roster—for the final and definitive analysis—harming or helping the Ranger Force? Company captains had as much trouble controlling him, as he had handling his own sizzling temper. Somewhat uncharacteristically for a Ranger, he battled bad guys, but likewise he wrangled with more than one county sheriff—and even pistol whipped one. His unbreakable bitterness towards a fellow Texas Ranger was hot-blooded and unpredictable: Bosses feared sudden detonation and explosion and an uncalled for funeral. The managerial tactic of hastily transferring him to West Texas failed to tame him. Recurrently defending some of his oppressive enforcement actions was a heavy lift—for practical politicians and perturbed administrators—too heavy. It all makes for a good criminal justice story though, gloomy but meaningful and informative.

Frequently—all too often—in writings focused on lawlessness the term "organized crime" is loosely bandied about. Preconceptions and misconceptions abound. Haphazardly or purposely portraying selected individuals as kingpins is one means of juicing a story. A reasonably simple blood feud—even one of lengthy duration—for some has more pizzazz if conspiratorial subplots, warlords, and grand schemes are pitched into the mix—notwithstanding a paucity of evidence. Sometimes contrived heroes need dragons to slay: Sometimes shaky avers need red meat to exist.

Organized crime tales are toothsome. Occasionally they make the gristly truth go down easier for folks crying to unduly cast blame. In truth, few ascended the ladder from gangster to godfather. There were exceptions, though, even in an Old West setting.

Herein is the tale of a top dog. Thankfully from a historic perspective his footprints may be followed: Starting with humble and honest beginnings right through to the role of a misfit and murderer and mercenary. He proved to be an apt pupil at cunning nefariousness; clawing, shooting, bribing, and double-crossing his way into commanding a legitimate, well, an illegitimate organized crime empire as of then unequaled in the American Southwest. A little bluff and bluster and notoriety may be useful tools in upholding stature as a big-time crime boss. That said, eventually super inflated egos give way to disproportionate negative publicity and humiliating embarrassment for politicians, calling their hand and forcing them into action. This thug's undoing would not come to pass by standing toe to toe with a gunfighter lawman of large or even speciously puffed repute. Toppling this crime boss would, in the end, take all of the monetary and manpower resources a distraught governor could muster—and even then it was no easy task.

There too is another sad true tale tucked into the pages of *Bad Company and Burnt Powder*. Concocted melodrama fashioned by profit-oriented entertainment moguls continuously pits the ever stalwart Old West lawman against the dark-eyed mean-natured bad man from Bitter Creek. Such overblown prattle makes for spine-tingling episodes, to be sure. Though, in many cases the embellishment dances the reader—or viewer—right out of the theater of reality. Dynamite comes in small packages, of that there's no argument. God may have created all men, and Sam Colt may have made all men equal, as the old saw goes, but the clichéd axiom is flawed. Then or now, sometimes it isn't the grown men grabbing six-shooters and bending to inane madness. Beardless teenagers' itchy trigger-fingers can set off catastrophe just as calamitous as the scruffy ne'er-do-well with scraggly whiskers and an evil grin. Herein is the chronicle of a kindhearted lawman and family man. Contrary to contrived Wild West hoopla, he took pride in keeping his duty pistol holstered. Unruffled diplomacy, in his mind, was much preferred to exchanging blows or expending bullets that couldn't be pulled back. Did he miscalculate, undervaluing a wayward son of poverty and misfortune and prejudice? Had he thrown caution to the wind? Was his not opting to offhandedly gun down a fleeing felon, a youngster, such a commendable—but imprudent—demonstration of self-restraint: Leaving a mourning widow and sorrowful children? Or, was his number just up?

It seems fitting to wind up *Bad Company and Burnt Powder* with an inspirational story of sorts, one sketching the life story of a Wild West lawman. Not by mere chance he also happens to be baby brother of the Texas Ranger and Texas Panhandle rancher underscored in Chapter One. Dissimilar to his four male siblings, for this guy disobedience reared its ugly head during those wearisome and often difficult adolescent, teenage, and early adulthood years. That somewhere in his psyche a wild streak flourished is most likely true. To be sure his preaching daddy had sermonized, trying to set him on the straight and narrow path. Until rescued by an older brother he was idly standing at the crossroads: On the brink of choosing between persistent stupidity or enduring good sense. The tale's encouraging angle is grounded in hard reality— a pleasing truth: Unlike the leopard that cannot change its spots, this chap shed the skin of rebelliousness along the way. He signed on as a Texas Ranger and his life forevermore changed—for the better. Comparable to his two brothers with stints as Rangers, he would live to tell about gruesome gunfights with saddled-toughened *mal hombres* hellbent on killing him. He, like they, would witness and assume a key role in quite a few newsmaking Texas stories. Whereas those two Texas Ranger brothers—after time—enthusiastically cast off the daily wearing of six-shooters to engage in other means of making a constructive living, this stalwart stayed in the policing game: A fully charged Colt's six-shooter appended to his hip. If truth be told his story is somewhat emblematic. Not just a few rookie lawmen had first teetered—skirting nebulous boundaries separating the checked prudence from the wild rambunctiousness—prior to actually pocketing their policing commissions. Career lawmen are inexplicably pulled into the job. Willingly taking on risks, greeting hazard and horror as an integral part of the profession is a baffling phenomenon defying cogent explanation.

So, as previously noted these chapters taken separately may stand alone, each exemplifying a thrilling Wild West narrative— a story worthy of preservation. In the aggregate these true tales unfasten the panoply of topics and rhetorical questions that may be associated with the practical application and implementation of a criminal justice system in the nineteenth and early twentieth century American Southwest. Optimistically there will be a few tidbits of relevance for the committed professional educator, historian, criminologist, or sociologist. But, more importantly, the outright objective is really to assemble an everyday language and well-documented platform for the general reader, a not negligible audience yet captivated by the nonfiction Western genre. They too are invited to sample the fare, hopefully scavenging a scrap of relevance for their lives. If the past really is prologue, then this Old West compilation facilitates the cracking open of a doorway—just a little bit—shining a clear spotlight on humankind, its compassions and cruelties. In the real world, and that's where we live, life's cards are dealt by chance: Sometimes an Ace, sometimes a Deuce. *Bad Company and Burnt Powder* owns its fair share of winners and losers.

Assuredly, whether this multi-year end product actually makes a meaningful contribution may be subject to honest deliberation and maybe even spirited debate. With a bit of luck, supplemented with thoughtful and impartial reflection, perhaps a touch of affirmation will have been met. There is an irrefutable hard truth, an unbendable bottom line. And, it will not suffer even the slightest challenge from anybody—anywhere. These historical cards were not dealt down and dirty, but face up, the ante of so very many players—all in. There are no games without participants, no histories absent enthusiastic helpmates. *Bad Company and Burnt Powder* is the end product of so very many and their contributions are truly appreciated and never undervalued. Prior to enumerating them by name, a simple but heartfelt acknowledgement is proffered: Thank you, my friends.

And, too, preceding singular mentions, remarks of gratitude should be—must be—extended in whole to personnel at Texas Ranger Hall of Fame & Museum (TRHF&M), Waco, Texas. Owing to deliberative appointments by the State of Texas Legislature, TRHF&M has long been the Official State Hall of Fame and Repository of the Texas Rangers. Much more recently, however, June 4, 2013, the Department of Public Safety Commission of the State of Texas by means of a formally crafted Resolution designated the TRHF&M as the official representative and steward for the forthcoming Texas Ranger Bicentennial, an endorsement of foremost significance and genuine esteem. The honor is homage to the dedication of TRHF&M's entire staff and their unparalleled roles in preserving and promoting the history of Texas Rangers and, by easy correlation, history of the Lone Star State.

An all-embracing and/or proficient study of Texas law enforcing issues calls for an edifying trip to Waco. TRHF&M is not only home to the Hall of Fame and Museum, but other components of the picturesque complex are the beautifully appointed Tobin & Anne Armstrong Texas Ranger Research Center, and the Robert K. Mitchell Education Center. Maintaining and operating such an extraordinary facility on a daily basis is no easy task, one demanding the credentialed expertise of a simply outstanding cadre of career-minded professional employees. TRHF&M employs only the best, a fact well known by a mass of lucky researchers, writers, movie-makers, scholars, students, and happily mesmerized visitors. It's first-rate in every regard.

Before the pleasure of tendering a name specific roster of those lending a helping hand, it is but appropriate to express appreciation—sincere appreciation—to Western artist extraordinaire Donald M. Yena, San Antonio, Texas. Real life Old West lawmen charged after desperadoes and ne'er-do-wells and nitwits: Chasing hell-bent on horseback all the while miserably chafing in slick-forked Texas saddles, spitting kicked-up dust, and sometimes scarily dodging a bullet—or bullets. The thundering narratives—in most instances—wind down with a good guy capturing a bad guy, but it's a scene fleetingly fashioned from imagination and words. Don Yena captures the moment, for keeps! His artwork is matchless. Many are the talented painters specializing in the Old West genre. Their artful depictions of lonesome cowboys stepping down and opening gates, or leaning from the saddle and kissing the girl, or lazily following a herd of Longhorns toward the rising or setting sun or through a mirrored river reflecting inverted visuals are great. Few, however, have bridled an ability to impose on spectators the horrors of real life excitement. Of feeling particles of gunpowder stipple sunburnt skin as hot lead sends splinters flying or the fear of intentionally baling off a gutshot horse, before the topsy-turvy gyrations suspend the rider upside down, a fancy gal-leg spur hung in the stirrup. Don's mental Wild West storehouse is jam-packed. Thankfully, somewhere along the way, from deep within he draws from that wellspring and puts brush to canvas. Looking into the depths of a Yena we may be scared, we may taste the fear, and it's likely we might want to break and run when—and if—uninvited company turns bad, and rudely sets to burning powder. Studying a book's dust-jacket graced with Don's work or standing in the gallery before one of his treasures, we may not actually be numbed or truly injured by that nasty and bloody gunshot wound, but we'll sense nauseousness. The realism is palatable. Yena's intrinsic genius is stunning, his breathtaking work genuine—the Real McCoy. We are the beneficiaries.

Also deserving mention by name would be: the late David Albright, Ballinger, Texas; Elvis Allen, Fruitvale, TX; Mary Jo Apodaca, Doña Ana County Sheriff's Museum, La Cruces, NM; Jan Appleby, Mason County Historical Commission, Mason, TX; Daniel Aranda, Las Cruces, NM; Bruce Archer, Dallas, TX; James Baird, San Francisco, CA; Dr. John T. Baker, Dallas, TX; Rans Baker, Carbon County Museum, Rawlins, WY; Michael Barr, Gatesville, TX; LaVerne Benton, Menard, TX; Mary Bird, Gadsden Museum, Mesilla, NM; Lynn Blankenship, San Saba Historical Commission, San Saba, TX; Jim Bradshaw, Midland, TX; Donaly E. Brice, Texas State Library & Archives Commission, Austin, TX; Jeffrey Burton, England; Clifford R. Caldwell, Mountain Home, TX; Bill Cavalier, Portal, AZ; the late Amos and LaDorna Chenowth, McNeal, AZ; Amy and Lynn Chenowth, Cienega Ranch, Rodeo, NM; Charles Chenowth, Santee, CA; Christa Claveria, Texana & Genealogy, San Antonio Public Library, San Antonio, TX; Mika L. Coffey, Program Analyst and Financial Officer, TRHF&M, Waco, TX; Leslie Cotton, ex-Sheriff, Navarro County, Corsicana, TX; Shelly Crittendon, Collections Manager, TRHF&M, Waco, TX; Amanda Crowley, Research Librarian, TRHF&M, Waco, TX; Sharon Cunningham, Samburg, TN; Lisa Daniel, Visitor Services Manager, TRHF&M, Waco, TX; Dan Davidson, Director, Museum of Northwest Colorado, Craig, CO; Ronald G. DeLord, Georgetown, TX; Kirby Dendy, Assistant Director Texas Department of Public Safety and Chief, Texas Rangers, Austin, TX; Jan Devereaux, Maypearl, TX; Beryl Jean Dreiss, Kerrville, TX; Candice DuCoin, Round Rock, TX; Doug Dukes, Liberty Hill, TX; Kim Durst, Gillespie County District Clerk's Office, Fredericksburg, TX; Casey Eichhorn, Education Coordinator, TRHF&M, Waco, TX; Robert Ernst, Perkins, OK; Randy Fancher, Mustang, OK; Todd Garrison, Sheriff, Doña Ana County Sheriff's Office, Las Cruces, NM; Coi Drummond-Gehrig, Denver Public Library, Denver, CO; Jan Gerber, Assistant Director, Museum of Northwest Colorado, Craig, CO; West Gilbreath, Sanger, TX; Carl Hallberg, Wyoming State Archives,

Cheyenne, WY; Robert W. Haltom, Porter, TX; Charles H. Harris III, Las Cruces, NM; Linda Harwell, Grand Saline, TX; Letta Rutter Hawks, Commerce City, CO; E. Dale Herring, Talpa, TX; Jane Hoester, Mason County Historical Commission, Mason, TX; Terry Humble, Bayard, NM; Paul Jenkins, San Angelo, TX; the late Dorthy Jesse, Carlsbad, NM; Harold Jobes, Cedar Park, TX; Byron A. Johnson, Director, TRHF&M, Waco, TX; David Johnson, Zionsville, IN; Kathy Katelin, Lincoln, NM; Lewis A. Ketring, Jr., Tucson, AZ; Kathy Klump, Sulphur Springs Valley Historical Society, Willcox, AZ; Daniel Kosharek, New Mexico History Museum, Santa Fe, NM: Mark Lane, Amarillo, TX; Josh Lehew, Waxahachie, TX; Ellis Lindsey, Waco, TX; Dakota and Sunny Livesay, Publishers, *Chronicle of the Old West*, Showlow, AZ; Augustin V. Lopez, Anaheim, CA; Kate McCarthy, Collections Assistant, TRHF&M, Waco, TX; J.P. "Pat" McDaniel, Director, Nita Stewart Haley Memorial Library, Midland, TX; Jo Ann McDougall, Llano County History Museum, Llano, TX; Rick Miller, Bell County Attorney, Ret., Harker Heights, TX; Kay Mooring, Quartzsite Historical Society, Quartzsite, AZ; Debbie Newman, Arizona Historical Society, Tucson, AZ; Nick Olson, XIT Museum, Dalhart, TX; Florene Parks, Parker, AZ; Sherrie Parks, Sweetwater, TX; Chuck Parsons, Luling, TX; Phyllis Poehliman, Lometa, TX; Bob Pugh, Trail to Yesterday Books, Tucson, AZ; Julia Putnam, Albany, TX; Gary B. and Jeri Radder, Alamo, CA; Clay Riley, Brownwood, TX; Shirley Aten Roberts, Amarillo, TX; Christine Rothenbush, Marketing & Development Coordinator, TRHF&M, Waco, TX; Karylon A. Russell, Llano County History Museum, Llano, TX; Louis Ray Sadler, Las Cruces, NM; Cathy Smith, Nita Stewart Haley Memorial Library, Midland, TX; Rhetta Smith, Parker, AZ; Robert W. Stephens, Atlanta, GA; Christina Stopka, Deputy Director and Head of the Tobin and Anne Armstrong Texas Ranger Research Center, TRHF&M, Waco, TX; Warren Stricker, Director, Research Center, Panhandle-Plains Historical Museum, Canyon, TX; Michael Toon, Associate Professor and Librarian, Ret., The Texas Collection, Baylor University, Waco, TX; Physical Plant Manager Paul Torres and staff, TRHF&M, Waco, TX; John R. Troubaugh, Thurmont, MD; Joseph H. Troubaugh II, Carlisle, PA; Doug Turner, Lindale, TX; David Turk, Historian, U.S. Marshal's Service, Washington, D.C.; David Ueckert, Ballinger, TX;

Deen Underwood, El Paso, TX; John Versluis, Director, Historical Research Center, Texas Heritage Museum, Hill College, Hillsboro, TX; Clara Vick, Castro County Historical Society, Dimmitt, TX; Ed Walker, Brownwood, TX; Sally Walker, Shallowater, TX; Susanne Waller, Trinity County Museum, Groveton, TX; Pat Watkins, Ballinger, TX; Shirley Weaver, Wortham, TX; Teddy Weaver, Weaver Ranches, Wortham, TX; Harold J. Weiss, Jr., Leander, TX; Jim Willett, Director, Texas Prison Museum, Huntsville, TX; J. C. Wilkerson, Winters, TX; Charles Wright, Customs & Border Enforcement, Las Cruces, NM; James Wright, Whitney, TX; Donald and Louise Yena, San Antonio, TX; Bobbie Young, Executive Director Navarro County Historical Society and Curator, Pioneer Village, Corsicana, TX; and Jeremy Youngs, Assistant Manager, Visitor Services and his dedicated crew, TRHF&M, Waco, TX.

Books undoubtedly have a starting point in an author's psyche and then morph into full-fledged manuscripts, but it's the publisher that converts same into an end product worthy of home on a purchaser's bookshelf. The University of North Texas Press is accomplished at doing a masterful job—making handsome and authoritative nonfiction books from the submitted reams of loose-leaf pages and old-time photographs. Making it all work smoothly—and effectively maintaining the first-class reputation UNT Press owns is the duty of hardworking folks, four of whom warrant particularization herein. Director Ron Chrisman, long and favorably known in academic publishing circles, runs the show and shepherds—quite regularly—the outfit's array of Old West books into winner's circles, earning fine-looking engraved plaques for the authors and keen admiration from competing publishers. Sustaining those high and enviable standards is the work—part of the work—of Karen DeVinney, Assistant Director/Managing Editor. Her behind-the-scenes editorial touch is the epitome of journalistic proficiency. Karen's easygoing and pleasing personality complements her level of competency. Paula Oates, Director of Marketing, affably tackles her projects with enthusiasm and expertise; assuring advertising and promotional matters are handled timely and properly. Lori Belew, Administrative Assistant—a real credit to UNT Press—is atop the operational process, tying up loose ends and aiding patrons with a smile.

CHAPTER 1

Battle at Bullhead Mountain

Cal Aten was a gentleman—and a gentle man. For a time, he was also a gutsy Texas Ranger. In annals of Old West literature he is scarcely mentioned. And though Cal sits prominently in one of the iconic and most widely published nineteenth-century Texas Ranger photographs, Winchester in hand, his presence is hardly noticed. He's overlooked due to foolish penchants for presupposing guys with baby faces own timid and unruffled dispositions. Cal was no showboat. Cal Aten would leave the swashbuckling to others. In truth, persons of that ilk, swanking and puffing about taking a life were not people worthy of emulating. Cal had been in tight places but talking big about those times was childlike, not manly. Certain things were—for the most part and to most folks—best left unsaid.

First seeing light of day on December 7, 1868, Calvin Grant Aten came into this world the sixth of seven children born to Austin Cunningham Aten and his lovely wife Katherine Eveline.[1] Like Cal, none of the Aten children would be native Texans. They were products of Illinois, Cal and his younger brother Edwin Dunlap having been born near Abingdon.[2] That the Atens were a close-knit bunch is evidenced by their next move—a real move. When but seven years old Cal and the rest of the family relocated to Texas. Whether the train trip had been filled with merriment or flooded with misery goes unspoken, but the passenger coach had been jam-packed with Atens. Making the trip besides Cal and his parents was the oldest sister, Margaret Angelina "Angie" Elizabeth and husband Americus Jerome "A. J." Kimmons along with their first born, Virginia May, more often than not just called "Virgie." Also managing the journey was Cal's sister Clara Isabel

1

"Belle," plus both of his widowed grandmothers. Cal's three older brothers Thomas Quinn, Franklin Lincoln, and Austin Ira, were a part of the menagerie, as was baby brother Eddie. On the twenty-ninth day of October 1876 the whole crew detrained in the Lone Star State, settling into their newfound home just inside the northern Travis County (Austin) line. For practical purposes such as socializing and church going and acquiring commercial niceties, the closest trade center was Round Rock, Williamson County.

Situated but a reasonably short distance from the Texas State Capitol, Round Rock and her surrounding hinterlands was a good place to raise a promising family: A town large enough to host merchants and blacksmiths, bankers and dressmakers, barbers and butchers—and preachers. And that latter profession had earlier beckoned Mr. Austin Cunningham Aten. He answered the call, becoming first a circuit-riding man of the cloth, but later a full-fledged minister with a farm outside town to boost income from his parishioners' tithes. Away from town the countryside was neat: gently rolling lands scattered with shade trees—right at the eastern edge of the picturesque Texas Hill Country with her springtime carpets of bluebonnets. Drained by the San Gabriel River and her tributaries, the whole of Williamson County was a veritable playground—for a boy, especially a boy with a gun or a fishing pole—and curiosity. There were deer and rabbits and squirrels to be bagged for the table, beehives to be robbed for the sweet-tooth, and arrowheads by the thousands to be polished and pocketed.

Cal Aten, at eight years old, perhaps sitting on a big rock alongside the creek savoring the deliciousness of a wild plum, had no inkling about a more grown-up fellow eager to gather a few plums for himself—right out of the Williamson County Bank, the old Miller's Exchange Bank. Sam Bass and his gang were in the neighborhood, ready to taste a little sweetness before greenbacks in the bank soured and spoiled.[3] The would-be Godfather coughed up blood, instead. Since the tale has often been told, quite proficiently, the recap herein is skeletal—decidedly so.

The long and the short of the story is this: On July 19, 1878, a Friday afternoon near four o'clock, outlaw Sam Bass, escorted by six-shooter-wearing Seaborn Barnes and Frank Jackson, slithered into Round Rock with larceny in their hearts. They were scouting, laying the blueprint for a bank heist. Unbeknownst to them their mission was no secret. They had been conspiring with a snitch in their midst, one who had tipped off the Texas Rangers. Major John B. Jones, the Ranger's big boss, was in town as were several of his fearless men, ready for action but keeping a low profile.[4] All were clued in on the likelihood of a highjacking. Without delay—in policing jargon—it turned "Western." Prematurely it may be argued, but, nevertheless, gunpowder was exploding. It was not a good day! Williamson County deputy sheriff, Ahijah W. "Caige" Grimes was killed outright. A visiting deputy from Travis County, Maurice B. Moore, lending a helping-hand, was critically—though not mortally—wounded. The bad guys did not fare well either. Seaborn Barnes was dead, a Ranger's bullet having plowed into his head, just below the left ear. Twenty-seven-year-old Sam Bass suffered two fingers being shot off his right hand, plus a bullet missing his spine but raggedly exiting three inches left of his bellybutton. Sam Bass, severely injured, made it out of town, but was captured the next day. Considering the hellfire of Ranger's bullets Frank Jackson's feat seemed miraculous—he had made a clean getaway.[5]

How does this play in the story of Cal Aten? Significantly it may be reasoned. Next day at Round Rock the good Reverend Austin C. Aten was on routine errands with two of his sons, Frank and Ira. He was besieged by church goers to carry the word of God to the brigand reposed on his deathbed in the tin shop, a makeshift hospital. Minister Aten finally acquiesced, agreeing to visit Sam Bass. Seventeen-year-old Frank was allowed entry into the tin shop with his father. Fifteen-year-old Ira was not. He was, according to the Texas Ranger posted as guard, just too young to personally witness death's doings. Turned away at the door, Ira Aten peeked though a window. Teenagers are generally impressionable, and the excitement was washing across Ira's imagination, swirling, drowning his formerly held aspirations. He would later write of the pivotal moment: "The Rangers were there in town with six-shooters on, swaggering around there. I thought it would be nice to carry a six-shooter and thought I would just stop the cowboy business and join the Rangers."[6]

Ira Aten stopped the "cowboy business" and the clock just stopped for Sam Bass. He was a dead man by the afternoon of July 21, 1878. Although explicit conversations are lost to history, there would be nothing amiss at speculating Frank and Ira had big tales to tell little brothers Cal and Eddie after returning home. Good guys battling bandits was not everyday goings-on at Round Rock. It was newsy. It was thrilling. It was heady stuff for farm boys—or any other boys. So, while dramatic quotations are mislaid, there are hard truths: Austin Ira Aten would become a legit Texas Ranger and Cal, following in his brother's footsteps, would too. Little brother Eddie would also become a Ranger—but that came later and begs for a breakaway story.

At age nineteen, on the first day of April 1888, Cal Aten enrolled in Company D of the Frontier Battalion.[7] The company was then headquartered deep in South Texas at Realitos, Duval County. Commander of Company D was Captain Frank Jones, and the top noncom was 1st Sergeant Ira Aten. By this juncture Ira had already earned five years' experience as a seasoned Texas Ranger. He also owned a favorable statewide reputation as a real lawman, not a fallacious self-promoter. By the time Cal had enlisted, Ira Aten had survived four gunfights, hunted fugitives, and worked undercover snaring fence-cutters. There was nothing counterfeit about Ira's law enforcing days.[8]

After a swearing in ceremony before an agent empowered to administer oaths—and the payment of his 25¢ fee—Cal Aten was a private citizen no more: He was official, a real Ranger.[9] He was in tough company. In speaking of his Company D subordinates Corporal J. Walter Durbin would remark that he had some pretty good men, even if they could be a "little fussy and dangerous" when drinking.[10] Private Aten was not a drinking man, probably not very fussy, but when necessary Cal could be dangerous—if he had a gun.

Cal had arrived at the Ranger camp unarmed, wholly unprepared. Quickly Sergeant Ira Aten corrected the embarrassing deficiency: "Just think of my joy that first evening when my brother Ira handed me (A Belt Four Inches Wide). . . .full of cartridges with a scabbard and a .45 six-shooter in it. He told me to put it on and on it went. I wasn't afraid Ira would joke me. I looked around and saw that every man there, ten or more had their guns strapped on. It seemed to be a tradition that rangers must go armed and stay armed and about the only time we took off those guns were when we were asleep."[11]

Private Aten had been in camp less than a week when a letter to Texas Ranger headquarters portended an upcoming and defining event in the young lawman's life, but little could he—or anyone else—have known it at the time. The sheriff of Uvalde County, Henry W. Baylor, had messaged the adjutant general at Austin, W. W. King. Part of the letter said: "If convenient I would like to have a detachment of Rangers sent to this place as there is plenty of work for them. Some in Edwards and Zavalla [Counties], as the horse and cattle thieves Seem to have broken loose afresh. . . ."[12]

There was other trouble on the near horizon, however, along the meandering Rio Grande in the ever hazardous Texas/Mexico borderlands. Working out of their camp near Realitos in southern Duval County, Company D Rangers were positioned perfectly for enforcing the law in several counties bordering the Rio Grande. And although Duval County's line did not actually touch the river, it was an important base for Rangers for two nuts and bolts reasons: First, Duval County had a long history of lawlessness. Second, it was at a primary geographical junction for commercial traffic. North/South commerce between San Antonio and Brownsville moved through Duval County—and vice versa. After start of the Mexican National Railway—Texas Division, East/West traffic from Corpus Christi to Laredo moved through Duval County—and vice versa. Duval County was gaining socioeconomic meaning, an international crossroads.[13] As the population increased so, too, did the trouble. Ne'er-do-wells hound for the easy money.

Private Aten was overjoyed when approached by Captain Jones during the evening of his sixth day in camp. Cal was advised that at first light a three-man scout would be leaving for the border. Nineteen-year-old Ranger Aten was to accompany the Captain and his older brother, Gerry "Dude" (also called "Dood" by family) Jones on the trip.[14] Next morning after packing the company's mule, Old Pete, "older in ranger service than anyone there," the trio set course in a southerly direction for their destination, Carrizo (now Zapata), Zapata County.[15] Until reaching Carrizo their camp rations would be "a piece of salt bacon, a few pounds of flour, baking powder, salt, sugar, and coffee." The excursion would be memorable for Cal—for more than one reason. It would be his first overnight camp while on a scout. No sooner had they pulled in for the night when tenderfoot Ranger Aten goofed. After unsaddling Cal placed his carbine, still in its scabbard, against a mesquite bush, muzzle to the ground. "I remember how mortified I was when the Capt. said, 'Cal you didn't do that right. You should stand your gun stock down as if it rains the scabbard will keep your gun dry.' Then I noted my mistake." Cal also noted something else early-on during this outing. Though he kept his own counsel at the time, it was Private Aten's private assessment that Dude Jones was "grouchy and a little wrong in the head. Fell out of a tree when he was born . . . . He was, I think the original Gloomy Gus . . . ."[16]

After arriving at Carrizo the three Rangers were given a tour of the Zapata County Jail by Deputy Sheriff Thatcher. Cal's observations are not only interesting, but telling as later events about this scout to the Rio Grande unfold and reveals:

> I have seen a good many jails since then, but none as crude as this one, a great stone dungeon with iron rings set in the concrete floor to chain the prisoners legs to at night. In daytime the prisoners would be loose with chains dragging. They looked to me like wild animals. But I was young and just beginning to see things. Everything around me seemed like a new world and was interesting, wonderfully interesting.[17]

Making sure his guests received the best in borderland hospitality Deputy Thatcher escorted the Rangers across the Rio Grande and into the Mexican city of Guerrero. Cal was thoroughly impressed with the "beautiful little city" though he did not understand "how a town of this size, and stores full of beautiful goods could be supported in a country so barren as this." He was in a foreign land and made comparative notes, particularly about architecture and tradition: "All windows in Mexican houses have iron bars like our jail windows and I thought that there must be lots of thieves in that country, but I guess it is just ancient custom . . . . All Mexicans I think sit on the floor as I can't ever remember seeing a chair in a Mexican house." All too soon the cross border visit was over and the tourists returned to Carrizo.[18]

On the morning of their departure, making ready to head back to the Ranger camp near Realitos, the echo of a pistol shot reverberated between adobe walls. Then, almost immediately, Deputy Thatcher's ten-year-old son rushed up to Captain Jones notifying him that prisoners were escaping and that his father had been wounded. Rushing to the county jail, which was but 100 yards away, the Rangers found "Mr. Thatcher holding his hand with a red handkerchief around it, a bullet had cut the flesh between the thumb and first finger." Although he could not let his emotions show at the time—a real lawman's not supposed to—Cal Aten was near busting with happiness inside: "Maybe it was for the boy ranger, anyway there was going to be excitement and that was what I was always dreaming of."[19] And excitement there would be for a rookie Ranger; Cal was going to get to shoot his gun.

Updated, the Rangers had learned that during the night four prisoners had somehow sawed through the chains, grabbed Thatcher's six-shooter from a bench where he had laid it prior to preparing breakfast, shot the deputy, and were at the moment racing for the river. The Rangers, now giving chase horseback were but three or four minutes behind the fugitives. Promptly they were met by Sheriff Robert A. Haynes and a deputy who had captured an escapee, the one with the Thatcher's stolen Colt's revolver. Aten's preconceptions surface: "The man with the gun had emptied it straight up through the tree tops. That is the way with a Mexican they like to make a show unless they have all the advantage." Again, Cal Aten's innermost feelings come to light, "That was disappointing to me, there couldn't be any more fun hunting men I know were unarmed."[20] Green as a gourd, Ranger Private Cal Aten was determined—dead set—on having some "fun!" Ranger Aten tenders more of the rousing story, and as legit history it's a gem:

Well, there were three others at large and we went down through the river bottom to the river. We expected them to try to swim the river. The river was up a little and was nearly a quarter mile wide with some drift floating in the middle. I spied a man's head amongst the drift about the middle of the river downstream from us. I asked the Capt. "Can I shoot at him?" He studied a moment and said "Shoot his head off." He then rode away, and I commenced shooting. However every time I would shoot Dude would grumble and tell me to quit. The Capt. knew I had no chance of hitting the head in the water at least five hundred yards away with the guns we carried those days, but he wanted me to have the fun of trying. When I had shot four or five times the fellow came to a narrow island with small willows. As he crawled out on the island I shot again. Then he stood up apparently naked and commenced shaking his fists at me and jumping up and down and I knew what he was saying about one wasn't nice.

I took careful aim and shot again. I never could tell where
my bullets were striking the water as it was very muddy and
broken by waves and drift but this last shot must have come
pretty close to him as he immediately dragged into the willows and I never saw him again. One of the others crossed
on the ferry and the other was drowned while trying to swim
a swollen arroyo several miles east of town. By noon the fun
was all over and we were on our way to home camp.[21]

As they were riding along, Captain Jones turned to his newest
Ranger and made a salient point: "Cal, I have been with the rangers a good many years and seen many rangers come and go, but
you are the first one I can remember of getting to shoot at a man
on his first scout."[22] Little did he know it then but Cal Aten would
learn what was fun today might not be fun tomorrow.

When Cal Aten signed on with the Texas Rangers big trouble
had already been brewing in the borderlands, in fact, just the year
before. Viviano Díaz and Cicilio Ybarro, suspected kidnappers,
had been liberated from the sheriff of Starr County (Rio Grande
City) and lynched by "a party of men." Though not made public,
Captain Frank Jones' comment to Adjutant General King might
have added fuel to the fires of animosity by now raging, had they
been broadcast: "They were very bad characters and the good
citizens here, American and Mexican, are greatly rejoiced at their
taking off."[23] Captain Jones' narrow-mindedness complicated
sound thinking. Catarino Erasmo Garza Rodriguez was not rejoicing "at their taking off." Catarino Garza may have been a patriot
or Catarino Garza may have been a firebrand—but, either way, the
highly educated and articulate newspaperman was vociferous and
he had a following—a real following: Sometimes a gun-carrying
following. Garza harangued incessantly about perceived inequi-
ties, and it has been proficiently and truthfully theorized that he
".... had enjoined a small but tempestuous revolutionary cell that
stood—twenty years ahead of their time—in open opposition to
the dictatorial Porfirio Diaz regime in Mexico."[24] Catarino Garza,
too, was not shy or disinclined about hurling journalistic barbs at
borderland lawmen—hoping they would stick—and sting!

Hardly had Cal Aten enrolled with the Texas Rangers when a
Company D comrade resorted to unlimbering his Colt's .45 and
spitting out finality. Captain Frank Jones updated headquarters:
"Private Dillard shot and killed a Mexican, name not known to

me, at Rio Grande City on the 16th inst. The man killed was implicated in the kidnapping of Manuel Guerrera. Dillard was compelled to kill him to prevent his escape. District Court is in session in Starr County, and the matter will be fully investigated. I am confident that Dillard will be exonerated."[25]

When time came to prepare Company D's Monthly Return for May 1888, Captain Jones knew the deceased fellow's identity, Abraham Recéndez. Although it's sometimes written that it was Inspector of U.S. Customs at Rio Grande City, Victor Sebree, who killed Recéndez, Captain Frank Jones' version leaves little room for ambiguity. Under the Monthly Return's heading of Recapitulation of Arrests Made by Company the following is particularized: "Date, May 16; Name, Abram Recendez; Charge, kidnapping; Where Arrested, Starr County; By Whom, Dillard; Result, Killed when attempting to escape."[26] The company commander may have genuinely thought the Ranger private would be exonerated, but he may have had a change of heart, as reflected in the following month's report: "A. Dillard discharged June 30th by Capt. Frank Jones."[27] Later and legally, the District Court's jurymen could not agree unanimously on Private Dillard's fate. Half were championing a courtroom conviction, and half advocating for an acquittal: Mistrial.[28] Be that as it may, by any reasonable man's standard the state of affairs in the Lower Rio Grande Valley was a wretched mess.

Company D reconnaissance scouts to the section along the river were necessary and frequent, tiring and sometimes sickening— literally. Although the malady is not diagnosed with medical specificity, while on one such undertaking in Starr County, Private Cal Aten was knocked out of commission "when he became quite sick." The other Texas Rangers on this perambulation had to leave Cal behind at Rio Grande City under the care of Doctor Kenedy, "who positively forbade his return to camp horseback." Later, after the obligatory recuperation period, Cal was allowed to make the return trip to the Company D headquarters camp via a stagecoach.[29]

Regardless the outcome of any brouhaha concerning Ranger Dillard's killing of Recéndez, or the illness of any particular Texas Ranger, Catarino Garza was yet active, yet livid, yet firing off his wordy torpedoes tipped with vitriol. He was a master at venting his spleen.

Though the overall story warrants retelling in certain treatments, this is not the platform for such an inclusive breakdown. Simply it may be said Inspector Victor Sebree was one of those fellows suffering verbal mutilation inflicted by a ranting Mr. Garza. Inspector Sebree, resorting to a serious gunplay, not accidently but seriously wounded Catarino Garza. Then, just ahead of a vengeance-minded crowd, Inspector Sebree hotfooted to nearby Fort Ringgold where he hid behind the U.S. Army's protective steel skirts—and their great big Gatling Guns.[30] The fort's commander, Colonel Clendenin, had received no nonsense orders to not blink and to "use his force if necessary to protect lives and property from mob violence," so said a newsman penning for the widely read *Laredo Times*.[31] Personal perspectives may differ, but for the Texas Ranger's hierarchy, aftermath of the shooting and the chase and the standoff inflexibly equated to a "riot." But it was sure not a One Riot, One Ranger job. En masse Company D was promptly dispatched to Rio Grande City, Private Cal Aten among them.[32]

By the twenty-ninth day of September Company D's manpower muscle had been marshaled and was ready to flex. The Rangers were on duty at Rio Grande City. Their presence was speedily beefed up by the appearance of a remarkable detachment of hardened Texas Rangers from Company F, led by Lieutenant James Abijah Brooks. The Rangers found, much to their collective dislike, that "there was still a strong undercurrent of excitement and Americans do not feel safe, that is those who have families."[33] Assuredly some long-time South Texas residents weren't feeling too safe. In what today might be termed an "investigative sweep" the Texas Rangers rounded up a mass of supposed rioters at Roma and downriver at Rio Grande City, charging them with Conspiracy and/or Conspiracy to Murder. The luckless and flabbergasted prisoners—43 in number—were then ensconced behind bars on the north end of Bratton Avenue, within the detention facilities of a near brand new Starr County courthouse and jail.[34] A percentage of those folks swept up in the dragnet were some of Starr County's and Rio Grande City's "prominent ranchers and local businessmen," but at the time such an exasperating truth was of little import to Texas Rangers. Grim-faced state-paid lawmen were handling official police business—and they meant business. They made sure there was no damn squabble about that! Perhaps it was summed up best for any doubters or would-be resisters in the language of Company D's forever straight-talking corporal, J. Walter Durbin: "The Rangers will attend to all the killing in this county for a while."[35] A few Indictments were returned by the grand jury, but they were not followed by convictions in a courtroom: That's what really counts. Fittingly the facade of peace retuned to the Lower Rio Grande Valley for awhile—a little while. It was peaceful enough. So, the biggest portion of the Company D Rangers were redeployed to their old base of times past in Uvalde County, Camp Leona. Three Company D Rangers, however, did not make the November 1888 move: "Privates Rogers, Fusselman, and Aten remain on duty in Rio Grande City with Lieut. Brooks."[36]

Speculatively it could be postulated that Private Cal Aten celebrated Christmas eating hot tamales and skipping rocks across the Rio Grande into Mexico. Factually it may be reported that by the sixth day of January 1889 he had rejoined Company D at Camp Leona. For that is the day he and another Ranger, Private Charles Barton, arrested Bud Sanders and Blake Rowland for Burglary, locking them in the two-story steel-barred rock hotel operated by Uvalde County Sheriff Henry Baylor.[37]

By now Cal Aten had shed his status as a raw recruit—a rookie. Although there is a mottled haze around his actual role, in one way or another Cal had aided his 1st Sergeant brother Ira with a headlining murder investigation: A real whodunit? It was a humdinger; four unclaimed bodies floating in the Rio Grande had to be identified. By means of decidedly competent sleuthing and smart employment of forensics—the first time used in Texas, maybe anywhere else—Sergeant Aten effectively identified the fatalities by uniqueness of their dental work and by testimony of a dentist. Once Sergeant Aten knew who the victims really were, he traced backwards following their movements till those intersected with explicit alibi machinations of the supposed murderer and a whopping catalog of circumstantial evidence. All of which led Sergeant Aten to the prime suspect, Dick Duncan. For whatever the actual reason, "Privates [John R.] Hughes & Aten went to Burnet County as attached witnesses in the Duncan murder case."[38]

That Cal Aten had matured as a Texas Ranger and was capable of independent assignments can be illustrated by noting the young lawman single-handedly located and arrested J. C. Gibson in the hidden recesses of Uvalde County, a man charged with Murder.

Private Aten checked his dangerous prisoner into Sheriff Baylor's lockup.[39] Three fellows were not locked down tight, and they were soon-to-be ex-Texas Rangers. Corporal J. Walter Durbin, as well as Privates John Reynolds Hughes and Bazzell Lamar "Baz" (sometimes Bass) Outlaw had opted out of the outfit. They had communally decided there was better opportunity for fattening their wallets in Mexico guarding valuable shipments of ore, than there was roaming around Texas taking dire chances and drawing piddling quarterly pay warrants—and those were discounted from face value. At the time, such resignations were not uncommon and hardly caused a Company D ripple. Within two days they were replaced with the enrollment of brand new privates, Alf Morrow, Carl Kirchner, and G. W. Rennick. Private Cal Aten's lot in the natural pecking order moved up a notch—well, three notches.[40] Although it might fly in the face of hyperventilated prattle, at the time, being carried on the Texas Ranger books was commonly considered but a steppingstone into more lucrative law enforcing or gun carrying work. It was not a long-term career job. Even the good Captain Frank Jones would actively seek—though in vain— to trade his Ranger captaincy for the title of U.S. Marshal for the Western District of Texas.[41]

Troubling as it is, a lot of ground must be covered within tight parameters of an anthology. Scarcely enough attention can be allotted to recapping details of the Jaybird/Woodpecker Feud at Richmond, Fort Bend County. The mêlée would impact the Aten family significantly, Ira more so than Cal, but his steadfast service as a Ranger would be brought into play too. The warring political factions, at loggerheads for years, opted to do with bullets what they could not do with ballots. A peace-keeping squadron of Texas Rangers under the command of Sergeant Ira Aten could not— and did not—prevent the streets of Richmond from running red with blood that day of 16 August 1889. When the smoke cleared and the bullets stopped flying the county sheriff was dead, on a list with several others who had given up the ghost, not counting the folks nursing survivable gunshot wounds. Fort Bend County was in want of a sheriff, and therein created the dilemma. The Woodpeckers nominally in control of county government had the authority to appoint a new sheriff—until the next election cycle— but lacked the financial wherewithal to guarantee his bond. On the other hand, the Jaybirds were flush with cash, but short on the lawful say-so to fill the position. Potential candidates for the sheriff's job were being blackballed by one side or the other as soon as their names were put forward. In everyday Southwestern lingo it was a Mexican Standoff. Neither bloc would budge.[42] The governor, who had managed the quick trip to Richmond, had a solution. Ira Aten whispers of the smoke-filled backroom doings:

> . . . .Governor Ross said, "This is my last chance with you. You will appoint Aten sheriff of this county or I will call martial law. I have spent two days here . . . . You know Aten. Appoint him or I will put you under martial law." Governor Ross went out. Attorney General Harrison staid [*sic*] there with the commissioners court. They wrangled awhile and said, all right.[43]

On August 20, 1889, Sergeant Austin Ira Aten's name was removed from the Company D roster.[44] At Richmond a dozen men, acting in Ira's behalf, personally and formally pledged the three requisite assurance bonds—$40,000—and Fort Bend County had a new sheriff. With no deputies now on the county's payroll, Sheriff Aten was in dire straits. It was a shortfall quickly noticed by Captain Frank Jones. He graciously detailed two Texas Rangers to serve as Sheriff Aten's interim deputies until empty slots could be permanently staffed. One of those Rangers, not unexpectedly, was Private Cal Aten.[45] Before forgoing his provisional deputyship and returning to Camp Leona, Cal and other Company D Texas Rangers would assist Sheriff Aten with the arrest of twenty-three Fort Bend County folks—charged with Murder as aftermath of that untidy and untimely street-fight.[46] Then, for Cal Aten it was back to Rangering out of Uvalde County.

By November 1889 we find Cal in the Texas Hill Country tracking suspected horse thief Frank Stewart somewhere along the South Llano River. After four days and 111 miles of saddle weary riding, Cal returned to camp—empty-handed—Stewart had given him the slip.[47] The next month other wanted guys would not get away and it would be exciting and scary and momentous.

Will and Alvin Odle were mean. Will and Alvin Odle were "thieves and murderers" who may have chosen the wrong path to be sure, but thieves and murderers they were, nevertheless.[48] Their older brother John had cold-bloodedly gunned a man down and was on the dodge in Mexico or Arkansas, or somewhere. Left to their own devices Will and Alvin Odle became *the* crime wave in Burnet and Edwards Counties. The boys burglarized homes, stole horses, and with murder in their hearts assaulted people—and did fatally bushwhack their sister Lizzie's husband. Gangsters Will and Alvin Odle were handy at something else too, jailbreaks![49]

As early as April 1887 they had had a brush with an Aten. Rangers Ira Aten and Frank Jones had located and placed under nighttime surveillance a kinsman's house habitually visited by Will and Alvin. Since, from time to time this real episode in Edwards County is somewhat garbled with another of Ranger Ira Aten's more noteworthy adventures in Williamson County, maybe it's simply best to hear from him: "We got there after night. We judged from the saddles and horses that they were in the house. Captain Jones wanted to make a raid on the house that night. I said, 'Cap, let's don't do that. They are very dangerous. You have a telegram that they are very dangerous men, and have killed a man.' I said, 'Let's wait until daylight and go in just as they get up. They are off their guard then and the house is unlocked.' The Captain said, 'Well, maybe you are right. We will just stay here.' We were at a spring about 100 yards from the house, where they carried their water from. The next morning about daylight here come a boy down to the spring after a bucket of water. Of course we held him. We got ready and ran around the house and I went in the back door. I said, 'Cap, I will go in the back door.' I went in the back door, in the kitchen and the Captain was at the front door. Had one of these strings that pulled. Odle was just waking up. There were two of them. I covered them with my six-shooter and arrested them, opened the door, pulled the string, and the Captain came in. . . ."[50]

There is little doubt Private Cal Aten had heard the story before, second hand. But now he was a Ranger in the Texas Hill Country—and Will and Alvin Odle were again on the loose, fugitives. In fact, they had not shed their larcenous dispositions, but they had maneuvered themselves into the business of stealing livestock on a wholesale scale. Cattle and horses stolen in Texas were herded to the river and crossed into Mexico—right fast. On breakneck return trips Will and Alvin pushed stock purloined in Mexico ahead of them.[51] It was profitable. It was a neat racket. It was a risky game they were playing, though. There were unsympathetic and quick-triggered Rangers on the prowl. Some of those cagy guys wore the stripes of tigers and were man-eaters in a scrap. One in particular, for the story at hand, Baz Outlaw, had forsaken the pleasures of Mexico and reenlisted as Texas Ranger with Company D.[52]

Captain Frank Jones knew Baz Outlaw had gumption and grit: "He is a man of unusual courage and coolness and in a close place is worth two or three ordinary men."[53] His former corporal distilled the characterization of Baz Outlaw down to but a few a words, as was so typical for J. Walter Durbin, saying Baz was ". . . . the worst and toughest man I'd seen."[54] One of his personal friends, fellow Texas Ranger Alonzo Van "Lon" Oden was forced into admitting the truth, that when his friend was hitting the bottle he ". . . .was a maniac, none of us could handle him, none of us could reason with him, we just stayed with him until he sobered up."[55] A politely disposed and refined lady, Laura Oden, applauded Baz then chided with a cautionary warning: ". . . .he was a true Southern gentleman, soft spoken, well educated and courteous. We loved to talk to him and to have him in our home but several drinks made a beast of him." During those times, which were quite often according to Mrs. Oden, ". . . .the doors were locked, children brought in off the street and all of us kept silence and hoped for the best."[56] A newspaperman added his two cents' worth in a piece for the *El Paso Times*:

> Outlaw has been in western Texas several years, much of the time an officer of the law, and all the time a terror to good citizens . . . . He was said to be a good natured man when sober, but he always wanted to shoot some one when he was drunk. And these periods of drunkenness were not infrequent.[57]

Also not infrequent was the criminality of Will and Alvin Odle. Even the state's chief executive had been besieged with complaints and petitions requesting that rewards be posted and labors be increased at carrying justice to the Odle brothers. Edwards County, hilly—even mountainous to some Texans—drained by the Llano and Nueces rivers was geographically crisscrossed with spring-fed creeks, winding canyons, hidden caves, and underground caverns. Game trails were all over the place. Will and Alvin knew the country well, advantaging themselves of its natural cover and seclusion. Tasked with issuing Will and Alvin a little justice was a special detachment of Company D Rangers. In charge of this special unit was John Reynolds Hughes, who like the others had found the grass not so green south of the Rio Grande, and had opted to take Ranger's pay again. His two working partners for this assignment were Privates Baz Outlaw and Cal Aten. However, carrying law into the wilds of Edwards County was no cakewalk—absent a snitch.

The county sheriff had an informant. Timely for Sheriff Ira Wheat an Indictment had been retuned charging a "prominent local rancher" with knowingly buying stolen cattle from the Odle brothers. Unluckily for the cowman, he had two distasteful choices: A trip to prison or squealing. He chose the latter. He knew just where and just when Will and Alvin would be delivering several stolen horses. Now, Sheriff Wheat knew too! The site would be near Bullhead Mountain. The time would be Christmas Day 1889, after dark.[58]

Not wasting valuable time, a posse of local citizens was deputized, led by Sheriff Wheat's real deputy, Will Terry. In turn Terry notified the Rangers, and Hughes, Outlaw, and Aten made ready for war—Will and Alvin were already "bought and paid for" which in policing talk denotes they were dead-game *mal hombres* and if they wiggled wrong they would just be dead.

Skirting the nearby community of Vance so as not to raise suspicion and picketing their horses at a safe distance, the posse was in place at the eastern foot of Bullhead Mountain by dark. The wait was short. Near eight o'clock iron horseshoes scraping across ground loosely scattered with white rocks was as if an alarm bell had been rung. The hidden posse had been given fair warning. Will and Alvin would not be so lucky. Now and then it's written that Texas Rangers would shoot first—ask questions later. On that cool and crisp Christmas night near Bullhead Mountain there were no questions in want of any answering. And, yes, the Rangers shot first! Cal Aten was not mealy-mouthed when owning up to the truth: "I am responsible for [missing word] but you will understand that it pertains to the time when the Odle boys were assassinated. That is all it was just plain legal assassination. However, there would have been someone else assassinated if we hadn't got the first shots."[59] Aten's rationale is easy to understand. The lawmen were going up against desperate men, men on the dodge, men known to have murdered. In the minds of the posse-men it was simply a case of them or us—and better them! Second place finishers in a gunfight are losers. Nevertheless, at least by one report, Jim Rhodes wanted the whole world to know he didn't want anyone calling him out for being too quick on the trigger: "He ejected every cartridge from his Winchester to prove that it had not been fired."[60]

Ranger Aten was more concerned with comforting a dying desperado. Will Odle and his horse were killed outright. Unmistakably, Alvin Odle was struggling to hang on, breathing his last. The end was near. Nobody, not a man among them, however, wanted to step on his neck and hurry the inevitable. They weren't murderers. Cal Aten sat down, raised Alvin's head and "held the dying outlaw in my [his] arms. One of the worst ever-known in the Southwest."[61] Whether or not the criminal realized what he was doing or not is lost in the fog of delirium and history. Yet near death, Alvin Odle would recognize Cal Aten's kindheartedness and sincere compassion. Alvin was not dying alone. Even in this gathering of saddle-toughened Texans the young Ranger was not scared or self-conscious about empathizing with the free-spirited guy who had chosen to live outside the law. Knowing he would never ever need it again, Alvin gestured or spoke indicating that Private Aten should take and keep his Colt's .45, ". . . .a wonderfully beautiful gun then without a blemish on it, beautiful engraving." Cal even acknowledged, somewhat reflectively: "I was sorry for that boy. Just a few years older than I."[62]

Lawmen killing folks is newsy stuff. Ranger John Hughes wanted to make sure the word got to his bosses timely, before they read gruesome details in the dailies. He also wanted to assure them it was, as the saying goes, "a good shooting." Within two hours from the fireworks going off, Hughes picked up the pen, writing Adjutant General W. W. King:

> Ten O'clock P.M. With the assistance of Deputy Sheriff Will Terry and a few good citizens We succeeded in trapping Will and Calvin Odel [sic sic] who are wanted for murder and theft. They resisted arrest and made a hard fight and we had to kill them in self defence [sic], also killed one horse and shot an other through the neck. It took place about 8 O'clock tonight. We will hold an inquest in the morning. Outlaw & C. G. Aten were with me.[63]

In his first writings about the shooting Captain Jones, somewhat inappropriately for officialdom in an official report to Ranger headquarters, broached the subject with droll witticism, cavalierly: "I guess you have seen in the papers where some of my men celebrated Xmas day by Killing the two Odles in Edwards County. It is a great strain off that country and the good people are rejoicing. John Hughes, Outlaw, and young Aten and some citizens did the work."[64] Reading between the lines is not too difficult regarding his report of but two days later. The overall tone had undergone a tweaking: "I have no particulars of the Killing of the Odles' except that they drew their pistols when commanded to surrender and then the firing began. Hughes, who is in charge of the Edwards County detachment, simply stated that they made a hard fight and they (the Rangers) were compelled to Kill them."[65] Fortunately the "hard fight" put up by the six-shooter wielding Odle brothers netted them zip on the scorecard for Ranger casualties.

Even Sheriff Aten was attuned to hard truths: the real possibility of forthcoming doom for Cal when the next grand jury met: "I will write to Ira Wheat about not having you boys indicted in Edwards co.: I wish I had time I would go up there & could tell in a short time which would be best, to have you indicted now or not. I expect Wheat would like to make some fees in the matter. . . ."[66] In the end the Rangers came clear—legally. Alvin's death troubled Cal—evermore.

In the short term there would be something else troubling Cal, the move to far West Texas. He was a still a Ranger, but a Ranger working with a detachment in Presidio County covering the Big Bend area. It was a far cry from the home-place lushness of Williamson County or the Texas Hill Country speckled with sparkling brooks. In making a report to Captain Lam Sieker, the young Ranger duly noted the working conditions in an around Shafter, Cal penning that the area was populated with countless craven killers and cutthroats and cow thieves.[67] Nope, working this thirsty and treacherous territory wouldn't do!

Sheriff Aten noted his brother's disappointment: "I am sorry you don't like that country but I always had an idea it was a very poor country, especially for Rangers."[68] There is little misgiving with suggesting Ira could tap into Cal's thought processes about continuing life as a Texas Ranger; he was then having—and had

been for a long time—his own personal qualms about the law enforcing life: "I expect some of these days to stand up before a
fire & shake off my six-shooter & Winchester & Kick them in &
watch them burn & go up in the pan-handle & settle down on a
little farm & go to nesting, be a better boy & read my Bible more.
When I am called up-on by an officer to assist him in making an
arrest, I will out to the barn & get a pitch fork or the hoe & follow
in behind the officer like old grangers do. . . ."[69]

Tracking Private Aten's footsteps throughout the Big Bend
Country and along the Rio Grande is doable—reasonably so.
However those archived Ranger records that shed such light do
not reveal Cal Aten was personally involved in any more gunplay.
That doesn't mean other Rangers were not suffering such horror.
Two of his working Ranger cohorts and personal buddies, Charles
Fusselman and John Gravis, would forfeit their lives riding for
Texas. Both were on the Company D roster in West Texas with
Cal. Those incidents are stories within themselves. Suffice to say
Private Cal Aten had accurately gauged the tough section, not-
ing that killing a Ranger was product of "the Deviltry of a lot of
cowardly thieves and murderers in which this country abounds."[70]

And although it conjectures up speculation, there is a logical basis for wondering if Ranger Fusselman's murder rekindled
inquisitiveness—and/or—guilt about the Odle brothers' undoing.
Private Aten made an inquiry to Captain Lam Sieker at Ranger
headquarters: "Dear Sir and Capt. You will pardon the liberty
I take in offering these few lines. I would be pleased to Know
whether or not Sheriff Ira Wheat of Edwards Co. received any
reward from the State on Will and Alvin Odle, who were Killed on
the 25th of Dec. 1889, in Edwards Co. by Deputy Shff. Terry and
Rangers Hughes, Outlaw, and myself. If it is too much trouble,
let it drop as it is but little more than curiosity on my part."[71] Is
interpretation of the letter up for grabs? Plainly, Cal Aten did not
overtly lay claim to a piece of the pie, should a reward have been
paid. Baz Outlaw and John R. Hughes would have been up to
snuff on that, if they had taken a cut. They were his pals. It would
not be illogical to theorize that perhaps—just perhaps—the "curiosity on his part" was due to an issue that tenaciously, like a can-
cer, kept creeping into his head: Was it a blood-money plot from
the get-go? Cal had a conscience and those could be troublesome
things—scruples.

By the end of June 1890 the three youngest of the Aten clan, Ira, Cal, and Eddie, had made a crucial decision: They would seek their fortunes—one way or another—in the Texas Panhandle. While on a leave of absence from hectic Fort Bend County, Sheriff Aten made an exploratory trip to the section, writing to Cal from the Panhandle: 'I will look for you a section close to me & if I locate up here. So you can come & go on it just as soon as you please. Eddie wants to come up here too & I am going to get him a section also . . . . I will enclose you an application & obligation to the state when a man takes up school asylum or State lands. I have filled one out so as to give you an idea of things.'[72] It appears Cal Aten, then stationed at dirty, dangerous, and desolate Presidio, just opposite the Mexican border town of Ojinaga, was already standing in the starting-gate just waiting for such news—a good excuse for saying *adios* to the Texas Rangers. He voluntarily separated from Company D on the last day of August 1890.[73]

Ex-Ranger Cal Aten had surely blueprinted a move to the Texas Panhandle, and would eventually make such a jump, but a stopover at home near Round Rock had temporarily knocked him off course, bumped him sideways. There was good reason to tarry—Mattie Jo Kennedy. Although she was eight years Cal's junior, Mattie Jo was brainy and vivacious and gorgeous and shapely and, perhaps, most importantly—available. That is, she would be, when she turned eighteen—so said her mama and papa. The courtship rituals were set in motion. In that interim period between front porch kisses goodnight and the May 2, 1894, march down the chapel's aisle Mr. Cal Aten earned his livelihood—part of it—from fees made performing duties of an area lawman, at least so says one conversant scribe.[74]

Cal's and Mattie Jo's dream, as later facts confirm, was not to have Cal spend his life toting a six-shooter and wearing a badge seven days a week. He was a man drawn to livestock and land. Brother Ira, after leaving Richmond had migrated to the Texas Panhandle, come through unscathed during a ghastly gunfight in the little burg of Dimmitt, served a stint as sheriff of Castro County, and had then picked up reins as Superintendent of the Escarbada Division on the mammoth XIT Ranch. It was the perfect opportunity for Cal to make his move. XIT pay records reveal that by 1899 Cal was cowboying on the Escarbada, Deaf Smith County, pocketing $25 a month and earning a lifetime's worth of cattle country experience. Cal was steadily banking knowledge and a good name, one that would allow him credit enough to buy his own piece of ground. And he did. Cal and Mattie Jo purchased a 2,560-acre spread near Adrian, Oldham County (Vega) not too terribly far west of Amarillo. There he later registered his brand at the courthouse, the 8N, a rather clever phonetic appellation for "Aten."

Though we'll not delve into the specifics of dates and places of birth, it is but appropriate to note that Cal and Mattie Jo lovingly raised something aside from cattle and horses and the occasional mule—a family, a large family. They would become the button-poppin' proud parents of eight children, Cassie, Calvin Warren, Darrell Lamar, Rena May, Quinn, Lannie Lillian, Austin Turner, and Moody Evelyn. Not unexpectedly then, with such a large family, over time it would seem as if grandchildren were sprouting like wildflowers on the Panhandle prairie. One and all, those grandchildren would adore Cal and Mattie Jo, and cherish the time spent visiting and vacationing on the new farm near Lelia Lake, Donley County, which would be the couple's last land acquisition. Cal Aten acquired something else, too, a short-lived turn in harness for the State of Texas.

Six months short of his 50th birthday Cal raised his right hand and took the oath of an unpaid Loyalty Ranger on 1 June 1918.[75] His job, though he carried all rights and privileges of a Texas peace officer, was not to physically arrest rip-roaring drunks and/ or jug behind-the-scenes embezzlers. America was at war with Germany and the possibility of security breeches from spies and/ or the likelihood of demolition by saboteurs within the confines of the country—Texas too—was real, at least the perception was real. Cal's assignment was "to assist our government in every way possible during this war . . . . work under cover as much as possible, and in a secret capacity, report all disloyal occurrences to this office for instructions." Additionally, when called upon by local law enforcement for any reason, as a Loyalty Ranger, the middle-aged Cal was to lend a helping hand, six-shooter and Winchester at the ready.[76] Thankfully the war ended, as did Cal's tenure as a Loyalty Ranger. He put his Colt's .45 six-shooter, the one once belonging to a disreputable and dangerous Texas desperado, back underneath his feather bedding at Lelia Lake, as evidenced by this individual illumination: "The same pistol I keep under my mattress now."[77]

Appreciating historical significance of such a six-shooter, and with commendable forethought knowing the weapon would be passed down through generations of his family, Cal found a small piece of paper. With his own hand he scribbled an explanation, placing it inside the Colt's grips by the mainspring.[78] The inscription read:

> Taken from hand of Alvin Odle as he lay dying at East foot
> of Bullhead Mt. Edwards Co. Tex. Xmas night 1889.[79]

As a father and grandfather Cal Aten prospered. From all appearances he prospered financially as well. When a certain piece of Uvalde County property came on the market, Cal did not hesitate. Within fence-line boundaries of this tree-shaded piece of real-estate was the old Ranger campground, Camp Leona. Cal, according to Ira, had become "quite attached" to the spot, and rather than let a stranger close the deal, he "bought the place and it made a good ranch for his boys . . . . The sentiment of letting anyone else have the old camp was too strong for him." Later, on a trip from his home in California to Texas, even Ira waxed nostalgically about Cal's act of generosity: "The boys have cleared out the brush and the old camp looks as natural as life, Fifty years ago. The old live oaks and pecan trees are standing as sentinels over the past. The scar on the old tree I nailed the feed box on and tied my horse to for nearly four years is still there."[80]

Time is not an ally. It's relentless and it's unstoppable. Like old men do, as he aged Cal Aten began the backwards glances at his life. Plainly it may be noted he was most proud of his family. Too, he was certainly not ashamed of his service with the Texas Rangers, but maybe somewhat embarrassed in a peculiar way. He had marked time with Rangers who had—in the line of duty—forfeited it all. Men gunned down on the job. Ranger buddies like Charley Fusselman, John Gravis, and his Company D captain of days gone by, Frank Jones. Cal Aten had been lucky:

> It seems to me as I look back I never had any thrills compared to famous Rangers. I was never shot, wounded, and never even had my horse Killed under me.[81]

The end was near. On the first day of April 1939, ironically the anniversary date of his enlisting with the Texas Rangers fifty-one years earlier, Calvin G. Aten passed to the other side.[82] He was seventy years old. After a memorial service, he was laid to rest in Clarendon's Citizens Cemetery. In life or in death, there wasn't a pretentious bone in his body. He had not been a vain showboat. Cal Aten had lived the life of a gentleman—and a gentle man.

Aten family following their move from Illinois to Texas. Standing L to R: Austin Ira, Clara Isabell, Thomas Quinn, Margaret Angelina Elizabeth, and Franklin Lincoln. Seated L to R: Calvin Grant, Reverend Austin Cunningham Aten, Katherine Eveline, and Edwin Dunlap. Ira, Calvin, and Edwin would earn records of distinguished service with the Texas Rangers. *Courtesy Armstrong Research Center, Texas Ranger Hall of Fame & Museum.*

Studio pose of Austin Ira Aten. Though the photo is somewhat deceptive, there was nothing timid or retiring regarding Ira's true grit. He survived several gunfights, standing alone, a claim not shared by some of the better known lawmen hawking their puffed up stories to Hollywood during twilight years. As a Ranger Sergeant he welcomed younger brother Calvin Grant into the service, handing him a Colt's six-shooter and a belt full of cartridges. *Courtesy Jeri and Gary Boyce Radder.*

An iconic photograph, the Texas Rangers of Company D. Standing L to R: Jim King, Baz Outlaw, Riley Boston, Charles Fusselman, Tink Durbin, Ernest Rogers, Charles Barton, and Gerry Jones. Seated L to R: Bob Bell, Cal Aten, Captain Frank Jones, J. Walter Durbin, Jim Robinson, and Frank Schmid. *Courtesy Armstrong Research Center, Texas Ranger Hall of Fame & Museum.*

Another classic Texas Ranger image: L to R: Private John Woodward "Wood" Saunders and the ever energetic Corporal J. Walter Durbin. Corporal Durbin was proud of the Company D Rangers, but did candidly admit they could be a little "fussy and dangerous when drinking." *Courtesy Nita Stewart Haley Memorial Library and J. Evetts Haley History Center, Midland, Texas.*

Company D Texas Rangers at Camp Leona near Uvalde, Texas, cordially posing for a traveling shutterbug. From L to R: John Hughes bringing up the rear with pack mule, Ernest Rogers, Jim Robinson, a dismounted Gerry Jones, Frank Schmid, Jim King, Baz Outlaw, Charley Fusselman, Calvin Grant Aten, Walter Durbin, and Ira Aten at the staged ensemble's forefront. *Courtesy Jeri and Gary Boyce Radder.*

A formal portrait of Calvin Grant Aten. *Courtesy Sally Walker.*

Texas Ranger Bazzell Lamar Outlaw, "a man of unusual courage and coolness and in a close place is worth two or three ordinary men," said Captain Frank Jones. Ranger Baz Outlaw was sometimes mean, sometimes drunk, and always dangerous. Along with Cal Aten, he would participate in a Christmas Holiday gunplay with the outlaw Odle brothers near Bullhead Mountain, Edwards County, Texas. *Courtesy Armstrong Research Center, Texas Ranger Hall of Fame & Museum.*

Standing L to R: Texas Rangers Bob Speaks and Jim Putman. Seated L to R: Lon Oden and John Hughes. Along with Privates Cal Aten and Baz Outlaw, Hughes would also take part in the Texas Hill Country gunplay with outlaws. *Courtesy Armstrong Research Center, Texas Ranger Hall of Fame & Museum.*

Elaborately engraved Colt's .45 six-shooter taken from desperado Alvin Odle after he and his brother Will were killed during an Edwards County gunplay with secreted Texas Rangers and a sheriff's posse. *Courtesy Joseph H. Trobaugh II.*

Handwritten note of Calvin Grant Aten regarding the revolver taken from Odle: "Taken from the hand of Alvin Odle as he lay dying at East foot of Bullhead Mt. Edwards, Co. Tex. X Mas Night 1889." Assuring the significance of this Colt's historic meaning, Cal placed the note behind the revolver's grips, next to the mainspring. His thoughtful preservation is appreciated. *Courtesy Joseph H. Trobaugh II.*

Wedding photograph of Calvin Grant Aten and Josie Kennedy. *Courtesy Sally Walker.*

Although cowboy Calvin Grant Aten cannot be positively identified in this group of XIT Ranch cowboys, it is a representative image and Cal Aten was on the payroll as a hard-riding and fast-roping XIT Ranch cowboy. *Courtesy Nita Stewart Haley Memorial Library and J. Evetts Haley History Center.*

Cal Aten and family at his first ranch near Adrian, Oldham County, Texas. *Courtesy Shirley Aten Roberts.*

Brother Edwin Aten, seated, visiting with Cal Aten at his 8N Ranch near Lelia Lake, Donley County. *Courtesy Shirley Aten Roberts.*

A Modern Hercules to the Rescue

Too frequently, emphasis in authentic Outlaw/Lawman history is predicated by a dogmatic categorizing of biographical subjects, awarding them with unfitting and/or misleading labels. First-rate examples of the phenomenon are easily illustrated. If one opts to stick with irrefutable evidence and forgo folklore, the skin of embellishment may be pulled back exposing truths. Resultantly, when standing naked—unclothed from the hype—not just a few of the Wild West's lawmen and outlaws let slip reality. Many of the so-called lawmen were less than admirable characters and many of the outlaws were simply that, outlaws—mean and despicable. Sometimes a fellow wore both hats, jumping back and forth across legality's line, which makes for a not very romantic understanding of the Southwest's frontier era, and, too, shoots to smithereens naive notions about that mythological, but overstated and overrated Code of the West. Securely grounding Old West criminal justice studies with facts, sans the sensational fiction, recalibrates our grasp of reality and expunges contrived romanticism.

John Nathan Hittson was neither a bandit nor professional badge-wearer, although he did pull a short stint as an overworked but truly less than inspiring Lone Star State sheriff in Palo Pinto County. Therefore in the stirring annals of gunfighters and guttersnipes his name is not notorious or well-recognized. His decisive and, at the time somewhat controversial, measures appreciably put the wholesale kibosh on an illicitness that had stayed alive and uninterrupted for years—and years—and years. John N. "Cattle Jack" Hittson was a Texas and Colorado cattleman, big-time. And John Hittson was fed-up: Fed-up with cow thieves and the bargain-hunting buyers of purloined Longhorns. His striking story has been told before now, brilliantly, but not in the framework of Outlaw/Lawman sagas or Criminal Justice studies. This facet of the rousing tale has not been told too often, or with too many particulars.[1] What follows is not a comprehensive biographical sketch of a man in the round, but rather an inspection of the technique one cowman employed to put right a profitless deficit, one that was steadily devastating his personal livestock empire, one that was progressively milking his financial wherewithal dry.

The well-regarded J. Evetts Haley wrote, "Of all the arrant horse-thieves that depredated upon the changing frontiers of Texas, the Comanche Indians were the worst and most numerous."[2] Unmistakably author Haley was right. This journalistic try is not a piece designed to dissect all the sociological dynamics of the Comanchero Trade. A quick glance is not out of place, however. Simply put, the Amerindians never shaped a manufacturing base, nor incorporated an ability to mass produce highly prized implements forged from steel.[3] Racing advances in technology did not go unnoticed by the wily Comanches. They, not at all dissimilar to any other evolving cultural subgroups, sought an upgrading from primitive physical standards of living by integrating into their daily lives the latest newfangled gadgets: iron kettles, sharp knives, shiny mirrors, or firearms. Once exposed to the man-made niceties that made everyday living just a little easier the Amerindian was hopelessly hooked.[4] There were but two logical recourses left open to envious Comanches: raiding and trading. Comanches who were preying first on horse herds, and then the cattle they shrewdly pilfered from frontier Texas ranch lands, soon learned that out on that ever lonesome and forlorn-looking Llano Estacado, somewhere in that timeless void of skullduggery between unlawful acquisition and unscrupulous disposition prowled Comancheros.[5]

Hollywood directors have somewhat skewed truthfulness with their epic portrayals of the Comancheros. It is effortless to picture Comancheros as drunken greasy-faced crisscrossed bandoleer-wearing ne'er-do-wells: Desperadoes capable of cold-bloodedly gunning down tenderfoot tourists and then savagely ravishing their broken-hearted widows, daughters, and sweethearts, before mercilessly cutting their screaming throats or swapping them into a wicked life of depraved whorehouse debauchery. Josiah Gregg, the early Santa Fe Trail trekker, the person credited with coining the term *Comanchero*, painted a slightly different portrait of the typical Staked Plains trader:

> These parties of *Comancheros* are usually composed of the indigent and rude classes of the frontier villages, who collect together several times a year and launch upon the plains with a few trinkets and trumperies of all kinds, and perhaps a bag of bread and maybe another of *pinole,* which they barter away to the savages for horses and mules. The entire stock of an individual trader very seldom exceeds the value of twenty dollars, with which he is content to wander about for several months, and glad to return home with a mule or two as the proceeds of his traffic.[6]

A protracted historic examination of the long enduring mercantile intercourse between impoverished New Mexicans and fearsome Comanche fighting men is not necessary for this narrative. Long before John N. Hittson came into a nineteenth-century world the trade had existed. As time went by the illegitimate traffic increased in historic proportion. Capitalizing on the nefarious commerce, as would be expected, were some wealthy New Mexican merchants and financiers. Lurking in the shadows and not chance-takers themselves, they were more than willing to buy stolen horses, mules, and cattle delivered to the very doorsteps of their immense ranges. The trade in stolen livestock and to a lesser extent human captives thrived.[7] During and after the Civil War this clandestine industry mushroomed. Helpful is but one example: On September 7, 1867, Captain George Letterman, U.S. Army, confiscated from Comancheros 800 head of misappropriated cattle, and was loose herding them near Fort Bascom, eastern New Mexico Territory, waiting for ranchmen to prove lawful ownership.[8] Comancheros and John Hittson, although neither knew it during the turbulent 1860s, were on an immovable and irreversible High Plains collision track.

On October 11, 1831, at Nashville, Tennessee, Jesse and Mary Ann Beck (Hart) Hittson had adoringly welcomed their first-born child, John Nathan.[9] The steadily growing family tarried not too long in the Volunteer State, and before he was six years old, John and his siblings were living in Monroe County, Mississippi.[10] By the time he was twenty (1851) John, his father Jesse, and younger brother William "Bill" were optimistically looking for a meaningful future in Texas. Four days after Independence Day, 1851, John married fourteen-year-old Selena Frances Brown at Henderson, in deep East Texas.[11] Three years later, John's brother Bill wed Selena's aunt, Martha, and the three Hittson families in due course moved farther west to the Brazos River country of Palo Pinto County.[12]

Formally carved from Navarro and Bosque Counties during 1856, Palo Pinto County wasn't organized until 1857.[13] The county seat was first named Golconda, but changed to Palo Pinto in 1858.[14] Regardless of the name changes, picturesque but broken and hilly, Palo Pinto County (west of Fort Worth) was thoroughly known for two qualities: it was first-rate cow-country, and it was the bleeding target of seemingly incessant Indian incursions. It was at the western edge of a brutal Texas frontier.

During the first county elections in the spring of 1857, John Hittson was elected sheriff of Palo Pinto County.[15] An evenhanded and painstaking biographer candidly characterized John Hittson's stab at executing official law enforcement duties as a dismal failure.[16] Over the last few years several adroit Old West writers have meandered—in spite of living descendants' disavowals—and watchfully navigated around the submerged mire and muck traditionally linked with wide-spread vigilante justice. There, however, will not be a journalistic thrust directed herein at traveling the well-worn trail of accusations, counterclaims, partisan innuendo, cleverly chosen omissions—and a few downright lies. Others have splendidly penned the gripping story. To be sure it's a good one. Simplistically, there may have been at one time a bona fide need for the Old Law Mob or its counterparts on that jittery North Texas frontier, a sparsely populated expanse that beckoned not only hard-working pioneers but an overabundance of unsavory and lawless rogues as well. Brand-blotching and cow stealing were commonplace, murder and mayhem epidemic. Vigilante justice was the recognized prescription, prompting one country editor to postulate an unfussy remedy for dealing with cutthroats and livestock stealers: "Hang 'em first; then if they persist in their innocent amusement, cremate them. If that does not put the kibosh on 'em, we don't know what will."[17]

Much of what has been written about trademark vigilante justice has been centered around events in Albany, the eventual shire town for Shackelford County and in her up-the-road neighboring

burg; a fractiously disposed hell-roaring civilian community commonly known as The Flat, just downhill from an Indian fighting installation, the U.S. Army's Fort Griffin. The squalid mess
spilled over like a tidal wave to the adjoining counties, Palo Pinto
included. Sheriff John Hittson's self-preservation perceptions
were astute. He quickly recognized "the raw, simple power of
armed men to solve difficult problems," subsequently becoming
a vigilante principal himself.[18] Hittson's overt sympathies, at the
time, were with the O.L.M. and its illegitimate offspring, outfits
bent on the righting of wrongs—on the spot—not necessarily an
appropriate position for a sheriff elected and sworn to administer
the rule of Constitutional Law.[19] John Hittson resigned as the top
lawdog for Palo Pinto County during 1861 and moved even further
west to unorganized Throckmorton County, joining his brother
Bill and settling into a drafty picket house at an abandoned federal
fortification, Camp Cooper.[20] Whether or not John Hittson herded
some 500 head of Longhorn cattle from Palo Pinto County to his
new stomping grounds goes unrecorded, but the nucleus for his
future livestock operations blossomed at this juncture.[21]

There might have been another justification for forsaking the
sheriff's job and ambling even further into a geographical world
of remoteness: Dodging the Confederate Army's relentless scrutiny. Distinctly it has plainly been written that "the Hittson brothers actively avoided the Confederate authorities," where out there
on the frontier's edge they were sensibly safe from the perambula-
tions of army recruiters and soldiers on the hunt for slackers and/
or deserters.[22] While others may have been squinting over muskets'
imprecise sights, rallying forth or retreating during blood-spattered
battles for the Blue or the Gray, John Hittson was not an idle man.
Everyday he hunted "wild cattle," roped and burnt into their sear-
ing hides his distinguishable and soon to be notable, Three Circle
brand, "a round ring on the shoulder, one on the side and one on
the hip."[23] John Hittson gathered through these tireless labors a
sizable herd, but as to whether he was "branding ownerless cattle"
as has been indifferently written, might well have been a point
argued by a hapless conscripted Texan, far away from his own
ranch, fighting in the war.[24] Be not fooled though; John N. Hittson
was not lily-livered and primary source evidence fails to even
imply he shirked hard work or hazard. Visionary, however, he was.
Opportunistically he, like so many of the celebrated Southwest

cattle-kings, craftily engaged in cow catchin' while the cow-creatures were there to be caught. Egotistically and profitably it was much more lucrative to be an entrepreneurial "cowman" than a wage-working "cowboy."

Hittson was remarkably industrious. Unmistakably for a budding cow-country capitalist he was at precisely the very right place—at the very right time—notwithstanding the continual Comanche forays. Through the 1860s John knowledgeably managed his ever-increasing herds, and eventually made the center of operations for his mushrooming venture near Battle Creek, in the surveyed but yet to be officially organized Callahan County (east of present-day Abilene). "The headquarters were used only when cattle were rounded up from surrounding lands, and only consisted of corrals, branding pens and a small shelter."[25] Eventually John Hittson's bovines increased in such numbers that they were ranging throughout an eight-county area.[26]

Comanche depredations seemingly went unabated and on several occasions while in the isolated reaches of his vast domain Hittson and his cowboys engaged in skirmishes, and more than once he suffered stinging punctures from the "red-devil's" whizzing arrows.[27] So bad had Indian raids become that temporarily Hittson and others were forced to "fort-up" in a civilian compound they jointly constructed on the Clear Fork of the Brazos, Fort Jefferson Davis.[28] Interestingly, from an Outlaw/Lawman standpoint, it was here that John Hittson and a respected frontiersman at the time lived as "next-door neighbors." Later the fellow resident, John Selman, would make his marks in the history books as a ranch-country rascal and man-killer of record.[29]

Several other Texas cattle-tycoons seemingly have captured the attention of biographers and Old West writers; men such as Charles Goodnight, Oliver Loving, John Simpson Chisum, C. C. Slaughter, John W. Iliff, Robert K. Wylie, and the likes, but an interested reader must not be misled by unfamiliarity. Each of them, one and all, were John's contemporaries, they knew him and he they, and it's been written that at one time Hittson "operated on a grander scale."[30] In fact, becoming one of the leading trail drivers of the period, John Hittson for several years, beginning in 1866, drove annually 8,000 head of Longhorn steers to New Mexico and/or Colorado.[31] Later it was estimated that he had as many as 50,000 head in Palo Pinto County alone.[32] At any particular time having as few as 50,000 head and as many as 200,000, at least according to one report, John Hittson was known as "one of the foremost ranchers in the West."[33] John N. Hittson by 1870 had metamorphosed from a scratching neophyte dirt-farmer in East Texas into a legendary self-made man, an indisputable Southwest beef-baron. When he had to be, which wasn't often, John Hittson could be refined in demeanor—for a time—but was on "the record as vulgar and abusive to his adversaries," as he was "quiet and withdrawn" around his relatives and friends. Leathery-faced and somewhat bow-legged from years spent in a slick-forked Texas stock saddle, John Hittson was not a man to monkey with. There are unsubstantiated rumors that he had killed several white men, and according to at least one specialized Old West scholar, during the iniquitous Lincoln County War in tumultuous New Mexico Territory, John Hittson "lurked as a shadowy figure in the background—his presence was felt but rarely noted."[34] To be totally sure, John Hittson was no mealy-mouthed, temperance-minded teetotaler; literally he "was excitable when drunk."[35] John Hittson was cut from rough stock and "Cattle Jack" could issue ruthless punishment.

Historically major events occur not in a vacuum. So, while John N. Hittson was busily engaged amassing his fortune and staking his claims, others were too. Namely, Comanches, their intermediaries the Comancheros, and at the top of the pecking order, wealthy New Mexicans, both Anglo and Hispanic, were cheering them on and mightily pirating and profiting from their despicable and sometimes bloody handiwork. By the end of the Civil War the illicit trade in stolen cattle had become big business. No longer was it a pitiable project of indigent peasants eking out a meager living. Only having to wink and licentiously look the other way, buyers on the one end knew perfectly well where rightful title to the vast herds of livestock belonged—and it wasn't with the Comanchero middle-men. But what the hell! Texas was far, far away!

Among his other attributes and in spite of his shortcomings, Texas cattle-king John Nathan Hittson was a prophetic man. During 1870 he began transferring his cattle interest to Colorado, anxious to take advantage of the escalating Denver livestock market. He established a ranch at Deer Trail east of the "Mile High City" on Middle Bijou Creek.[36] When questioned about reasons for making the northern migration, Hittson simply proffered what most Westerners already knew, "cattle will do as well there [Colorado] as in Texas, and there was freedom from thieving in a comparative degree."[37] The comparative degree of cow-pilfering had become pandemic in that adjacent country bordering the gargantuan and secretive and unforgiving Llano Estacado and its ageless hideaways. Hittson estimated the number of cattle spirited away from the northwest Texas ranges and sneakily traded to the increasingly furtive Comancheros in excess of 100,000 head.[38] Another legendary and conversant cattle-king, the well-known Charles Goodnight, tripled the guesstimate.[39]

Long had John Hittson suffered abuses by the ceaseless raiding of Comanches and the resultant loss of his livestock through their conspiratorial conduit for cheating rightful ownership, the Comancheros. The uncontrollable pandemonium touched him personally, on more than one occasion. A case in point: John's seventeen-year-old son, Jesse, a top-hand cowman himself, was managing a ten-man roundup crew near present day Ballinger, Runnels County, Texas. The county, not to be organized until 1880, was barely populated and miserably vulnerable to the onslaught from fast-riding warriors.[40]

About forty Comanches struck young Jesse Hittson's platoon of cowhands. After a gruesome and frightening four-hour battle the Indians jubilantly made off with seven hundred head of cattle, insultingly leaving behind but one friendless and pitifully bellowing heifer. Sardonically, Jesse had the creature roped and tripped, and with a blistering running iron branded into her side a back-country billboard:

7-11-72
Indians Thick as Hell
J. H.[41]

Daddy John Hittson was not amused. He had had it! His belly was full, plumb full! In Hittson's mind and, justly so, there were three separate components comprising the disreputable traffic in stolen cattle and horses. Naturally, at the bottom were the prowling Comanches and allied Indian *compadres*; on the next rung up a hierarchical ladder stood the Comancheros, who he irreverently characterized as "a low desperate class of Greasers," and at the top of the list, "First and Chiefest" were a set of New Mexican merchants who were occupying "prominent and responsible position before the public."[42] Furiously determined to solve his problem—his way—and perhaps reminiscent of an acquaintance with vigilante justice, Cattle Jack Hittson decisively opted to cut the head off the snake and chop where it hurt most, the pocketbook.

Reports that Hittson actually somehow acquired deputation from the Governor of Texas is dubious and, if in fact there were any documents of authorization they seem to have been made historically invisible.[43] Likewise, and it may be at least partly true, that with legal formality he was granted Powers of Attorney from nearly 200 fellow cattle ranchers as claimed, perhaps not, but he assuredly had their blessing and backing from the get-go.[44] Well, at least most of them; somewhat curiously Charles Goodnight, for whatever reason and indeed the unvarnished truth might prove most intriguing, "refused to sanction his moves."[45]

John N. Hittson, come hell or high water was unshakable though. By his mulish reasoning at this stage cheap talk and impotent threats were just damn foolishness. From his Colorado headquarters, John Hittson began pulling together a regiment of hard-boiled and well-seasoned stalwarts. The company when finished was imposingly muscular: ninety men.[46] The outfit was basically divided into three unsentimental detachments. When it was all said and done, the list was comprised of several Old West notables: Hittson's close friend and trail-driving companion, James E. Patterson; Thomas L. Stockton, the owner and operator of the legendary Clifton House; the "Wolf of the Washita," Robert Clay Allison; an eternally feisty and fearless John "Chunk" Colbert; and several gunfighting men from the Clear Fork country, "John Larn, the four Wilson brothers, and Tom Atwell."[47] And although hanging out in New Mexico at the time, rounding out the list were two Brazos River brothers well-known to the tough lineup, John and Tom "Tomcat" Selman.[48] Another member of the team setting out to be a righter of wrongs was the noteworthy Hugh Martin Childress, Jr., a hard-edged Texas cowman and formidable fighter of the first order:

> There are few drovers, or for that matter few men, of the
> peculiar type of Childress. A convivial, jolly fellow, always
> full of fun and frolic, with a heart as large as that of an ox.

He will walk boldly into death's jaws to relieve or avenge a
friend; has a nerve of iron, cool and collected under fire; is
a deadly pistol shot, and does not hesitate to use one effectively when occasion requires; yet would always rather avoid
a quarrel than see one, but will not shrink from facing the
most desperate characters. Nevertheless, there are few more
kind-hearted men more true to friends than Childress. But
to his enemies he presents, in anger, that peculiar characteristic of smiling demonically whilst he is plainly and openly
maneuvering to shoot them through the heart. However, the
reader will be in error if he concludes that Childress is a desperado, for he is not. . . .[49]

During the warmth of an 1872 summer, Texans swept across the
plains of eastern New Mexico Territory ruthlessly rounding up
suspected stolen cattle and horses ahead of them. United States
Army commanders, tactically, and by design, supported John
Hittson's mercenaries. In at least one instance they were ordered to
furnish "surplus arms" to the avengers.[50] Later, on August 1, 1872,
cooperative instructions to field officers were tightened, and their
efforts were to be overtly directed only toward the prevention of
"bloodshed,"—*if possible!*[51] Predictably the spilling of a few buckets of blood was called for, well, at least from the warped reasoning of the Texas crowd. The compassionless contingent of Chunk
Colbert and platoon recovered a herd of stolen cattle and "arrested"
two suspects near Cimarron (Colfax County). A bothersome court
hearing was not in the cards; the two detainees were fatally gunned
down on the road back to town.[52] Not surprisingly, a Coroner's
Jury of area citizens, in light of the daunting options, fastidiously
but speedily determined the killings were not unwarranted.[53] In
an additionally reported homicidal happening, although anecdotal
but undeniably having a ring of believability, it was reported that
near Anton Chico the Texans recovered fifteen hundred head of
cattle wearing the wrong brands. After a hard fight they took one
of the culprits, an *Americano*, into momentary custody, nonchalantly lynched him, and then briskly galloped away leaving the
lifeless corpse dangling under the shadows of a lonesome pine
tree.[54] There are, however, other casualties of the wicked little war
that suffer the misfortune of an indiscernible identity.

One splendidly agitated rancher, another *Americano* by the
name of Simpson, defiantly refused to forfeit possession of his

herd to the retaliating cow-hunters. After all, he sensibly surmised, the beeves had been legitimately paid for with hard-earned U.S. greenbacks, albeit tendered to Comancheros, but where they got hold of the cattle was categorically none of his worry. Perhaps it should have been. Maybe he should have adopted a more conciliatory tact. Simpson didn't, though, and belligerently chided that nobody was going to cut and sort his cattle. The ever intractable Jim Duncan, from the opposing team, unambiguously proffered to Simpson that "they were damn sure going to take them." Executing a skillful maneuver, unsmilingly a Texan leaned from his saddle and opened the corral gate, intent on liberating the pilfered livestock. Simpson audaciously jumped into the breach.[55] Calmly "the Texans shot him down and cold-bloodedly drove the cattle out over his body."[56]

On the face of it, it seems that abruptness and meanness were steadily spiraling out of control. Don Miguel Otero, formerly the Territory's delegate to the United States Congress and father to a future New Mexico governor, made a hasty trip and, timorously, "went to the raiders' camp where he urged their leader to have greater regard for the property of the citizens of New Mexico."[57] John Hittson made clear the warring Texans' rationale and Otero was advised in no uncertain terms:

> These God damn greasers have been stealing our horses and cattle for the past fifty years, and we got together and thought we could come up this way and have a grand round-up, and that is why we are here. What is more we intend to take all the horses and cattle we come across and drive them back to Texas where they belong. My advice to your fellows is: Don't attempt to interfere with what we are doing unless you are looking for trouble.[58]

Even the Indian fighting military was beginning to confess a degree of frustration. Colonel Ranald S. Mackenzie, a noted frontier campaigner, for quite some time had been cold-trailing specified Comancheros across the Llano Estacado based on the rock-solid intelligence provided by a previously captured informant, Polonis Ortiz. Disappointedly for Mackenzie, at the village of Pureta de Luna (New Mexico Territory) he found that the suspects had scattered; "to escape an even more feared foe than the troops. John Hittson, one of the largest cattle owners in Texas, with a force of ninety cowboys and gunmen. . . ."[59] Wholly apathetic toward any pitiable local citizens' distress, and undisturbed by the U.S. Army's qualms, John Hittson's soldiers pressed the chase and the case, unmercifully.

At Loma Parda, on the banks of the Río Mora, twenty-five miles north of Las Vegas, New Mexico Territory, the Texans on September 8 found seven head of John Hittson's misappropriated steers standing where they shouldn't be. Because their force was undermanned at the time, recovery efforts were sternly rebuffed by an adamant Edward S. "Sam" Seaman, the local postmaster and constable, a salty ex-mountain man who in the past had fought alongside another illustrious New Mexican, Christopher "Kit" Carson. Smartly, the thoroughly perturbed Texans gave ground, but only for awhile. Two days later they returned, sixty strong, rip-roaring and more than ready to "whip ass and take names!" Straightway, Julian Baca was ordered to surrender two horses. He didn't. He paid dearly for the noncompliance. Grabbed from behind he was pistol-whipped severely, "until his body was black." Baca's crying wife pleaded for help. A neighbor, Toribo Garcia, rushed to her aid, a six-shooter in hand. The act was heroic; the misjudgment colossal. He was mortally gunned down. Seaman, with commendable bravery in light of the poor odds, but wretchedly impractical, raced toward the trouble only to be curtly questioned: "What are you doing here, you damn son-of-a-bitch?" Before he could interject a coherent retort into the homicidal hubbub, he was sledgehammered to the ground by a "slashing blow" from a rifle barrel, "cutting a deep gash across the cheek bone, and putting out the left eye." Knocked senseless, confusingly he ran into, rather than out of the cow-pen where the cantankerous Texans had congregated. Insolently grabbed one more time, somehow he wrenched himself loose and ran for the comfort and safety of his adobe abode. For his trouble, he "was shot from behind, falling forward on his face—the ball entered the back part of the head and came out just above the forehead tearing away quite a large piece of the skull, and causing instant death." Their rush from adrenaline thoroughly ignited, raging, the incensed "Cowboys" madly charged about rowdily firing Colt's .45s and purposefully gathering all the cattle in town. The tiny hamlet's *alcade* nobly registered his remonstrations, and he, too, was gratuitously gunned down, "callously shot through both legs." Then they left, leaving the "tortured town to its misery."[60]

Though perhaps thoroughly exasperated by the Texans' bold and brutal methodology of righting wrongs, a New Mexico Territory newsman hinted at underlying truths:

> Within the past few weeks the town of Loma Parda is known to have lost four of its citizens by violence. They became too intimately associated with their neighbors stock, and were strung up by the sufferers who had more faith in a stout lariat than stone walls.[61]

Naturally, every coin has two sides, and from the underside the aggrieved and run amok Texans saw the clamor in subjective shades casting a drastically differing light. James E. Patterson penned a letter to the Santa Fe *New Mexican* illuminating and justifying that local gendarme Seaman was only cut down after he had made vile threats, passionately stirred the near riotous riffraff of a crowd, and menacingly brandished a scary looking six-shooter.[62]

Before Patterson's version is simply written off as a face-saving and wholly shambled excuse, it must be recalled that a delightfully quaint and sleepy little New Mexican village, Loma Parda was not! More precisely, if a feminine appellation is not too impolite, she was known far and wide as "Sodom on the Mora." Basically Loma Parda was a Hispanic community, and an infamous "gathering place for sheepherders and Comancheros. . ."[63] At the time of John Hittson's raid she was familiarly branded as the "most notorious 'Hog Ranch' for soldiers" stationed nearby at the U.S. Army's Fort Union. Bluntly, post commanders were continually, although not very successfully, declaring the bawdy and tawdry sin-city off-limits.[64] Even a thoroughly pragmatic New Mexico Territorial newspaperman was forced—by the facts—to sensibly concede "there is a soreness on the part of the innocent purchasers of the stock, but they cannot deny the justice of the Texans' claims."[65]

For a short time it appeared if at least one of the Texans would be forced to honor a date with the Blind Mistress of Justice. There, in fact, was a technical arrest, after one of the shootists surrendered. There, too, was some very transparent bribery and an escape, causing a newspaper editor to sadly lament, though not correctly, "it was safe to say that he will never again be heard from in our Territory."[66]

Too, it was reasonably safe to pronounce that John N. Hittson and his Texans, at least from the pure public relations standpoint— exterior to the New Mexico Territory borderline—came out on top! As faraway as New York City and Chicago, the story about operations against the "border-thieves" was journalistically reported, and it was unconditionally declared that, "our bold, honest and wealthy stockman has gained a national reputation by the effectiveness of his method, and its entire want of red-tape."[67] John Nathan Hittson was even being widely dubbed "A Modern Hercules to the Rescue."[68]

An old Comanchero, even after confessing that he had taken bread, *panocha*—a sprouted wheat pudding—whiskey, guns, cotton fabrics, beads, knives and other articles out onto the Llano Estacado and traded with his *friends*, the Comanches, somewhat lamely tried to justify his disreputable mercantile business:

> The Comanches resented the moving of the Texans and other stockmen with their cattle into their land. Stealing cattle was the means of revenge which the Indians used against the cattle owners . . . . The Americanos around us were the real racketeers in the business. They did the buying from us, then they would drive the loot to Colorado, Kansas, Nebraska, or to California where they sold it at great profit . . . . In trading with the Comanches, we rounded up the cattle at night by the light of the moon and we drove them on a fast run. We made thirty miles by daylight. A party of Comanche Indians would stay behind to fight and hold the Tejanos back in case of pursuit.[69]

And pursuit is the genesis of this Old West story. Pursuit of stolen cattle. Pursuit of the outlaws on horseback. Pursuit of unprincipled sideline profiteers. Pursuit of freedom from financial ruin. Pursuit from a psychological devastation: the abject failure of protecting one's own property. Pursuit of dreams. When it was all said and done John Hittson and his assemblage of gunfighters and *mal hombres*—some good men too—rightly or wrongly, had pursued, confiscated, and driven away between five and six thousand head of stolen hoofed and horned stock: worth at the time some $60,000 to $70,000.[70] Although the individual body count is bafflingly shrouded, hidden from historical exactness, it must be accredited that several Comancheros or Comanchero sympathizers or, maybe even just a few unfortunate innocents, had unceremoniously been gunned down, compelled to draw their last breaths to sate retributive punishment's gnawing appetite. Incontestably, too, some rich New Mexican *rancheros* were tidily demoralized, and were pondering the real wisdom of purchasing those animals spirited across the Llano Estacado in the dead of night. No matter how cheap the outlay, if the cow-creatures were only to be confiscated and lost to a profitable tally, the shady deal had not been a bargain—at any price. John Hittson's methods and motives could yet be passionately queried and/or squabbled about. No doubt, at least in his own mind, John Nathan Hittson was a triumphant conqueror. Pragmatically though, in the larger picture of Southwestern frontier development, the finishing work for tapping out the troublesome Comancheros' lights was not to be the enduring legacy of Cattle Jack Hittson. That job was left for the blue-coated soldier; the wanderin' buffalo hunter; the thrifty shopkeeper; the cat-eyed underground miner; the hard-scrabble sod-buster; the overworked husbands and the undervalued wives; and the carefree and sometimes sassy schoolchildren: Mamas' unremitting cry for stability and civility—that's what, in the end, killed the Comancheros' illicit traffic and tamed the West.

And of John Hittson, personally? In Colorado he hammered out a cattle-kingdom and a gold-plated reputation—eventually surrendering both! On the national front there had been an economic downturn and, too, for John Hittson there had been the abysmally creeping erosion, psychologically. Sound judgment was abandoned to periodic "spreeing" when, as was often the case, he "became excited by liquor." Then he became sinisterly dark and "was a dangerous man to cross." On one occasion at Deer Trail, Hittson, armed with a shotgun, and J. M. Maxwell, sporting a six-shooter, traded hot lead. The upshot? A slightly wounded Maxwell suffered for awhile, an unscathed John Hittson rejoiced—briefly—for quickly it was learned an utterly unconcerned bystander, a little boy named Brown, had caught a wildly spent bullet in the foot. Cattle Jack, well, he caught the blame— big shame—and the bail bond, $4,000 worth. With his mind "unhinged" during another senseless argument with somebody over something, Hittson once again fell back on a six-gun settlement. Attempting to get off a speedy shot, this time his intended human target was a smidgen more nimble, and ferociously administered an excruciating thumping to John's weathered face and graying head with an unbending Colt's barrel.[71]

On a frosty Christmas Day, 1880, near an iced-over Bijou Creek, traveling by himself, fifty-nine year-old John Nathan Hittson, an authentic Texas borderliner, a cowman and Comanche fighter of "the old school," had a disastrous wagon wreck. He died. Three days later, at chilly Denver, Cattle Jack Hittson and a slice of history, the real Old West kind, were reverently buried—together.[72] Strangers they were not!

John Nathan "Cattle Jack" Hittson, a dominant force in the Texas and Colorado cattle industry. He would take the law into his own hands with overwhelming and injurious results—to cow thieves and their money hungry contacts. *Courtesy Western History/Genealogy Department, Denver Public Library.*

Buffalo and Comanches competed with John Hittson for the Open Range country west of the Brazos River. Here, at Weatherford, Texas, the region's trade center, a wagon train of buffalo hides is being brokered. John Hittson, for a time, was sheriff of adjoining Palo Pinto County. *Courtesy Nita Stewart Haley Memorial Library and J. Evetts Haley History Center.*

Although this is a latter day image, notorious man-killer John Selman, the shootist liable for ending John Wesley Hardin's disreputable career, during earlier days "forted up" with John Hittson when both were seeking defense for their families from marauding Comanches. *Courtesy Nita Stewart Haley Memorial Library and J. Evetts Haley History Center.*

John C. Jacobs, a Real McCoy buffalo hunter and cowboy and Wild West lawman. He hunted for hides and herded cattle and chased after fugitives on the Open Range where Hittson grazed livestock by the thousands. *Courtesy Nita Stewart Haley Memorial Library and J. Evetts Haley History Center.*

Though photographed later in life, J. Wright Mooar was one of the most celebrated buffalo hunters of all time. He, too, roamed the West Texas countryside with the likes of John Hittson and the Comancheros. *Courtesy Nita Stewart Haley Memorial Library and J. Evetts Haley History Center.*

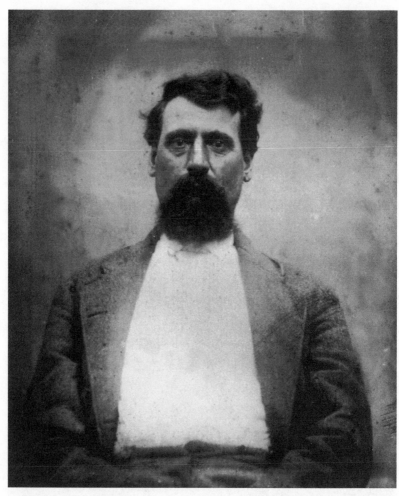

Hugh Martin Childress, Jr. He accompanied John Hittson on the New Mexico "cattle raid." Mart Childress was not a man to trifle with: "He would walk boldly into death's jaws to relieve or avenge a friend . . . . has the nerve of iron, cool and collected under fire. . . . is a deadly pistol shot. . . . presents, in anger, that peculiar characteristic of smiling demoniacally whilst he is plainly and openly maneuvering to shoot them through the heart." *Courtesy Paul Jenkins.*

3

Murders and Madness at Millican

Brazos County in Central Texas can lay legitimate claim to more than her fair share of the Lone Star State's history. Named for the Brazos River, the county could tout being an heir to Stephen F. Austin's second colony. After a quick but necessary designation or two the little village of Bryan blossomed as the seat of county government, due solely to the Houston & Texas Central Railroad bypassing the modest burg of Boonville. The region was agriculturally rich. Bottomlands of the Brazos and nearby Navasota Rivers assured prosperity for the industrious farmer tending his crops and overseeing his slaves. It was Plantation Country for the well-fixed landowners. For others, the hard-scrabble farmers eking meager subsistence absent financial wherewithal and the unwillingly ensnared workforce, Brazos County was yet profitably suitable agricultural real-estate. Motivated and hardworking Brazos County settlers eyeing their future could—and did—find their niche. It, too, in a later timeframe, would become home to the Agricultural and Mechanical College of Texas, Texas A&M, now nestled within the confines of Bryan's suburb, College Station.[1]

In the southern stretch of Brazos County lay the little hamlet of Millican. For awhile it was the northernmost railroad terminus in Texas and was so at the time Civil War hostilities erupted. As such the settlement, known then as Millican Crossroads, could proudly claim an active grist mill, hotel, restaurant, stagecoach station, small drugstore, a general merchandise store, churches, a subscription school, tin shop, and post office, manned by its first postmaster, Arthur Edwards. It was for a time the largest city north of the burgeoning metropolises of Houston and Galveston. At the time Millican Crossroads was the epicenter for Brazos County

commerce. During its lifespan, before the railroad reached farther north, Millican Crossroads was a town recognized statewide.
Threat of a hostile Indian incursion, though very troublesome during an earlier era, was a danger no longer faced.[2] Other trouble
was on the near horizon.

When time arrived for Brazos County folks to fish or cut bait
there was hardly evidence of hesitancy; the vote for secession was
decidedly lopsided, 215 to 44. Although the majority of landowners owned fewer than five slaves, nevertheless Brazos County laid
claim to 118 slaveholders and in an aggregate the slave population
exceeded 1000.[3]

Understandably from a geographic perspective Millican
Crossroads' position as a Confederate shipping funnel was
noteworthy. Valuable cotton ultimately destined for sale in Old
Mexico went south via the railroad from Millican Crossroads. A
nearby training and recruitment site, Camp Speight, served as the
platform for boys mustering in under the Secessionist's flag. After
unit organization and instruction the new recruits and their officers disembarked for grueling duty in Arkansas and/or Louisiana.
Other comrades entrained at Millican Crossroads for the docks
nearer Houston and Beaumont, then transshipment to more distant battlefronts.[4]

Following the South's capitulation and the boys in gray stack-
ing their muskets, Millican Crossroads underwent U.S. Army
occupation during Reconstruction when federal troops arrived
during 1865. With its heavy population of recently free black citizens, Brazos County on the whole and Millican Crossroads in particular, suffered a gratuitous spell of racial turmoil. The scorching
residue of insensitivity was not scrubbed away quickly. Bearing
witness to the fact that racial tactlessness in Brazos County died a
slow death—by employing a chronological fast-forward—is evidenced by an 1889 edition of *The Bryan Eagle*.

Troublesome Coons

Negro toughs have been giving the officers considerable
trouble during the past week. On Saturday [a] burley brute
resisted Deputy Marshall Bowman's authority and cursed
and dared him to attempt to take or strike him, and when
the officer gave him a gentle reminder with a cane he made

vigorous use of a large wagon whip, striking the official several heavy blows. Other officers came to the rescue and the tough was run in. On Monday City Marshall Nall was compelled to use the knock-down argument on another one, and did it in first-class workman like shape. On the same day, Sidney Bradley, a "bad man" from the country, stole a sack of meal from a white man's wagon, a trunk and contents and some other articles from some negro women, put them on his own wagon and left for home. He was overhauled about a mile from town by Deputy Marshal Bowman and the colored policeman Levi Neal. Bradley made fight and struck Neal with a heavy wagon standard. Several blows from Neal's six-shooter and Capt. Bowman's "billy" brought the villain to knee, and he was lodged in the county jail—though when he passed our office on the way—we mistook him for a freshly butchered beef, and expected the wagon to stop at the market house.[5]

And though the present narrative could rightly reach back with genealogical tentacles to days of the Alamo and San Jacinto, it is in the post-Republic of Texas days that harkens our interest. The town of Millican Crossroads was namesake for the Millican family, originally from South Carolina, via the patriarch's trans-Atlantic voyage from Scotland. Robert Hemphill Millican had married Nancy McNeill, and from that union, among other children, two sons were born: William Templeton Millican, a political powerhouse when the birth of a Texas nation was at hand, and Elliot McNeill Millican, at maturity a practicing physician and, too, a heavy-hitter on the field of local government and statewide policy making. Early on, unsympathetic tragedy had stalked the Millican clan. Robert Hemphill Millican passed away from pneumonia on the banks of the Trinity River near the settlement of Liberty during the well-known Runaway Scrape, while Sam Houston was busy marshaling his forces to do battle with Antonio López de Santa Anna at San Jacinto. William Templeton Millican died from exposure in 1848 while serving as a part-time and provisional Texas Ranger in the days when such service was commendable, but preceding the time a fledgling outfit was officially tasked with law enforcement duties. On the other hand, his brother Dr. Elliot Millican picked up the peace-keeping and tax-collecting reins of early day Brazos County, becoming its first sheriff. Additionally Dr. Millican, on more than one occasion and in more than one capacity, served as a member of the Texas State Legislature.[6]

Unashamedly at the time—during the Reconstruction era—Millican Crossroads was a fertile hotbed of racial violence and a literal killing ground for insensitive hotheads. A black Methodist minister, George E. Brooks, who also doubled as the voter registrar, had begun arming, organizing, and drilling as a militia, companies of freedmen in their nearby but segregated neighborhoods. Former slaves and their kinfolks deemed it but an appropriate and not unjustified measure of self-protection. White-robed and hooded Ku Klux Klansmen were about, blatantly marching in defiance with an in-your-face attitude, protesting Union League meetings and making threats. Alarmed whites supposed that the black military-type maneuvers were the rumblings of an anarchic volcano about to blow, one erupting with white folk's blood spurting high. Pigheadedness was mutual. The Freedmen's Bureau agent, Captain N. H. Randlett, issued his ultimatum: No armed groups, organizations, or secret outfits, would be allowed to operate in Brazos County. With narrow-mindedness in their heads, neither side gave an inch. Randlett's edict was impotent. Pandemonium was predictable.[7]

During the ensuing gunpowder mêlée craziness overrode common sense and sanity. It's not necessarily inaccurate to postulate that a freedman fired the first shot, at least so concluded Captain Randlett, but not surprisingly whites would fire the last—and there would be many, too many to enumerate. Responding to rumors that a black man had been killed by a white, Reverend George Brooks had dispatched a posse of armed freedmen under the command of one of his lieutenants, Harry Thomas. They surrounded the residence of the prime suspect in the alleged murder, threatening to lynch the fellow. As soon as the news broke at Millican Crossroads, a rescuing posse of whites with the mayor and a Brazos County deputy sheriff riding in the forefront had rushed to the scene, confronting Harry Thomas and his vigilante troops. In the end, talk turned to terror as both sides cut loose with their hand-held artillery. Harry Thomas died, as did a number of his freedmen volunteers that fifteenth day of July 1868. Guesstimates place the number at between four and fifteen. Whites suffered no casualties.[8] The mindless volcano of violence had erupted.

Over several days the body count of luckless freedmen grew, some say five—Republican leaning newspapers say half a hundred or more were killed in the vicinity of Millican. Another matter could be reported with more clarity: Preacher George Brooks was lynched. And with fortuitous irony, the U.S. Army, who had been called in to tamp down tensions and provide safety to the defenselessly vulnerable population, had, in the end, actually afforded whites the real protection and unintentionally awarded the freedmen's gravediggers backbreaking work. There was a quantifiable outcome—a favorable outcome—linked with the dreadful Brazos County bloodshed, at least according to an esteemed writer and educator, an expert in the field of study: "The violence at Millican for all practical purposes brought an end to the Ku Klux Klan as a statewide movement. The Klan had not produced good political results."[9]

After the mournful loss of his first wife, Elizabeth Clampitt Millican, Dr. Millican married Amanda Marcella Boyce Triplett, widowed with a small child. From that coming together four sons would issue, half-siblings to the good doctor's first eight children.[10] Unfortunately three of those eight and two of the four would be subjected to violent deaths. And it is the six-shooter drama of those Millican boys, brothers and half-brothers, that founds the genesis for this chapter.

The first near unspeakable dustup was sad, pitiably so. Exacting details are sketchy, perhaps purposely swept under the genealogical rug. Elliot Millican, Jr. would be killed by one of his own brothers, William Hemphill "Bill" Millican. Through the murkiness of time and obfuscation it may be fittingly said that Bill Millican would claim self-defense, not suffering any legal penalty. But, during an unrelated brouhaha, Mr. Bill Millican, serving as a Brazos County deputy sheriff, would forfeit his life.

During a spate of riotous behavior, white prisoners in the Brazos County jail were set free. The only black inmate in custody was not awarded his liberty. He was summarily lynched. Colonel (a presumed honorary title]) Robert C. "Bob" Myers, no doubt an ex-Unionist sympathizer but then a local saloon owner and "radical carpetbagger," accused Deputy Bill Millican of overtly cooperating with the infuriated mob. While certainly not defensible then or now, it is paramount to keep in mind that at the time local lawmen willingly cooperating or knowingly turning the blind eye to mob or vigilante justice was not necessarily an anomaly, especially in

Central Texas. In fact, though somewhat disheartening, often the community's prominent populace stood at the forefront of a mob's loosely interwoven leadership model. Or, in specific instances, influential citizens formed the top tier of mobs more intricately and secretively structured: That "Leaders of these mobs, more or less, were the Southern-minded economic elite of a community," is not misguided rhetoric. And in fact, "Most Texas mobs operated with the knowledge and tacit approval of law enforcement. Because organized mobs or vigilante committees could never exist without the help and support of local law enforcement, basically, approval was given for them to do what the law was otherwise powerless to do . . . . The Southern mindset viewed participation in vigilante mobs, although it was illegal, as necessary and legitimate. It was an exercise in their self-protection in the hostile and isolated region of Central Texas."[11]

Deputy Bill Millican had shied away from doing his duty, acquiescing to madness, so maintained Bob Myers. Colonel Myers' son-in-law, Benjamin F. "Ben" Boldridge, who had helped the colonel in organizing the Brazos County chapter of the Loyal League, an outfit bent on seeing Reconstruction work in Texas, was vocal in his outrage—real or feigned, partisan or fair-minded. After accepting the position of sergeant in the decidedly unpopular Texas State Police, Boldridge had messaged the equally unpopular Texas chief executive, Governor Edmund J. Davis. In the missive Boldridge advised that his district was decidedly Republican due to a lopsided black voter turnout, but that countywide Bryan with its larger white population could wield the Democratic stick with aplomb. Having noted the demographics somewhat accurately, Sergeant Boldridge furthermore highlighted that "the desperadoism has been allowed to run unchecked here from the time of the [Confederacy's] surrender." He noted that Millican Crossroads had been the scene of "many murders," specifically of so-called Union men. Boldridge spotlighted the death of Morris E. Lyons, claiming his assailant, Jesse Blair, "shot him down in the streets like a beef." Another, the son of a local judge, he said, was hanged from a stout live oak limb by a crowd overwhelmed with hate.[12] In Boldridge's mind the town of Millican Crossroads had simply run amok. And Sergeant Ben Boldridge was not alone.

Doctor John C. Gill, a Unionist, without a second thought it seems, openly declared that Millican Crossroads was "a miserable cut throat hole," and that everyone there "carries a large bowie knife and revolver strapped to him."[13]

Colonel Myers in regard to the jail liberation and coldhearted lynching of the black prisoner demanded a formal investigation be made and rightful punishment be administered, forthwith. Naturally that supposed complicity of Deputy Bill Millican would be the focal point of any nonpartisan inquiry—so thought Bob Myers. For his trouble Colonel Myers reportedly received numerous death threats. Bill Millican's terrorization added to the din—perhaps. Some few openly declared, so it's been written, that Bob Myers, "a damned old Republican anyhow" must die. Though counseled by his friends to flee for his life, Myers decided to lock and load, to stay hitched no matter the outcome. On February 6, 1870, Deputy Bill Millican waltzed into the Colonel's drinking emporium. Maybe he was a little or a lot tipsy, but for sure he had a cocked Colt's percussion six-shooter in hand. What hot vocals were exchanged is lost to history. The loudness of Myers' reply is not. He cut loose with both barrels of his shotgun, the scorching loads of buckshot hammering the life out of Brazos County Deputy Sheriff Bill Millican.[14]

Not unexpectedly Bob Myers was arrested and charged with the killing, as were his codefendants, David Myers and G. W. "Wash" Hardy. They could count on little sympathy with an all-white jury of dyed-in-the-wool Democrats, and in light of the time and place and crime, the verdict of guilty came as no shocker, but the subdued sentence of but six years at hard labor was. Shouldn't they all be hanged for killing a deputy sheriff, several mused? Many supposed the convictions and light sentences were only the result of their "sympathy for a foully murdered colored man." Governor Edmund J. Davis was not impressed one iota with Brazos County justice, convicting men of simply defending themselves from an oppressive and mulish officer of the law: One who *may have been* wholly complacent about the extralegal execution of a powerless freedman. At least the governor rationalized it that way, or damn close to it. No, that would not stand! Colonel Robert C. Myers—along with the others—was granted a Governor's Pardon within two months of the original conviction.[15] Myers could walk the streets of Millican again, free as a bird—a game bird. The Millicans were hunters. The Millicans were hungry.

A saying has it that revenge is sweet. William's brother John Earl Millican, also a Brazos County deputy sheriff, thought so. More than ever when served cold with gunpowder and lead. Bob Myers was fatally gunned down by John Earl during May 1871. There is a certain amount of obscurity as to whether or not John Earl faced the legal music for killing Myers, but it matters not very much in the overall story of a Texas feud.[16]

Colonel Bob Myers's grown children wanted to sate their taste for vengeance, too! So, on August 29, 1872, some sixteen months after the killing of their father, Allen Myers and his married sister, Nannie Boldridge, advantaged themselves of opportunity.

The *Cleburne Chronicle*, among other newspapers in Texas, carried the story. Deputy John Earl Millican after attending a local temperance meeting was but thirty yards away from the doorway to his residence when two shots rang out, in double quick succession. He stumbled and crumpled. Thirty seconds later a single charge of 00 buckshot found its mark, all nine pellets penetrating his torso. Two pitiless assassins fled into the shadows of looming darkness. Neighbors and/or family carried John Earl into his home, trying to make him as comfortable as possible. John Earl remained conscious until near the bitter end, just long enough to manage an official and legally admissible Dying Declaration, unambiguously fingering Mr. Allen Myers and Mrs. Nannie Boldridge as his coldhearted revenge-minded enemies and as the triggermen, well, triggerman and triggerwoman. Then he died! Although later arrested and held under a $7000 bond for awhile, the brother and sister skipped paying a legal price for their bushwhacking due to jurymen not being able to reach a unanimous verdict—a hung jury—a mistrial.[17] Settling scores outside a courtroom was okay. Texas was blood-feud country.

The following year, 1873, a Central Texas fellow from Leon County was arrested in Bryan, Brazos County, just up the road from Millican Crossroads. A newspaper snippet about the arrest is both amusing—as it was intended to be—and rightfully indicative of not just a few Texas boys' ingrained deportment:

> On his person were found the following side arms: two six-shooters, one derringer, a pair of brass knuckles, a poker "full"—three tens and a pair of sevens—a large knife and seven or eight morphine powders. He was prepared either to kill or cure.[18]

And that feuding mentality ran through the blood of two of Dr. Elliott Millican's boys by his second marriage, Marcellus Randall "Pet" Millican (01-27-1856) and his younger brother by two and a half years, Wilbur Ashley "Will" Millican (08-25-1858). Their older full brother Leander Randon "Lallie" (or Lally) Millican (08-23-1853) would in time gain favorable notoriety through- out Texas as a leather-slappin' bronc-ridin' man of the cloth, known far and wide across the Lone Star State as the "Cowboy Preacher."[19] According to his own words, Lallie Millican "grew up as 'Wild as a Cowboy' and ran my [his] own boat."[20] Lallie Millican by any measure was tough as the proverbial boot, but he was not rattlesnake mean. The youngest of this quartet of boys was named Elliott McNeill Millican, Jr., in honor of his father and the half-brother who likewise had the same name, but had been killed years before by his brother. Sorrowfully, the second Elliott McNeill Millican, Jr. died during infancy.[21]

Pet Millican, too, at age thirty-three, was a Brazos County lawman, holding title as the Constable of Precinct 1, a position he had nailed down on 12 September 1881. The Christmas spirit may have been in the mindset of most Brazos County folks that December of 1889, but not for one Mr. Charles "Charlie" Campbell. At the behest of the Curd brothers, Ezekiel aka Zeke and Dick, aka Poker, the ever so malleable Mr. Campbell was naively duped into a plot or paid hard cash dollars to assassinate Pet Millican. As yet an undisclosed motive sleeps in the abyss of uncertainty. Details are murky, the outcome isn't. On the fourteenth day of December the calculated bushwhacking took place. Constable Pet Millican was killed outright. Seemingly the criminal investiga- tion was of but extraordinarily short duration, perhaps in large part due to Charlie Campbell rolling over on his coconspirators and becoming the state's superstar witness. Jurymen were not im- pressed with the prosecutor's reasoning or his argument or his plea for the imposition of justice. A confirming declaration that the Curd brothers had connived with Charlie Campbell to kill Pet Millican was not demonstrated beyond that tricky legal standard of Reasonable Doubt. The claim that Zeke and Poker had hidden a gun, to be retrieved and used in the premeditated murder by Charlie Campbell, was, likewise, not at all provable above and beyond that sometimes elusive, but mandatory legal benchmark. A hard fact that the two Curd brothers were elsewhere when the crime was committed, however, was sustained—even if it might have been as was probable—an alibi by design.[22]

The acquittal may have surprised the district attorney, but his outrage was not shared by Zeke and Poker Curd. They were set free to go about their Brazos County business, though they'd best be watchful. Looking over their shoulders was but prudent. Texas feudists did not prefer the gavel to the gun. Handling their personal business was personal—and predictable. Pet had family. Needless to say, Pet Millican's younger brother Will was not in very high spirits. He was real mad, damn mad—madder 'en Hell. Will Millican's frosty threat to the Curd brothers was unmistakably plain, compassionless and unforgiving: Leave the county— for keeps—or endure the penalty. Millican wasn't fooling. Will said what he meant, and meant what he said![23]

An old-timer sets forth what happened next, well, what he was told happened next—a smattering of oral history. Constable Raymond Day elucidated: "There was an old man here by the name of Will Millican. He was a pretty tough old man . . . . He was pretty tough. He killed two or three men in his life . . . . Will Millican, the Will Millican that I know of, had killed one of the Curds right down here in front of the saloon . . . . There was one Millican named Pet Millican, and there was two of the Curd brothers. They was supposed to have killed this one that was named Pet Millican. Well, I don't know if they really proved anything or not, but old man Will Millican told them to leave Millican [Crossroads] and never come back. If they did, he was going to kill them. Well, this Zeke Curd had some kinfolks that lived up here and he come into Millican one evening and said that he was going to the saloon and get a drink of whiskey before supper. So he went down there and somebody [George Dunlap] came up here [and told Will] . . . . Will Millican was staying here and was told that Zeke Curd was at the saloon . . . . Will saddled his horse and came up here. Old Zeke Curd had a gun on him but he run out the front door and he grabbed an old man by the name of Taylor Bean. He was holding him up between him and Will Millican. That old Taylor Bean was having a fit trying to get loose. He said old Will told him, 'Goddamn it Taylor! Be still! I ain't going to shoot you!' So directly, he [Will] got a shot at him [Zeke] and plugged him and killed him. So that was the end of that story."[24]

Adding a touch of historical framework will not change the story, Zeke Curd was dead, and Will Millican was one tough fellow, a dead-game *hombre*. Supplementing Raymond Day's account with a few added details is not inappropriate.

Will Millican learned that the Curd brothers, at least one of them, had not heeded his warning and was foolishly partaking of a drink in Millican Crossroads at the Green Front Saloon, an imbibing establishment under the proprietorship of the Yeager boys, Fritz and Alfred. Saddling his horse and rounding up a helpmate, a nephew, Leander Marcella "Lee" Thompson, Will and Lee headed for the Green Front Saloon, blood retribution on their minds, fully charged Colt's .45s handy. Will Millican was quite literally not a man to monkey with, having for several years guarded inmates, possibly even having killed one or two. He was attuned to that scheming convict subculture filled with lame excuses, ploys, bluffs, lies, and violent acts of pure meanness, and the resultant corporal punishments. Prison predators can be ruthless. Their keepers need be tough. Will Millican was tough—bootstrap tough! Will and Lee reined up in front of the Green Front Saloon, primed for a bear hunt—or a Curd.[25]

Outside, Will instructed Lee to go to the rear of the Green Front, and not let their prey have an avenue of escape. Will braced up, not precisely knowing what to expect, and walked through the saloon's front door with but one thought seared into his mind— making dead meat. There really are two versions as to what happened next, but they blend quickly into an agreement. Zeke Curd espied Will Millican walk in and knew any socializing would be with six-shooters. Rather than test his skill with a Colt's revolver, Zeke sought cover—a human shield. He grabbed Guy K. Bean around the neck and started inching toward the back door, a frightened but fast sobering drunk between him and Will Millican. Earing back the hammer on his six-gun, calm and collected, cool and certain of his marksmanship talent, Will straightened his arm and touched the trigger. Zeke hit the floor, lifelessly waiting, but never knowing when or if a Millican Crossroads' mortician would arrive. In another version, the two Curd brothers were in the Green Front Saloon and Will tapped out the running lights of both Zeke and Poker. The *Bryan Eagle* of June 26, 1890, is silent about Poker giving up the ghost, but hesitates not the least, not even a smidgen with crediting Mr. Will A. Millican with ending the life of one Zeke Curd.[26] Will Millican, again keeping with the blood-feud tradition of Texas, was given a free pass, legally. After all, Zeke had killed his brother Pet, hadn't he?

Will Millican's grit was just the gruel he needed for his next job, a hard-riding and hard-charging assignment with the Texas Rangers of Company B, commanded by Captain William Jesse McDonald. At forty-six years of age Will, a single man, had enlisted with the Ranger Force in Madison County on the twenty-fifth day of April 1905.[27] Apparently the place of enlistment was due to expediency and to the fact a Texas Ranger presence was needed for some high-profile district court business then underway. The actual headquarters for Company B at the time was in faraway West Texas at Sierra Blanca.[28] Although it cannot rise above the level of conjecture, it is not at all unjust to believe that Private Will Millican was not adverse to a posting west of the Pecos River. Will's preaching cowboy brother, the good Reverend Lallie Millican, was riding circuit and ranching at Allamore, just east of Sierra Blanca and just west of Van Horn above the Rio Grande. Whether Ranger Private Millican wanted to make a home in this section of far-flung West Texas is unknowable at this point—and immaterial.[29]

Headquarters for the company soon shifted to the South Texas town of Alice, then in Nueces County, now Jim Wells County.[30] Situated less than fifty miles due west of Corpus Christi, Alice had long been the headquarters locale for first this, then that, company of Texas Rangers. Geographically the Rangers posted at Alice worked that untamed and woolly territory between the Nueces River on the top end and the Rio Grande on the bottom end, real-estate popularly known as the Wild Horse Desert or the Nueces Strip. The semi-tropical weather was generally balmy—sometimes damn hot. Energetic mosquitoes were a constant aggravation—sometimes damn bothersome. Rattlesnakes were near everywhere—damn nerve-racking. Morally lacking cutthroats and desperadoes, Hispanic and Anglo, were reliable; their ill-behavior was always bad—damn bad. In fact, a newspaperman for Austin's *Daily State Journal* not lovingly avowed this particular swath of South Texas was the platform for "a vagabond population, inured to rapine and violence, and who make it the theater of incessant lawlessness."[31] It was a good site for Texas Rangers—a damn good place.

On the twenty-first day of July 1905, at Alice, Will Millican's state paperwork was updated and he was issued his Descriptive List, that Ranger Force document granting official peace officer status.[32] The paper trail for Will Millican's tenure as a Texas Ranger is spotty, but a reasonably accurate account may be gleaned by examining the Company B Monthly Returns and the Company B Correspondence Files. Perusing those archived Ranger Force records is—as it always is—fascinating. In the case of Private Will Millican those documents are revealing on two fronts.

First, piecing together the days of Will's service with the Ranger Force discloses he was seemingly in constant motion. After helping out with security for District Court in Madison County, Private Millican was dispatched northeast of Buffalo, Texas, to the little community of Oakwood so he could "look after cases there." Finishing that task Millican reported for duty at Sierra Blanca, temporarily, soon transferring with Company B when they took up their new station at Alice. Seemingly Private Millican was busy as a beaver in Nueces County, arresting horse thieves. Will Millican jugged another fellow, John Gleason, for Disturbing the Peace and Cursing Rangers. Then on what was but a routine "scout" in Duval County at San Diego, Ranger Millican arrested a slobbering and wobbling drunk, removing him from the public streets and further embarrassment. Then it was back to Nueces County where he safely arrested "Poncho" Garcia, "a bad bad man" for Disturbing the Peace, turning him over to local deputy sheriffs who locked him away in the Nueces County Jail. Next the tireless Texas Ranger chased after a horse thief—caught him—and then testified in court at Corpus Christi. Soon thereafter on the gargantuan King Ranch he captured another horse thief.[33]

Secondly, those tucked away documents also confirm that although Private Will Millican's Texas Ranger work by any standard was justifiably commendable, it was not the spectacular drama worthy of "dime novels." A proven man-killer he was—but not as a Ranger.

Unlike many of the better-known Old West personalities—a few Rangers in the mix—Will Millican was not a self-promoter, speciously puffing. Thus far in this stage of his policing career he had come though unscathed. There was an adversary he couldn't handle though, sickness. The malady is not specifically identified, other than fever, but during the latter part of January 1906 Ranger

Private Will Millican received an approved furlough allowing him travel to Millican Crossroads for rest and recuperation.[34]

Subsequent correspondence indicates Will was on the mend at Millican, but ostensibly he, too, was prospecting for a change for the better, a job paying more than $120 per quarter in sweltering South Texas. In the meantime he returned to duty at Alice and was fit enough to assist Captain Bill McDonald arrest two owl-hoots for Fighting. Shortly he backed-up another Texas Ranger with the apprehension of a chap charged with Assault to Murder and for Carrying A Pistol.[35] Next it was back to San Diego where he picked up two convicts for delivery to local authorities before resuming his "scout" to the area of Mathis, San Patricio County.[36] Private Millican may have been a Texas Ranger but ever since the trip back to Millican Crossroads other thoughts had been creeping—then racing—in his mind, as evidenced by Will's letter to his circuit riding brother Lallie at Alamore. On Company B letterhead Will Millican penned:

> Dear Bro. Your kind letter of the 17th inst. received and in reply will say that I will try and come to see you. Some of my friends in Brazos Co. want me to run for the Dist. Clerk Office, it is a very nice position and pays from $900 to $1200 per year. This is a very nice income. I have not fully decided yet to make the race, but waiting for further developments and would like to get a ranch in that country and put goats on it. When I come to see you I will talk the matter over with you. I got a letter from George. He says they are all anxious for you to write them. I am in good health at this time. I do not want to spend another summer down here. Hoping this will reach you all well. Give my love to all. Your Bro. [signed W. A. Millican][37]

Clearly the magnetism pulling him back to the Brazos County country was strong—it was home. Too, there was also a chance— at the minimum—of near doubling his monthly salary, not even factoring in the likelihood of supplemental income from rais- ing cattle, hogs, sheep—or goats. Many are those Central Texas raised boys that would find living in humid South Texas not their preference. Not everyone is agreeably charmed by a muggy sub- tropical climate, intermittently punctuated with squalling hur- ricanes. Texas Ranger Private Millican's enlightening remark, though short on the word count, says a lot: "I do not want to spend another summer down here." And he didn't.

Private Millican, in writing, submitted his resignation from the Texas Rangers—giving thirty days' notice—to Captain Bill McDonald on June 1, 1906:

> Dear Sir: I tender my resignation from the Ranger Force, to take effect on July the 1st, as satisfactory arrangements has been made at home for me to make the race for Dist. Clerk. . . . .[38]

Long had been the penal practice of working the daylights out of inmates on the farm; the prison farms and/or county farms. A snippet in *The Dallas Morning News* of December 12, 1889, is illustrative, and may play itself into the story at hand as it pertains to Brazos County's near neighbor adjoining on the northwest, Robertson County and its smart little settlement of Hearne: "A train of five passenger coaches attached to No.11 freight passed here Monday loaded with 300 negroes from Torboro, N.C. Their destination is Hearne, where they will cultivate the farm recently vacated by the state convicts." That same month in Brazos County *The Bryan Eagle* made mention of their facility:

> Officer R. H. Smith took Ed Allen from the county jail on Monday to the county farm in the lower end of the county [Allenfarm just southwest of Millican], and turned him over to the proprietor, Mr. Harrington, to work out a fine and cost assessed against him in a fighting case.[39]

Early on, if the 1880 U.S. Federal Census and the family's oral history and a newspaper story are accepted—there's no reason to doubt them—Will Millican had earned regular paychecks as a "Guard" while yet in his twenties, long before his brief tenure as a Texas Ranger.[40] From the best evidence at hand, which admittedly is sketchy, after voluntarily separating himself from the Ranger Force and prior to diving headfirst into Brazos County politics, Will Millican returned to guarding fellows doing hard time.[41]

A fellow guard, Sergeant Henry S. "Ham" South and Will Millican had a history of sorts, and not necessarily an agreeable one. Earlier, George W. Dunlap had updated Millican regarding a brouhaha between Will's nephew, Leander Marcella "Lee" Thompson, the young man who had backed Will's play in the revenge killing of Zeke Curd. Subsequent to horrific Brazos County flooding during July 1899, a red-hot dispute had arisen between Lee and Ham's kinsmen John South: Dunlap said, in part (with minimal editing):

> . . . .It was over a place that was not covered [with water] in 1853—8 or 10 feet deep. Harrington persuaded South to keep men and mules in there until Saturday—lost several mules. Harrington helped him get them out and let the free [non-prisoner] Negroes alone until Sunday at his Gin House. I thought they were out. I only had one boat and it was so rough through my field could hardly get there. Went over to Harrington's Saturday night. Walter Knox came in with a boat belonged to John South at 2 o'clock in morning. Brought no one out, but just prowling around in the bottom. I told Lee Thompson to get it and go bring my Negroes out. Next morning at Harrington Gin House when he got there John South and Harrington was there and South just thought he would take the boat away from Lee. Lee told him if he would let him have the one he was in [he] could have it. South said was his and would take it and told the ones with him to come and we would take it. I had given Lee a pistol when he started, satisfied they would try to buck about the boat when they met him. Lee waited until South got in a few feet of him and threw the gun down on him and told him to stop. South threw up his hands . . . . said he was not armed and pulled on back. After that he exchanged boats with Lee, [and] told Lee that was not the last of it. Lee told him he could find him anytime he wanted to. . . . .[42]

Family feuds fester. Feudists don't forget. Sometimes, well, opportunity just knocks, opening wide the door for settling old scores. Although it cannot historically rise past a reasonable degree of conjecture as to motive, there is a hard bottom line. On November 16, 1906, Ham South somehow managed to disarm Will Millican at the guard shack—fatally shooting him; killing him with his own Colt's six-shooter.[43] Were one or the other drunk? Was it murder or self-defense? ¿Quién sabe?

In those rich Brazos County bottomlands near Millican, murder and madness were not occasional visitors. Personal warfare was common place. Too, more than her fair share of those doggedly unbending and tough Millican boys lived by the gun—and died!

Texas Historical Commission Marker: William Templeton Millican.
Courtesy La Verne Benton.

Dr. Elliott McNeil Millican, a descendant of Stephen F. Austin's "Old Three Hundred" and the first sheriff of Brazos County, Texas. *Courtesy Phyllis Poehlmann.*

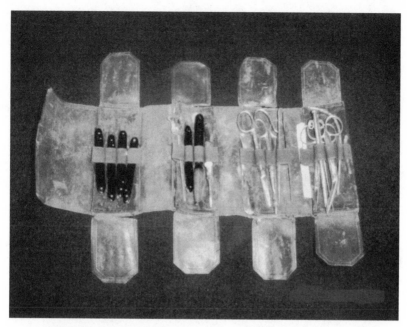

Remarkable photograph of a frontier era surgical kit, this one belonging to Dr. Elliott Millican. *Courtesy Beryl Jean Dreiss.*

U.S. Post Office, Millican, Texas. *Courtesy La Verne Benton.*

Leander Randon "Lallie" or "Lally" Millican, favorably known throughout West Texas and the Big Bend Country as the Cowboy Preacher; a free-spirited minister taking pleasure in "running his own boat." *Courtesy Phyllis Poehlmann.*

Marcellus Randall "Pet" Millican, Brazos County Constable. The coldblooded murder of Pet would spark revenge, Texas style—first rate Wild West drama. *Courtesy Beryl Jean Dreiss.*

Wilbur Ashley "Will" Millican, photographed subsequent to exacting mortal six-shooter revenge for his brother's murder. His genealogical linkage to Texas history is splendid. W.A. Millican would serve as a Texas Ranger and prison guard. On the ground, closer in time, he and his brothers and half-brothers would live—and die by the gun. *Courtesy Phyllis Poehlmann.*

The eye-catching Susan Millican, half-sister to Will, Pet, and Lallie Millican. *Courtesy Phyllis Poehlmann.*

Rangers at Alice, Texas, one of the spots where Will Millican was stationed. Was the photograph for show, or were the lawmen actually engaged in mandated target practice? *Courtesy Armstrong Research Center, Texas Ranger Hall of Fame & Museum.*

Wilbur Ashley Millican loaded for bear—or an escaping prisoner. *Courtesy Phyllis Poehlmann.*

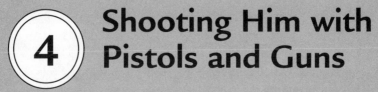

Shooting Him with Pistols and Guns

Gideon Christian "Gid" Taylor by several versions was one tough customer, but by no means was he an outlaw or desperado. Gid went about his everyday business armed, most of the time with his well-oiled Colt's .41 caliber six-shooter. The pistol was part of his overall persona and a necessary tool of his trade. Gid Taylor was superintendent of the Navarro County Poor Farm.

Named after José Antonio Navarro, a big-name player during that earlier period while Texians were severing ties with Mexico, Navarro County was smartly chiseled from whopping Robertson County during the springtime of 1846. By summer, Navarro County was politically and demographically equipped for organization. On the thirteenth day of July 1846 it was official, and burgeoning Corsicana was selected as the county seat.[1] James A. Johnson was named the first sheriff.[2] Of that early era perhaps one of the best-known characters was Navarro County's third sheriff, James Buckner "Buck" Barry. Barry in later writings helps set Navarro County's geographical and sociological stage: "The county, as a part of the frontier, covered all the territory between the Brazos and the Trinity Rivers, west to New Mexico. Court was held in a log cabin. We had no jail, consequently, I had to chain the prisoners like so many pet bears inside a log cabin."[3] Pinpointing when that double-walled single-room calaboose finally gave way to more progressive penal evolution has thus far eluded an answer. Sooner or later, as with the overwhelming majority of Texas' 254 counties, old jails were demolished, replacements were built, supplanted with structures more befitting the times—Navarro County not excluded.[4]

Relevant to the story at hand is the Navarro County Poor Farm. In addition to county jails, many of the heavily populated counties found it helpful to incorporate into their blueprints for enlightened thinking a concept prevalent throughout Texas during the late nineteenth and early twentieth centuries—the poor farm. Navarro County's borderline neighbor to the north, Dallas County, had one. Why not Navarro County? The elected county judge and county commissioners set in motion the hunt for suitable land at a suitable price. By 1884, after closing a cash price deal for $4,000, Navarro County owned 976 ½ acres near the community of Petty's Chapel, not too far east of Corsicana.[5]

In reality the poor farms were but clearinghouses for societal predicaments: What to do with persons at least temporarily unfit or unhealthy enough to be integrated into the county's general population. The Navarro County Poor Farm is paradigm. Initially there were but two houses built on the farm: one designated for paupers and one for certain county prisoners. Shortly, however, three more houses were constructed: one for persons with acute mental impairment, one for smallpox quarantine purposes, commonly called "pesthouses," and one to serve as home for the superintendent.[6] The Navarro County Poor Farm was a farm, and as would be expected, in addition to living quarters for the displaced and a lockup for the inmates, there was a whole working complex of barns, stables, corrals, and not just a little acreage devoted to garden plots, orchards, and fields of corn, millet, wheat, oats, and cotton. Hogs and cattle were slaughtered, cows were milked, and henhouses robbed of fresh eggs in a worthy scheme of upholding self-sufficiency at the poor farm.

Nonetheless, within the context of this storyline, it is the convicts that might merit attention. In place at the time was a rather common policy. Some of Navarro County's sentenced inmates had the option of laying out their fines in an austere jail cell at Corsicana, or working at the poor farm as trusties, having $1.00 a day deducted from their fines. A number of these prisoners were even eligible to earn that dollar credit by laboring on private citizens' farms in the surrounding area. Of course that was a dubious policy begging abuse and in due course would be outlawed. Progressive penology cried for experimentation, and poor farms filled a gap.

When the position for a new superintendent opened up, Navarro County Sheriff J. M. Weaver, who had the authority to make the appointment, was not in a quandary. Weaver's deputy, forty-three-year-old Gid Taylor was in good standing with the community and was in good standing with the sheriff. During 1891 Taylor was named superintendent of the poor farm. Although a large part of Superintendent Taylor's work was administrative in nature—overseeing everything—it was yet a gun-carrying job. By basic definition lawbreakers are not societies' best; some embody its worst. The Navarro County Poor Farm, notwithstanding its other missions, was a correctional facility. From time to time Gid Taylor would have to chase down a nitwit—an escapee—one who had reneged on the court's or sheriff's charitable deal. And, on occasion, sometimes a tightly clinched fist or hardwood nightstick was necessary for protecting oneself from quarrelsome and confrontational convicts. In that regard prisons and poor farms were on equal footing. Wardens had to stand their ground. It should come as no shocker, threats against Taylor's life, while not everyday happenings, were not rare and were acknowledged as part of the job. So much a part of the job that as a practical matter Gid Taylor purchased a $2,000 life insurance policy.[7]

Though but hearsay, it's alleged at least two of those inmates making threats can be identified by name: Alex Breadland had threatened Superintendent Taylor because he shot at him during an incident when he had been re-arrested. And, Ben Younger was "expected to kill Taylor for whipping him while on the poor farm." On another occasion Gid Taylor "had fired upon and wounded a poor farm convict, who was endeavoring to escape." Purportedly, Gid Taylor was well aware and to some degree apprehensive knowing "that some of the convicts or escaped convicts on the poor farm would kill him; that he had to whip a great many negroes on the poor farm, and they had threatened to kill him."[8]

As the big chapter in Gid Taylor's life unfolds it may be announced that at age twenty-three, and half-dozen years her senior, he had married Miss Pattie G. Haden, the nuptials taking place in Navarro County on July 18, 1875.[9] By the time Gid promoted into the top job at the poor farm the loving couple were the proud parents of seven children.[10] The two oldest girls were teenagers, racing towards the day they would be grown, gone, and married. The remaining brood was yet close to the nest, carefree, contentedly strutting towards those distant days of adulthood. For Gid and Pattie life was but a bowl of cherries. Whether or not Gid delighted in amusing his children with local lore is lost. Perhaps he told them why Cryer Creek was named. How early day settlers thought the rushing water cresting over a small waterfall sounded like a woman's crying—creepy. Or, even less eerie, but downright funny, was how Mesmeriser Creek allegedly earned its moniker. About that self-proclaimed hypnotist who tried to hypnotize a wild buffalo bull. The snorting and pawing animal was not mesmerized and stampeded. Quite literally the hypnotist was buffaloed and the nearby creek had a new nickname.[11] As far as is now known, Superintendent Taylor was a family man, living a wholesome life—not dancing to the iniquitous tunes of self-indulgence. The same might not be said of Jim and Tom Murphy.

On Saturday, September 22, 1894, the brothers embarked on an extravaganza within the corporate limits of Corsicana. Today's term barhopping would be likened to the young men's saloon schlepping spree. The boys had come to town to have some fun. Tom, the eighteen-year-old, making sure he was set for answering any affair of gravity or triviality had a six-shooter tucked into his waistband. Twenty-year-old Jim was well-heeled financially—but not well-heeled like a typical feral Texan on a bender. He didn't possess a pistol. It was a deficit in want of a fix. Downtown at Harry Kaufman's pawn shop Jim bought a Colt's .44-40 caliber six-shooter, one with white—ivory or pearl—grips. He also bought a box of .38-40 cartridges, which could be loaded into and fired from the newly purchased revolver.[12] Mixing liquor and gunpowder and youthful impetuousness makes a good primer for mischief—or mayhem. As the blood/alcohol percentage in their bloodstreams went up, the level of good sense spiraled downward. The ribald hilarity, the hysterical guffawing and laughing and snorting produced a terrible nosebleed. Tom borrowed a handkerchief from a friend, but the owner flatly refused to take back the bloody rag.[13]

As if it was birthright, virtually all drunk Texans like to shoot guns—Tom was a drunk Texan. Out came his Colt's revolver and the bombardment begin. Responding to the racket, Corsicana officer T. J. Luster came out too. Apparently Jim had his brand new Colt's .44-40 hidden from view, but Tom was not as smartly disposed as his brother. Right fast the fuzzy minded Tom Murphy was arrested, his six-shooter was impolitely confiscated, and he was criminally charged with a misdemeanor, Discharging a Firearm Within the City Limits.[14]

The drunkenness, well, Tom could just sleep that off in jail. When the sun came up a local judge would take charge of dispensing the justice, deciding what best be done with the big bad man from Bitter Creek. Nominal would be any jail time sentence, trifling would be any cash fine. So, the night passed. Slowly allowing soberness to try and overtake him, Tom stayed up all night just waiting to post the obligatory bail bond. Meanwhile, Jim whiled away nighttime hours hanging around until his brother would be turned out of the hoosegow. Then they would go home and leave Mr. Tomfoolery and Miss Corsicana's persnickety policemen on the back trail.

At the poor farm on the morning of September 23, 1894, Gid Taylor saddled his horse, making ready for the short trip into Corsicana. Kissing Pattie goodbye and waving to the children he stepped into the stirrup and was off. Whether he was tending to workaday chores or simply going to town for socializing is unclear. With sharpness it may be reported that he had "a world of friends" in the city, in fact, throughout Navarro County. By way of eyewitness clarity it may be reported that while in town that Sunday morning he amiably "chatted with friends."[15]

Exactness of the hour is elusive, but the jail door swung open and a bleary-eyed Tom Murphy staggered out—the sobering-up was a work in progress. Whether he posted a cash bond or was released on his personal recognizance to appear in court later is vague—but in any event he was free as a bird, a jailbird no more. His wings had been clipped though. He had been turned out unarmed, police officer Luster preserving possession of Tom's six-shooter. His brother Jim was waiting nearby and the boys made ready to go home, but inexplicably they were now in need of a conveyance. By what means they had managed the trip to town in the first place is a mystery. Shortly before noon they rented or borrowed a "top buggy" and started on the road for home. Fortuitously—in so far as known—Gid Taylor left town shortly thereafter, probably not even knowing the Murphy brothers were ahead of him.[16]

As they ambled or trotted along, the Murphy boys always in the lead and Taylor anywhere from 800 to several hundred yards behind, the fellows did not go unnoticed. Several adults, Fred Fleming among them, saw the travelers marking time on the road leading to the poor farm. Jimmie Griggs, "a negro boy ten years old" was playing in the yard with friends and watched both parties pass by.[17]

In but a moment or two little Jimmie heard several gunshots, and soon saw two men in a buggy, "coming rapidly down the road . . . . and as they passed him he noticed that one of the men had a pistol in his hand, which he seemed to be examining." Next, after the buggy was entirely out of sight, a horse yet saddled, stirrups flopping, but no rider astride came into view. Quickly and quite commendably young Jimmie Griggs caught the horse, tying it to a fence, perhaps not even noticing that its shoulder and mane bore powder burns.

The Murphy brothers had raced to the residence of their brother-in-law, Eugene Meador (Meadows in certain legal filings), which was about a mile and a quarter northeast of the Navarro County Poor Farm. Their sister and Eugene were about to partake of dinner (lunch), affably offering Tom and Jim seats at the table. The boys begged off, declaring they hadn't been to sleep and were ready to crash. The Meadors made note—little could they help it—that the boys, both of them, "appeared to be under the influence of liquor, especially Tom." Compliantly and hospitably their sister rearranged the bedcovers. The boys retired and went to sleep.[18]

Meanwhile on the poor farm road there was no catnap dozing, things were astir. On the implied pledge of their return two trusties were on a Sunday after-lunch stroll. To their utter disbelief they discovered the lifeless form of Superintendent Taylor sprawled in the road, bloody, his .41 Colt's six-shooter in the dirt, his clothing yet afire. Without delay a messenger was sent to summon authorities. Directly Sheriff Weaver and a bevy of citizens and a physician were onsite. The sheriff dutifully began reconstructing the crime scene. Obviously Superintendent Taylor was dead. Taylor's smoldering clothes mute testimony to the closeness of burning muzzle blasts. Bullet wounds, evidently .44 caliber, revealed that he had been shot five times, and from their placement—in conjunction with injury to his horse—it could be deduced that his assailants were afoot and he horseback when the fireworks had rocketed him to the ground. It had been, at least for a split-second, a fierce fight. The smelly spent load in Gid Taylor's wheel-gun disclosed he had fired one round. Sheriff Weaver did find where a bullet had "cut a fence post" but while such was helpful in plotting a spent projectile's trajectory, its evidentiary value was minimal. Rather progressively for the times, by order or request, a certified surveyor later examined the crime scene, made a scale drawing, in this particular instance an inch equaling 400 feet and unimaginatively titled, "Map of the Scene of the Gid Taylor killing."[19]

Truthfully, meaningful forensic evidence was in short supply. Eyewitness testimony to the actual shooting was not there. Yes, there were folks in the neighborhood who had noted both young men in a buggy and the mounted Gid Taylor traveling the poor farm roadway, but not together and not at exactly the same time. Yes, they reported hearing some gunfire. That, in and of itself, was not too bizarre. Within rural Texas—then or now—a few gunshots are not cause for worry. Just who was shooting, at just what, was up for grabs. A headlong rush to resounding booms of someone popping a few caps was not warranted—not in the countryside and the road between Corsicana and the Navarro County Poor Farm was in the country. The dead body had been discovered by happenstance, not purposeful inquiry. The shocking slaying of Mr. Gideon Christian Taylor, an obvious murder, was in the colloquial slang of on-the-ground lawmen a bona fide whodunit?

Sheriff Weaver rather quickly concluded—and rightly so—that the closest he had to an actual eyewitness to the crime was what youngster Jimmie Griggs could remember. Whoever was in that buggy the "little negro" had seen was obligated to shed light on what had happened. Sheriff Weaver and a posse began following fresh tracks made by the buggy. That trail led straight to the Meadors' dwelling. There, at about four o'clock, Jim and Tom Murphy were not courteously rousted from their slumbering stupor. "When aroused both men seemed to have drank heavily; one was still drunk and the other showed evidence of the after effects of drink."[20] Neither had a six-shooter, but Tom had a speck or two of blood on his forehead and splotches of blood on his clothing. They too found the casing of a fired .38-40 round on the floor underneath the Meadors' cleared-off dinner table. Outside, lawmen discovered a few more spent .38-40 hulls in the buggy. How much Sheriff Weaver actually pondered the finer legal points is blurred, but his gut instinct told him the brothers owed him a trip to town—in handcuffs. In truth, the sheriff had sufficient Probable Cause to make arrests, but was yet far short of hurdling another benchmark, that of Guilt Beyond a Reasonable Doubt.[21]

Jim and Tom Murphy didn't help themselves any by their somewhat cocky attitude. When appraised by lawmen that they had been taken into custody for murdering someone they just laughed, not even making inquiry as to who they were alleged to have killed. Was it a big joke?

All too quickly the Murphy brothers realized the sheriff wasn't fooling. They were locked deep in the bowels of the Navarro County Jail at Corsicana. There would be no piddling away time at the poor farm for these fellows. Compounding their desolation was the fact that—wisely on the part of Sheriff Weaver—they had been separated: Jim Murphy was held in a downstairs cell, brother Tom was ensconced upstairs in a steel-barred cubicle. The boys were cut off from communicating with each other, unable to slyly synchronize stories—or prefect plausible alibis. This became noticeably apparent to the public and woefully evident to the brothers after Sheriff Weaver—with nothing to withhold—permitted an inquisitive correspondent writing for the *Dallas Morning News* access to the prisoners. It was obvious from that point forward that the brothers understood the gravity of their predicament. There were noticeable discrepancies between the accounts given the newspaperman, but on one point the boys were in agreement: Both disavowed murdering Gid Taylor.[22]

While the Murphy boys languished in jail babbling to a reporter, near the community of Dresden west of Corsicana, a quite prominent Navarro County settlement on Richland Creek, preparations were underway for saying final goodbyes to Gideon Christian Taylor. On September 25, 1894, two days after the murder, Pattie Taylor and children watched their beloved husband and father lowered into the grave at Dresden's cemetery. Saddened onlookers—there were many—wept.[23] In careers centered on law enforcing and corrections work an officer's death doesn't equate to downtime or a holiday from accountability. Rather quickly the sudden vacancy at Navarro County's poor farm was filled. D. A. DeWitt was appointed to pick up the reins as superintendent.[24]

Not only did an inquisitive journalist interview the proposed defendants, so did the sheriff. Although Weaver's interrogative technique is not authenticated, the quantifiable consequence is. A trip back to the Meadors' residence was called for. There, secreted inside a trunk, the sheriff retrieved a Colt's .44-40 caliber six-shooter with white handles, just "where Jim Murphy said it would be found."[25] At Corsicana, pawnbroker Harry Kauffman identified it as the pistol he had retailed to Jim Murphy on September 22, one day before the homicide.[26] The State of Texas' murder case against the Murphy brothers was seemingly airtight—circumstantial to be sure—but airtight, nevertheless. An Indictment was sure to issue forthwith. And it did![27] Grand jurors found that Jim and Tom Murphy "then and there unlawfully and with malice aforethought kill G. C. Taylor by shooting him with pistols and guns."[28] Now, the crux of the matter was out of the sheriff's talons, lawyers were ruling the roost.

Understanding the Navarro County prosecutor's tactical style and the trial judge's edicts are critical for telling the story—the whole story. Within that context are truths, hard truths, about how the nitty-gritty game of criminal justice is played—sometimes. Although the grand jury returned true bills—Indictments—against both Murphy brothers it would be Tom who would stand trial first. Severing the cases, only trying one fellow at a time, was not out-of-the-ordinary. In this instance, with two defendants, should one manage to slip through the Blind Mistress of Justice's fingers with a verdict of Not Guilty, the district attorney had another bite at the apple. Gauging older brother Jim's clear cooperation by informing Sheriff Weaver where the Colt's .44-40 six-shooter was stashed, no doubt guaranteed Tom would go first—perhaps the legal groundwork for a Plea Bargain of sorts, if you will. Should Tom's goose be cooked it might not even be necessary to rekindle the fire and roast Jim.

Tom Murphy's case, a felony, would be decided by twelve jurors. Theoretically they would be impartial at the outset, slowly drawing opinions as evidence unfolded before them. Vying for their attention and favor in America's adversarial system of justice would be prosecutors and defense attorneys scuffling to include or exclude this piece of evidence, that person's testimony. Supposedly—if the system worked right—the jury's verdict would be resolved solely on what was ruled admissible and presented in the courtroom. Simply put, in theory, what the jury heard while sitting in the jury box was all that counted—all that could be used to make up their minds. District attorneys wanted to get something before the jury, defense attorneys whined and objected—and vice versa. In *The State of Texas vs. Tom Murphy* the district court judge at Corsicana would determine what jurymen could hear and what they couldn't—the battle lines were drawn![29]

The state's murder case was a snap, so championed the prosecutor. Jim and Tom Murphy had come to Corsicana to have a whale of a good time. Aside from getting liquored-up, at a city pawnshop Jim bought a .44-40 pistol and .38-40 cartridges which could be fired in said gun. Later, Tom drunkenly creating a disturbance was relieved of his own six-shooter by a legally sworn lawman. Tom spent the night in jail. Next morning the two wobbling brothers rented a buggy and departed the city of Corsicana, ostensibly heading for home. Following closely, but not necessarily purposefully, was Superintendent Gid Taylor who likewise was heading for home. All three travelers were seen—at one point or another—by unconcerned parties, including Jimmie Griggs, that "little ten year old negro boy." But none saw them together. When Tom and Jim were overtaken by Taylor, he noticed one of the boys had a pistol, and in his role as a legally constituted Texas peace officer Gid had tried to make an arrest for Unlawfully Carrying a Firearm. There was resistance and the superintendent was killed, heartlessly gunned down. While reloading Jim's pistol several cartridges were spilt, toppling onto the buggy's floor as they raced for their brother-in-law's house. Jimmie Griggs saw them bouncing along in the buggy, one of the men, he knew not which one, "had a pistol in his hand, which he seemed to be examining." At the Meadors' house Jim hid the gun in a trunk and the brothers, yet somewhat intoxicated, passed out or feigned sleep. Oh yes, the flustered Tom unintentionally overlooked washing Gid Taylor's blood from his clean-shaven face and clothing before hitting the sack. They were next abruptly awakened and lawfully taken into custody by Sheriff Weaver who had—properly—banked sufficient Probable Cause. Subsequently, after competent interrogation at the Navarro County Jail, Jim told Sheriff Weaver where that Colt's .44-40 six-shooter was tucked under the folded bedding in his sister's trunk. Dutifully the revolver was uncovered and seized. What more did a jury need to know than that?

Well, plenty! The legal team representing Tom Murphy had a lengthy laundry list of bits and pieces jurymen should know—were permitted by law and a virtuous sense of fair play to know. And therein was the rub. Over vociferous objections, from the court's bench the judge ruled that the jury would not be allowed to hear certain items the defense lawyers deemed pertinent to their case. All Tom really wanted—they avowed—was a fair shake.

What any defendant standing at the court's mercy was entitled to, protections promised by adoption of the U.S. Constitution's Bill of Rights. Though the whole of their arguments will not be repeated herein, a few of the points Tom's attorneys wanted made known to the trial jury are cited.

Perhaps first and foremost, since it really was but a circumstantial evidence case, and despite the fact that Tom and Jim Murphy were prior to the homicide "on most friendly terms" with Taylor, excluded was the fact other persons had made public threats against the superintendent's life. It was important for the jury to know, according to Tom's lawyers, that some folks in the poor farm community or who had previously lived there "entertained feelings of hostility and bitter animosity against" Taylor. The defense team could and would name two—with proof, if allowed to. Could either of them have encountered and killed Gid Taylor while traveling the poor farm road? The jury would not know of their existence, much less their threats of bodily harm. Or could the crime be attributed to that unknown fellow seen by Mr. Hickey and his wife just a few minutes after the shooting? That "copper-colored negro, whom they did not recognize, [and who] passed their house riding a sorrel colored horse most rapidly from the direction in which the shots had been heard." Certainly there was indication some folks had an axe to grind with Gid Taylor, but not a shred of evidence that there had ever been a hard word spoken between he and the Murphy boys, never ever, a cross-word between he and Tom. Zip![30]

Given that a prosecutor was explicitly suggesting during the act of committing the homicide small quantities of the superintendent's blood splashed onto Tom's face and clothing, would it not be relevant a jury know he had had a nosebleed the night before? Could it have been Tom's own blood? Tom had even had to borrow a handkerchief from a friend to staunch the blood flow. The jury would never hear of the nosebleed.[31]

Was little Jimmie Griggs, a mere child, really competent to offer sworn testimony, capable of understanding false testimony would be an act with prescribed "pains and penalties" for perjury? Not that he would willingly lie, but would little Jimmie have sufficient intelligence to understand the obligations of said oath, the consequences of his actions? Capping that, if little Jimmie could not even positively identify which man in the buggy was "examining a pistol," was not the threshold of any evidentiary value for his eyewitness testimony rather low? The problematic legal bar for allowing prepubescent children to testify was high.[32]

And how was that Colt's .44-40 revolver purchased by Jim in a Corsicana pawnshop and secreted by Jim at his brother-in-law's home linked to Tom in the first place—or the last place? Or even the homicide? It was, after all, prior to the days of forensic and ballistic matches. Had not officer Luster taken Tom's hot-barreled Colt's six-shooter from him the night before Gid Taylor met his death—and kept it? If truth be known, didn't it really somewhat logically demonstrate that "on the occasion of the homicide, he was very likely not armed, and that his brother, Jim Murphy, only had a pistol."[33] If Tom Murphy were a triggerman, admissible evidence was the channel for putting a gun in his hand. In that regard the prosecuting attorney was firing blanks.

There was a specific judicial accountability in this type case—one resting on a bottom of inferred evidence—"in a case wholly depending on circumstantial evidence, it is the duty of the jury to explore every reasonable hypothesis consistent with the innocence of the defendant before they would be authorized to convict him . . . . In other words, if the evidence reasonably shows that some other person than the accused committed the offense charged, it is their duty to acquit; or if the circumstances which tend to show that some other person may have committed the crime are sufficient to raise a reasonable doubt of the defendant's guilt, an acquittal should follow."[34] Unsaid is a touch of common sense: Jurymen are only able to examine evidence allowed in the courtroom. Inadmissible evidence by definition goes unseen, and therefore is of no value to a juror.

Untenable was a good explanation as why Taylor had been killed. Defense counsel knew that several folks, stemming from their days at the Navarro County Poor Farm, had long-held a deep-seated hatred for the superintendent, but they could not get that incontrovertible fact before the jury. For topping off his murder case just right, the prosecuting attorney was in dire need of a motive—a plausible motive. The prosecutor would set in the jurors' minds his premise that Gid Taylor was foully murdered while trying to disarm Tom Murphy. He would not do it with admissible evidence but by implication. He requested the judge include within the framework of his formal Jury Instructions: "If an officer sees any person with any pistol, carrying the same unlawfully, such officer has the right, without warrant, to arrest such person; and if such person so unlawfully carrying said pistol shall resist arrest by such officer, and in so doing shall such officer, though such officer is attempting to arrest him without warrant, and although it may be necessary for such officer to use force in making such arrest, provided that such officer use no more force or violence than was reasonably necessary to effect such arrest, yet such killing would be unlawful and will be murder in the first degree, or murder in the second degree, according to whether the same is committed with express malice or implied malice, as explained to you [the jury] in the main charge."[35] Noticeably absent from this directive to the jury was a most important detail: A person was legally permitted to transport a pistol from the place of purchase to his/her home or business. In this instance then, there was no criminal offense regarding the unlawful carrying of arms. It was a rather slick ploy, but there was not in the court's record or anywhere else a scintilla of evidence showing Superintendent Gid Taylor was killed while attempting to arrest gun-toting Tom Murphy, "not one word."[36] Such slipperiness would shortly haunt Navarro County's legal officialdom.

Superintendent Gid Taylor, as far as the upstanding folks in Navarro County knew was a genuine family man—hard working and honest to the bone. Steel-nerved and tough when he had to be, compassionate and bighearted when he needed to be. And maybe it's all true. Tom and Jim Murphy, as far as the decent folks in Navarro County knew were free-spirited and ornery when it suited them. While on a lark they could howl at the moon like coyotes and shoot at the stars with recklessness. Tom and Jim couldn't be good. And maybe that's all true. The old saw "perception is reality" is not wide of the mark—especially in the courtroom. Would it be a case of competing assessments of mortal men's moral fiber? What role would character, reputation, and integrity really play? Legally the criminal case was styled *The State of Texas vs. Tom Murphy*. In a matter-of-fact sense it was in actuality *Gideon C. Taylor vs. Tom Murphy*. The verdict came as no shocker:

> We the Jury find the defendant Tom Murphy guilty of Murder in the second degree and assess his punishment at 34 years in the state Penitentiary.[37]

The Navarro County prosecutor had won! And so too had Jim Murphy. With brother Tom declared the evil murderer of Gid Taylor there would be no political problems or public angst with the prosecuting attorney simply holding open the case in his prosecutorial files. Justice had been served. Or had it? Tom and his lawyers thought not. Perhaps a second look was in order; one by the Texas Court of Criminal Appeals, the last rung of hope within the Lone Star State's criminal justice system. The necessary paperwork and court records were properly filed, the appellate process initiated. Prisoner Tom Murphy's fate was in their hands.

Based solely on testimony and/or evidence presented to jurors in the jam-packed courtroom, their unanimous verdict should have not been unexpected. Gideon Taylor had been a Navarro County favorite, somebody had best pay—of that there was not doubt. Those Murphy brothers were but "notorious characters," so had exclaimed lawyer E. O. Call who handled the state's prosecution.[38] Conversely though, justices hearing the appellate case were cognizant of what had been excluded from that same jury's thoughtful deliberations. They had been placed on the appellate bench to insure fair play: To rein in the abuse of overzealous prosecutors and limit the chicanery of defense lawyers.

The high court's binding and written legal opinion, likewise, should not come as any bombshell. For a whole array of reasons—most cited above—the Texas Court of Criminal Appeals issued their finding: The criminal case against Tom Murphy was Reversed and Remanded. Meaning the stunned Navarro County prosecutor could retry Tom Murphy—or forget the whole damn thing. Murder conviction number one was for naught. The prosecuting attorney was a tiger, he'd set his teeth, he'd not let go.[39] Now that nobody was legally settling up for Gideon Taylor's killing, all bets were off: He'd bite Jim Murphy, too.

Realizing the unlikelihood of finding twelve wholly open-minded jurors in Navarro County, Tom's and Jim's defense team prudently begged the court for a Change of Venue. The motion was granted. The second trial would take place at Athens, Henderson County, Navarro County's eastern neighbor just across the bordering Trinity River.[40] This time, careful not to make legal errors of inclusion or exclusion, the trial of Jim Murphy commenced on the twentieth day of September 1896, two full years plus since the homicide of Superintendent Taylor. After hearing testimony for eight

days, the jury acquitted Jim Murphy. E. O. Call was flabbergasted—
and mad. Jim Murphy was, as the saying goes, free as a bird. In
fact, had he wanted to, ducking behind the Bill of Rights' protection regarding Double Jeopardy, Jim Murphy could have now
kept his constitutionally guaranteed immunity and even admitted
to having killed Superintendent Taylor, without having to pay any
penalty—whatsoever. He didn't and wouldn't squawk.

Fate's twists can prove mysterious and unexplainable. At the
subsequent trial of Tom Murphy beginning on the second day
of October, making use of the very same evidence, the outcome
would be diametrically dissimilar. It was yet a purely circumstantial case, but even circumstances can add up quickly, sometimes
with overwhelming and persuasive enormity. The second trial jury
thought so. They promptly retuned a verdict of Guilty, Murder in
the 2nd Degree. Tom's sentence was accessed at seven years' confinement. Hard time would be spent in the state prison at Rusk,
Cherokee County; then a penitentiary unit, now a facility for committing the mentally ill.[41]

Tom Murphy, after exhausting all immediate legal remedy in
the Texas courts, entered the prison entity at Rusk on July 12,
1897.[42] Once again, even though Tom was imprisoned, lawyers
would begin preparing paperwork initiating the appellate process, thinking their struggle an uphill battle, but a battle worth
waging nevertheless. There were many matters to contest, one of
which was the fact there was no evidence in the record of Tom
ever having possession of a pistol after his had been seized during the arrest for Discharging a Firearm Within the City Limits at
Corsicana. Provably, though, Jim had one, the pistol he purchased
at the Kaufman Pawn Shop. Defense attorneys parried, "What did
that prove?" Though it interrupts the chronological story, lifting
a witty paragraph straight from the legal brief being prepared in
Tom's behalf is indeed worthwhile—and comically engaging:

> It is true that Jim Murphy had a pistol, with which he could
> have killed Taylor, but his does not prove that he did kill him.
> To illustrate this, if the Court will indulge us, we relate an
> anecdote of an Irishman. He was charged with burglary. The
> evidence was circumstantial. He protested his innocence,
> but the Court told him, "You had burglar's tools upon you
> when you were found." To which the Irishman replied, "That

may be true, your Honor, but suppose I was accused of rape, would your Honor convict me because I had the tools upon me with which the crime could be committed?"

Tom Murphy was not, according to prison records, a model prisoner. Judging from afar is knotty. Perhaps inmate Tom Murphy was somehow justified in "cursing a fellow convict" but hardened correctional officers thought otherwise: He was punished for the odious infraction, two days in the hole.[43] Outside walls in what convicts call the "free world" not just a few folks in Henderson and Navarro Counties were being punished: Their consciences were hurting. Had Tom Murphy, in fact, been railroaded?

What happened next may or may not measure as having set a record in the annals of Texas jurisprudence—but if not, it must come close. There was a concentrated move underfoot to see that Tom Murphy was awarded a Governor's Pardon. Many folks thought—and perhaps rightly so—that if Jim Murphy was not suffering in prison for Gid Taylor's murder, neither should his younger brother Tom. A lone voice seemed to be E. O. Call the Corsicana attorney who had headed the prosecution team. He hammered out a letter of protest to the governor, which in part said that the people in Henderson County were sympathizing with the Murphy brothers, and were bordering on rising "up in Arms against the State."[44] His hyperbole was rich.

There was no talk of warfare, though there were plenty of petitions and letters fired off to the state's chief executive at Austin, and not just from that misty-eyed out-of-control bunch of liberal do-gooders in Henderson County, as lawyer Call wanted the good governor to believe.

To prove beyond reasonable doubt that Tom Murphy owned an incredible overabundance of backing is easy. Enumerating the bombardment landing on the governor's desk is near effortless. A partial list of the folks championing Tom Murphy's appeal for clemency would include: All twelve Henderson County jurors that had found Tom guilty; all twelve Henderson County jurors that had found Jim not guilty; Henderson County Sheriff K. Richardson; J. T. Deen, District Clerk for Henderson County; Henderson County Judge W. F. Freeman; Henderson County Clerk Ben F. Warren; Henderson County Tax Collector L. N. Foster; W. H. Gill, District Judge of the 3rd Judicial District of Texas; District Attorney John S. Jones, 3rd Judicial District of Texas;

Athens attorneys Paul Jones and A.B. Watkins; John F. Cook, ex-Sheriff of Henderson County; Physician J.C. Hodge; W. T. Carroll, Real Estate & Insurance; and a petition containing in excess of 350 signatures by private citizens of Henderson County.[45]

The din for granting Tom Murphy a pardon wasn't solely emanating from Henderson County. The noisy chatter was echoing to the west in Navarro County, too. J. D. Roberts, a dealer in coal and feed at Corsicana petitioned the governor suggesting if either of the Murphy boys had "Killed Taylor, Jim did it . . . . and Tom is not the man to be punished any further. Jim Murphy has had his trial and has been acquitted—therefore I have no hesitancy of saying that I want every guilty man punished to the reasonable extent of the Law but firmly believe that the punishment of Tom Murphy is already excessive. . . ."[46] T. J. Barron made his feelings known to the governor in no uncertain terms: "I was familiar with the case or witnessed from its incipiency & have never Known a Case with as much prejudice on the part of prosecution . . . . That Jim Murphy, Brother of the one in whom interest I now write, was the one who had the pistol and did the shooting. He has been formally acquitted of the charge of Murder & is a free man. Now I am sure it will be but right to pardon the Innocent."[47] Other Navarro County folks agreed. Just short of 1000 Navarro County citizens signed a petition, praying to the governor for a pardon:

> . . . . Tom Murphy is now serving in the State Penitentiary at Rusk . . . . Jim Murphy was placed on trial in the District Court of Henderson County, charged with the same offense and that Jim Murphy was duly arraigned and a jury was duly selected by the State and the defendant, and a trial was had, taking in all, eight days to try said case and that the jury heard all the testimony, that the State was able to rake and scrape against the said Jim Murphy for the last three years, and the arguments of counsel and the charge of the court and retried and duly considered their verdict, and that all of said jury voted unanimously to acquit the said Jim Murphy . . . . And we would further most respectfully state that it was the belief of most of the citizens in this, Navarro County, that if either of the Murphy boys killed the said G. C. Taylor, that it must have been Jim Murphy, who was acquitted. That therefore we fear that Tom Murphy must have been convicted more upon prejudice than upon evidence . . . .[48]

Perhaps the straw that broke the camel's back—so to speak—was not the near mindboggling number of pleas from Henderson and Navarro Counties' populace, officeholders and private citizens alike, but from Mr. R. K. Smoot and Mr. Henry E. Shelly. These two heretofore unheard from gentlemen jointly thought because there really were "grave doubts of the applicant's guilt" and since he had already served hard time in the penitentiary—probably unduly—that Murphy's application for clemency must be given favorable consideration. The pardon should be granted by the governor, restoring all rights of citizenship to Tom. Yes, these fellows' judgments carried real weight: They were the Board of Pardon Advisors, State of Texas.[49]

Request for a Governor's Pardon did not gather dust after the Board of Pardon Advisors penned their recommendation. Tom's prayers and plea for mercy were answered on September 23, 1899. Lieutenant Governor Browning, sitting as acting governor, signed the proclamation granting Tom a Governor's Pardon, restoring full citizenship status and the right to vote.[50]

There is a truism often overlooked: Then or now trial juries do not return an official verdict of "Innocent." The jury is charged with either making a finding of Guilty or Not Guilty, resultant on what was presented in the courtroom. If the Guilty verdict is brought it means the jurors were won over by that tough standard of Guilt Beyond a Reasonable Doubt. In other words, jurymen believe in their heart of hearts that the defendant did the deed, committed the crime. Return of a Not Guilty verdict doesn't automatically equate with a conclusion that the defendant is innocent, but rather that the state's arguments did not measure up to that higher—but necessary standard. There are instances wherein an innocent defendant is convicted, and cases wherein a guilty defendant is acquitted. Persons guilty of a crime may be pardoned. Persons innocent of a crime but found guilty may be pardoned. So, for deciding judiciousness of the final outcome in this storyline, *The State of Texas vs. Tom Murphy* readers may now step into the jury-box and sit tall. The decision is theirs'.

Gideon Christian "Gid" Taylor, the strikingly popular Navarro County deputy sheriff and penal farm administrator. *Courtesy Les Cotten, former Sheriff of Navarro County, Texas.*

Prisoners' quarters at the Navarro County Poor Farm, on the eastern outskirts of Corsicana, Texas. *Courtesy Les Cotten, former Sheriff of Navarro County, Texas.*

Although this image leaves an impression of peace and tranquility on the streets of Corsicana, Texas, the Navarro County town was anything but peaceful for a spell. *Courtesy Navarro County Historical Society.*

Wagons carrying barrels of beer or whiskey were not an uncommon sight on the streets of Corsicana. *Courtesy Navarro County Historical Society.*

Inside a Beaton Street taproom at Corsicana, proprietor Jim Stockard with pistol in waistband stands ready to dispense beer, booze—or bullets. *Courtesy Les Cotten, former Sheriff of Navarro County, Texas.*

Has a Wolfish Look, Is Bold to Recklessness

5

John Wesley Hardin earned high marks as one of the Wild West's notorious gunfighters. His dexterity in handling smoking Colt's six-shooters was A+. If idiomatic terminology is loosely applied, Wes may be tagged a graduate student in the fine arts of personal survival and man-killing, attaining degrees in infamy and misplaced admiration. He, too, was a schoolteacher.[1] As a contracted educator Master John Wesley Hardin was scarcely older than some of the class under his tutelage, but unlike his darling little charges the teacher already had bona fide cuts on his notch-stick. At least one fellow, the subject of this vignette, Alfred "Alf" Rushing, would follow suit. With a fine example standing before him at the blackboard, Alf would learn his lesson well, that part about dodging the law. In fact he would surpass his schoolteacher's talents in that regard.

Alf's parents, Calvin and Harriet J. (Griffin) Rushing had made a pre-Civil War migration from the Volunteer State, Tennessee, to Texas, settling in Navarro County at the Spring Hill community during 1853.[2] The modest settlement was the oldest in Navarro County, a stick building covered with rawhide serving as its first church and school.[3] On the southeast, Navarro County butted up against Freestone County and its little community of Wortham. The tiny locale would play a not insignificant role in the story at hand. Wortham, too, was not terribly far north of Fort Parker where Comanches had raided and ridden away with their most celebrated captive, nine-year-old Cynthia Ann Parker.[4] This strip of Texas was situated at one of those geographical crossroads where the eastern forests and thickets were gradually giving way to western expansiveness: the seemingly endless rolling prairies directly in front of mountainous West Texas and the pancake-flat Llano Estacado.

Not unexpectedly, before the invention and incessant stringing of barbed wire, it was Open Range country: a time-frame and setting where strict adherence to bothersome ethics often took second place for the industrious fellow skilled in tossing the wide loop.

A few astute—some might say selfish—fellows had opted to forgo participation and remain in Texas while their countrymen had put their names on the Confederacy's dotted line, temporarily abandoning private livestock interests in the name of state's rights patriotism. During the war's lifespan, back in Texas, nature had been taking its course and free-roaming cattle were appreciably increasing in numbers. The ratio of cowmen to unbranded cows was pitiably out of whack. The few stockmen skipping service in a gray uniform couldn't keep up—no matter how hard they hunted or how often they unlimbered a catch-rope, though some few did chisel out individual beef bonanzas. In the main, however, there were plenty of loose cattle not wearing a burnt hide nametag. Subsequent to the Big War a race for tattooing mavericks with claims of ownership, a brand and an ear mark, became ubiquitous on Texas' vast public pastures—the Open Range. An unbiased U.S. Army officer stationed in the Texas Hill Country during Reconstruction hammered home a truism: the competition to mark and brand mavericks was fierce, men actually living in fear that one of their neighbors would gain the upper hand.[5] One fellow, a ranchman and local politician, squawked that even heretofore respectable folks were knowingly partaking in a slight dab of "irregular branding," making sure to get their unfair share before all the at large cattle had been expeditiously gathered "by the most active adventurers from wheresoever."[6] Periodically, contemporary newspapermen were not reticent or bashful. This one writing for the *San Antonio Daily Herald*, chided:

> There are men in the country who never bought a cow in their lives who now have large stocks, and they get them by branding other peoples stock entirely, and if you will show me a man who cow hunts or lives in the country away from a butcher shop who does not brand calves or eat meat not his own and contrary to law, I will show you nine men to one that does do it.[7]

Old-time cowman Ike Pryor didn't dabble with any hollow self-serving excuses: "I say that any cowman of open range days who claimed never to have put his brand on somebody else's animal was either a damn liar or a damn poor roper."[8] Perhaps even more germane for the story at hand, since it involves Alf Rushing's soon to be kinfolks by marriage, is an inquiry made to James L. Swink as to why his brother Henry A. Swink owned more land, more cattle, and more wealth? Absent even hint of a smile or a half teaspoon of humor, the steely-eyed James L. succinctly replied: "That's easy, he's better with a rope."[9]

Born into cow country on the seventeenth day of September 1856, Alf Rushing was the second child and only son of Cal and Harriet.[10] He had an older sister, Mary Ann, and Alf's birth had been followed by arrival of the twins, Evaline N. "Evie" and Josephine S. "Josie" two years later on October 12, 1858. Family lore has fourteen-year-old Alf, Evie, and Josie as attendees in John Wesley's one-room schoolhouse, at least for the three winter months Hardin laid off the six-shooters and picked up the instructional pointer and chalk sticks.[11] The fact that these three Rushing kiddos were students is somewhat underscored by Hardin's autobiographical remarks: "In January 1869, I went with my father to Navarro County and engaged in school teaching near Pisgah. I had about twenty-five scholars, both girls and boys, from the age of 6 to 16. I taught school for three months. . . . While living near Pisgah, in Navarro County, I had made the acquaintance of nearly everybody there at that time. . . . I knew the Newmans, the Tramels, the Rushings; the Andersons and Dixons were cousins of mine."[12] According to at least one fascinating remembrance, teacher Wes Hardin was highly regarded by the student body, although he was pretty strict and "prayed before class every morning."[13] Alf Rushing—as far as now known—did not leave any clues as to whether or not he turned toward Heaven for comfort in those days. Though, shortly, it is a reasonably safe bet he, too, prayed every day—prayed he wouldn't get caught. Alf, an adept pupil, knew the ABCs of building and pitching a loop.

By the time he was physically mature the sandy-headed Alf Rushing topped out at two inches above the six foot mark, tipped the scale at 175 lbs. and owned, besides his florid complexion, three criminal indictments in Navarro County for cow stealing.[14]

Details of the alleged crimes are indistinct and the sketchy information is drawn partly from a Texas Ranger's fugitive notebook and partly from a letter from the Navarro County District Attorney. Was Alf accused of stealing three head or several head during three different episodes? Could it have been a mistake, a misunderstanding: a case of roping and tripping and innocently branding and ear-notching the wrong bovine? Three times? Did he knowingly sell three head or three herds minus Bills of Sales? ¿Quién sabe?[15] There are very few quantifiable facts, but it may be reported with clarity that the Navarro County Sheriff, James H. Brent, in the short term had not arrested Alf Rushing during 1874 when the offenses were alleged, nor in 1875 after the grand jury returned its three livestock theft indictments.[16] Alf, by and large hanging out across the county line in Freestone County for good reason was by definition a real cowboy—and a real fugitive. He was also yet a teenager. Then as now, boys in Texas cow country grow up fast: straightforward familiarity with guns, cold-backed cow ponies, and skittish mossy-horned cattle are not reserved for the age of majority. During adolescence, to parrot a phrase, is when most Texas bred cowboys earned their spurs. Alf Rushing was a native Texan.

After quite some time Alf either made the mistake of accidently acquainting himself with a Navarro County deputy sheriff or voluntarily surrendered to one. In any event he was arrested, taken to Corsicana and lodged in the jailhouse until others in his behalf posted the requisite bail bond. Then he immediately returned to what he must have interpreted as the safe environs of ridges and draws and the rich bottom lands along the line separating Freestone and Navarro Counties, namely Pisgah Ridge and its cobweb network of out-of-the-way caves.[17]

The extent of their business interplay must remain in the realm of speculation but there are a few hard facts begging mention: namely that Alf Rushing's younger sister Evie, one of the twins, married the aforementioned Henry A. Swink. Like Alf, Henry had received minimal formal education in a "subscription school" but by the age of nineteen was a genuine cowboy. Drawing wages of $18 per month, young Henry had trailed beeves to the Indian Nations and to the Kansas cow towns before quitting the stinky and dusty grind of following the tail end of another person's cattle. He went into business for himself, which, reading between the lines, might accent the words of brother James' characterization that Henry was pretty handy with the lariat rope. Henry and Alf also had another common denominator. Both Henry and James Swink were under indictment in Navarro County, at least according to that Texas Ranger's list of wanted fugitives. James had been indicted in 1876 for "Theft of a cow" and Henry during that same year suffered indictment for "Theft of cattle."[18] Indictments, relatively speaking, are rather easy for a prosecutor to come by, and it's frequently claimed by defense attorneys that a good district attorney could indict a ham sandwich. Which is a play on words for, "Where's the beef?" What's the meat of the case? Is evidence palatable or just waste and gristle for a trial jury to chew on? The return of an indictment does not equate to guilt Beyond a Reasonable Doubt; nevertheless, any prudent man would not willingly welcome any grand jury's handiwork.

The next installment in Alf Rushing's story puts meat on the bone. Although there are many as yet unanswerable questions, there is an ineradicable bottom line. And it's not pretty. Nor is it a pretty story for Wortham, that sometimes pleasant little burg in the northwestern stretch of Freestone County.

Cataloging the little town and the area as being pleasant, sometimes, is not an unintentional slip-up. Wortham, inside and just outside the city limits, would herald 1877 a banner year for badness. On March 2 just five miles east of town, Dr. J. S. Webb was mortally gunned down by an unknown assassin or assassins when he answered a nighttime knock at the door. Most believed, if the newspaperman was correct, that the coldblooded killing was the result of an "old feud of long expanse."[19] At Woodland, just to the southeast of Wortham, near Kirvin, for some reason as yet indistinct, on the fourteenth of July a Mr. Harralson was killed by W. P. Johnson. The following week another fellow killed his brother-in-law at Davids' Mills.[20] Doing it up right, cowboy style, on or about December 1, 1877, a young yahoo named Whittaker tanked up on whiskey and rode his horse into the Woodland grocery store of P. E. Waters, twice. After the forced evictions Whittaker laid in wait for Waters. After closing his shop Mr. Waters found himself accosted by Whittaker who was armed with a scary looking knife. Undaunted, so it would seem, the storekeeper jerked out a long-barreled revolver and whopped his assailant aside the head, "inflicting, it is feared, a mortal wound." Several days later young Whittaker "was still insensible from the blow and had considerable fever. The wounded man is [was] a stranger about Woodland, not even his first name being known. He is [was] apparently not over twenty-five. The only paper found on his person was a bill of goods bought of Mr. J. J. Beckham of Mexia."[21] Yes, for good or bad there weren't many sissies in northwestern Freestone County.

On the third day of December 1877, a Monday evening, hell popped again at Wortham. Riding into town with twenty-one-year-old Alf Rushing were Harvey "Harve" Scruggs and Frank Carter. The boys were not strangers to town. In fact, they were quite well known. All three were prototypical men of the 1870s Texas range: hard-bitten cow hunters with leathery faces and lanky frames—and an overabundance of pluck. A few years of cow country tradition had permeated their very hearts and young souls: Bad bulls, bad weather, bad brush, and bad horses had toughened them to the bone. Be it man or beast, they'd not show the white feather. They had come into town eared back at the half-cock notch. All three fellows carried double barreled shotguns across pommels of their double-rigged Texas stock saddles. Alf Rushing was young, headstrong, and particularly primed for impetuous warfare. The boys reined in at the Wortham mercantile of J. J. Stubbs shortly before dark.[22]

There are competing versions as to a detail or two, but inside the store a disturbance burst forth. Generally it's written—in contemporary newspaper accounts—that the brouhaha stemmed from merchant Stubbs removing a Colt's .45 from saddlebags Harve Scruggs had sometime earlier left at the store. The cowboys demanded that storeowner Stubbs fork over the six-shooter or seventeen dollars—or pay with blood. Stubbs maintained he knew nothing of which they spoke. The argument waxed hot, with enough elevated vitriol to attract attention of Jackson T. Barfield, the town of Wortham's fifty-seven-year-old city marshal. Officer Barfield did what a good lawman was supposed to do: something. He walked to Stubb's store intent on putting a damper on unrestrained tempers and nasty talk. In what was described as "a friendly manner" Barfield asked the wound-tight fellows to "not raise a disturbance and to be more quiet." Witnesses, and there were many, thought the city marshal had done just that, successfully defused a potentially explosive row. They and Barfield were wrong—dead wrong.

The ruffled feathers were not smoothed; the bitter feelings were not soothed. Doused with a sprinkling of the lawman's common sense admonishment, the three cowboys stepped into a stirrup of their caques—their saddles—and mounted their cow ponies.[23] As soon as Marshal Barfield turned his back to walk away, Alf Rushing raised his shotgun. When Alf touched the front trigger a sizzling orange blast from the scattergun's muzzle lighted up shadows drawn by the fast setting winter sun. The range was so close that all nine buckshot ripped into Jackson Barfield's back, "three inches below the left shoulder blade," with at least three balls plowing through sinew and into his heart.[24] City Marshal Jackson T. Barfield was killed instantly, a dead man falling.[25]

Wheeling their horses in a perfectly orchestrated half circle, the three rogues hightailed out of town "at full speed under a shower of buckshot." To an outsider, pandemonium may seem to have washed over Wortham, but to tough Texas townsmen it was but a call to arms. And in 1877 Texas—or today—handguns and rifles and fully charged shotguns are always fairly handy. The citizens' posse was horseback and on the hunt in but a heartbeat. Racing for their lives the boys, now first-rate desperadoes, could see the posse would soon overhaul them so they stopped and turned about, hoping to check the advance with a shot or two. For Rushing and Scruggs it may have been a moderately wise move, for Carter it was catastrophic. The citizens would not passively accept being shot at. During the ensuing return fire they managed to kill Frank's horse outright and put at least one bullet into Carter. Though wounded and leaking blood he hotfooted across an open field. But, alas, outrunning a horse would at any time be problematic, more especially while weighted with burning lead. The burden was simply too much. Frank was quickly corralled by unsympathetic pursuers and made a prisoner. Alf and Harve made good their getaway.[26]

Reportedly Rushing, after separating from Scruggs, had hastened to the vicinity of the Pin Oak Creek bottoms. He was being secreted by "those who sympathize with him, and are supposed to use every means to aid him in escaping the hands of the law."[27] History will bear witness that Alf Rushing would have plenty of friends. And though it may not be said unequivocally, which they readily acknowledge, family lore passed down through the years adds another motive for the killing of Barfield. Some think Alf

Rushing, who was yet facing charges in Navarro County for cattle theft, killed Wortham's city marshal due to a personal animosity arising from those indictments.[28] The Frontier Battalion's Major Jones thought Alf's killing of Barfield grew from and was but "continuation of an old feud between Mr. Pisgah in this county [Navarro] and Wortham in Freestone."[29] Alf Rushing was a killer, wanted by the law, regardless the reason.

Meanwhile back in Wortham a town was in mourning. Margaret Barfield was a widow. Citizens had lost an honorable and respected peace officer, an asset to their frontier community. Reverently the slain city marshal was laid to rest in what was then known as the Crouch Cemetery plot, in a fenced area adjacent to the Lindley Cemetery.[30]

Subsequent to the dignified formalities of a funeral and interment, Freestone County's and Wortham's legal trustees refocused on apprehending Alf Rushing, the person all witnesses had fingered as having heartlessly gunned down Marshal Barfield. Mayor W. M. Seely of Wortham telegraphed Major Jones:

> Rushing is at Jim Newman's, Henry Swink's, or Frank Polk's at night. He, Rushing, can raise fifty men to back him in half a day.[31]

The short staffed Freestone County sheriff, twenty-four-year-old James P. Robinson's back was against the proverbial wall. He needed help because, as he advised the Texas Adjutant General, William Steele, "Rushing is still in Navarro Co. harbored about Mt. Pisgah & backed by some Forty Five of Fifty men. . . . As to the character of these parties we refer you to Maj. J. B. Jones who can also give you an idea as to the number it will require to make the arrest."[32]

And, indeed, the Frontier Battalion's Major Jones in all probability could offer valuable insight to the AG concerning the standing certain fellows had in the community—he was from Navarro County. The section around Pisgah was home turf to some of Navarro County's best citizens—and some of its worst, well, toughest and meanest. There were several caves nearby and one, known as the White Elephant, was outfitted with a fireplace, gambling tables, and no shortage of homemade whiskey. It was a well known and popular hangout for those skirting imposition of the law. Whiskey and gunpowder and immaturity are a volatile mix. Pisgah Ridge hosted all three—in spades. Once, according to local lore, a tenderfoot made an appearance on Pisgah Ridge. Somehow he had managed to arouse the anger in some area toughs, and they simply packed him into a pickle barrel, pushed it over the ridge and took potshots at it while making the thirty-degree drop.[33] Chaste history is vague whether or not the greenhorn dizzily recovered and ran away—or the hogs ate him! Spotless history, too, reveals that one of those Dixon boys, Simp, would eventually be gunned down by a tenacious posse. Two other Dixons, Thomas K. "Tom" and William A. "Bud" would be mobbed from the Comanche County courtroom, along with that former Pisgah Ridge teacher's brother Joseph G. "Joe" Hardin. Those boys were lifelessly suspended from the stoutest limb of a nearby live oak, while two other hapless fellows were fatally shot while sleepily reposed on their woolen blankets.[34] Yes, they grew 'em real tough around Pisgah Ridge.

What Major Jones could not do, however, was to pull an entire company of Texas Rangers away from pressing duties to hunt for just one outlaw, no matter how bad Alf Rushing was, or was purported to be. On the last day of December 1877 Major Jones, in writing, informed Wortham's Mayor Seely and Sheriff Robinson of his dilemma, and a stopgap solution: "I Send Lieut. Arrington of my Command to look into the matter of arresting Alf Rushing. I have no Company that I can Send So far into the interior, at this time, all of them being now on the extreme frontier. Lieut. A. is a discreet officer. He will investigate the Situation and if he concludes that the arrest can be made by three or four men I can send that number to him. Even in that event I will have to ask the citizens to mount his men as they will have to go from here on the Rail Road. Please give Lieut. A. such advice and assistance as he will require in the business."[35]

Although the governor of Texas had issued a reward, and the dollar amount had been augmented by outraged citizens from Wortham, no one seemed overly eager to rush headlong into Alf's stronghold and perhaps suffer a six-shooter standoff with those forty-five or fifty hard-edged cowboys and kinsmen haunting the vicinity of Pisgah Ridge. Lieutenant George Washington "Cap" Arrington, who himself had run away from a murder charge in Alabama and since adopted a wholly new persona, traveled to the vicinity and made the initial inquiry.[36]

Lieutenant Arrington was not a man to take lightly though, especially if one was to think the lawman didn't have plenty of determination and sand. As time edged by, Ranger Arrington laid his traps and made big plans. Alf must have thought himself a pretty smart cookie, but Cap Arrington had greased the pan—and maybe the greedy palms of a snitch. During the first nine days of January 1878, in and around Freestone County, near Wortham, and assisted by eight other Texas Rangers, including N. O. "Mage" Reynolds, Lieutenant Arrington "scouted" after Alf Rushing.[37] Their hard charging went unrewarded. The dough had soured. Alf was either not in the country or had been productively tipped off to Texas Ranger movements by friends and relatives.[38] A newsman writing for the *Luling Signal* had a different take on the lawmen's seemingly lackluster performance:

> .... their commander, reports that he found Rushin [*sic*] too strong for him and his men, having arrayed his whole neighborhood on his side and also a strong force from Navarro county. They have bought all the Winchester rifles they could find and offer defiance to the State of Texas. It is presumed the Rangers will at once be reinforced and give Rushin and his outlaws battle.[39]

Though the newspaperman may have been a touch over dramatic, the manhunt was temporarily abandoned. Sooner or later, somehow, actionable intelligence would surface that would be the undoing of Mr. Alf Rushing—so the Texas Rangers thought and hoped.

Certainly the possibility that Alf had fled the state of Texas was believable, at least for one fellow. C. H. Graves, an attorney from Freestone County, had received a letter "from a man in Dallas" asking for a requisition for Alf. It seems that this man—which in all probability was the noted bounty hunter Jack Duncan—had information Alf was out of state, but given twenty days could have him in irons and bound for Texas.[40] The clue, good or bad, fizzled and fell into the abyss of nothingness.

Another shooting incident at Wortham grabbed the headlines. One of John Wesley Hardin's *amigos*, Frank Polk, who even Wes described as a "notorious desperado," had an axe to grind with the city's mayor, William Marcus Seely. Frank, not to be confused with Frank M. Polk the brother of sometimes Old West lawman Cal

Polk, had ridden back into town after an arrest two days earlier. On 23 September 1878, a Monday, Frank Polk had not a hatchet in hand, but a fully charged Winchester. He had killing on his mind. The city's replacement for the slain Jackson T. Barfield, City Marshal Charles Powers was on duty. As he should have done Officer Powers tried to prevent trouble, but all too soon was embroiled in a shootout. During the exchange of gunfire, lawman Powers managed to kill Polk's horse and hit his target. Frank, though suffering gunshot wounds, killed policeman Powers. Mayor Seely, who also carried commission as a Freestone County deputy sheriff, jumped into the hot affray. Major John B. Jones in recounting the incident to headquarters at Austin in part detailed the shooting scrap by noting that ".... Polk, who killed Powers and was himself killed by the Mayor, Seely...."[41] A smattering of oral history which spices up the story suggests—and it may be true—that Mayor Seely issued Frank Polk a coup d'état while he was pinned beneath his saddle, unable to extricate himself. Some folks thought Seely should have to legally answer for killing a man while he was down. He was indicted by a Freestone County Grand Jury for manslaughter. Mr. Seely had an explanation, a justification: That he couldn't go through life always looking over his shoulder, just waiting for Frank Polk's guaranteed act of revenge. After all, Polk was known throughout the area as that "notorious desperado." Common sense dictated that the mayor should shoot Frank Polk when he had a damn good chance, not just lethargically wait until he himself was bushwhacked. Neighborhood citizens bought into the uncomplicated logic and not altogether impractical reasoning.[42] Mayor Seely skated across the bar of justice, no penalty, no fine.

Months had passed fruitlessly in the search for Alf Rushing. About the time Frank Polk met his death there was a sparkle of optimism, for a little while. On furlough, reporting from his homeplace near Corsicana, Major Jones updated Adjutant General Steele on September 25, 1878. He had dispatched a Texas Ranger to Wortham to apprehend Rushing, but regrettably learned that Alf had probably—about a week earlier—skipped to Lampasas County. There, according to the major's best information, Rushing was thought to be hanging out with saddle hardened relatives, the celebrated or condemned—depending on perspective—Horrell brothers: Sam, James Martin "Mart," Tom, Benjamin F. "Ben," and Merritt. The Horrells were tough to the limit and perfectly pigheaded, a set "who were raised to horses, cattle, whiskey and guns."[43] Major Jones followed up: "Have given notice at Lampasas and have men there now on the lookout for him."[44]

Texas Rangers should have been looking elsewhere, had they the wisdom of hindsight. By the best data now available, and certainly then, after a lapse of time Alf Rushing was on the dodge in Boone County, northwestern Arkansas, utilizing an alias and headstrong about any forced removal to Texas. Reportedly—and maybe mistakenly—Alf was by now running with George Harris, twenty-six, a heavy-drinking fellow wanted in Texas for a cold-blooded murder committed on December 12, 1877. Thirty-eight-year-old Elias Olenick, a Jewish immigrant from Poland and now Austin dry-goods merchant, and George Harris had become mixed up in a bitter argument over the payment for two shirts at the Pecan Street store. Conclusively it may be noted that Harris, according to the *Galveston Daily News* then, and a subsequent courtroom conviction, "drew a pistol and shot him [Olenick] in the head inflicting a mortal wound. Harris mounted his horse which was hitched near by, and was gone immediately."[45] According to Boone County Deputy Sheriff Moore, the two, Rushing and Harris, were lying low in the neighborhood of Harrison, Arkansas. Moore reported that George Harris had assumed a new identity; he was then calling himself J. P. Harris and Alf was using the surname Johnson.[46]

There is room for error in Deputy Moore's thinking or it might be that the once good information he had been given about George Harris by an ever industrious private eye was a wee bit stale. In keeping with at least one newspaper account, Harris had already been arrested and hand-delivered to Travis County authorities by the Hill County Sheriff, John P. Cox.[47] Likewise, at the time Deputy Moore wrote his June 3, 1880, letter to the governor of Texas inquiring about reward monies, according to the Convict Record Ledger as maintained by the Texas Prison System, Harris was already doing time as inmate No. 8491: And had been since entering the penitentiary on the twenty-third day of March 1880. Deputy Moore may have come up short regarding fresh data about Harris' whereabouts, but he was seemingly on target about Alf.

Recognizing the necessity of complying with demanding legal formalities Boone County Deputy Moore had requested that the Texas governor make an official extradition request to the governor of Arkansas.[48]

Made aware of the possible location of Rushing, the Freestone County Attorney, B. S. Gardner, made his thoughts known to the governor, recommending he promptly issue a requisition for the breathing body of Alf: "Nearly all of the witnesses to this murder are living in and about Wortham and I have every reason to believe if captured that Rushing could be convicted of Murder." Working within the letter of the law's framework—in this case—was very important. Rushing was worth $1000 to the fellow that made the capture and returned the outlaw to Texas.[49] Persnickety legal rules had best be obeyed.

Even though hard and fast details are at best murky, there are a few documentable facts. George Harris and Alf Rushing had—if they were ever together—already parted company. Alf rushed into the Indian Territory west of the Arkansas line—at least temporarily—while George Harris was beginning his ten-year stretch—doing hard time in Texas.

The aforementioned Jack Duncan had, by steadily working his extensive network of confidential informants, been apprised that Alf Rushing was cowboying north of the Red River in the Cherokee Nation. County Attorney Gardner requested that private detective Duncan of Dallas be named the agent for the Texas Department of State's Extradition Warrant No. 605.[50] Just how much effort was placed on executing the warrant is nebulous. With clarity, however, it may be reported that lawmen missed capturing Alf Rushing in the Cherokee Nation—he had skipped, once again.

It seems that Major Jones' assertion that Alf Rushing was in the company of one or more of the Horrell boys was spot on. Some of the boys, though, were not slinking around in Lampasas County. At this time they were in southeastern Colorado, across the North Fork of the Cimarron River, fifty miles south of Granada. Alf Rushing, temporarily using the name John McFarland, was riding with Sam Horrell. There, on the prairie, they had a chance encounter with Cal Polk, who was doggedly intent on lending a helping hand to an incarcerated cousin. Cal Polk, who never won the blue ribbon at a Spelling Bee, was a fearless bronc buster and up-for-anything cowboy. He wasn't bashful about the undertaking:

> . . . I looked up a little creek and saw a wagon at a camp[.]
> I road up there and asked if I could get Dinner from them
> [and] they told me to get Down [and] make myself at home[.]

I staked out my horse and while Resting there [told them]
that I had a kindsman in Jale at the next town By the name of
Alf Polk for killing 2 men and wanted to assist him[.] They
was 3 men at the camp and they would look at one another
and smile[.] In a few minutes 2 of them walked off to one
side and Begain to talk Lo and then called the other one[.]
this caused me to think they was some thing [wrong]. I got
up and buckled on my 45 Colts and started to get my horse
to leave and while I was untying him I looked back and [saw
them] coming to warge me. . . . He come up and says . . . we
are good friends of Alf Polk. [We intend] to brake him out
of Jale tonight . . . my Rite name is alf rushen [Alf Rushing]
I am . . . wanted in . . . texas for murder [and] they is a Big
Reward there offered for me[.] [The] oldest mans name is
Sam Harl[,] he is wanted in [Lampasas ?] co texas. We came
from the Indian territory to take him [Alf Polk] out.[51]

Cal Polk's newfound friends were hell-bent on freeing Alf Polk
from jail. Or, barring that, they would unconditionally "whirp
everything in granado [Granada]." Whether or not Cal Polk was
hoodwinked or knowingly entangled himself in a plot to participate in the jailbreak is ill-defined. He did agree to serve as a
reconnaissance agent, slip into town and map out escape routes.
Perhaps to everybody's good fortune, Alf Polk had, by the time
Cal reached town, made bond and was no longer in the lockup.
Also falling into place was a job for Cal and Alf Rushing. Alf Polk
had agreed to take charge of one of the JJ cow outfits, operating
for Jim Jones, one of his bondsmen. He hired as part of his cowboy
crew cousin Cal Polk and Alf Rushing, "who went by the name of
Mcforlin [sic: McFarland]." Sam Horrell and the other toughened
fellow—a guy named Bob—opted to seek their dubious fortunes
elsewhere. They drifted northwest toward the Canadian line.[52]

    For the next few months Alf Rushing and the carefree cow-
boys worked cattle and hurrahed a small village or two with
their childish—though sometimes dangerous—tomfoolery. Then
things spiked more serious. Out of the blue it was learned that
Alf Polk's bond had not been in fact properly secured, and he
was now a highly sought fugitive—just like Alf Rushing, aka
John McFarland. The boys were on the dodge, avoiding the bigger
towns, jumping back and forth across the Colorado/New Mexican
border hoping to always land in an actually identifiable section of

real-estate, "No Man's Land."[53] Cal Polk, in later life, did carry part of the story forward, highlighting a six-shooter dustup heretofore unnoticed:

> But to keep on the look out for all officers and not Be arrested we got Down there [New Mexico Territory] and found that they was to Be Some Pony Races at a small mexacan town the next Day which was Satterday. So we went to the Races and win some monnie off of the mexacans then went Down on a Spring Branch in front of a mexacan house to Eate Dinner. Just as we Set Down to Eat I saw a mexacan lope up to that house and go in it. In a few minets we could here a woman crying and Beggin and could here some one whirping her. All at once mackforlon [Alf Rushing aka McFarland] Jumped up and said you Boys make out your Dinner while I go up there and kill that mexacan for whirping that woman and off he went. Just as he went in the house we heard 3 shots fire and saw mack [McFarland] step out of the Door with a smokeing 45 colts in his hand and start and talk to the woman for a few minets. He then come on Down and said I got him. He wont whirp any more wimen soon. But I whish I had let him Beat her to Death for as soon as I shot him she wanted to Jump on me for it.[54]

For this noteworthy case it seems Cal Polk's story—though standing alone—rings true, perfectly aligned with the family's oral history. Although many of the Rushing clan may have been devout churchgoers and religious most of the time, they lived by an uncomplicated cow country dogma: If a damn mad Rushing said he would shoot you, he damn sure would![55]

Later, after the sojourn on the JJ, owlhoot Alf Rushing worked his way north. Exercising his cowboying talents and cleverly concealing his true identity and status as a Texas fugitive, Alf wormed his way into Wyoming. Shortly thereafter he landed himself a foreman's job at the Sugg brothers' cattle ranch on the Powder River in Johnson County. Of course, he had continued using an alias. Alf was still popularly known as John McFarland.[56] Someone, apparently learning Alf's real name, real story, and real repute, spilled the beans.

The governor of Texas had wired the sheriff of Johnson County that there was an outstanding warrant and reward for Alf

Rushing, aka John McFarland. Arrest him, hold him, and a deputy or sheriff would make the long trip to picturesque Buffalo at the southeastern base of the Big Horn Mountains, the county seat. Then he would take physical custody of Barfield's killer for a legally sanctioned extradition back to the Lone Star State.

The Johnson County Sheriff, Frank Canton, and the fugitive Alf Rushing owned at least two common denominators. Both had left real seedy reputations and their real names in Texas. The sheriff of Johnson County was, in fact, none other than Joe Horner, an outlaw shootist with confirmed kills and jailbreak on his back trail. The no nonsense Sheriff Canton was certainly man enough to jug Alf Rushing. Cleverly and deceitfully the good, well, sometimes bad, Frank Canton had set his trap. Cozying up to Alf Rushing in a Buffalo barroom, the sheriff invited Alf to share in partaking of a few "stimulants." The alcohol induced haze of diminished vigilance comfortably wrapped around the duped Texas fugitive. The sheriff's cocked six-shooter insured peaceful compliance: Alf Rushing, aka John McFarland was jailed.[57]

Behind iron bars Alf Rushing paced. On the other side Sheriff Canton paced. Both were waiting the arrival of a lawman from Texas. Two weeks passed. There was no word from Texas. There was word from the cowboy pals of Rushing; they were not necessarily thrilled with news of Alf's imprisonment. Many began drifting into town, Winchesters in their saddle scabbards, Colt's revolvers beneath heavy woolen coats, and icy stares to punctuate their cold displeasure. The undercurrent of trouble wasn't thawing. At last, after seventeen fretful days, a magistrate acted. With his bronc-bustin' buddies present in the courtroom, Alf Rushing stood before the bench of Judge Blair four days after Christmas 1885, eight years after Officer Jackson T. Barfield's death. Alf was set free. The judge's ruling was based on the seemingly lackluster outlook of authorities in Texas. They'd been given plenty of time to get Alf—if they'd really wanted him. Obviously they didn't!

Alf's release unleashed a celebration, cowboy style: whooping and yelling, carrying Alf out of the courthouse atop their shoulders and the brandishing of Colt's six-shooters. Sheriff Frank Canton was not any too happy. He'd been forced to feed and care for and guard the prisoner around-the-clock at Johnson County's—or his expense—and there would be no collection of any reward monies whatsoever. Somewhat testily he penned a letter to Alf's sister Josie, who was now living in Sweetwater, Nolan County, Texas, herself married to the county's future sheriff, James F. "Jim" Newman, who was then heavily and actively invested in the eastern New Mexico Territory cattle business. Part of Sheriff Frank Canton's missive was a stern admonishment, putting Texas authorities on notice:

> J. L. Walton [Navarro County Sheriff] of Corsicana, Texas, is the man who was sent-up after him. He came as far as Cheyenne, Wyoming. I think he was to [*sic*] cowardly to come any farther for he stopped there 10 or 12 days & I think he then went back to Texas, if he wants any more men in this country arrested he can come up here & arrest them himself. I am sure I will not arrest another man by his order.[58]

Knowing he wouldn't—or might not—come clear the next time should Wyoming lawmen knock at his dugout door, Alf Rushing scooted for a warmer clime—maybe. Exactly how he received the investigative lead is foggy, but Jack Duncan had suspicion enough to think Alf Rushing was back in the Indian Nations. Telegraphers' fingers were busy. United States Deputy Marshal Sam Sixkiller thought, based on Duncan's lead, that he had Alf Rushing located. The fugitive was now going by the name of Ed Brown, working on a ranch in the vicinity of Webbers Falls, southeastern Muskogee County. Employing a usable ruse, Marshal Sixkiller and Deputy Bill Drew "gathered up a bunch of cattle, and driving them up, asked permission to put them in a yard [corral] there for the night." The newsman continues the Wild West narrative:

> The request was granted, and Brown was called from the crib where he was at work to help pen them. While driving them Sam worked around to where Brown was, and throwing down on him, took him completely by surprise, and he could offer no resistance. The cattle were then turned loose. Brown denies he is the man wanted by the officers, but they are certain they have the right party, and he is being held here awaiting the Texas officers.[59]

In this specific instance Ed Brown, or whoever he was, was damn right—he was the wrong man! It was an embarrassing fact confirmed in pages of the *Dallas Morning News*. Pulling no punches the reporter acknowledged the arrest had been made "by instructions of Detective Jack Duncan." The newspaperman elaborated. Freestone County Sheriff Henry J. Childs had made the trip to Muskogee. He, no doubt, had been absolutely delighted that finally he would be able to handcuff and shackle one of the state's most wanted fugitives. The euphoria was short lived. Sheriff Childs and witnesses traveling with him quickly learned that the arrested Ed Brown was not Alf Rushing. For Texas lawmen it was a disappointment. For bounty hunter Jack Duncan it was humiliation. He was forced to step up: "Mr. Duncan states that he will pay the expenses incurred by the men who made the arrest and that he proposes to catch Alf Rushing or land his existence in the rural regions of Sheol"—a Biblical place in the depths of the earth conceived of as the dwelling of the dead.[60] At this time, really, where Rushing was, was anybody's guess. The law had not a clue, and would not have a viable inkling of his whereabouts for years.

Then there was a new and maybe creditable lead. Circa 1890 Alf Rushing, or someone thought to be Alf Rushing, was arrested in California. Freestone County authorities were notified and the wheels of legalese began turning—well, spinning. Unfortunately there was a hitch, a slipped gear, best explained by the Freestone County Attorney, R. M. Edwards, to Texas Governor C. A. Culberson: "citizens have paid out of their pockets about 500$ to get Mr. Rushing but have failed. Our sheriff 8 or 10 years ago located Rushing in California had him arrested and before he could get there he was released under a writ of Habeas Corpus."[61] Still on the dodge, Alf Rushing had eluded pursuing lawdogs—again.

How the information surfaced is mysterious. Somehow, for some reason, officialdom thought they had Alf Rushing pinned down in California once more. The investigative lead was based on criminal intelligence furnished in a letter from J. M. Glass, Chief of Police, Los Angeles. Requisition No. 516 was applied for by R. M. Edwards, County Attorney, Fairfield, Freestone County, Texas, on July 13, 1898. The requisition on the governor of California, named H. H. Powell (Sheriff, Freestone County) as the person appointed to "receive and return said fugitive, without any expense to the State of Texas under this appointment. (ACTUAL NECESSARY EXPENSES not exceeding the sum of $200 will be paid by the State upon delivery of said fugitive to the proper officer inside the jail of Freestone County, Texas, upon sworn itemized account and upon proper of evidence of said delivery.)" On the same day, Capias Arrest Warrant No. 1088 issued from Freestone County, commanding the arrest of Alf Rushing, "charging him with Murder." Furthermore there was sworn certification that Sheriff Powell "has no private interest in the proposed arrest."[62]

Well nigh two decades had elapsed since the back-shooting murder of Jackson Barfield. Alf Rushing was still footloose and fancy free—though preoccupied by the ever looming threat of apprehension. Despite the fact he'd been arrested in Wyoming and California and wiggled loose each time Alf was yet on the run. He had been for twenty-plus years. Dodging lawmen was now part of his makeup, in his bloodstream. While much may be factually known within family circles—though somewhat shushed—remnants left for the studious historian are but scraps of speculation, well-grounded speculation, but speculation nevertheless. Alf had help—maybe?

One of Alf's twin sisters, Josie, had married the aforementioned Jim Newman. After the section around northern Freestone and southern Navarro Counties began "settling-up" Jim Newman had migrated to the open range country of the Texas Panhandle where there was no barbed-wire to hem in his tempestuous spirit or his untamed cattle. Like his brother-in-law Alf Rushing, Jim Newman was bootstrap tough, wedded to the cow country culture. For the steep price of $60 Newman had purchased the old Causey buffalo camp, owning the sod house headquarters and grazing rights of the range, but no clear title to any land.[63] When the XIT began methodically building its 6000 miles of fence, several of the open-range cattlemen were forced—crowded—outside the wire. Old-time cowhand Sid Boykin, who worked for Newman, said it in plain English: "When the fencing started we began getting out."[64] Jim Newman moved nearly 3000 head of cattle to the free grass country near Portales Springs in east central New Mexico Territory just outside the Texas state line. Having Jim Newman as a new neighbor—competing for overgrazed grass and scarce water—did not set well with Doak Good who had a small cattle herd and sometimes hunted vanishing buffalo or chased after wild mustangs or delivered mail just to makes ends meet. Purportedly and, there's not reason to doubt it, Jim Newman and Doak Good swapped shots with each other using long-range buffalo guns. Neither marksman scored blood.[65]

Though he did miss hitting Doak Good with a bullet, Jim Newman did score a big name for himself as a cattleman. During free range days, before eastern New Mexico Territory was opened up to titled settlement, Newman held dominion over nearly 10,000 head of cattle grazing across a thousand section ranch, though his principal residence was at Sweetwater, Texas.[66]

The outlawed Alf Rushing, according to family lore and other sources, found a home in New Mexico, cowboying or cooking on the DZ Ranch and/or the H-Bar Ranch, both heavily invested in by Jim Newman and Tom Trammel, another relative by marriage.[67] Keeping within character for a wanted fugitive from justice and, illuminating of cattlemen and cowboys' willingness to hold sacred an open secret, is the fact that Newman's and Trammel's in-law was an outlaw. Many Open Range folks knew Alf was once again operating with an alias. Cowboy George Root later remarked: "Alf Russian [*sic*] ran the DZ outfit at the Salt Lake and was the brother-in-law of Jim Newman. He was under the assumed name of Harry Blocker."[68] That the lonesome countryside along the borderline was inhabited by a few hardened *mal hombres* is evidenced by the simple remark of cowman J. Frank Yearwood: "You could ride up on the west side of the Capitol and Blackwater pastures and spit over into New Mexico. We had some hard characters that were dodging back and forth."[69]

In one sense Jim Newman's next move may not be relevant to Alf Rushing's saga—but then again—it might. Eventually cowman Newman gained political status at Sweetwater, Texas, becoming the Nolan County Sheriff, a job he held onto through several election cycles.[70] By any standard Jim Newman and Tom Trammel were influential players in West Texas and Eastern New Mexico cattle and banking affairs. Pitch the sheriff's position into the equation and it's not difficult to aver that Alf Rushing had friends in high, well, reasonably high places. Though for the time being it remains shadowy, it undoubtedly does seem that at some point, either due to influential tinkering in the murder case, or an abject disinterest in pursuing Alf any longer, the charge was dismissed. The decades-old criminal case lodged against Alf Rushing for the murder of Jackson T. Barfield simply washed away—evaporated.

With specificity it cannot be said when Alf quit hiding and surfaced, abandoning aliases and once again donning his birth name. Clearly Rushing was not dodging the law in 1920 when, at 63 years of age, he was enumerated in the federal census, living with his widowed sister Josie and her grown children in Sweetwater. Ten years later, the enumerator found him at the same address, though his occupation was then "retried."[71] Retired shootist? Retired fugitive?

As his health began failing and at the insistence of family members, Alf Rushing returned to live out the remainder of his allotted time in his old stomping grounds, Navarro County. Over a half century after his killing of Officer Barfield, Alf, who had never taken a wife, passed to the other side on December 12, 1930. He was buried at the Richland Cemetery.[72]

At fourteen years of age, squirming in the classroom on Pisgah Ridge listening to Master John Wesley Hardin harangue about the day's lesson plan, Alf Rushing would have had no idea that he, too, would find his biographic profile outside legality's line. As a victorious fugitive from justice in Texas the guardedly tiptoeing Wes Hardin was a failure. Unlike his schoolteacher, Alf Rushing had managed to avoid a trip to the Texas penitentiary at Huntsville, dying in bed and not facedown on a grimy barroom floor with a notorious West Texas gunman's bullet in his head.

Henry A. Swink, Alf Rushing's brother-in-law, was an authentic Texas cow hunter: Saddle toughened, plucky, and handy with a catch-rope. *Courtesy Teddy Weaver, Weaver Ranches, Wortham, Texas.*

George Washington "Cap" Arrington, a noted Texas Ranger who had left his birth-name and an unsavory shooting incident in the past. Although Arrington was an efficient and brave Texas Ranger, fugitive Alf Rushing gave him the slip in the rugged creek bottoms and hidden crowns of Pisgah Ridge south of Corsicana, Texas. *Courtesy Armstrong Research Center, Texas Ranger Hall of Fame & Museum.*

Henry A. Swink's expertise in the beef business stretched from the catch-rope to the chopping-block. Pictured is his Richland, Texas, meat market. *Courtesy Teddy Weaver, Weaver Ranches, Wortham, Texas.*

Here Alf's oldest sister Mary Ann is standing with her husband Ambrose Hilburn to her right. The two fellows at left are unidentified, but by any reckoning the whole Rushing/Swink/Hilburn clan by blood or marriage were pretty tough customers. *Courtesy Teddy Weaver, Weaver Ranches, Wottham, Texas.*

At far left Alf Rushing's father Calvin. Alf was on the run, a fugitive from justice. Henry Swink is flanked by his son Bertie and his wife Evie, one of Alf's twin sisters. At far right is the Swinks's oldest child, Allie. *Courtesy Teddy Weaver, Weaver Ranches, Wortham, Texas.*

Alf Rushing and twin sisters, Evie Swink [L] and Josephine Newman [R]. Unlike his former schoolteacher, the ever self-justifying and self-promoting John Wesley Hardin, Alf Rushing managed to evade capture and lasting incarceration for his crimes, living his final years in Texas among protective family and hospitable friends—dying boots off! *Courtesy Teddy Weaver, Weaver Ranches, Wortham ,Texas.*

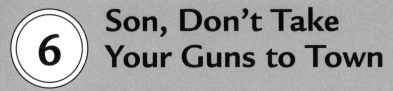

Son, Don't Take
Your Guns to Town

It should not be surprising to committed aficionados of Outlaw/ Lawman tales that, even at this late date, there are yet many rousing Old West stories in want of tellin': particularly ones with germane sociological commentary vis-à-vis criminal justice and/or criminal injustice issues. All too often the driving force of well-intentioned writers is recapping or reanalyzing previously published biographical profiles and the resultant blood and thunder episodes. Even though the approach is sometimes overworked, fortunately, we now know in exacting detail so very much about days gone by. There is also, thankfully, no shortage of divergent conclusions and/or opinions. However there is a steep price to pay for the reexaminations of the stale and clichéd Wild West stories. Frequently other tumults with the law and its enforcers receive but scant notice. The purpose then of this simple story is to feature a lesser-known Western melodrama: encapsulating the essence of a caring father's admonitions; accenting the affectionate devotion of a pioneering woman hopelessly in love; and spotlighting the courtroom trials, and conspicuously self-imposed tribulations— and heartbreaks—of a dangerous West Texas stockman, father, and fugitive—an unyielding fighter.

An appropriate spot to begin the narrative is with George Washington Clayton, the son of Warren and Mary Ann "Polly" (Ratleff) Clayton. George was a Southern boy through and through, born in Jefferson County, Alabama, in 1834. For the all too briefest time—about six months—George received a smidgen of formal education in Itawamba County, Mississippi, when the family moved to Mooreville. George remained at home working on the family farm until age eighteen. Then he married the stunningly attractive Amanda Jane Redding, three years his junior, from Monroe County, Mississippi.

With meager ownership of but four homemade chairs, a feathered bed, one saddle-pony, and five reasonably domesticated cows, the newlyweds set up housekeeping. Ever so slowly, George began renting farms, working hard, and in but rather short order had modestly added to his inventory of material possessions. George Washington Clayton was an industrious farmer and, too, a genuine virile husband. His family was growing, appreciably so. Amanda gave birth to five children: Benjamin Jerome (1854), Finis Ewing (1855), Laura Julina (1857), Loveday Rebecca (1859), and Dorinthia Salone (1861), before life drastically changed for the Clayton household. Civil War cannons bucked and belched in numbing recoil and nationalistic minded Southerners rushed to join the Confederate Army, George Washington Clayton among them.[1]

Proudly, he enlisted with Company C, Fourth Mississippi Cavalry, under command of Colonel James Gordon.[2] Seeing action in several "pitched battles and skirmishes," luckily George came through the bloody ordeal unscathed, never suffering a debilitating gunshot or shrapnel wound. Incredibly, he legitimately garnered an official permit from "regimental and brigade officers to supply the soldiers with whiskey." With accommodation from neighborhood distilleries George Washington Clayton was able, financially, to provide for his family and return home after close of the War with enough spare money to buy a farm outright with Confederate dollars.[3] He was a renter no more. Nineteenth-century life was on the upswing for George Washington Clayton.

George, little by little, multiplied his assets and his offspring. Amanda gave birth to George Washington "Wash" Clayton, Jr. (1864), Oliva "Ollie" O. (1867) and Emmett Anderson (1868). Sadly, as result of complications with the birth of their eighth and last adored child, Amanda's health worsened and shortly thereafter, on July 10, she died. There is little wonder that with eight children to care for, George Washington Clayton had not time to squander mourning. And he didn't! On August 27, 1868, he remarried, tying the matrimonial knot with Esther (Pruitt) Skinner—a Civil War widow—in Lee County, Mississippi. Their nine-year age difference was handy; the new bride had now, with an effortless "I do" inherited a rompin' and stompin' brood. Substantial energy she needed, more especially when George Washington

Clayton, Sr. decreed that the clan was to up and vacate Mississippi and rearrange their lives under the flag of a yet wild and woolly place, 1868 Texas.

Crossing the Red River into northeast Texas, George Clayton acquired land in Lamar County (Paris) and began an extensive farming operation. Maybe it was pure wanderlust or just another sound economic judgment, but, whatever the reason, during 1876 George moved again, to the surveyed but yet to be organized Runnels County (Ballinger).[4]

The county, on what was then still considered the Texas frontier, was but sparsely populated. Carved from the gargantuan Bexar Land District in 1858, Runnels County was ranch country.[5] The county was rich with history.[6] Much of that history, in one way or the other, revolved around this or that Comanche raid, lost cattle—and burnt ranch houses.

Not too very long before George Clayton's arrival, Jesse Hittson, son of the renowned cattleman John "Cattle Jack" Hittson, had a bloody all-day skirmish with screaming raiders near "old Picketville on the Colorado River."[7] Although they lost some ten or twelve of their own number, the Indians managed to make off with all the cattle—save one heifer—and before their flight wounded several of Hittson's cowboys. Clearly throughout the state, in pages of the *Texas Almanac*, it was reported that Runnels County was "fine stock country, but too far on the frontier, and too much exposed to Indians for settlement." The Texas Adjutant General, because of the Comanche and Kiowa menace, ordered Captain William J. "Jeff" Maltby, Company E, Frontier Battalion (Texas Rangers), to establish headquarters in nearby Brown County for the sole purpose of protecting Runnels and Coleman Counties, as well as the surrounding area. The Rangers on more than one occasion successfully dealt with marauding warriors, killing, scalping, and even skinning them. Reportedly, one of the Texas Rangers "made some beautiful quirts out of the hide[s], trimmed with ornaments from Indian hair."[8] Too, it has been written that the hard-edged Captain himself paid twenty-five dollars for a quirt made from a particular Indian's skin.[9] It was tough country, settled by tough people. The timid went elsewhere.

Shortly after George Clayton meandered onto the scene, Runnels City was beginning to blossom. It could, or soon would, claim three dry goods and grocery stores, a drugstore, two hotels, a bank, a blacksmith shop, saloons, a livery stable, a saddle shop, three land offices, a school, and several churches. After the county was formally organized in February of 1880, it had its very own lawman, John M. Formwalt.[10] The newly installed Runnels County Sheriff, Formwalt was a thirty-one year old, six-foot four-inch stalwart who was just as disposed to shoot out saloon lights as were any lively cowboys ambling the town on a drunken toot.[11] The sheriff was one of those Old West lawmen seemingly devoid of fear, a man not at all disposed to take a backward step when facing personal danger. Recapping but one episode is illustrative.

An unruly U.S. Cavalryman was in town on a whiskey drinking tear. The bluecoat was aimlessly firing his government issued holster gun, moving down the block—reloading—and then shooting again and again and again. A local constable kept sheepishly maneuvering for an advantage, but in the face of gunfire would always give ground, a not necessarily foolish strategy, but not particularly helpful either. Sheriff Formwalt, accompanied by the sheriff from nearby Coleman County, "came along through the crowd and walked right up to the soldier."[12] Formwalt nonchalantly disarmed and arrested the mischief maker, and broke up a crowd of several hundred people that had been—as spectators— "having lots of fun . . ."[13] John Formwalt was not too much troubled by killing men either.[14] Nor was the local editor of the *Runnels County Record* bothered by the sheriff's unflinching and well-publicized wildness, who, in reflecting a generally favorable public opinion, wrote: "John Formwalt always fetches 'em."[15]

Purchasing a tract of land for a $1.00 per acre, George Washington Clayton established his 5000-acre ranch and kicked off dabbling in the cattle business. Later, discovering the profitability of raising sheep, he expanded his ranching operations. He, too, had grown his family, fathering two children by Esther, a son, Abner (1870), and a daughter, Mary Elizabeth (1881). There is not any historic information to indicate a favoring of one child over the other, but unquestionably it may be correctly reported that George W. Clayton doted over his children, especially the girls, and particularly for this Old West saga, twenty-year-old Dorinthia.[16] She was pretty. She was naïve. She was untaken.

The endlessly promoting newspaperman was haranguing about the promising future to be had in opportunity-loaded Runnels County and at Runnels City. He did bemoan two bothersome anomalies, however; the lack of a "calaboose" and a "plethoric overplus of unmarried men," and that it was all "bosh" when a man proclaimed he couldn't marry for "the world is filled with chances."[17] Into town—always ready for trouble—and willing to take one of those "chances" rode Ruben (Rueben) Flanoah "Noah" Wilkerson. Dorinthia Clayton would exalt the day. George Washington Clayton would rue the day.

The admittedly handsome Noah Wilkerson was born on February 13, 1861, in Fairburn, Fulton County, Georgia—just a short skip southeast of Atlanta. Noah was the child of Frances Marion and Sarah (Miller) Wilkerson.[18] The exactness of just when and just how, or just why Noah ended up in Texas is muddled. Simply it may be said, based on family legend and hearsay, that by the time he was sixteen he had left home for the Lone Star State and was cowboying in Coleman County as early as 1877.[19] By the time he was twenty he was a stockman and property owner in Runnels County, details rooted in factuality. Noah grew into manhood owning two idiosyncratic attributes: an uncanny knack for raising first-class Thoroughbred race horses, and an unyielding disposition. Due to Wilkerson's inherent temperament, he was known as a man that "you couldn't run over," a man not to trifle with.[20] And although it's oral history, by one account it has been whispered that the "Kids run from him—saying here comes Noah and his guns."[21] Subsequent events will more than passably corroborate the handed down family beliefs and the Outlaw/Lawman folklore.

Exactly when Noah Wilkerson met Dorinthia Clayton is indeterminate. Not subject to question is the fact, though, that Dorinthia tumbled head-over-heels for the slender and self-assured Wilkerson. Likewise, Noah was utterly smitten with the enticing charms of Dorinthia. The peppery romance was no secret. Particular details of the exhilarating courtship are vague. However, when Dorinthia broached the subject of marriage with her father and stepmother, her euphoric imaginings spewed into a dehydrated fountain of disenchantment. George Washington Clayton put his boot down, hard! He wanted no part of Noah Wilkerson for a son-in-law, never![22] Whether he actually knew something sinister or could somehow futuristically read the proverbial handwriting on the wall goes unrecorded. By damn, not in his house—not in his lifetime! George Washington Clayton may have been right, and history seems to sustain the wisdom of his arguments, but, he too was wrong. Young love is seldom encumbered by a rational thought process, not even in frontier Runnels County. Fearing not in the least George Washington Clayton's wrath, an always plucky Noah Wilkerson simply spirited Dorinthia over to Runnels City in a disobedient elopement, and the couple were legally married on January 17, 1881.[23] The ever gritty Noah Wilkerson sought not a blessing, nor needed permission from anyone to do anything. Likely G. W. Clayton mused: "Child, he's nothing but trouble!"

Dorinthia set up housekeeping at Noah's 1,071-acre northeastern Runnels County ranch near the community of Crews, just west of the Coleman County line. And although the looming threats from marauding Comanche had subsided, the area was still regarded as untamed country—inhabited by wild animals and rough-edged men. Dorinthia was fashioned from sturdy stock though, and soon she was making a loving home out of haunt—and making babies, too! Dorinthia, over time, would give birth to nine children fathered by Noah.[24] From Dorinthia's lifelong and heartfelt perspective, the delightful sparkle of her marriage to Noah Wilkerson faded not—ever! She had found her soul-mate. That she was dead sure of.

Noah was dead sure about some things too. He, from the bottom of his very being, was a racehorse man. Steadily his herd of blooded horses multiplied, and his successes at brush tracks and, even at the larger ones, say, at Abilene, Texas, were escalating. Wilkerson horses warranted the reputation as serious contenders—at any race meet. Noah was dead sure about another thing too. He would not idly stand by and suffer an imagined or actual affront from anyone, be they neighbor or total stranger. So, while congenial Dorinthia tended hearth and home, gracefully laying the comforter of adoring gentleness around rambunctious kids and her cherished husband, Noah earned bitter enemies and a viable livelihood.

George Washington Clayton, during 1883, once more opted for making a relocation. Selling land he had once paid a $1.00 an acre for, now brought him $2.25 and with the tidy profit he invested in an Abilene livery stable, and then into a general merchandise store of substantial consequence, becoming the city's most prominent early merchant.[25] Undoubtedly he fretted over his precious daughter's defiant decision to spurn his advice and marry that poisonously coiled Noah. George Clayton, however, wasn't the type of man to mockingly chide, "I told you so!" As a dutiful father he wished for Dorinthia the very best, but from his very core George Washington Clayton knew trouble, unsmiling trouble, was on the Runnels County horizon—near Crews.

He was prophetic. On the morning of May 2, 1886, brothers Ben R. and George Wilson stopped by the Wilkerson residence. Noah was not at home, but Dorinthia and the children were. The Wilson boys told Dorinthia they had come to remove two fresh cows and their calves from the Wilkersons' crudely fashioned milking pen. Earlier the animals had been temporarily loaned to Noah by the rightful owner, Jim Lewis. Way out in the ranch country, dairy cows were in short supply, a rarity, and unquestionably a hard-to-come-by commodity. Noah and Dorinthia, at that time, had a four-year-old son and a three-year-old daughter, and both liked the taste of sweet milk. Caught off guard and not knowing what to say—or do—Dorinthia told the Wilson brothers, "I guess it'll be all right." She was mistaken! George and Ben left the Wilkerson's ranch driving the pairs ahead of them. It is not necessary to elaborate with expletive dialogue, but when Noah returned home and was updated, he turned hot—his blood boiled.[26]

Jumping back onto his horse, Noah headed for the Wilsons' ranch. When he got there, at their cow-pens, he boldly dismounted and as if in but one fluid motion drew his Winchester from the saddle scabbard, snappishly levering a round into the chamber. The Wilson boys, who had been hotfooting it to the stock-pens, drew up short. Noah "took down the gap [wire gate]," removed the cattle, and pointing his rifle square at the bewildered boys, said that "he would shoot us [them] if we [they] crossed the fence."[27] Wilkerson told the Wilson brothers that "he had verbal authority to take those cows and calves," and "that whenever we [they] could show up better authority than he had, that we [they] could get the cows and calves at anytime."[28] Somewhat ironically, and in a seeming whopping understatement, later Ben Wilson swore under an oath, "All this was not spoken in a very friendly way."[29]

Ben and George Wilson were not gunfighters and, so, instead of chasing after Noah with blood in their eye, they headed straight for Ballinger, the recently created county seat of Runnels County. It was there that they filed their Complaint. During the District Court's October term (1886), the Grand Jury handed down a

Criminal Indictment charging Noah Wilkerson: Assault With Intent to Murder.[30]

And, although the courthouse records are meager, it seems that Noah, one way or the other, was arrested by Sheriff John M. Formwalt. Whether or not Noah posted bail or languished in the newly constructed *hotel de lockheart* is hazy. Even with the establishment of a railroad, the Gulf, Colorado & Santa Fe, and a modicum of encroaching civility, Runnels County and John Formwalt were yet still wild and woolly.

During the early afternoon of March 29, 1887—Noah was still awaiting trial—Sheriff John Formwalt, not surprisingly, shot off his six-shooter in an area saloon. Later the sheriff was still tipping a few with another certifiable man-killer, Mannen Clements. The sheriff, in his cups, became more and more disorderly. So much so that his anxious deputy, Joe Townsend, decided he must disarm his boss. The law enforcement action did not go smoothly. Clements interjected himself into the hubbub on behalf of the sheriff, pulling his revolver as he cursed his way into tragedy. With unerring aim Joe Townsend killed him, shooting Clements square above the left eye.[31] Joe Townsend and Sheriff Formwalt came clean on the shooting affair, legally.

The very next year, on October 22, 1888, a trial jury found Noah Wilkerson "not guilty" regarding his altercation with the Wilson brothers.[32] Apparently in West Texas simply pointing a Winchester's muzzle at someone's pounding chest was really no big deal, especially when crying babies wanted that nourishing sweet milk. Wilkerson's tilts with Texas justice were yet in their infancy.

Simply because there is no paper trail to follow, does not necessarily mean something didn't happen. Many are the barroom brawls and feisty back country confrontations that swirl out of control—momentarily—then fizzle into the shadowy abyss of anonymity and omission. Absent the complaint to a peace officer, or the formality of bringing prosecutable charges, many crimes go unreported and unrecorded. That fact does not erase some very real realities.[33] The historian may only measure what is measurable. So, in Noah Wilkerson's case, it would not be irrational to suggest that there were altercations and arguments, rows and rubs that were hushed. Unassailable data discloses that not everyone liked Noah Wilkerson. It has been written that he was "anxious to impress [everyone] with his badness," and that he "bore a bad reputation in that country [Runnels County] and was frequently in trouble."[34]

Although it falls far short of factual verification, rumor and gossip persist to this day that Noah, after an argument with "Old Man" Pendleton, acted abruptly and ruthlessly. He burned Pendleton's house to the ground. No actual crime was provable, nor was Noah arrested, so, perhaps it didn't even happen. But, it's best not to ask a Pendleton![35]

Another of Noah's "troubles" is historically quantifiable. There are two accounts to choose from, though. Most descendants opt for the less wicked of the two scenarios. Part of Noah's real-estate holdings were in Coleman County. A neighbor, Sam Gray, owned an adjoining unfenced pasture. During an exceedingly dry spell, Noah advised Gray that he could no longer water his live-stock at the Wilkerson water tank; he simply didn't have the water to spare. Sam was up the proverbial dry creek without a paddle— at least his bawling cows were. So, under the cover of darkness he continued using Noah's precious water. Wilkerson was a fighter, not a dummy, and by plainly reading the clear-cut sign could figure out his neighbor's sly stratagem. Noah simply hid in the brush until Gray herded his cattle in for a drink. In the resultant fight Noah pistol-whipped Sam severely. At least that's what Gray later told inquisitive lawmen. Noah's version was somewhat at odds with Sam Gray's, and he denied even having a six-shooter, later telling family that he had used a chain. He never disavowed the warfare, just the implement of war.[36]

Version two is radically simple. Noah and Sam fought due to personal affections, not over cattle watering or monetary motives. A newspaperman wasn't ambiguous when he characterized the battle: "It was jealousy over the woman whose picture Wilker-son had ... which was the beginning of all the trouble. Wilkerson assaulted a man who was also intimate with this woman..."[37] Which version is authentic truth? Could there even be a hint of believability in amalgamating both anecdotes? ¿Quién sabe?

Clearly though, Gray filed a formal Complaint against Noah in Coleman County and, once again, Noah found himself facing sobering criminal charges.[38] Seemingly, he was his own worst enemy. Noah posted bail and, through his lawyers, initiated a series of legal machinations and requests for Continuances calculated to forestall final imposition of the law.[39] Perhaps, in retrospect, Noah Wilkerson should have welcomed a respite hoeing cotton or polishing brass bars at the Texas penitentiary in Huntsville. His life was about to change, forever—and it wasn't for the good!

Dorinthia, now the mother of eight, was ever mindful of maintaining and nurturing a warm home front, despite the misadventures of her beloved husband. She was with conviction a true stand-by-her-man kind of woman. Her devotion would prove an admirable, but emotionally pricy proposition.

On August 24, 1898, Crews area resident Ben Slate, accompanied by Frank Moore, his brother-in-law, headed for Ballinger with a load of firewood. The duo camped about three miles short of their destination, spreading a canvas for bedding. Sometime just before or just after midnight, a revolver barrel was pressed against Slate's snoozing forehead and the cocked hammer dropped. Slate's sleep was instantly made everlasting, as were the brain matter and blood stains powerfully permeated into the wagon sheet. Frank Moore awakened absent a solitary clue, but was the next day arrested for what was a straightforward execution. According to Inquest data the "bullet penetrated the head of [the] deceased above the right eye, passing down and through the brain and out just behind the left ear."[40] Shortly after his arrest, Moore arranged to have a note passed to Noah Wilkerson, who in turn posted a message on the door of Slate's widow, she being away at the time. Noah Wilkerson recovered Ben Slate's remains for burial, and returned them to his place, about twenty miles northeast of the crime scene. Two days later, on the twenty-sixth, at Noah's ranch headquarters twenty-one-year-old Texas born Randal "Tump" Eldred was arrested for Slate's murder by the then current Runnels County Sheriff, R. P. Kirk. Frank Moore was turned loose.[41]

On September 2 another Complaint was filed by Sheriff Kirk. An arrest warrant was issued and Noah Wilkerson was taken into custody sans any melodrama or ferocious gunfight. At a Preliminary Hearing on September 7 it was determined: "that the proof is evident and Sufficient to require the defendant Noah Wilkerson to answer before the District Court of Runnels County, Texas, for the offense of murder in the First Degree and Said offense not being a Bailable one it is ordered by the court that the Said Noah Wilkerson, defendant, be committed to the jail of Runnels County, Texas and there safely kept to answer for offense before Said District Court …."[42]

Obviously Tump Eldred had squealed or lied—but either
way—he'd turned state's evidence. This time Noah's fat was
in the fire. Dorinthia's premonitions were frightful and tearful.
Never was there an allegation that Noah actually pulled the trigger. Tump Eldred entered into a Plea Bargain agreement with the
District Attorney, and in exchange for a reduced charge and a predetermined prison sentence, he agreed to swear that Noah had
furnished him the six-shooter and ammunition to do away with
Ben Slate.[43]

At that October term of the Runnels County Grand Jury, Noah
Wilkerson was indicted for participating in Ben Slate's murder:

> and the grand Jurors aforesaid upon their oaths aforesaid do
> further present in said court that Noah Wilkerson on or about
> 24th day of August—1898 and prior to the commission of
> said offense by the said Randal Eldred, in the County and
> State aforesaid did unlawfully, knowingly, willfully, and of
> his malice aforethought advise, command, and encourage
> the said Randal Eldred to commit said offense and said Noah
> Wilkerson did further at time and place aforesaid and prior
> to the commission of said offense by said Randal Eldred did
> prepare arms and aid in the way of a Horse, Saddle, Bridle,
> pistol ammunition and Rope to the said Randal Eldred for
> the purpose of assisting said Randal Eldred in the commis-
> sion and execution of said offense....[44]

Why did Noah want Ben Slate dead? Today that remains an
unsolved and more than puzzling mystery. Unquestionably, many,
many Wilkerson family members then—as well as now—even
those unsentimentally accepting of the fact that Noah was sometimes pigheaded, and on occasion downright troublesomely dangerous, question the bona fide credibility of a criminal prosecution
based on seemingly uncorroborated evidence. A careful reading
of trial transcripts and appellate arguments, admittedly—and with
some legitimacy—fuels the fire for speculative conspiracy theo-
rists. Clearly from the trial testimony, there were several identifiable persons in the neighborhood of Crews who could very well
have wanted to see Slate dead. Statements in sworn testimony
leave begging many open-ended questions: "My little daughter
6 years old told me that Slate tried to have intercourse with her.
I didn't know whether to believe or not." Or, "I heard that Slate

tried to have intercourse with my little sister six years old." And, "I did not ask Mally [Cox] what Tump was going to do with a pistol. I supposed that he was going to steal horses, and I told Mally that he had better put our horse up." Or, "and started to pick up a club when he grabbed him. Said he [Slate] slapped the old man [Polk Cox] down. Said the old man told his son … to pick up a chunk and knock him down, and that Mally started to do so when Noah Wilkerson interfered and prevented him."[45]

Historically speaking, it really matters not a whit whether Noah Wilkerson was ganged up on by malicious public officials; those who saw a chance to rid themselves of a terminal pain in their law-enforcing ass. Nor is history dramatically changed due to the fact that Noah might have been figuratively crucified by a pitifully whining and lying Tump Eldred, in a desperate move to save his own neck. Even if there were some grand horse-stealing scheme, one involving Eldred, or Slate, or Wilkerson, or several others, the insinuation cannot rise above the level of guesswork. That type of unsupported hypothesizing alters not what happened, judicially. Plainly there is a bottom line:

> We the Jury find the defendant Noah Wilkerson guilty of Murder in the 1st degree as charged in the indictment and assess his punishment at confinement in the penitentiary for life.[46]

Continually locked away in Runnels County since the gruesome murder, Noah was quickly transferred to the Coleman County Jail. He still had charges pending regarding the pistol-whipping brouhaha with Sam Gray. A fitting disposition for that case was being called for, too. And it was resolved. The trial jury determined that, indeed, Noah had had a six-shooter and lied when he denied having one. They found him guilty of Perjury and sentenced him to two years in the penitentiary.[47] Seemingly Noah Wilkerson's goose was cooked—barbecued: two felony convictions—one a life sentence. His lawyers filed a spate of legally worded motions, but still, Noah had to remain in jail until there was a Court of Criminal Appeals ruling.[48] Undeniably, George Washington Clayton heard of the guilty verdicts, and no doubt inaudibly mused about his earlier prophecy: "Child, he's nothing but trouble." Trouble or not, the eternally steadfast Dorinthia couldn't and wouldn't watch her man simply wither and waste away. If she couldn't have him—the state of Texas couldn't either!

The call for help went out from Dorinthia. For this business she couldn't turn to her father, or his sons—her brothers. By some accounts Noah's three brothers, Zan, Milton, and Ed, rushed to Ballinger. If so, they had but one thought on their collective and conniving minds. Other family members assert, and it's probably the most reasonable, that brother Zan quietly slipped into town and held a huddled counsel with Dorinthia. Zan, much like his brother Noah, wasn't a man to monkey with. Purportedly he was always armed with a six-shooter and wouldn't back down from a fight with any man, for any reason.[49] Clearly though, under these circumstances it would be preferable to outwit lawmen, rather than outfight them. Receiving word that the higher court had upheld Noah's conviction set the conspiratorial scheme in motion.

Traveling to Coleman, Dorinthia once again presented herself at the county jail for a visit with her husband before he was to be hustled off to prison—forevermore. Knowing Noah would soon be whisked away to begin serving his sentence, even hard-hearted jailers—while they didn't particularly like confrontational Noah—sympathized with Dorinthia's anguishing plight. She was granted privacy. In the dank and dark lockup, all so quickly, a loving and truly devoted wife gave her husband two things: a hacksaw and an interlude of the most personal kind.[50] Then she left!

Busily, at times when a locomotive was nearby and nosily switching boxcars, Noah and others put the smuggled saw to work. Often they added to the din by singing and whistling while they worked. The native inmates caught the fine metal shavings and/or sawdust on a piece of paper, "then [they] would use soap to cover up the places where they had sawed."[51] If the 1900 Census enumerator had waited six days before he listed prisoners in the Coleman County Jail on his tally sheet, he would have missed identifying Noah and several others, notably William "Bill" Taylor, locked up for an abortive train robbery. As it were, he counted them on June thirteenth, but on the nineteenth they made good their getaway. Whether or not it's true is uncertain, but purportedly Bill Taylor was so big and the opening was so small, that his fellow escapees had to grease him with soap before he could be extracted for his breakout. Once outside, the jailbirds parted company for their liberating flight.[52]

It is at this point in Noah's thorny chronicle that family folklore and clear logic bump heads, although it's wholly understandable. Charitable tradition, through passed down oral history, implies that Noah raced back to his ranch and hid for several months, almost in plain sight. Supposedly, because Noah was a crack shot with a rifle and was of daring repute, area lawmen were too frightened to come and fetch him. That might be true. Sensibly though, remembering that Noah's escapades many times before had resulted in his arrest seems to somewhat devalue the assertion. There is not evidence to support a conclusion of timidity on the part of local lawmen. Assuredly if they needed help they could have called on a whole company of Texas Rangers had they known Noah's actual hiding spot. It, too, seems unlikely that the Governor of Texas, Joseph D. Sayers, would authorize a $500 reward for Noah's capture if his whereabouts were widely known, but authorize the bounty he did![53]

Thankfully for this Old West tale there is a plethora of primary source documents, and it is relatively easy to peel back the truth. With his escape Noah attained status as a fugitive, and overnight accepted the merit of assuming a false identity. Ruben Flanoah Wilkerson was no more: Lee Escue had taken his place.[54] Somewhere along the winding owlhoot trail he armed himself with a brand new Savage hammerless rifle and a Colt's six-shooter, .41 caliber.[55]

While exacting details are frustratingly scarce, at least two contemporary sources credit Runnels Sheriff Kirk with no dereliction of duty or tentativeness about hunting Noah. According to these published reports, Kirk received information that Wilkerson was "working on a ranch in the mountains near Roswell, New Mexico." Apparently he traveled to the area, and after some competent sleuthing located the place where Wilkerson was working for cowboy wages. Riding horseback to the location, Kirk espied Wilkerson, but unfortunately for the lawman, Noah saw the sheriff, too. Who fired first is jumbled and the newspaper reports leave it at "some shots were exchanged between the fugitive and the officer." The long and the short of it is that neither of the duelists damaged their intended target and fugitive Noah—Lee Escue—made good his escape. The crestfallen Sheriff Kirk returned to Ballinger.[56]

Historically tracking Wilkerson after an ineffectual shootout with the sheriff is not at all problematic: Noah kept a diary.[57]

During late July and early August 1900, Noah was gradually and surreptitiously winding his way northwest through West Texas and New Mexico Territory. On August 12 he rode out of Portales, New Mexico Territory, and traveled all day to the rip-roaring cowtown of Liberty, "a wild frontier hamlet" with her own iniquitous personality, one well suited for a man on the dodge, a tough spot that "never had a constable or lawman." There he came down sick, rested, and then traded for a fresh horse before moving out for Clayton, arriving there six days later.[58] Crossing into Colorado, Wilkerson moved almost due north through Trinidad, Walsenburg, and Pueblo.[59] On the night of September 15 he overnighted in Colorado Springs. Finally, after passing Denver, he turned west and headed into the mountains. He particularly took note that it was a part of the country "where the Ladies all ride horseback astraddle [sic]."[60] Evidently, after getting into the higher country, he leisurely meandered along, hunting—killing grouse, sage hen, ducks, and Mule deer. By October he had managed to make it to Parachute, southwest of Rifle, Colorado. There he decided to stay for the winter, working "at anything that he could get to do."[61]

Hearing that Joe Erimmer (or Trimmer) was making a trip into Wyoming, Noah asked for the "privilege" of accompanying him. On the afternoon of November the seventh the men struck out and "a little after noon" arrived at Perkin's Store near Dixon, Carbon County, Wyoming, on the thirteenth.[62] For the whole of Noah Wilkerson's forty years on this earth, it would prove his most fateful journey.

Dixon, almost straddling the Colorado/Wyoming borderline, had been named after Robert "Bob" Dixon, a "trapper who lived to old age," but who was later killed by Arapahoe Indians.[63] At the time Noah arrived in Dixon, however, another "Bob" was there. He was every ounce as hard and tough as Noah Wilkerson. Robert D. Meldrum was his name, and carving out a turn-of-the-century, man-killing reputation was his game. As a *mal hombre* he was legit, the real deal.[64]

The England-born Meldrum had up to this point—and it would carry forward—lived an undoubtedly colorful, though not necessarily nice life. In Montana around Forsythe, east of Billings, he had seen active service as a horse thief. At Deer Lodge he had spent time as a convict in the Montana penitentiary. Some may have characterized Bob Meldrum as not being "overly bright," but all considered him viperously treacherous and poisonously dangerous.[65] Meldrum, in addition to the foregoing, was many things: a pretty good saddle and harness maker; a sometimes Pinkerton Detective Agency undercover operative with a secret code name; a thoroughly committed hard liquor drinker; a letter-writing friend of the notorious man- and boy-killing Tom Horn; an all-around nasty guy and conscienceless killer who would unhesitatingly shoot prior to any of the silly warnings a mythical Code of the West was alleged to have called for; and relevant to this Outlaw/Lawman criminal justice story, an officially sanctioned and sworn Carbon County Deputy Sheriff.[66]

Meanwhile, back around Ballinger, Sheriff R. P. Kirk had not been an idle man, for in addition to everyday Runnels County business he was trying to keep up with Noah Wilkerson's movements, but usually he was coming up just a day or two short. Although it cannot arise past the level of speculation, it is more than likely that Kirk was receiving vital criminal intelligence with the clandestine help of an obliging local postmaster. Whether or not the sheriff actually was afforded an opportunity to steam open an envelope addressed to Dorinthia—or someone receiving mail in her behalf—cannot be conclusively proven—or disproven. Somehow, either by that investigative methodology or by utilizing an informant—a family member or a supposed good friend—Sheriff Kirk, sitting in Texas, tracked his man to Wyoming. Kirk's slick detective work can be confirmed from Bob Meldrum's own mouth:

> That on Oct. 7th I received a letter from the Sheriff of Carbon County ordering me to arrest a man named Noah Wilkinson [*sic*] accused of murder—with description and photograph of said Noah Wilkinson [*sic*]....[67]

On the sly, after learning that Wilkerson might be traveling to the vicinity of Dixon, Sheriff Kirk had messaged Carbon County Sheriff McDaniel at Rawlins, enclosing Noah's photograph and promising a $200 cut of the reward money.[68] The note and photo were forwarded to Deputy Meldrum at Dixon. Forewarned, then, to be on the lookout for a stranger fitting Noah's physical description, Bob Meldrum was primed and ready when he finally saw Noah about 9:00 a.m. on November 14. From afar he studied Noah and reexamined the photograph. Since he "wished to be positive as to his identity," Meldrum sashayed up to Noah and initiated a conversation. He did not, however, tip his hand that he held a deputy sheriff's commission in his topcoat's pocket.[69] At last, Bob Meldrum was thoroughly satisfied. Slipping away he called on Charles E. Ayer to assist him in making the arrest. Ayer agreed.[70]

Later, all three, Wilkerson, Meldrum, and Ayer were at Charles Perkins' warehouse. When he thought it was right, Bob Meldrum said to Noah, "throw up you hands, you are my prisoner."[71] Noah tersely shot back, "No, I guess not!" Audaciously civilian Ayer grabbed Noah's wrists plainly admonishing, "Yes, Yes—He means it." Unconvinced, Noah slung Ayer to one side "whirling him like a top."[72] Noah snatched his Savage Model 99 which was nearby, and Bob Meldrum, too, clutched the blue-steel octagon barrel. While the two scuffled over the rifle, Ayer was snapped back to reality when he heard the gun discharge, the .303 bullet burrowing into the dirt underfoot. Ayer boldly jumped back into the frantic mess. Meldrum finally gained control of the Savage hammerless, trying to lever another round into the chamber, but the "catch had caught and he could not work it."[73]

Throwing the rifle to the ground, Bob Meldrum drew his .41 Colt's six-shooter. Likewise, as Noah was making his break, "edging away sideways," he was also trying to get his long-barreled .41 Colt into blistering action. Unfortunately for Noah, his gun caught in the scabbard he was wearing between his outside shirt and an undershirt. Bob Meldrum "got there first." His shot struck Noah in the face or mouth, and Wilkerson started running away from the deafening and scorching blast. Meldrum fired once more, again striking Wilkerson. This time the ball entered "in the back between the shoulders and [the bullet] exiting the right side of the mouth, breaking the spinal cord in its passage."[74] Noah Wilkerson had made it approximately seventy-five feet before he collapsed, dropping his fully loaded six-shooter onto the mucky and bloody street.[75] Death, if it didn't come instantly, came quickly.

On the fifteenth a Coroner's jury was impaneled. They inspected Noah's body and under oath examined several witnesses, Bob Meldrum and Charley Ayer among them. Their finding was no surprise:

> That the deceased, supposed Noah Wilkerson, came to his death by a gun shot from a .41 Colt's revolver fired by

> one Robt. Meldrum deputy sheriff for Carbon Co. State of
> Wyoming while resisting arrest. . . . Robt. Meldrum while
> acting in the capacity of sheriff was justified. . . . and it
> was justifiable homicide and we exonerate the said Robt.
> Meldrum from any and all blame in said cause.[76]

Even today the killing of Wilkerson generates acidic sentiment, chiefly among Noah's descendants, which is understandable. Knowing that Noah Wilkerson was a wanted murderer, should Bob Meldrum have simply "throwed down" on him once he knew he had the right man? Would Noah, looking into the terrifying depths of a Colt's barrel, have chosen to lay down his arms in deference to his other options: fight or flight? Dispassionately those questions are not answerable. Adding to the conundrum, for some, is the very real fact that Bob Meldrum, as opposed to some other high-profile Old West gunfighting personalities, didn't give his adversaries a choice: "He just gunned his victims down, usually without warning."[77] Later, Bob Meldrum added other cuts on his notch-stick, and one, the killing of "Chick" Bowen, smartly earned him a personalized identification number—2370—at Wyoming's penitentiary.[78] So, when it's from time to time written in the modern-era that he "murdered" Wilkerson, smoldering embers ignite into a flickering flame of conspicuous antipathy— chiefly from Noah's bloodline descendants.[79] However, just as Noah Wilkerson was found "not guilty" in the squabble with Ben and George Wilson, and with renderings of "guilty" verdicts regarding the pistol-whipping of Sam Gray and the murder of Ben Slate, there is that sometimes troubling bottom line; a contemporary and legally constituted Criminal Justice System decided, and impartial Wild West history is evermore stuck with the unbending outcome. In this instance, Deputy Sheriff Bob Meldrum was lawfully vindicated.

Sheriff Kirk was messaged that Noah had been killed, and he rushed to Wyoming, tasked with making the requisite formal identification of the body. While there he took possession of Noah's personal property, including the Savage rifle and the Colt's six-shooter, which had been properly recorded and inventoried.[80] After the body was prepared, he accompanied the coffin back to Runnels County.[81] Back in Texas, and because the lawman's prisoner was dead and he was unable to accomplish "the delivery of the said

R. F. Wilkerson to the Superintendent of the Penitentiaries at Huntsville Penitentiary, inside the said Penitentiary," as the Proclamation of Reward stipulated, Kirk was forced to suffer the stinging humiliation of a duplicitous state government: Bounty money— denied![82] Bureaucracy's backstabbing was costly and rude.

While winding down Noah's story and dropping the curtain on his attention-grabbing days, it is not inappropriate to again mention Dorinthia. Not unexpectedly, she was devastated by the news she had received from that Snake River Country of Wyoming. Notwithstanding Noah's character flaws, he was the absolute love of her life. No doubt Dorinthia's family and friends were concerned not only with her emotional well-being, but, too, with her physical health—she was carrying Noah's baby. Happily, during the next year's first quarter Dorinthia delivered a son, Loyd. Sadly, the little boy grew to estimable manhood never knowing his daddy.

Dorinthia's struggles can hardly be imagined. Despite the ups and downs, financial and otherwise, Dorinthia hung on, scratching out a living and devotedly mentoring her nine children. Over time, ever so gradually through pure grit and determination her lot improved. Life became more bearable, even comfortable. In fact, she carried on Noah's passion for raising first-class racehorses and diligently established a highly favorable regional reputation in that risky business. More importantly, she raised good children. Dorinthia never forsook Noah's memory. She had made her commitment to him, and no other. She never remarried. A full half-century after Noah's death, on October 21, 1952, Dorinthia passed peacefully to the other side. At long last, once more she lay beside the man of her dreams, interred at the Norwood Cemetery, in the ranch country northeast of Ballinger.

George Washington Clayton, with the very best fatherly intentions, had appealed to Dorinthia—"Child, he's nothing but trouble!" Perhaps, in retrospect, it would have been apropos had another father been able to plea—"Noah, don't take you guns to town, son. Don't take your guns to town!"

Ruben Flanoah "Noah" Wilkerson, unfortunately lived life at the half-cock notch. *Courtesy Pat Watkins.*

Dorinthia Wilkerson and two of her nine children fathered by Noah. *Courtesy Pat Watkins.*

Runnels County Sheriff R. P. "Bob" Kirk, left, and Robert C. Goodfellow, Texas Ranger. Sheriff Kirk ineffectively traded shots with Noah in eastern New Mexico Territory. Productively, without having to even leave the Lone Star State, he cleverly tracked murder fugitive Noah Wilkerson to Wyoming and aided in orchestrating his undoing. *Courtesy David Ueckert.*

Robert D. Meldrum, a genuine bad man, ex-convict, future convict, and the Wyoming deputy sheriff who would confront outlaw Noah Wilkerson for the last hurrah. *Courtesy Museum of Northwest Colorado.*

Noah's granddaughter Pat Watkins with Savage Model 99, .303 caliber, the rifle Noah Wilkerson had at the time of his death—struggling with Deputy Meldrum while resisting arrest. *Author's photo.*

Local Brownwood, Texas, historian Ed Walker, left, and Noah's grandson J. C. Wilkerson examine Noah Wilkerson's .41 caliber Colt's six-shooter: the pistol he tried to pull on Bob Meldrum. *Author's photo.*

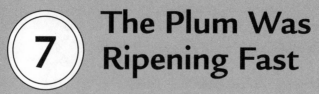

The Plum Was Ripening Fast

Phillip Cuney Baird was topnotch—tough, tenacious, and tactful: good traits for a lawman. Had he really wanted to, Baird, popularly just known as P. C., could have cashed in when early twentieth-century Americans stampeded to box-offices lining up to live through and savor the Wild West experience—vicariously! Other folks could madly hound after the Hollywood movie producers and scriptwriters and novelists, pushing and puffing their stories for profit while pumping those melodramas plumb full of hot air. There was no need for Baird to step on the truth; he was legit.

The fourth day of March 1862 closed with P. C. crying his way into the Central Texas world, the third child and first born son of Milton Coleman and Nancy Ann (Lee) Baird. Milton Baird was a hardscrabble farmer, and from the very beginnings of life P. C. had been instilled with everyday work know-how, the practical brand.[1] Absolute specificity regarding his formal education is elusive, but as an adult it will be perfectly clear he had pretty well mastered reading and writing and arithmetic. A horsemanship knack was elemental. If standing by graduated marks on the back of a door, the somewhat ruddy complected P. C. would top-out at five feet, ten inches.[2] Aside from hard work toiling on the family farm, by necessity P. C. had honed his skill with firearms and woodcraft, hunting along Coryell County's hillsides and creek banks, supplementing the family's fare with deer, turkey, squirrel, rabbit, and, perhaps, occasionally a treed raccoon or greasy tasting possum. He gathered nuts free for the taking from beneath huge pecan trees and garnered sumptuous catfish from the snaking Leon River. Though in later life he would be drawn back into large-scale agricultural endeavors, at twenty years of age P. C. Baird did not yearn to stay on the farm, or drive stage-coaches, or hustle customers while clerking in a hardware store at Gatesville, the county seat. An inexplicable phenomenon was tugging—gnawing—at his insides. Young Mr. P. C. Baird craved a few thrills.

By order of Adjutant General Wilburn Hill King, P. C. Baird and four other recruits were to be placed on the Muster and Payroll for Company D, Frontier Battalion. The young men impatiently reported to company headquarters, Camp King, seven miles west of Uvalde, Uvalde County on September 4, 1882.[3] After swearing their oaths of office they became full-fledged Rangers. Civilian Baird had reported for duty unarmed. Ranger Private Baird was right fast issued gear by the state. The cost, based on a preset pricing schedule, was to be deducted from his quarterly pay. Proudly the rookie took possession of a model 1873 Winchester .44-40 lever-action carbine, $20; a gun (saddle) scabbard, $1.75; a Colt's six-shooter, .45 caliber, $13.50; and a pistol belt and scabbard, $3.50.[4] Cartridges were issued at no charge, as was the liberal ration of beef, beans, bread, and coffee. The company commander was Captain Lamartine Pemberton "Lam" Sieker, a no nonsense go-getter and gritty lawman who would back his men during a hard play, but one wedded to the notion that truly good Rangers held sacred a genuine sense of duty. In Captain Sieker's blueprint for proficiency and professionalism there was not a smidgen of space reserved for whiners or sissies or bad Rangers.[5] P. C. Baird would make a good Ranger.

Little did he realize it then, but the young private had signed on with a unit that was making and would make a brilliant name for itself in the annals of Texas Ranger history. Sadly, it would also be Company D that would earn a heartrending distinction: That of losing the most Texas Rangers in the line of duty during the nineteenth century.[6] If P. C. Baird wanted action, he'd darn sure chosen the right spot and the right company of Rangers.

P. C. Baird did not jump the tracks of tradition. It takes a few months for his name to be enumerated in Company D's voluminous stream of paperwork. He was young and he was untested. Rangers already hardened by real time experience would be his tutors. Such is an expectant attribute of seniority. Though Baird's name is not particularized per se, it would not be unreasonable to suggest that as a rookie he took part in a few of the arrests accomplished by Company D Rangers for the month of November 1882. The defendant list is long; the broad variety of felony and misdemeanor violations is enlightening: Unlawfully Displaying Firearms, Attempted Murder, Swindling, Theft of a Gun, Burglary, Assault, Gambling, Disturbing the Peace, Embezzlement, Selling Beer Without a License—and incredibly, Masturbation.[7]

Clearly Private Baird was an apt pupil and fast learner. Not far into 1883 he was making arrests on his own. He and several Rangers—on temporary detail—were working the Rio Grande country in and around Eagle Pass, Maverick County. At that time and at that place the handiwork of P. C. Baird begins to shine—illustriously so. He is personally credited with arresting folks and transferring them into the custody of Maverick County Sheriff Thomas L. Oglesby, himself a former Ranger captain. Private Baird's five arrests in this instance were for serious legal infractions: Assault to Murder and Assault and Battery, and a solitary incarceration for Disturbing the Peace.[8] The following month he was back in Uvalde County, where he arrested one fellow for Robbery and another for Burglary.[9] Private Baird was exhibiting so much law enforcing talent that before summer kicked off he was promoted to 2nd Corporal, a position allowing him to lead—but also be held accountable for—Ranger scouts.[10] Shortly thereafter the Company D camp was relocated to a spot five miles southeast of Uvalde on the Leona River, and designated Camp Leona.[11] Numerous are the scouts Corporal Baird, riding as the headman, led throughout the Texas Hill Country. In the short term maybe his most notable arrest was when he took into custody eight folks at Uvalde for Gambling, one of the players being the notorious Texas gunman John K. Fisher who was in town concurrent with a session of District Court.[12]

On the fifth day of December 1883 Corporal Baird headed an eight-man scout to Llano County. He was to maintain order while the District Court was sitting at the county seat, Llano. As time permitted he was to patrol the surrounding countryside.[13] The undertaking would prove notable for the life of P. C. Baird, for several reasons. He made the acquaintance of an attractive and alluring feminine flower, seventeen-year-old Kittie Margaret Holden, and he also became acquainted with a thus far unnamed person—an informant—that professed strategic possession of theretofore unknown criminal intelligence: the alleged whereabouts of highly sought fugitive Frank Jackson, the guy who had given Rangers the slip at Round Rock during the gunplay with outlaws Sam Bass and Seaborn Barnes. Baird personally wrote to Adjutant General King:

> Will you be pleased to inform me what reward there is offered for the Arrest of Frank Jackson of the Bass gang. If any, by whom are they offered. I have him located. He is, however, not in this State. Will you let me off and assist me going after him. If so please get for me the appointment of Dept. U.S. Marshal for that purpose. Please let me here from you at once as I want to send a man to him so as to have all things ready before I start after him which it will take some time to arrange before I shall want to start. There also were two other outlaws with him. One of which Killed a man in Williamson County but whose name I do not at this time remember. I should like to see you personally on the subject and by your permission come to see you.[14]

Unfortunately for Corporal Baird and maybe luckily for Frank Jackson, the adjutant general did not buy into the creditability or urgency of the appeal. King scribbled his answer in longhand at the top of Corporal Baird's letter: "Answer him that I Know nothing of any reward, that the matter is too uncertain & difficult for his request to be granted at this time."[15]

While Corporal Baird and his detachment were extraordinarily busy at Llano keeping the peace and arresting miscreants, things were ginning at Austin. Texas Governor John Ireland had called a special session of the legislature. There was but one topic on the agenda, fence cutting. Rural Texans were literally at war with each other because of wire—barbed-wire. Monetary losses were staggering, registering on the plus side of $20,000,000.[16] Catchy sales pitches touting that barbed-wire was "Light as air, Stronger than whiskey, and Cheap as dirt" or that it was "Pig tight, Horse high, and Bull strong" were overstatements falling on deaf ears and unfastened pocketbooks.[17] Lest there be undue misunderstanding, many communities were divided—50 percent favoring the stringing of the newfangled prickly ribbons of steel, and 50 percent thinking it was but Lucifer's work. One free-grazing stockmen's hyperbole was not hesitant, downheartedly fantasizing that it would be his dream come true if "the man who invented barbed-wire had it all wound around him in a ball and the ball rolled into Hell."[18]

Ranchmen in San Saba County were not unjustly concerned that barbed wire would injure their cattle, because: "in warm weather the screwfly is so destructive to stock that it is impossible to guard against its ravages while stock is being cut to pieces by such fences."[19] Local politicos listened to their predominate and important livestock raising constituency: "Be it resolved by the Commissioner's Court of San Saba County that our members of the Legislature be requested to use their endeavors to prevent the passage of any law making such fences legal, and to secure the passage of a law making it a penal offense for any one to use or own any such fence."[20]

During the same year P. C. Baird was promoted to corporal, 1883, half of the 171 thus far organized counties in Texas reported fence-cutting episodes—and in select sections it was near pandemic.[21] At Brownwood, Brown County, that same year some 200 armed partisans converged on the courthouse square, threatening to burn the town if the sheriff, William Nelson "Uncle Bill" Adams, didn't do something about the big cattlemen fencing them off of the Open Range grasslands and precious waterholes.[22] Many folks sided with "Knights of the Knippers."[23]

On the other hand, there can be no doubt where the sympathies of Governor Ireland were: He had been a victim of nighttime nippers of wire.[24] Times were changing and so, too, were days of the Open Range model for raising and fattening livestock. The state legislature stayed abreast. When lawmakers left for their respective homes that early part of 1884 there were new laws on the books: Simply said, it was now a felony to destroy someone's fence or purposely torch their pasture, a one to five year stretch in the penitentiary for the cutters or arsonists; persons could only fence land they had legal right to, and certainly not Texas' public school land; any fence crossing a public roadway must now have a gate every third mile, granting ingress and egress for those traveling to the courthouse or post office or railroad depot or to attend a wedding in an adjoining county. Of particular interest for P. C. Baird's story, due to the lackluster performance or political costs or downright ineptitude of a few local law-enforcing officials, the Texas Rangers now held jurisdictional authority to suppress fence cutting and/or apprehend cutters.[25]

After an absence of 41 days in Llano County, Corporal
P. C. Baird's detachment returned to Camp Leona.[26] Little did he
realize it then, but P. C. Baird's fellow noncommissioned part-
ner, Company D's 1st Corporal, Louisiana-born Benjamin Dennis
"B. D." Lindsey, a crackerjack lawman, had scouted into Edwards
County. There, twenty miles northeast of the future county seat,
Rocksprings, at Green Lake, Corporal Lindsey may have made
the very first arrests after enactment of the fence-cutting statute.
He and two Texas Ranger privates had taken into custody Henry
Wood, J. D. Creech, and E. Beech, turning them over to a justice of the peace.[27] Fearing that he might face hard time, one of
the arrestees cut a deal. Captain Lam Sieker messaged Adjutant
General King at Ranger headquarters: "Corpl. Lindsey has a man
who has turned states evidence in the Edwards County fence
cutting . . . With him conviction is sure."[28] Well, it wasn't quite a
slam dunk!

In recognition for the hard work being carried out by his two
corporals, when a vacancy presented itself, B. D. Lindsey was
promoted to sergeant for Company D and P. C. Baird was moved
up a notch to 1st Corporal. Wood Saunders moved into Baird's old
2nd Corporal spot.[29] Though he had been working in overdrive,
leading scouts, inspecting suspected herds of burnt or blotched
cattle, and supervising arrests, the pace was about to pick up for
Corporal Baird.

The drought that had started during 1883 had not abated.[30]
Texas was hot and Texas was dry. Grass was short and scarce.
Creeks were bone dry. Cattle were dehydrating on the hoof.
Water, what little there was, was precious as gold and horded. It
boiled down to bottom-line simplicity: If your cow creatures or
sheep and goats could drink you'd probably get by—if not you'd
watch your herds and bank account dehydrate and die. Greediness
was not an issue; core survival was. At the aforementioned Green
Lake in rocky Edwards County there was yet water, not an ocean,
but priceless water nevertheless. There, too, were two gentlemen
with clear title to Green Lake, the Greer brothers, William Joseph
"Joe" and G. B. aka Green. They were sheep men.[31]

The Greer brothers had fenced off Green Lake. Neighboring
cowmen were not any too happy, most especially offspring of the
Brunson and Burton bloodlines, along with rough and tumble
cowboy M. D. "Mark" Hemphill.[32] In the dead of night the Greer

brothers' fence surrounding Green Lake, at least a section of it, came down. Although there was no shortage of fingers pointing at the culprits' true identities, there was, unhappily, scant admissible evidence to place in the hands of a game district attorney. At an earlier juncture when their fence had been cut down the Greer brothers had willingly but unwittingly made a deal with the Devil, having accepted $125 cash from one of the cutters as restitution, accompanied by a formalized pledge not to criminally prosecute.[33] They had been hoodwinked.

Their fence had been cut again. They were loathe to rebuild, it was expensive to continually replace the fence, but in their eyes financial survival extorted that they protect what water was yet pooled in Green Lake. Green Greer turned to Governor Ireland: "Sir, as I am almost certain that my fence is going to be cut as Soon as I close it, I will wait one week longer before closing it. I would respectfully request you to Telegraph Capt. Sieker to Send Some men & let them come at Knight & Secret themselves So when I close it we can Ketch the fellows, they are going to be very Sly this Time as they have been caught once. . . . "[34]

Within the week Corporal P. C. Baird left Camp Leona straddling his saddle-horse, Pinto Grande, heading for Green Lake and a rendezvous with fence cutters—he hoped. Baird was accompanied by Privates W. A. Mitchell, W. W. Baker, and Oscar D. Baker. The Baker boys were not related by blood, but were brothers of the badge.[35] Under the cover of darkness, as requested, Corporal Baird and men pulled into the Greer ranch during the night of 28 July 1884. The Rangers' horses were secreted about two miles away from the downed fence wire so any whinnying or snorting or pawing would not give them away. From the Rangers' nicely concealed position it was now a touchy game of hurry up and wait—quietly.[36] Luckily their timing had been impeccable.

While the next morning's sun was coming up Green Greer instructed foreman John Landigan to rebuild the fence. Mr. Landigan gathered the necessary barbed-wire and tools and set to work. At about straight up nine o'clock—it was already scorching hot—Landigan looked up, mopping sweat from his brow. Coming towards him were about 150 thirsty beeves, herded by four men: Mark Hemphill, Henry Burton, John Brunson, and John Bailey, a convicted murderer and escaped convict who was using an alias of John Mason. Hard thinking was not required to decipher the quartet's intent. Landigan's orders from the boss were plain: Fix the fence and deny permission to anyone hankering to cross it—period. Mark Hemphill was in no mood for a Mexican Standoff. He jerked out his Colt's six-shooter, cocked the hammer and told Landigan he'd best step aside right quick or he'd kill him. Mr. Landigan was no fool, nor was he foolhardy. The cowboys and herd passed through the as of then unrepaired gap in the barbed-wire fence; the cattle feverishly drank from Green Lake.

What from the Rangers keeping deathly quiet nearby? Corporal P. C. Baird had this to tender: "I witnessed the above fact from where I was concealed about 150 yds. from where it occurred but thought it best to remain silent until I had a sure case against them as I was confident they would cut the fence down again as soon as it was closed. . . ."[37] Admittedly Baird had the legal Discretion to act. What he would do and how he would do it would be a Judgment call: ignoring a crime taking place in his presence, waiting for an actual fence-cutting violation to materialize. Clearly Baird's three Rangers were eager to pick fruit, a few rotten fence cutters:

> At this juncture it took quite an effort on my part to hold the boys down, as they were "raring to go" and anxious to open the ball; but in my judgment the time was not ripe for such action, owing to our position being at a disadvantage at this particular stage of the game. I could see that the "plum was ripening" fast, and when the opportune time came to be plucked, business would pick up, and get much warmer than it was on this already hot day.[38]

The opportune time came that afternoon. About four o'clock the four yahoos reappeared, this time with a cavvyard of 50 thirsting horses. Landigan had finished his work. The downed fence had been fixed. This time, instead of whipping out a six-shooter, Mark Hemphill whipped out a pencil and paper. Hurriedly he wrote a note to Green Greer, saying he was doggedly set to water his horses and that if a gap in the fence was not made for him, he would make one himself.

Green Greer "refused to accede to his demands."[39] The plum had ripened. Stepping down from their horses, the cowboy owl-hoots cut the fence. Then they rounded up their horses and drove them through the fresh gap in the wire and on towards Green Lake. According to Corporal Baird he had now witnessed a "bold and unlawful act." It was now time to "discharge his duty." Afoot the four Texas Rangers advanced toward the fence cutters. When the Rangers were spotted the lawbreakers dismounted and took cover behind a low rock wall, making ready to fight.

Corporal Baird could see Winchesters aimed in his direction, and he distinctly heard the dare: "Come on & take us in you damned sons of bitches." Seemingly with ice-water in his veins Baird advanced hollering time and again for the skunks to surrender. At Corporal Baird's fourth plea Mark Hemphill "made the only & following reply. 'Go to hell you son of a bitch' which was instantly followed by the report of their Winchesters: Hemphill firing the first shot."[40]

Not unexpectedly the Rangers replied in kind. The fight waxed hot for ten minutes—real hot. Atop a nearby hill and from a place of safety Green Greer witnessed the war, and a war it seemed to be with the expenditure of—in his estimation—at least 150 shots. He particularly noted that P. C. Baird was "ever ready with words of encouragement to cheer on the brave boys under his command." Greer also was in a position to watch and hear Private W. W. Baker cry out in pain as a bullet tore through his left side . . . making him very "weak from the loss of blood" and forcing him to "retire from the field." As Privates W. A. Mitchell and Oscar Baker tried to outflank the desperadoes Mr. Greer watched the cutters readjusts their position and pour a withering fire on the two unprotected Rangers. Greer was worried, fearing that "they were going to get the worst of it." Wholly flabbergasted Greer watched as Ranger O. D. Baker mistakenly tried to load a .45 Colt's pistol cartridge into a .44-40 Winchester's loading gate, a serious human malfunction at a most inconvenient time.[41] Crouching "behind a small liveoak sapling" Ranger Baker finally "finished the act of extracting the pistol cartridge from his gun."[42] He was back in battle mode.

During the horrific gunfight a fence cutter was silhouetted while trying to jockey for a better shot. Green Greer saw it all: "Mason stepped from behind his bush and raised his gun to shoot Mitchell. Baker's gun cracked and Mason staggered back with a bullet in his breast. Quick as lightening Mitchell planted another one in his bosom. Mason moved back behind the brush, but in doing so he exposed himself to Baird's fire and soon the smoke boiled from that gentleman's gun and down went Mason with a bullet in his brain."[43] P. C. Baird picks up the fire-belching narrative: "the rustlers were soon rustling for cooler and safer quarters, making a dash for their horses near by. . . . Had I been supplied with ammunition I would have killed their horses, placing them on an equal with us as to mounts, but as I thought it best to save what I had for men in case of continued trouble, instead of killing horses."[44]

Surveying the scene Corporal Baird took in reality: Three cutters had made a clean getaway, one had been killed, and he had a wounded Ranger to care for. There were legal matters needing attention, too. Joe Greer, using Baird's horse, was dispatched to make the thirty-five-mile trip to Junction, Kimble County, summoning a medical doctor, notifying a justice of the peace, and "to get five hundred cartridges with which to replenish our magazines and belts." There were rumors circulating that the *mal hombres* would gather reinforcements and avenge the loss of their crony. The bad guys didn't return and the local magistrate was out of pocket. When he returned the next morning Joe Greer was accompanied by Drs. Burt and Vaughn, and saddle bags bulging with ammunition. After carefully examining Ranger Baker's wound and declaring it survivable, Doc Burt commented that the all night nursing care provided by Green Greer's wife Julia and the Rangers had been exceptional.[45] They had cleverly jerry-rigged a bucket and suspended it above Baker's lesion, with a continual drip through a nail hole, which kept "a small stream of water on the wound to keep down inflammation. . . ." [46]

Nine-year-old Tom Dragoo and another lad, Lee Smadler, after hearing all the commotion rode bareback to the Greer Ranch. There the youngsters saw the dead man stretched out on the ground covered with saddle blankets. Boys will be boys, and Tom had to steal a look despite the Ranger's warning: "But, I raised up the blanket, and if I live to be a hundred years, I'll never forget what I saw. It was July and the flies were bad. He had about ten days' growth of red beard, and I wish I hadn't looked. I picked up .22 shells that were shot during the fight."[47] Taking it upon his own in the absence of an official empowered to conduct a formal Inquest, Corporal Baird ordered that John Bailey's remains be interred. It had lain in the July inferno undisturbed for twenty-two hours. Afterwards—at the town of Mason—Corporal Baird thought it might be smart to update the boss. He sent a telegram to Captain Sieker:

> Send men to Green Lake, Edwards County. Had fight with fence cutters. Baker wounded. Bring wagon to move him. My wagon at Wright's. Please bring it. One cutter killed.[48]

Green Greer was tickled with the Texas Rangers' heroic performance: "Too much cannot be said in praise of the four Ranger boys who were concerned in this fight—And it is the earnest desire of all the good and law abiding citizens in this section that their action be sustained by the state government."[49] Unfortunately not everyone was feeling so benevolent. Frank Jones, at the time Company D's lieutenant, was on a scouting and fact-finding mission. What he discovered in Edwards County was not comforting: "I find the people up in the section of Green Lake very bitter against Rangers and say that they had no right to come into the country in the night. They say, and I guess truly, that if Hemphill had known Rangers were in the country he would not have cut Greer's fence."[50] Lieutenant Jones' observations were on target. Three days after writing that missive to the adjutant general, another letter, this one from Captain Lam Sieker, made it to AG King's cluttered maple desk at Ranger headquarters: "Burton's son who was one of the Green Lake fence cutters has made complaint against Corpl. Baird & squad for attempt to murder. I instructed them to go by Bull Head and wave [*sic:* waive] [preliminary] examination and give bond to appear before the Edwards Co. Grand Jury—we will make it interesting for them before they get through with it. Please see the Gov. about counsel."[51] It appears that Corporal Baird didn't get the message or didn't understand the legal strategy of waiving a Preliminary Hearing, letting the case go straight to the grand jury. Though Captain Sieker's legal terminology is imprecise, he was aware Company D's lieutenant was personally witnessing the theatrics in Edwards County: "Lt. Jones is now at Bull Head but has not established a camp yet. He is attending Justice Court there where Corpl. Baird & squad are being tried before the Justice for assault with intent to Killing young Burton at Green Lake."[52]

   Moving Corporal Baird's narrative forward obligates winding down the Green Lake saga. In the end the Rangers came clear of paying any legal penalty—as well they should have, it seems.[53] An argument that the four fence cutters did not know they were fighting Texas Rangers, but thought those scruffy-looking fellows with Colt's .45s and Winchesters were just hired-guns employed by the Greer guys is conceivable. Not just a few local folks thought so, especially since the lawmen had not been wearing uniforms or sporting badges. Corporal Baird and Private Oscar Barker made good on a personal promise and arrested John Brunson, delivering him into the hands of the Edwards County's first sheriff, Ira L. Wheat.[54] Somewhat later Lieutenant Jones and his scout arrested Henry Burton in Edwards County, turning him over to a justice of the peace.[55] Months later Mark Hemphill surrendered to a Ranger, Searce Baylor, who transported his prisoner to the nearest jailhouse, the one maintained by his brother, Sheriff Henry W. Baylor at Uvalde[56].

Following the Green Lake affair Corporal P. C. Baird may have conjured up ideas of a little rest and relaxation. If so, events beyond his control sent those silly thoughts to the back-burner of his brain—a news-making murder had been committed; treacherous outlaws were on the dodge. At once he left for Fredericksburg, Gillespie County. On 3 September 1884, during an armed robbery gone awry, the very well-liked fifty-five-year-old John Wolfgang Braeutigam had been cold-bloodedly gunned down. He left a widow, Christine, and now his eleven children were fatherless. Mr. Braeutigam's death was not only a genuine tragedy for the family, but the entire Gillespie County community as well. Collectively they had all been stabbed in the heart.

The murderer's hapless victim had been the proprietor of Braeutigam's Beer Garden, perhaps the most popular venue in the Texas Hill Country for celebrating social events such as birthdays, weddings, family reunions, county expositions, etc. It was a grand spot for those galas, due to the entertainment complex having a dance pavilion, a large grapevine-covered arbor, shaded picnic tables, and even a dirt race track for those Saturday afternoon contests where local owners could vicariously play the part of big-dogs in the Sport of Kings, horse racing. Mr. Braeutigam's uncalled-for death was a genuine heartbreaker! Made evermore so by the cheerless fact that it was Braeutigam's ten-year-old son Henry who had discovered the bloodied and lifeless body.[57] The Gillespie County Sheriff, John Walter, was overworked and understaffed and in dire need of capable help: Texas Ranger help. Company D's Monthly Return for September 1884 is explicit: "Corpl. Baird and 3 men made scout to Gillespie Co. to report to sheriff for duty."[58]

One of the Texas Rangers in Corporal Baird's team was Private Ira Aten, who would later be recognized as a gutsy and tenacious Ranger, but was now basically a tenderfoot lawman simply trying to earn his spurs. Corporal Baird's investigative thoroughness was commendable. By carefully piecing bits of circumstantial evidence together his men had a reasonably good idea as to who the killers were. They tracked the suspects south along the Colorado River to the vicinity of Travis Peak, in the northwestern part of Travis County, not too far from the Burnet County line. Trailing their prey—as exciting as it might sound—was not accomplished by following indistinct hoof-prints, measuring the freshness of horse droppings, or retrieving broken twigs, but by competently visiting with and interviewing folks along the way, further refining the physical descriptions and direction of travel. The Rangers were now confident they were looking for the right men: Jackson "Jack" Beam, William "Bill" Allison, Ede Janes, and C. W. "Wesley" Collier. Too, there was a shadowy possibility that Jim Fannin was a player too.[59] The work had morphed from a whodunit to a manhunt.

Barely had thirty days lapsed since commission of the terrible crime before a noose began tightening for Braeutigam's alleged killers. Developing his criminal intelligence and keeping his cards close to his vest Corporal Baird was ready to act during the wee hours of October 5, 1884. Ira Aten, perhaps wrapped it up best: "We rounded up their houses at night at two different places and caught them in bed."[60] Rangers had caught three snoozing suspects, Collier, Beam, and Allison.[61] With prisoners in tow Corporal Baird and his overjoyed men set their course for Fredericksburg. There the bewildered detainees were locked in the Gillespie County jail pending a Preliminary Hearing. Not unexpectedly bail was denied; the bad boys could just sit it out until the next Gillespie County grand jury met. And, also not surprisingly, Baird and his Rangers were treated as conquering heroes at the celebratory party hosted by the town's jubilant populace. Subsequent to the big doings, after consulting with Sheriff Walter, it was decided to transport the prisoners to the much more secure Bexar

County lockup at San Antonio. After depositing their three prisoners there, Corporal Baird's detachment retuned to Camp Leona.

Although Corporal P. C. Baird's part in the Braeutigam murder investigation is finalized, the aftermath proved to be an ongoing saga, involving manhunts, jailbreaks and jailhouse fires, and a gunfight. A skeletal recap would close that book revealing that Bill Allison burned to death while a prisoner; Ede Janes had been run to ground by Rangers Ira Aten and James V. Latham and thrown into the Gillespie County hoosegow; and mysterious Jim Fannin just seems to have melted, fading into the abyss of murkiness. The ever plucky Ira Aten interdicted the criminal careers of the last two: He captured Jim Beam, who caught penitentiary time, and when the idiot went for his six-shooter Ranger Aten tapped out fugitive Wesley Collier's running lights with a single bullet from his Colt's .45. The governor had personally told Aten to bring Wes in—one way or the other—dead or alive. Ira Aten had complied.[62] P. C. Baird's head was elsewhere.

After capably leading the manhunt and carefully managing the arrests of Braeutigam's killers, Corporal Baird's last Texas Ranger assignment was to make a scout to the vicinity of Mason, Mason County, scouring the countryside for the whereabouts of a slippery fellow wanted for Assault to Murder. The four-day trip netted him a zero, but may have paved the way for his new line of law enforcing work. Corporal P. C. Baird said *adios* to the Texas Rangers on the last day of November 1884, honorably and voluntarily discharging.[63] He pinned on a deputy sheriff's badge. By one account, because of Baird's sterling Ranger reputation and a gold-plated standing with the Texas Hill Country's public at large, Mason County's sheriff had petitioned Adjutant General King to release Baird from his term of enlistment.[64] Certainly it's true that Baird assumed responsibility as the chief deputy for Sheriff John Calvin Butler, but there may have been another logical reason pulling him out of Ranger service and tugging at his heartstrings.

Typically it's underplayed in many Texas Ranger histories, but since the Frontier Battalion's inception during the spring of 1874 an ill-advised policy with unintended consequences had hamstrung the organization's overall efficiency and retarded its march toward professionalism. Attaining that high level of proficiency is normally acquired through theoretical education and practical experience. An administrative diktat from the Frontier Battalion's hierarchy prohibited Rangers in the lower ranks—privates and noncoms—from being married. An exception was granted for its commissioned officers, the lieutenants and captains. While all seemed reasonable on paper—dashing young single men hunting hostile Indians and wicked outlaws—the policy had a quantifiable negative result: The turnover rate within enlisted ranks was atrocious. It was not a sound personnel management philosophy. There was at the time a hard bottom line. A worthy young man could be a Ranger without a wife, or a husband without a Ranger's pay.[65] Baird, at twenty-two, was career-minded and matrimonially inclined and in need of a paycheck.

Miss Kittie Margret Holden, at the time of P. C. Baird's separation from the Ranger service and his donning the chief deputy's hat, was yet living in Llano County, Mason County's immediate eastern neighbor. There are no grounds—not even shallow ones—to suppose that Kittie's parents, Frank and Emily, had any bad vibes about the brown-haired and blue-eyed lawman courting their daughter. Phillip Cuney Baird was a good man and a good Ranger when he had been previously detailed to Llano County near two years earlier. He yet was a good man. Perhaps during those earliest days it was naught more than flirtatious infatuation, followed by giddy puppy love, then raging hormonal issues not politely discussed in mixed company, and by now, 1885, true love had bloomed. Kittie had blossomed too. She was nineteen and the apple of Chief Deputy Baird's eye. Maybe there was just a touch of deviousness in P. C.'s proposal, a little insurance about never forgetting a wedding anniversary: They would marry on his birthday.

This far removed by time there is veiled mist as to whether or not the ceremony took place in a church's sanctuary or at the Llano County home of the bride's parents. Nonetheless it may be conveyed with clarity that the nuptials and P.C. Baird's twenty-third birthday matched perfectly. Owing to profiling P.C. Baird's law-enforcing life in but a chapter-length layout, though it breaks with an exacting chronology, now is an ideal place to mention that the March 4, 1885, union between P. C. and Kittie produced eight children: John Butler, Ola Ora, Asa Milton, Edna Earle, Robert Roy, Lee Russell, Lillian, and Audree Nadine.[66] When need be, lawman P. C. Baird was a fighting man. Forever he was a family man.

There were not just a few tough spots in Texas compelling its lawmen to be doubly tough. Mason County was one. For a time during the nineteenth-century ubiquitous gunplay and Mason were bedmates. Casually filliping pages of a generalized county history or meticulously studying Mason County specifics the viewer will be bombarded with a litany of brutality and bloodshed.

Mason County was home turf to hardened Texans provably able to gun down U.S. Army soldiers on the courthouse square; or storm the jailhouse, liberating inmates and hustling them to the hanging tree on the outskirts of town while a Texas Ranger impotently looked on; or murder a fellow washing his face, eyes covered by the towel; or from atop a horse shoot an unarmed man, jump down and stab him, then use the blood-spattered blade to take his scalp for a trophy; or discharge buckshot into a man approaching the city's barbershop, forevermore embargoing his need for a haircut. Few geographical or political subdivisions in the Lone Star State could claim with legitimacy—or illegitimacy—their very own named war, but this hardnosed setting could: The Mason County War, more popularly tagged in Texas speak as the Hoo Doo War.[67]

Disregarding the skullduggery of the Hoo Doo War feudists that lasted for decades, even into the twentieth-century, other tough characters haunted the barrooms and gin-mills of Mason. Perhaps one of the most notable was Zachariah "Zack" Light, a proven killer, one with both a human and buffalo tally cut into his notchstick. When sober he was a dead shot, when dead drunk he was near a maniacal demon. At Mason on Christmas Day 1884, the wiped-out Zack involved himself in a shooting at Tom Kinney's taproom: Life had been tapped out for Joe Kyle. After posting bond Zack was yet ready to take on the world while in his cups. He and the county judge, himself a one-armed and one-eyed fellow with a formidable fighting reputation, became entangled in a six-shooter saloon imbroglio, one wherein Zack drew blood but there was not need for a funeral.[68] Yes, the town of Mason and the county of Mason were damn tough spots.

Sheriff John Calvin Butler, a native Tennessean and a dealer in groceries and meats by trade, was sixteen years P. C. Baird's senior. Although he had served an interim appointment as the sheriff of Mason County, John C. Butler was actually voted into that office during the election cycle of 1882, the same year

P. C. Baird had enlisted with the Rangers.[69] Sheriff Butler had a made a wise choice when recruiting Baird for the job. The young ex-Ranger was favorably known throughout the Texas Hill Country for his tenaciousness.

After learning that a horse had been stolen from in front of the Methodist Church one Sunday night, P. C. assumed the role of a bloodhound. Having determined a peculiarity in one of the horse-shoes and the track it laid down, Deputy Baird cold-trailed (not hot pursuit) the horse absent an inkling as to who he was chasing or what the crook looked like: man or boy, big or little, black or white? Finally, northwest of Mason at Eden, Concho County, Baird interviewed the postmistress, a "small slender black-eyed woman with the eye like an eagle." She was nosy and she was newsy. Now owning a good physical description of the yahoo, the energized deputy sallied forth once more. At Runnels City, near present day Ballinger, Baird was forced to secure a fresh horse before continuing the hunt. Fifty miles later in Taylor County at Abilene the weary deputy seemingly caught a break—he had in truth made his own good luck. He found his man taking breakfast at a restaurant near the depot. After the owlhoot caught a glimpse of the Colt's .45 in Baird's waistband, execution of the arrest was trouble-free.[70]

The next morning with his prisoner and the stolen horse in front, Deputy Baird began the 175-mile journey back to Mason County. As nightfall began closing in, P. C. dredged from past knowhow: "I landed in McCulloch county at a sheep camp on Dry Brady Creek; here I had to resort to the old Rangers' jail, that of sleeping chained to 'my pal' during the night; with only two small boys in the camp to whom I turned over my keys and pistol, after locking myself and pal together."[71]

There's little doubt Sheriff Butler was pleased as punch when Baird and the horse thief pulled into Mason. County sheriffs enjoy returning purloined property to rightful owners—the voters. All wrapped up? Not quite! A few days later while he was attending court in Blanco County, Deputy Baird was posted about a "jail delivery" back in Mason wherein five prisoners had escaped, including his pal the horse thief. After returning to Mason and disentangling pressing business, P. C. Baird began his manhunt anew. Though this time the distances would be greater, the strain on his backside would prove less severe. Tracking by telegraph and traveling by train, Baird traced his man to El Paso. There, although he felt like "a country Rube" being "from the brush and cactus country," he cast his net and caught his limit—one taken aback horse thief. By a circuitous route Baird and his prisoner started for home, eventually detraining at Burnet's depot, thence taking the stagecoach via Llano, then into Mason.[72] Sheriff Butler was happy.

It's been written, and maybe it's true, that because of his determined demeanor and success at hunting fugitives Deputy Baird was awarded a nickname: "Old Sleuth."[73] Certainly P. C. Baird had transitioned from a neophyte lawman into a highly competent and respected peace officer. Texas had more than her share of wild human tigers, and P. C. Baird—to his credit—was smart. He had learned early on not to buy into that One Riot, One Ranger hooey. Sometimes a brave man, an intelligent man, needs help. When he needed it Deputy Baird wasn't too shy or unduly self-conscious about asking for it. P. C. knew he was a man. He wrote the adjutant general:

> There is a party in My County charged with Murder and other offenses elsewhere, who, I Would like very much to effect his Capture. It seems almost Impossible for Me to do the Work Myself owing to my being Known so well and the Locality and situation of things. If you Could favor me with Ira Aten's services a short time I could do the Work Without any trouble, as he is not Known in this Section. If you can let Aten help me to do the work please let Me Know as soon as possible. Also, Notify Aten to come anytime that I may call for him. I will Want to do the Work as soon as everything is in our favor. I have a hard set to deal with and will very probably be compelled to make a Killing, is why I want Aten to help Me and hope if possible You will assist me in this Matter. Hope to hear from You soon. Kindest regard to Your self and Capt. Sieker.[74]

Upon receipt of Deputy Baird's request AG King approved sending Ira Aten and one man to Mason County, although he did caution Company D's captain, Frank Jones, that the Rangers would have to go horseback not incurring additional travel expenses.[75] Within but short order Ira Aten and Ranger John Bargsley were scouting after Deputy Baird's purported desperado. On January 13, 1887, they did arrest a fellow in nearby Edwards County named William Connell, charged with Theft of Cattle, and returned him to Mason County and into the hands of Sheriff Butler. Whether or not this was the target of Baird's original request is thus far indeterminate.[76]

By any measure P. C. Baird was a respected and much admired member of the Mason County community, an assertion backed up by unequivocal truths. The question as to whether or not Sheriff Butler and Deputy Baird had beforehand worked out a mutual agreement would have best been answered by them. Absent their input, the hard facts tumble as they may. During the 1888 election Baird defeated Butler for the position of county sheriff. An application of common sense suggests Baird's running for sheriff was not an act of disloyalty or political treachery. The men just changed seats on the seesaw: Baird became sheriff, Butler his chief deputy.[77]

Sheriff Baird would hold on to that spot through the next four election cycles, which at the time were of two-year durations, rather than the present four. Following Sheriff P. C. Baird's footprints as he went about his daily business is not necessary at unraveling his workaday duties: He served subpoenas and summoned witnesses; seized property for delinquent taxes, then from the courthouse steps auctioned it to the highest bidder; attended sessions of district and country court; babysat grand jurors while they were in session; arrested misdemeanants and sometimes felons; brokered heated disputes between husbands and wives; counseled wayward teenagers; maintained a network of confidential sources; kept stray dogs and human vagrants off of Mason's streets; perambulated around town at night checking merchant's doors; stood at the forefront, ever ready to assist lawmen from neighboring jurisdictions hunt fugitives; continually crunched numbers for an underfunded budget; and expended no little effort overseeing the jail, feeding prisoners and keeping a tight lid on security. Sheriff Baird was a busy man.

Let there be no misunderstanding. When circumstances called for it, Sheriff Baird could still stay hitched during a gunplay, just as he had demonstrated during the shoot-out at Green Lake. Holding down the top spot in Mason County's law enforcing pecking order, Baird was called upon once more to act with finality. By 1889 Johnny Simmons had become the proprietor of the Garner &

Calhoun Saloon. It seems Johnny, rightly or wrongly, had become involved in a heated brouhaha with a customer and the uproarious fracas had removed from inside the saloon to the street. Johnny thumped his adversary, a fellow named Allison, over the head with a pistol. The saloon man stood over the prostrate man daring him to get up and suffer another dose. Standing on the north side of the courthouse square, Sheriff Baird and Chief Deputy Butler had seen it all. Rushing to keep the peace and hoping to prevent bloodshed, the two lawmen raced across the street, demanding that Simmons drop his six-shooter and settle down. Their plea for sanity was ignored. Instead of surrendering, the worked-up Simmons called out for his brother Jesse who was yet inside the saloon. The shouted message was stupid: Bring a shotgun and get outside and help me. Johnny Simmons raised and pointed the muzzle of his six-shooter just as brother Jesse stepped through the swinging doors leveling the twin barrels of his scattergun. Baird and Butler did not envision coming in last during a gunfight, dying in second place. Though just whose bullet struck who is unfixed, the outcome is not. Jesse Simmons fell where he stood with a bullet in his head, sledgehammer dead. Another bullet punched through both legs of Johnny Simmons. Although his death was not instantaneous the Grim Reaper paid him a visit two days later.[78] Sheriff Baird—or Butler—were not men to trifle with.

While his innermost thoughts cannot be excavated, there should be no doubt Sheriff Baird was perplexed beyond description by the death of Addie Kaufman. The youngster had been abducted and murdered during her trip home after school. Try as he might, Sheriff Baird could not develop sufficient clues to bring the guilty party to justice. Baird's not successfully doing so but thrusts reality to the forefront, putting a human face on its law enforcers. Even good lawmen don't win every time.[79]

P. C. Baird ostensibly took a break from the hectic life of lawman, but he just couldn't let go entirely: He applied for and was granted status as a Special Texas Ranger, a position absent state pay, but one upholding his status as a bona fide Texas peace officer. For Muster Roll and bookkeeping purposes—on paper—Special Ranger Baird was officially assigned to Company E, commanded at the time by Captain John Harris Rogers, headquartered at Alice, Texas.[80] The appointment allowed him to go armed. Any worth-his-salt lawman has a few enemies lurking within the ranks of crookdom. Devoting the years between 1896 and 1912 to ensuring financial wherewithal, Baird concentrated his intrinsic industriousness on attaining and maintaining a comfortable and worry-free life style. His private sector business achievements paralleled his success as a frontier era Ranger and, later, as a progressive Texas lawman transitioning into the modern twentieth-century. In addition to becoming a thriving stockman with numerous assets, P. C. Baird, through grueling hard work and uncompromising resolve, gained profitability and prestige as president of the First State Bank of Mason.[81]

Good lawmen can hardly abide a thief. Purportedly, as president of the bank Baird discovered an employee had been clandestinely dipping his fingers in the till and covering the shortage by cooking the books. Baird advised Judge Fulton he was going to confront the fellow. Noticing that Baird was "heeled," a six-shooter under his coat, the prudent jurist asked P. C. to leave his pistol behind and pick it up later. Baird acquiesced to his intelligent friend's entreaty. At the First State Bank of Mason the president and the purported pilferer had a meeting but not necessarily one of the same minds. After the fellow confessed his sins, P. C. Baird was fuming. So much so he issued Mr. Embezzler "a smarting slap to either side of his face."[82]

Sitting on top of the world P. C. Baird thought he would again pin on a Mason County badge. Subsequent to the November 1912 election, once more, it was Sheriff Baird. He moved his family into the first floor living quarters of the newest Mason County Jail, a solid sandstone structure built by general contractor L. T. Noyes for the Diebold Safe and Lock Company in 1898 at a cost of $8,500: a detention facility yet housing prisoners today.[83]

Again, it is not historically necessary to meticulously chase after Sheriff Baird's every move. He would stand election three more times—and win. We've already taken a measure of the man, but a few more examples will quantify that auspicious assessment.

One of Sheriff Baird's more noteworthy—at least more publicized cases—centered on a pair of career criminals, professional safe burglars. Though it's out of sorts for today's terminology, during the days of the story at hand and in detectives' and newspapermen's jargon these type crooks were commonly referred to as "Yeggmen."[84] Southeast of Brady (McCulloch County) and northeast of Mason town rests the quaint little community of Fredonia, just inside the Mason County line. There was a U.S. Post Office at Fredonia and inside that facility, as would be expected, a heavy iron safe. At the time daily bank deposits were unheard of—for most folks. Sometime after the moon came up and before the roosters started crowing, a delicately measured and deftly placed quota of nitroglycerine netted two Yeggmen $6,500 apiece. It was a huge haul! The crime was a humdinger, and though stealing from the U.S. Post Office was a federal offense, local lawmen were legally and morally obligated not to turn a blind eye. Sheriff Baird and an unnamed deputy responded immediately, racing towards the scene with horse and buggy. Along the way they met a drummer driving a Tin-Lizzie, aka Model T. The negotiations may have been or may not have been sweet, but they were short. That they commandeered the auto may be talk too strong; nevertheless the good Sheriff Baird and his man made Fredonia sitting on gasoline power not riding on horsepower.[85]

Sheriff Baird's crime scene investigation at Fredonia was revealing: The safe had been blown to smithereens and the crooks, whoever they were—and there must have been more than one, were gone. P. C. Baird had street smarts. He quickly deduced that those newly rich fellows would now yearn for putting *mucho* ground between themselves and the Fredonia PO, and right fast. Trains traveled fast. The nearest depot was at Brady. Both Mason County lawmen climbed into the auto, one of them stepped heavy on the gas pedal. At Brady's railway depot they learned the next departure would be hours away, about sundown. If at Brady, the crooks would have to kill time—somewhere. Where would burglars pass time without arousing unwanted notice? A nearby lumberyard seemed a good spot, so mused Sheriff Baird. Yeggmen had thought so, too. It was their undoing. At the point of his Colt's revolver, P. C. Baird rounded up the outlaws, relieving them of two loaded .45 calibers six-shooters, 52 loose cartridges, and all of the money less $7.00 they'd spent on a lunch—Oh, yes, and a vial holding twelve ounces of nitroglycerin.[86]

The following year, 1915, Sheriff Baird posed for a photograph with Ernest N. Kelly. Near the settlement of Katemcy in the northern reaches of Mason County a murder most foul had been committed.[87] An "old crippled fellow," Hugh Chamberlin, had been killed by treachery when Kelly had turned on the victim, a polite fellow who had been furnishing Ernest transportation; allowing him to ride on the freight wagon. At a noonday stopover for a campfire meal, Kelly struck Chamberlin a severe below from behind with a hatchet. To make sure he'd done the dirty work right, Kelly whipped out a butcher knife—one with a bone handle—and cut Hugh's throat from ear to ear. Ernest tried to camouflage the body with leaves but, alas, it was discovered. Through due diligence and dandy detective work Kelly was traced to and arrested at Brady trying to sell Chamberlin's wagon and its contents. Upon their return to Mason a shutterbug convinced the tenacious Sheriff Baird to stand for a snapshot—prisoner Kelly wasn't consulted. Peering out from beneath a cocked hat, there's little doubt, when Baird once fixed that blue-eyed stare he was a dead serious *hombre*— not a man to monkey with. Kelly must have thought so too. The wretched defendant was awarded a life sentence. No longer needed as evidence for the courtroom, the hatchet and the butcher knife were handed over to the deceased man's relatives. Chamberlin's family gifted Baird with the murder weapons as morbid souvenirs—they had no place for them, understandably so.[88]

Sheriff Baird certainly wasn't heartless. He had both compassionate and humorous depths to draw from. A young Mason County fellow, "one from a good ranching family" had been hired to dig a sizable number of postholes by hand for another, but older, cattleman. It was hard work. When the job was finished the cowman refused to pay off as agreed. Predictably a most heated argument ensued. During the dustup—it was Texas—a Colt's .45 spit blue flame and a hot pill!

The older man didn't die, but the younger chap was forced to stand trial. The Assault to Murder conviction in Sheriffs Baird's mind was unjust. Mrs. Baird thought so too, commenting about the young man's laborious job and her unsympathetic fault for the guy who caught the bullet: "that was about the hardest work anyone could do and the 'son-of-a-gun' got what he deserved." Taking wife Kittie and their youngest daughter Nadine with him, Sheriff Baird proceeded to Austin deferentially petitioning for an audience with the state's chief executive. The Governor's Pardon was granted. After returning from the trip to Austin, with the official paperwork tucked into his suit coat's inside pocket, Sheriff Baird thought he'd simply postpone telling "the perfect gentleman" locked away in the upstairs tier of cells. Cleverly, Baird thought, he would invite the prisoner to partake of Sunday dinner (lunch) with his family in the jail's downstairs living quarters. After the meal he'd tell the boy about how his future had changed. Halfway through the meal sheer "exhilaration" on the sheriff's part misdirected his initial plan: Baird could hold the secret no longer. He blurted out the good news. The absolutely stunned and crying and grateful prisoner was so gosh darn elated he "couldn't swallow another bite."[89] Sheriff Baird beamed, it was a good day to be a lawman—a good lawman.

Sheriff Baird, always in good stead with the Mason County public, remained in office competently handling administrative, civil, and criminal business for the sheriff's office, as well as serving a grand marshal for the town's 4th of July parades, until he opted out during 1916, formally replaced by George H. Willis as a result of the November election. Thereafter he maintained his extensive business interests.

P. C. Baird had lived a good life—a full life. Few were the men who could claim service as a gun-fighting veteran of the Texas Rangers, or multiple terms as a highly competent Hill Country sheriff, or as a prominent and proficient livestock producer, or as president of a hometown bank, but perhaps he was most proud of his family—and they were forced to say goodbye.

Philip C. Baird suddenly took ill, an out-of-the-blue downturn in his normal fit health. Medical attention was sought at San Antonio. Sadly his time was short. Mr. Baird died in the Alamo City on the ninth day of March 1928, five days after his sixty-sixth birthday.[90] Dissimilar to so many of the speciously puffed lawmen marketed for twentieth-century profitability, Baird was and always had been, like John Calvin Butler and Austin Ira Aten, the real deal, not a counterfeit bone in his body. He didn't need a publicist to push his story.

Philip Cuney "P. C." Baird, gunfighting Texas Ranger, Sheriff, Rancher, and Banker. *Courtesy James Baird.*

Texas Ranger Oscar D. Baker. He participated in the blistering gunplay with fence cutters at Green Lake. *Armstrong Research Center, Texas Ranger Hall of Fame & Museum.*

Mason County Sheriff John Calvin Butler recruited P. C. Baird to become his chief deputy. On a Mason street they jointly and successfully traded shots with drunken yahoos terrorizing the town. *Courtesy Mason County Historical Commission.*

Mason County Sheriff P. C. Baird. Paperwork is a never ending chore, even for early day lawmen, especially sheriffs and chiefs of police. *Courtesy Mason County Historical Commission.*

Mason County Sheriff P. C. Baird stands for a photographer with his prisoner, murderer Ernest N. Kelly. *Courtesy Mason County Historical Commission.*

Mason County Jail. Typically for the era, top floors were where prisoners were confined and the first floor was reserved for the sheriff's living quarters and office. For awhile Sheriff Baird maintained his personal residence at the county jail. *Courtesy Mason County Historical Commission.*

Mason County Sheriff P. C. Baird leading a 4th of July parade through downtown Mason, Texas. *Courtesy Mason County Historical Commission.*

Six-Shooters, Sermons, and Sour Mash

8

During the Wild West era, finding a preacher with a pistol was easy. For that time span, especially in the Old Southwest, Bible thumpin' and gunfire was not racket at cross-purposes. As certainly as some human wolves were clad in sheep's clothing, a few frontier ministers' mild-mannered meekness camouflaged a big and unhealthful sampling of gunfighting grit. Herein is the true tale of a Southwesterner who could tap out a guy's running lights on Saturday and eulogize at his gravesite on Sunday.

Thematically *Bad Company and Burnt Powder* is a treatment highlighting criminal justice—or criminal injustice—issues. Therefore, conscientiously adhering to that set-up, there will not be an undue emphasis wasted on piling wearisome genealogical minutia on the platform. All too often tediously regurgitating the pedigrees—tracing bloodlines from Adam and Eve, through fiefdoms of Medieval Europe, and then onto seesawing decks of the Mayflower—impedes and depreciates an otherwise real good Wild West story.[1] Although for the earnestly devoted storyteller it's troubling—and should be—to learn that bored readers skipped Chapters One, Two, and Three, history doesn't have to be tiresome. The Chenowth family-tree is tall, the aged branches many.

The subject of this biographical profile, John Augustus "Gus" Chenowth, could well be proud of his lineage, that part about ascendants' participation in what are now epic episodes of carving Texas into a freestanding Republic and wrestling it away from marauding or docile Indians.[2] But this is John Augustus' story, not his daddy's or grandfather's or even a distant second cousin's by marriage. As illustrious and gutsy Lone Star shootist John Wesley Hardin might say—Gus Chenowth's "tub could Stand on its own bottom."[3]

Tramping backward in time to rural Tennessee and peeking in on 4 October 1834 would near pinpoint the place and particularize the time of Gus Chenowth's birthday.[4] Registering and putting into crisp historical context the time of the boy's birth will be instrumental in later measuring the real mettle of a man. Mexico yet owned Texas and California. Comanche and Apache and other tribes' fighting men drew their toll—sometimes in blood—for traveling points between. Mountain Men were mapping, trapping, and exploring. Sam Colt's brain was spinning. Wheels for Butterfield's overland coaches had not turned. The Pony Express was but a notion. The American West was untamed.

Exactly when and how Chenowth got there is fuzzy, but subsequent to the stopovers in Arkansas and, purportedly Texas, at a reasonably young age Gus the man had luckily managed the hazardous trip to California. By one family account he had made the trip when but a teenager, hitching a ride with a westbound wagon train. Talk of the gold rush had captured America's imagination: Gus Chenowth had big ears and big dreams and a big plateful of pluck. Somewhere along the way, in that vacuum between adolescence and adulthood, Gus had picked up the knack for proficiently bullwhacking plodding oxen and cajoling stubborn mules: He was a freighter. Over but a short span of time Gus had learned there was more money to be made hauling rather than humping with pick and shovel in hand or swirling icy water, pursuing minuscule specks of gold in a pan. In but short order entrepreneur Chenowth could legitimately boast of owning wagons, teams of mules and spans of slow moving but dependable pulling oxen, laboriously tramping the Feather River Country of California.[5] Usually, in Wild West stories the protagonist looks toward the setting sun. Gus Chenowth turned his head east. He was hearing jingling coins and they beckoned.

Pauline Weaver, the legendary beaver trapper and mountain voyager, had somehow made it to the lower Colorado River country, but instead of setting steel traps he tapped into a discovery: Gold.[6] Though it hardly depreciates the fact Pauline Weaver was one of the discoverers, Isaac Goldberg writing in 1894 recalled that during 1863, Don Juan Quarez crossed the Colorado River into southern California with "a chunk of gold valued at $1,000. It looked exactly like the hand of a human being. He brought besides this rich and rare specimen, fifty ounces of smaller nuggets, all of them pure gold."[7] Of course, the particular site of the find leaked—purposefully or not—and the rush was on. Almost overnight La Paz was born.[8] Quickly planted on the Arizona side of the river, the little burg was figuratively and literally booming. Industrious guys could get rich at La Paz—or killed.

You see, in the beginning La Paz was a men's town. Though as time progressed they would be replaced with flat-roofed adobe structures, when a fellow stepped off a ferry and ambled the two miles into La Paz he would find "less than 100 primitive brush ramadas built mainly of mesquite and arrowweed: Two of these were outfitted as stores; 12 were saloons."[9] Girls? There were a few: "Mojave squaws, comely and vigorous women, did the housework and met the 'domestic needs' of the camp."[10] Ostensibly, and it may be true, in those earliest days at La Paz a newspaperman lamented that but one in a dozen men actually worked for a living: "The rest sponged off those who did."[11] Not mistakenly another adroit chronicler addressed real time reality in those early day Arizona Territory mining camps: "Greenhorns, gamblers, whiskey, and women rolled in and staked their claims along the streams or on the men who worked them."[12]

As with any new town burgeoning with an influx of single men, hot tempers mixed with hooch netted a dead body or two or three. There was the time Red Kelly shot and killed "a Texan."[13] During another high drama and high profile shooting spree William "Frog" Edwards, an ex-Confederate from Arkansas, cut loose on off-duty U.S. Army soldiers assigned to guard the steamer *Cocopah* moored at the Colorado River dock "which was some distance from La Paz." Privates Ferdinand Behn and Wentworth Truston, 4th Infantry, were slammed to the ground dead on arrival. A third boy in blue fled, leaving a profuse blood trail, while screaming in excruciating pain.[14] Frontier justice could take on a comical twist, not for the suspected perpetrator, but for those charged with chronicling the happening. Like at La Paz when a frequent troublemaker's lifeless body was discovered beneath circling buzzards in the nearby desert: the Inquest jury ruling that he clearly came to meet his death as a result of somebody—an unknown somebody—killing him in what must have been self-defense. Case closed.[15]

Just as quick as some drunken lunatic could jerk out his Colt's revolving pistol, Chenowth had noted the real profitable potential for hauling building materials and supplies to La Paz. Gainfully he began tirelessly tramping and intermittently popping his rawhide bullwhip between pretty San Diego and the desolate Colorado River crossing in Yuma County. La Paz grew as did Gus's roll. Fast in La Paz, "dry goods and liquor were abundant."[16] Wood was such a scarce commodity at La Paz the industrious and ingenious merchant Isaac Goldberg resorted to unpacking and selling the empty dry goods boxes to recoup his markedly inflated 15¢ per pound freighting expense: "Those boxes were used for coffins, furniture, and other purposes."[17]

Not unexpectedly, Gus and the hardscrabble miners and parasitical camp followers were not the only speculators to see that money—*mucho dinero*—could be made at La Paz. Shortly the population at La Paz was ballooning.[18] Some folks were maneuvering for political advantage, suggesting La Paz could and should become the capital of Arizona Territory. After all, it was by this time already the county seat of Yuma County: Why not saddle a radiant shooting star? Unquestionably with a presupposed public relations agenda, Arizona Territorial Secretary of the Treasury Richard Cunningham "Slippery Dick" McCormick was touting Yuma County when he authored and dispatched a glowing multipage letter to the distant *New York Tribune:*

> As yet its settlements are all upon the river. La Paz, the chief of these, is a busy commercial town of adobe buildings, with a population about equally American and Spanish. It has some stores that would not do discredit to San Francisco, and enjoys a large trade, extending up and down the river and to Central Arizona.[19]

Without doubt Goldwater brothers Mike and Joseph didn't want to miss a golden opportunity; they resolutely marched onto the scene opening one of their landmark stores.[20] Another redoubtable Arizona Territory pioneer, John G. Campbell, wanted to make it to the new arena of action at near any cost, financial or physical, hazarding "the desert to El Dorado Canyon, built a raft and floated down the muddy Colorado to the new gold strike at La Paz" where he soon began "merchandising."[21] Day in and day out Gus Chenowth marched, too—toward prosperity. At bustling La Paz coffee was bringing $.50 per pound and sugar was fetching

$.25 while flour was costing consumers $30-$40 per hundred pounds, which were "remunerative prices" for a shrewdly invested bullwhacker or mule-skinner.[22] Financial success in the freighting business demanded more acumen than just heaping a wagon full and maneuvering it down the rutted road to retail merchants' storefronts. Accomplishment of significance in that line of work called for wagons and teams and teamsters, tenacity and nerve. An insatiable demand for provisions—the necessities and the frivolous—was thriving.

Whatever else Gus was—as will become evident—he was a survivor and it didn't necessitate him reading tea-leaves to know that riverboat traffic on the Colorado River would all too soon economically overhaul his lumbering overland freight trains. He would forgo freighting from a southern California base. Settling in at La Paz he focused energy on transporting from the Colorado River docks those much needed commodities eastward to Wickenburg and Prescott and strewn mining communities there-abouts. The thoughtful geographical correction would prove more cost-effective—and dangerous.

Measuring with exactitude the extent of Gus Chenowth's monetary outlay in acquiring rolling and walking assets is not doable. Allowing for a smidgen of suppositional leeway and gathering of scattered facts, it's not unreasonable to suggest that after considerable capital expenditures Gus had wagon trains strung out between points of pick-up and final destination. Corralling relays of working stock at carefully selected and pre-positioned sites, along with tools and hardware for maintaining wagons, was but part of the game. With clarity, one such spot Gus invested in may be identified: Desert Station. Gus and William D. Fenter in some sort of amicable split—the percentages are unknown—partnered in Desert Station, located about a dozen or so miles southeast of present-day Quartzsite on the Ehrenberg–Prescott road.[23]

Be it removed several miles from the everyday dabbling in firewater or savoring an aroma of spent gunpowder at La Paz, even at forlorn Desert Station it could turn real Western, real quick. The record is silent as to whether or not Gus was even onsite, but it made not much difference to Willy Barr. During some brouhaha about something, he shot and killed "Gayatta John," last name unknown to history—and maybe even to Gus.[24] Other criminal violence along the La Paz Road may not have been an everyday occurrence, but happen it did: Mexican bandits killed a man in the process of digging a well and "just tossed over the corpse and windlass then spent some hours vandalizing the station." The next day a mail carrier, Mr. Duff, working his customary schedule happened on the scene discovering the ransacked station. Unbeknownst to the Mexican bandits, another man had been working at the bottom of the well—the mailman rescued him.[25]

Though, admittedly, the population numbers were scant in the vicinity of Desert Station, Chenowth did manage to garner a touch of public trust: He was appointed an Election Judge during May 1867 for the Los Posos Precinct. While it will forever remain buried in the abyss of the speculative, this local public service appointment may have sparked an interest in Chenowth for a future political gamble.[26]

One thing he was not content to gamble with, however, was falling behind schedule due to the slowness of oxen: Gus Chenowth transitioned exclusively to mules as draft animals of choice for his interior trips from Colorado River docks to settlements many miles distant. More costly in comparison, mules could cover the ground much quicker than oxen.[27] And covering ground was the name of the game for freight haulers. There was good money to be made offloading at Wickenburg/Prescott or points between and beyond, but it was a COD business—cash on delivery. At Prescott, the lively territorial capital, a pound of bacon or sugar or coffee was bringing $1.50, and that universal measurement, 100 lbs. of flour, sold for $50. A brand new pair of "ordinary boots" was worth $25—payable in gold, not currency.[28] If one was wishing to catch up on the latest West Coast happenings, that San Francisco newspaper would be but four weeks outdated by the time the pages were unfolded at Prescott.[29] And if one were really hungry for one not so fresh peach—which were scarce at Prescott—the price could be as high as $1.00—American money, if you please.[30] Typical freightage fees by this time netted 12¢ per pound, per 100 miles.[31] An energetic freighter could do well. Turnaround time was critical. Empty wagons were profitless. Thankfully for Gus and his fellow freighters, provisions were backordered at Prescott. There was no shortage of timber, though. Along the lower Colorado lumber was in short supply. Wasting brainpower was not necessary: Keep them wagons rolling—going and coming.

Mother Nature had no stake in the freighters' game. She was capricious and unsympathetic. Whether she was hatefully spitting or crying crocodile tears was of little consequence to those boys on the soggy ground: When she turned real naughty in season, wetness and misery and impassable roads were frequently her handmaidens. The desert needed gentle rain. Eroding torrential downpours, well, that was another story. Gus needed the money, storeowners needed the merchandise, but during late August 1868 their displeasure was shared—disgustingly so. Chenowth's outfit was observed more-or-less stuck—not high-centered—but immobile in the Kirkland Valley, southwest of Prescott. The roadway had been inordinately "cut up" by heavy and unremitting rainfall. The summer had been unusually wet, and on the California side of the Colorado River perturbed teamsters' wagons were "stacked up" and had been for three weeks. Wagon-master Chenowth was waiting for a break in the weather, not moving, waiting for other trains to catch up: With manpower and mules they'd jointly repair the road.[32] And it was a rough road to be sure. In fact, Army Inspector Nelson H. Davis reported that one frazzled Arizona freighter grumbled that he'd rather haul cargo from Leavenworth, Kansas, to Prescott "than from La Paz."[33] During fits of foul weather during those earliest days the teamster's travel time between La Paz and Prescott could be doubled—30 days.[34] Interruptions in the natural flow of commerce—supply and demand—manifested itself directly: Supplies stacked up at busy riverfront docks, and palpable shortages of provisions at the inland townships and mining camps now and again led to near panic and pushed prices upwards—sometimes outrageously high. The freighting industry was a community's lifeblood.[35]

Though it wasn't a bloodsucking insect, the generically dubbed Campo-Muncho, "something like a grasshopper but much larger and sometimes as much as three inches long" was a menace. It fed on the Galleta Grass which grew near the Colorado River, and much like the Blister Beetle which infest Alfalfa fields in certain Southwestern climates, "they are almost sure to kill any animal that eats them," especially horses or mules.[36] Combating the potential for problems in this instance is relatively easy. Instead of allowing animals to graze freely, cut bundles of grass and shake vigorously—until the creatures fall off—then, and only then, feed it to livestock.[37] Whether or not one of Gus Chenowth's trains blundered into this infested grass and he failed to take precautions goes unsaid, but a squib in the *San Diego Union* mentioned that he had three or four mules die on a trip to the Colorado River.[38]

The competent and conscientious freighter—the boss—was burdened with another incessant hindrance—from within. Hard people piloted those wagons. A percentage of people are pilferers. And those wagons from time to time carried desirable commodities, like molasses or sugar or tobacco—and whiskey. Shrinkage along the route between pick up and drop off could be pricey for the freighter. If he desired profit at the end of the day watchfulness and shrewdness and courageousness best accompany him every step of the way.

Sticky fingers, foul weather, bugs, and dreadful inland roadways, rudimentary as they truly were, presented nightmarish headaches for teamsters, but those challenges paled in comparison to maddening horrors doled out by hostile Indians. Mules were inviting targets, much more so than plodding oxen: They could be ridden or eaten or traded for things. Not all Indians were friendly. Upbeat travelers and/or isolated settlers had best be vigilant. Inattentive trekkers were fair game. Freighters, too, were vulnerable. In fact, not long after Gus Chenowth cleared the muddy Kirkland Valley, news, possibly rumors, was flooding the area. Purportedly King S. Woolsey's ranch had been attacked. Supposedly a group of miners had been murdered by Indians in the vicinity of the Castle Dome Mountains, 30-odd miles east of the Colorado River, northeast of Yuma.[39] Peace had not yet come to frontier Arizona Territory.

What was not gossip were the attacks on freighters caught in the open or off guard. Manuel Ravenna, a La Paz merchant, had consigned wagons to Prescott carrying supplies during the spring of 1867. Lurking warriors killed three of his teamsters, unharnessed 18 mules, repacking them with provisions totaling near $5000, then stealthily faded into the mountain shadows and secluded canyons.[40] On the thirteenth day of June 1868, an estimated 100 Indians assaulted a train, killing two teamsters, wounding four others, and making a clean getaway driving 38 mules towards the mountains. Another attack netted marauding Indians 80 mules subsequent to their murdering three men, inflicting injuries on others, and destroying two wagons—a raid costing the freighting partners near $12,000.[41]

Even if it may be tacked with a rusty hinge of the anecdotal, there very well could be a hard truth in the front line tactics of wagon-master Gus Chenowth. The logic is somewhat sound. Accordingly, Gus typically had his wagons painted yellow—from a distance they were more difficult to discern traveling across the sandy desert's floor. Up close or in the piney woods the yellow would stand out clearly—a bold message as to just who the train belonged to. There would be no flight, but a guaranteed fight: An attack would be repelled—at all costs. Indian pirates dubbed Gus Chenowth the "Yellow Devil." Blue-eyed desert desperadoes may not have given over to using that nickname, but must have really thought Jesus was with Chenowth. After all, that grizzly looking six-foot, four-inch, steely-eyed fellow always had his well-worn "Bible wrapped in a newspaper, in the jocky box" as well as several Colt's wheel-guns and a sure-sighted rifle for holding bears or bad men at bay.[42] The undercarriage for wagons was forged from tempered steel—so was Gus's backbone.

During one hair-raising episode Gus Chenowth and his wagon train, traveling with the Miller brothers' train for mutual protection, came upon a pinned-down cattleman. An obdurate party of outlaw Mohave and Maricopa Indians were demanding payment for passage: five head of cattle. The cowman would consent to forfeiting but one. By definition it was no Mexican Standoff, but neither side would budge. Scary nighttime hours finally gave way to dawn. The Indians attacked, "some with guns, others with bows and arrows." The freighters, all eighteen of them, carefully husbanded their ammunition, not having any way of calculating how long the contest might last. The senseless fight lasted all day. At nightfall the Indians disbursed as a group, taking their dead and wounded with them as they melted into the background. Purposeful rear guards, for the next few days, managed to harass the caravan as it slowly and cautiously made its way to Prescott.[43]

The owner/editor of Prescott's *Arizona Weekly Miner* shared what he believed sage advice with his readership: "Just now, our red brethren are awful thick hereabouts. They are seen in the woods, close to town in the rocks below town, on Granite Creek, in fact, everywhere . . . keep your powder dry and whenever you see an Indian that says 'Americano mucho bueno . . .' kill him, he don't mean it."[44] Perhaps written with tongue in cheek, maybe not, but Prescott pioneer William "Uncle Billie" Fourr penned that in the town's early day saloons and taprooms and sporting spots, Whisky Row, when tempers frayed to the tearing point and it was likely six-shooters would be a solution, "the crowd usually stepped in and disarmed them, and told them to go to it with their fists, that men were too scarce to go to killing one another."[45] For that 1860s section of sparsely populated Arizona Territory, particularly around Wickenburg/Prescott, to the pioneering denizens it undoubtedly seemed as if there had been an actual across-the-board and all-out role-reversal, an upheaval: "the whites lived on the reservation and the Indians occupied the country."[46]

Arizonians were not enthralled with the U.S. Army's weak-sister approach to solving their dilemma. On the one hand they—as citizens—were under a "hands off" admonition while a bureaucratic national government was pursuing its peace policy, trying to appease recalcitrant Indians into behaving, rather than punishing them and forcing passivity, so the settlers thought. Understanding concerns held by the majority population at La Paz is not difficult. Defending their straightforward course of action would be more problematic. An exculpatory letter from a resident printed in Prescott's *Arizona Weekly Miner* is self-explanatory and particularly name specific in identifying one of the sortie's foremost participants—Gus Chenowth.

On the night of Sept. 25th, 1868, a band of Apache Mohave Indians were camped about one-fourth of a mile from La Paz. They numbered some 25 or 30 warriors, and remained gathered in a circle, around a campfire, plotting for the purpose of destroying the citizens living on the outskirts of La Paz. They were overheard by spies who had been sent there to listen and observe their actions. The head chief, Cojackama, and his braves, called at the reservation on their way to La Paz and endeavored to persuade the red-skins there to murder the Agent and join in a grand scheme of robbery. Iretaba, the head chief on the Reservation, refused and warned the whites of their danger. Cojackama and his band of thieves then came on to La Paz, marched up in savage glee to Cole's store and demanded flour—they were refused.

The above facts becoming known to the citizens of La Paz they almost unanimously determined to wreak revenge on the copper demons for their many depredations. Only a short while had elapsed since some of Cojackama's band ambushed Mr. Wm. Brown in the canyon known as Granite Wash, and mortally wounded him. He died a few days afterward in great agony. Gustavos Chenowth, who was at La Paz with his train, took his brave boys and joined the residents. They were then guided cautiously to the spot where the demons were camped. Some two or three Chimhueva Indians led the advance. Precisely at 3 o'clock in the morning the attack commenced. Cojackama, old Captain Jack, and ten more of this band were killed. Some 20 escaped, but all were undoubtedly wounded, as pools of blood were found by a pursuing party.[47]

There was but a lone voice at La Paz condemning the raid, Manuel Revans (Ravenna ?). He was, according to the incredulously dumbfounded newspaper correspondent, raucously swearing like a "maniac." Manuel's haranguing was discounted by most La Paz folks due to the ethnically insensitive fact that "his squaw-consort had forsaken him—left him desolate—left his bed and board without cause or provocation, and joined her tribe."[48] As would be expected the U.S. Military hierarchy was not condoning predawn raids by civilians. Major William Redwood Price, 8th U.S. Cavalry, standing in as an investigator for the army, was not a happy camper.[49] Nor was he at all inclined to yoke his words with pleasantries, writing that there were civilians "with no more principle & almost as inimical to peace as the Indians, if they could depend on the Military for protection."[50] It had simply been, according to infuriated military men, "a cold-blooded cowardly murder committed by low-lived, drunken cowardly villains."[51]

Another guy was berating and blowing, too! Richard McCormick, now the territorial chief executive, was not hiding like so many mealy-mouthed spineless politicians would habitually do. His feelings were upfront: Declaring, in his mind, that the whole wretched affair was nothing short of a damnable "Indian murder." Although McCormick, probably more than anyone, was attuned to the actual futility of his bemoaning plea, he was insistent that everyone involved be arrested, prosecuted, and punished accordingly. No one now—this far removed—should be even a little flabbergasted at the barbed comeback. Folks from the lower Colorado River Country, principally at La Paz, were not in any mood for humor: For that wearisome multitude, politico Richard

McCormick's wrongheaded idea was utterly ridiculous, laughable: "This odious and tyrannical 'order' caps the climax. The Governor of our Territory arresting free white men for killing hostile Indians!"[52] Participants of the La Paz Massacre escaped punishment in the courts and, in many quarters, were seen as having done their duty—distasteful but necessary.[53] Historical judgment has been less compassionate.

What was not arrested was the immeasurable good will Gus Chenowth was carrying with the everyday folks—the working crowd, the guys and gals early to bed, early rise, scrimping pennies and looking hard for salvation—from recalcitrant bronco warriors who'd jumped the reservation. At the time a good number of Arizona people knew—those reading newspapers—Gus Chenowth was a standup guy: A man worthy of tying to in a tight, in the trenches or on a mountain top. Once interrogated as to how many Indians he had slain, Gus shied away from gory details but did grant he'd killed a few.[54] Gus was a doer, not a bragger.

And there were big doings down in the Salt River Valley in a locale that would shortly be called Phoenix. Absent resorting to chalking out a roster of the earliest movers and shakers steadily relocating, the picturesque valley's draw can be accounted for in a nutshell: Water. Farsighted fellows, Jack Swilling among them, early on recognized that properly harnessing the Salt River's steady current would lend itself to a bountiful agricultural bonanza. A blueprint—of sorts—was in place. In one form or another—although primitive by 1867 standards—Hohokam Indians had by hand scratched, scrapped, and chiseled from the Salt River Valley the biggest and most comprehensive prehistoric system of irrigation in North America. "Moreover, the Hohokam exercised a working knowledge of engineering and hydraulics in order to create the proper flow with the appropriate gradient of the land." The construction—a multiple century venture—was impressive not only in scope, 500 aggregate miles of canals supplying water to tens of thousands of surface acres, but by insightful technological achievements as well. Such progressiveness had not been a helter-skelter earth-moving project, massive as it was: There were "weirs of rocks and brush out into the Salt River, serving as diversion dams. Head gates were built with vertical log posts, then filled with brush and interwoven with reeds." Suitably it would seem, of the prehistoric period water carrying ditches, the largest, "the great canal," was tagged as the Montezuma Acequia.[55]

With a temperate climate and soils suited to growing and a promise of reliable irrigation the Salt River Valley had changed forever: "The canal craze had begun."[56] Gus Chenowth moved, divesting himself of "five ten mule trains for $8000," not a paltry price for that place and time.[57] His repositioning decision was intentional and intelligent: unintended consequences proved to be fortuitous and fixed. Gus Chenowth's life—for good and bad—would be marked forevermore. Right fast falling in line with what his encouraged comrades were doing, Gus staked legal claim on 160 acres in the Salt River Valley. Then he went to work as a "Superintendent" for one of the undertakings which would broadly be dubbed the Salt River Project.[58] With plenty of jobs to be had and unbridled optimism on a near horizon, the valley blossomed with new businesses and burgeoned with new faces. The formality of Phoenix actually incorporating would have to be forestalled—in want of a new county: First things first.

By an act of the Sixth Territorial Legislature meeting at Tucson during January 1871 the county of Maricopa was born: "Maricopa county was taken entirely from Yavapai county, and there was doubt expressed in Yavapai as to the ability of the people 'of Phoenix settlement' to maintain a county government, but there were no animosities growing out of the creation of the new county."[59]

The actual formation of a brand-new county may have been the impetus for Gus Chenowth and W. D. Fenter separating themselves from financial interest and ownership of Desert Station during March 1871. The two business partners transferred title to James McMullen, pocketing an undisclosed sum and/or carrying the mortgage—or a percentage of the note.[60] Both Chenowth and Fenter, at this time, were already hopeful Salt River Valley residents.

Maybe there were no "animosities" linked with birthing a spanking newborn county, but Gus might have argued there was plenty of discord about just who would govern the infant bailiwick. You see, Chenowth was popular, very popular. In actual fact, so warmly regarded he would be a contender in Maricopa County's first political race—a sizzling contest! Gus was vying for the sheriff's slot, a candidate backed by the Railroad Ticket, supporters shooting for Phoenix as the county seat. Gus Chenowth's no-nonsense opponent, James "Whispering Jim" Favorite, was the front man on the People's Ticket, his sponsors firing to have Mill City made Maricopa County's first shire town.[61]

Whispering Jim Favorite was pigheaded and John Augustus Chenowth, aptly so, was mulish. The political race waxed hot, mutual dislike blazed. The Arizona Territory frontiersmen were engulfed in an inferno—of their own making. On the morning of 21 April 1871 gunfire popped. There were eyewitnesses. With but a slight touch of present day editing, L. E. Williamson said:

> In the temporary absence of Chenowth at old Maricopa or Maricopa Wells, Favorite circulated a story of an amicable arrangement into which he had entered with Chenowth. According to the terms of it if Favorite should be elected, Chenowth was to be his deputy and vice versa. When he got back from Maricopa Wells and heard the story Favorite was telling, he went out to Favorite's ranch to ask him about it. Favorite denied having told the story but he refused to make a public statement denying it. In the quarrel that followed he shot at Chenowth with a double-barreled shotgun, but missed him. But he shot so close that the wadding from the gun fell into a pocket of my coat, which I had loaned Chenowth, and burned a hole in the bottom of it. Favorite then ran into a corral and Chenowth, with a revolver, shooting through the wide cracks, killed him.[62]

After the gunplay Gus, accompanied by five eyewitnesses, ambled back to town and surrendered to William A. Hancock who was provisionally tasked with an appointment as sheriff until Maricopa County voters could make their choice. Realizing he was holding a hot political potato, Justice of the Peace Charles Carter rather quickly conducted a Preliminary Hearing. Testifying in behalf of Chenowth—and no doubt telling the truth—all five onlookers under oath swore to "very similar accounts." Although the interim sheriff would bill Maricopa County $17.50 for fees and services rendered in *The Territory of Arizona vs. John A. Chenowth*, the criminal case was dismissed and the defendant was free to go.[63]

Where Gus didn't want to go was into politics. Subsequent to the killing of Whispering Jim, he willingly and timely withdrew from the sheriff's race. Perhaps Gus pondered if he had to kill a man to get the job, how many fellows would he have to kill to keep the job?[64] Moreover Gus had something else preoccupying his mind and occupying his time. Her name was Mary Murray.

Miss Mary was nineteen, pretty, and untaken. Gus was thirty-six, a bachelor, but not blind. The apple of Gus's eye had arrived in the Salt River Valley in 1870, the year prior to his killing Jim Favorite. Mary had not made the trip alone. Traveling with her widowed father and five sisters—plus 200 head of Texas-bred cattle—the family had been relocating from the Lone Star State to sunny California. Whether it was those promising rumors of unlimited potential in the Salt River Valley being the magnet that threw William Pinckney Murray off course, or he just stumbled into the valley by happenstance goes unrecorded. His expedition to California ended. Likewise unmentioned is what Mary Murray thought or had to say about Gus Chenowth's mortal mess with a political rival—she was a virtuous and a devoutly religious young lady.[65]

Details of the courtship are vague. Upshot of the courtship is not. In what very well may have been the city of Phoenix's very first officially recorded wedding ceremony, Gus Chenowth and Mary Murray were religiously united in matrimony on August 16, 1871, Reverend Franklin McKean, "A Minister of the Gospel," officiating. James Murray and Columbus H. "Lum" Gray served in the capacity of witnesses. Assuring the civil side of the wedding was properly addressed, Justice of the Peace Charles Carter, the very same fellow that in the Preliminary Hearing had ruled self-defense in Gus Chenowth's favor the year before, recorded that the "rites of Matrimony was [were] solemnized by me" and the official certification was made a part of Maricopa County's records.[66]

Naturally with the obligations of earning a living, Gus and Mary had no time to squander on something as superfluous as a fun-filled honeymoon, not a traditional starry-eyed honeymoon. They had ravenous mouths to feed and kids to clothe. Following the unexpected death of her mother, Mary, oldest of those remarkably resilient Murray girls, early on had been tasked with caring for her youngest sisters, ten-year-old Rilla and Eula, age five. Though thus far legalized custody documents have yet to be unearthed, Gus, at least informally, "adopted" his two youngest sisters-in-law and they made their home with him and Mary.[67]

Seemingly Gus was constantly on the road. An example of just one excursion will suffice. The *Arizona Weekly Miner* particularized: "Gus Chenowth arrived in town [Prescott] from the Salt River .... having freighted barley to Date Creek for the Miller Bros ... returned empty to Prescott and loaded lumber for Phoenix." Unhappily there was more news, distressing news, emanating from the Salt River Valley: Gus informed the newspaperman that there were about "13 Smallpox cases" at Phoenix.[68]

As late as March 1878 it may be reported that Gus was working "an 8 horse team" hauling freight, primarily lumber from the Curtis Sawmill, in vicinity of Prescott to the utterly blooming Salt River Valley.[69] From time to time Mary accompanied Gus on these, what were becoming necessary, but routine trips between Prescott and Phoenix.[70]

Gus Chenowth, a man ever industrious and always focused on diversification, planted a test plot of "Egyptian Corn" on his Salt River Valley acreage. After harvest an intact stalk was handed over to the local newsman for examination and editorial comment: "This variety of corn is being largely introduced from California and gives excellent satisfaction."[71]

Phoenix was most of the time hot, but metaphorically all was not bright and sunny in the lives of Gus and Mary Chenowth. They would be losers in real property. The distraught couple would be losers of colossal magnitude on another front, too! Although the particular maladies or details of unfortunate accidents are not now known, their first three Salt River Valley-born children would not attain adulthood: Orlena Mae, Ida, and Henry Lee. On the plus side the Chenowths would be able to celebrate Maricopa County birthdays and the precious lives of Ivy Pearl and Charles Augustus, during 1877 and 1879.[72] On that other front there was no cause for cheer.

Unfortunately, many of the "prominent Phoenix settlers were compelled to relinquish claims." The nuts and bolts are these. The National Homestead Act of 1864 allowed for the staking of a claim for free land, should the claimant live "on the land for five years. It also required some nominal land cultivation and the construction of a dwelling."[73] Therein was the crux of a real problem, a staggering problem. While the Salt River Valley was indeed a spider web system of dirty ditches and muddy irrigation canals, they were not as of yet all completed and operational: Water was not then flowing, everywhere or in profusion. Land absent water for sustaining life for crops and/or man was clearly not yet suitable for cultivation and was uninhabitable. Perhaps that is why the experimental plot of Gus Chenowth's "Egyptian Corn" had been downsized to but "an eighth of an acre" in size.[74] Claims filed too early could not be "proved up" and the stark remedy was plain: Relinquishment. Gus relinquished.[75]

Apparently Gus had not relinquished his total stock of wagons and teams, or had kept at least one stockpiled, making available a supplemental income by that old standby method for him, hauling freight. Snippets in regional newspapers were not hard to decipher: The reading public was keen on keeping abreast of Gus Chenowth's business and social activities. Reasonably frequent were his hard-driving freighting trips from the Salt River Valley to Prescott, nearly always warranting a favorable mention in the *Weekly Arizona Miner*.[76] On occasion, as previously noted, wife Mary accompanied Gus, particularly on the trips hauling lumber between Signal, Mohave County, and Prescott, Yavapai County.[77] Pinpointing with exactness what was said is undoable. Conjecturing that while perched atop the wagon's wooden bench, Gus and Mary chitchatted about the inspiration—pros and cons— of bidding adieu to Maricopa County is verifiable—by default. It was time to move. And they did, this time to bustling Pima County, that section that would in the near future become Cochise County, home to Tombstone and her odd assortment of miners and merchants and musicians—and a menagerie of misfit lawmen playing both sides of the line.

Plumbing the depths of Gus Chenowth's pockets is out of the question, but the workaholic had to hustle for a living—and he did. Gus set to freighting firewood and fir lumber from the saw mill in West Turkey Creek Canyon to Tombstone. Idleness was not his kin. Too, it's also about this time that he went to preaching.[78] There is room for doubt as to whether he was answering the Lord's call, or was breaking his back to appease Mary, but on the streets and in the bars and below brush-arbors and at out-of-the-way cowboys' camps Gus was carrying the word of God. As he saw it!

Mary Chenowth seemed to always have been carrying something, too: Babies. Interrupting the narrative's natural flow, temporarily sidetracking correct chronology is somewhat irksome for readers and writers alike, but word-count constraints for an anthology are tough. When Gus and Mary moved from the Salt River Valley to southeastern Arizona Territory quite expectantly young Ivy and Charles were a part of the ensemble. Other Chenowth kiddos would lay claim to Cochise County, Arizona, or Grant County, New Mexico, birthplaces. Appropriately, so it seems, this is a break in the story where they will be acknowledged by name: Howard Pinckney, Loyola Agnes, Clive Hale, Karl Murray, Mary Francis, Eula Bee, Isaac Earl, and Robert Graham. As a sidebar, spinning with a poignant perspective, from the very day Mary conceived her first child, until the birthday of her last son on 10 September 1893, she had been pregnant for 117 months. A few prayers for Mary were not unbefitting. She needed help.

Returning to the story at hand, it's easy to track Gus Chenowth's footprints, well, wagon tracks. They rolled east and into New Mexico Territory, just across the line, but Gus didn't know it at the time. By his logic Gus was yet in Arizona Territory. The section was/is nicknamed the Bootheel Country, that area where Arizona and New Mexico come together with the Mexican states of Chihuahua and Sonora. Geographically—then and today—it's real rugged real-estate. Demographically—then and today—it's dangerous ground, a sparingly populated gateway for smugglers and outlaws and fugitives jumping jurisdictions, thwarting detection and apprehension and extradition—or trying too.

The particular spot of ground Gus Chenowth ended up laying claim to was situated northeast of Galeyville, Arizona Territory, and southwest of Shakespeare, New Mexico Territory. Although the property was comprised of land in both territories, the headquarters complex and corrals were situated in Grant County (Silver City) at the time Chenowth arrived, but following creation of a new province, Hidalgo County (Lordsburg), that is where the homeplace was and is now staked. The expansive level plain beneath the Pelonicillo Mountains was identified then and today as the San Simon Cienega and Chenowth's claim came to be known as the Cienega Ranch.[79]

People of faint heart were better suited elsewhere. Most of the San Simon Cienega's human traffic was not overrun with whiners or wimps. Many were on the run though: Running from the law or from the U.S. Army's cavalrymen. The Bootheel was the corridor of choice for outlaws herding stolen livestock and bronco Apache who'd bolted the San Carlos Reservation.[80]

From days much earlier and exactitude is impossible, Spanish explorers had constructed an adobe corral with high walls near the water source which would later become the celebrated Cienega Ranch: It was "a relic" of their presence half a century before, but was still utilizable after Gus and Mary had acquired the property. In fact, on occasion, the thick-walled enclosure served as an open-air fortress for the Chenowth family and their anxious neighbors when reports of an Apache outbreak were whistling on the desert winds—carrying embellished prattle and/or horrifying bloody truths.[81] Absent backtracking and trying to cough up a broad spectrum discourse about the rights and/or wrongs of America's Indian policy, or spitting out lame, but politically correct excuses for Apaches marauding and murdering and skewering men, women, and little children on the spit of bloodlust, a to-the-point précis is fitting: Apache danger in the Bootheel was ubiquitous and real.

At Silver City understandably concerned folks resorted to the barbaric policy of their Mexican neighbors below the international borderline, a bounty. Many of Silver City and Grant County's prominent personalities willingly contributed, substantially juicing up an account that would pay $100 "for every head of any Indian that is connected with the band of Fiends who are murdering our fellow citizens."[82] In but short order a newspaper editor puffed:

> The Scalp fund shows up fairly. Enough is subscribed to pay
> for making good Indians of at least 20 of the red devils.[83]

Yes, Gus and Mary Chenoweth and their brood were parked in a perilous place. The locale was not the exclusive domain of "the red devils." The list of devilish white yahoos haunting the area was a Who's Who of the Southwest's borderland badness. Herein it will not be necessary to pause and profile each player, enumerating a partial roster of those living and/or passing through the Bootheel during Gus Chenowth's day will do. The list would include "Curly Bill" Brocius, John "Cherokee Jack" Rogers, Sandy King, William "Russian Bill" Tettenborn, Isaac and Billy Clanton, Johnny Barnes, Zwing Hunt, Arthur DeCloud Burtcher aka "Billy the Kid" Grounds the little brother of Alfred Burtcher aka "Hair-Trigger Johnnie" Dubois, James "Slim Jim" Crane, Bill and Ike Heslett, Milt Hicks, Charles "Pony Diehl" Ray, Jake Gauze, Charley Thomas,

John Peters "John R. Godalmighty" Ringo, William "Rattlesnake Bill" Johnson, Joseph Graves Olney aka Joe Hill, Jack McKenzie, Robert E. "Dutch Bob" Martin, Billy Leonard, and a ne'er-do-well deluxe, the son of Chenowth's nearest neighbor along the New Mexico/Arizona line Nicholas Hughes, Jimmy "Sweetheart of the San Simon" Hughes. That the Chenowths had staked their future lives in a rough neighborhood is borne out by witty 1881 doggerel published in the *Tombstone Epitaph*:

> *Once I owned a bronco*
> *And bought him for a song.*
> *He wasn't very handsome*
> *But he carried me along.*
> *But now I punch my burro*
> *All up and down the hill*
> *For my bronco's gone to San Simon*
> *To carry Curly Bill.*[84]

A later generation of crooks, train and bank robbers, would also sometimes take flight or light in the San Simon's Cienega Ranch vicinity. Gus would know them, too! The oldest Chenowth boy, Charles Augustus, in later life penned his remembrances, saying: "I have known 21 rustlers, all of whom were either hanged or killed."[85] The captivating and secluded Bootheel may have been God's country—but at times it seems even He took a vacation.

Purportedly, and it may be true or partly true, that while hauling rough-cut timber in and around Galeyville, Gus Chenowth had "met a man who offered him the temporary use of his jacal of adobe-plastered pickets at the upper end of the San Simon Cienega. Gus moved his family in, and his benefactor presumably never retuned to reclaim his shack."[86] Tantalizing though it might prove to be, it's not out-of-place to note that even before Gus Chenowth and family made a show at the San Simon Cienega, two of the above cited Wild West characters had together filed a claim on 320 acres. Mr. Joseph Isaac Clanton and Mr. John Peters Ringo knew their joint venture was situated in Grant County, making sure the paperwork was properly filed at the courthouse in Silver City. The aim, according to the documents, was to name their mutually held land the Alfalfa or Cienega Ranch.[87] Had a parson made a deal with devils? *¿Quién sabe?*

At any rate Gus and Mary had settled into the remotely situated Cienega Ranch, raising horses and cattle and children. With dexterity Gus could tattoo the loop of a catch-rope around the knurled horns of a young bull, trip him to the ground, rob him of manhood with a Barlow's sharp blade—and release a new steer to fatten and mature. And just as quick as he could step from the stirrup, at the drop of a hat Gus could issue personalized prayers and a double dose of scripture. He was—in his own way—quite religious, although not denominationally ordained by formality. Gus was a practical preacher—and a very practical man. His strategy for survival in a hostile land was straightforward: Except for quick roping someone into the corral of Christianity, Gus would doggedly stick to minding his own business, not poking around in others' dealings. Translation? Hunted outlaws running through or skirting the Cienega Ranch were most welcome to stop, water their jaded horses and partake of Mary Chenowth's biscuits, beans, and barbecue. As they mounted up to offer thanks and say goodbye, Gus and his family knew not if they headed toward a rising or setting sun—or Old Mexico? When hard-charging lawmen chasing despicable desperadoes made their way to the Cienega Ranch they were welcome to water their horses, sit on the front porch, wolfing-down Mary Chenowth's biscuits, beans, and barbecue. When mounting up to utter thanks and *adios*, they could still be tracking the right outlaw's route—or not![88] Making enemies in the Bootheel was not real smart. Payback could be hell! Neutrality was wise.

What about bronco Apache? They were not welcome at the dinner table, but Gus—the good Christian that he was—a practical Christian—always made sure a fat steer was standing in the cattle pens a good distance from the house. Apaches could butcher and barbecue right there, no need to come to the house, none whatsoever: The unwritten message was damn plain, don't molest me or mine, and I won't bother you or yours'. Cienega Ranch wagons were painted yellow or had a yellow stripe as a marker, a warning. Gus Chenowth was yet the "Yellow Devil." He would scrap or sermonize or kneel and pray for poor departed souls. Bronco Apache were practical people, too. They never raided the Cienega Ranch.

Cherokee Jack Rogers was not smart. Apparently he wasn't too spiritual. And he was a sorry excuse for a highwayman, though he wanted to be a bad ass. The following account, admittedly, is based on hearsay—like Wyatt Earp's assertion he killed Curly Bill—but Gus Chenowth's word was credible. On an overnight trip to town, Gus riding a hot-blooded borrowed horse was accosted by Cherokee Jack Rogers, an eared-back six-shooter in hand. Jack had the drop on Gus. The scalawag's motive was unsophisticated. He would simply trade horses and saddles with Chenowth—at gunpoint—and be on his merry way. With years on the tough road bossing profane tobacco-spittin teamsters, cajoling pigheaded mules, and dodging Apaches, Gus was not shaking in his boots—not due to any fear of a pup. He was the wolf. Feigning submission Chenowth parried: "You wouldn't take an Old Man's Bible, would you?" Cherokee Jack relaxed, figuratively gave himself an approving pat and holstered his handgun. Allowed to fish in the saddlebags—now on the ground—Gus reels in not the Good Book but a big-mouthed and ugly-looking Colt's .45. Cherokee Jack was now playing an upside-down game, and he wasn't laughing—the tables had turned. Gus Chenowth could have outright killed Cherokee Jack, and in that rough and tumble Bootheel sector would have been given a free pass, but he didn't. Gus barked an order for the would-be bandit to jump back on his horse and hightail it down the mountain trail. Cherokee Jack did so with zeal, prompting smiling Gus to verbalize: "Son, you'd make a good soldier. You take orders real good."[89]

Pat O'Day would not feel so benevolent toward Cherokee Jack. In a Galeyville mercantile the fight started and was near finished, O'Day having beaten Cherokee Jack senseless with a three pound single-jack (a miner's short-handled sledgehammer). The storeowner begged Pat not to kill him in the store, but drag him outside first. O'Day obeyed. Bystanders there were many, but Cherokee Jack was a constant troublemaker. He was friendless and his predicament was futile. Grabbing a Springfield .45-70 Trapdoor rifle, O'Day "dragged the inert body down to the slag heap by the Texas smelter, from where, moments later, a shot was heard . . . ." Right fast a legal Coroner's Jury was impaneled, and right fast they rendered their finding: "Death from gunshot wound at the hands of someone unknown to the jury." Dressed for his trip to the Pearly Gates or the raging inferno below, Cherokee Jack Rogers was rolled up in a dirty tarp and planted in a shallow grave "next to the road downstream from camp a little way."[90]

Another tale about Gus Chenowth may register as apocryphal—of dubious authenticity—but it is a deeply trenched part of the Chenowth family's folklore. Prematurely and categorically and condescendingly dismissing it out-of-hand might prove embarrassing for the writer or historian perhaps someday forced to address a new paper discovery inside that dusty trunk in an attic. Although not supported by creditable ironclad citation, it's been written and believed by not just a few, that on one occasion Gus Chenowth, "with his notoriously short fuse" was preaching and proselytizing behind swinging-doors of a Galeyville saloon. Purportedly a wandering nitwit had surpassed the sensible limit of tarantula juice, and in some form or fashion invoked the wrath of a lecturing lay preacher. Who threw the first punch goes unspoken; Gus nets credit for the last. The sloshed loud-mouth was pummeled to the hardwood floor by a powerfully arching blow to the jaw. Knuckles on Chenowth's bloodied and bruised right hand throbbed. Mr. Drunk just died.

The unfortunate fellow's necked snapped when Gus delivered his punch, or he broke it when he hit the floor, or least likely of all, he suffered a heart attack while fast tumbling into eternal rest. Next afternoon, the deceased in no condition to register the slightest protest, Gus "obligingly preached his funeral." Fact or folklore is not the issue. The tale, true or false, fit well with the public's down-to-earth picture of preacher Gus Chenowth.[91]

The public was not kept in the dark about another aspect of Gus Chenowth's absorbing life's story even though it's somewhat bizarre for a guy seeding and fertilizing the Good Lord's word. Gus Chenowth was fermenting something else. He was a whiskey maker: By some tallies a pretty darn good one too! His little operation behind Rattlesnake Hill opposite Cienega Ranch headquarters was not by any means elaborate, but the still's condensers reliably and regularly dripped efficiency. Taking into account the Cienega Ranch's geographical remoteness, for Gus and his helpmate sons, it was not crucial to slip behind Rattlesnake Hill under a shining moon. Distilling and distributing spirituous liquor dealt Gus no moral or ethical dilemmas. If wine in a goblet was okay for the Holy Land, whiskey in a tin cup was not too debauched for the Bootheel: Except that silly part about rendering unto Caesar. For that untidiness Gus balked. What that damn county tax assessor didn't know was okay. If God didn't snitch—Gus wouldn't either. Once one of those pesky fellows came to the Cienega Ranch snooping, inquiring and looking for those rumored taxable assets and prompt payment of the mandatory liquor licensing fee. Gus and Mary and the kiddos stood pat and quiet. The bureaucrat's search was vigorous but wasted effort. Climbing into his buckboard for the return trip to the county seat, the disenchanted deputy sheriff felt his leg bump against something, a burlap bag tightly wrapped. The cork peeking out the top stymied but did not eradicate the aroma—that pleasing and tempting fragrance—of sour mash whiskey wafting from the brown gallon jug. The perplexed tax man tilted his head and turned to Gus for an explanation. Chenowth winked. The tax man, eyes fixed to the front, picked up the reins and launched the wagon forward.[92] Maybe he'd just take a nip and a nap on the way back.

The Bootheel area was sparsely populated. Geographically the Cienega Ranch was isolated. Via uncomplicated linkage Rattlesnake Hill was, too, an out-of-the-way piece of rocky ground. Purportedly, and it's believable, on at least one occasion a wandering cowboy stumbled onto the still site. Or, he had purposely charted it as an objective. A stash of select whiskey went missing. At a regional Saturday night dance the slick profiteer was selling that siphoned bootleg whiskey. Unbeknownst to the dispenser of distilled spirits, and despite their blurred religious upbringing, Chenowth boys were in attendance. Girls were scarce in the Bootheel. The whiskey had not been repackaged or rebottled. It was identifiable as Chenowth whiskey—by Chenowths. Perhaps they hung their hats on Good Book chapter and verse for assessing a level of on-the-spot punishment. In the real world— apart from the theoretical playgrounds of weighty armchair thinkers—some things are best left unwritten or unspoken to most outsiders. The Lord works in mysterious ways. If need be, so did the Chenowth tribe. Liquor theft ceased.[93]

As introducing the offspring of Gus and Mary into the narrative was somewhat out of synch with an exact chronology, it is important to note that the senior Chenowth was not out of step with courthouse legalities. There would not be even the slightest injustice with asserting that his Salt River Valley "Relinquishment" profoundly influenced his concept of complying with land title laws and accessing his legal claims to precious water for irrigation. Voluminous are the entries in Grant County Deed Books

associated with Gus and Mary Chenowth's acquisition and disposition of financial interests in this or that piece of real-estate and
their partnerships with others concerning ownership and percentage rights to ditches and canals, such as the San Simon Farming
Canal, the Atlantic & Pacific Canal, the Cave Creek Reservoir, San
Simon Valley Land & Water Company, and the San Simon Land
and Cattle Company. Making sure the paperwork was up to snuff,
courthouse records reflect that even Gus and Noah Haydon guaranteed the validity of their personal transaction when the former
purchased "two wagons and six good work horses and harness"
from the latter for $400 at Steins Pass, New Mexico Territory.[94]

The reader captivated by Gus Chenowth's profile may effort-
lessly accept at face value, or if that's troubling, conduct first-hand
primary and secondary source research on their own, but the outcome, in the end, will register the same: The Bootheel was rich with
Apache history—good and bad, spellbinding and bloody. Gus was
tuned to reality—bronco Apache could strike at any time. One of the
most harrowing sorties came during November 1885, "a slashing
raid that rivaled the greatest such adventures in Apache history."[95]
A dozen warriors captained by Josanie (Ulzana in Burt Lancaster's
1972 movie *Ulzana's Raid*), brother of the noted Chiricahua
Apache raider Chihuahua, jumped north across the borderline, unit-
ing with a slightly larger band secreting themselves in the Florida
Mountain hideaways south of the Southern Pacific Railroad's tracks
connecting Deming and Lordsburg.[96] From that near impregnable
stronghold they sallied forth in a series of lightning strikes. One
of the unfortunate southwestern New Mexicans caught off guard
was the indomitable man-killing ex-Grant County deputy sheriff
Dan Tucker and his mining partner for the day, William Graham.
A blurb in the region's *Southwest Sentinel* alerted the readership:

> when a small party of Indians suddenly came on them.
> Tucker and his partner had no arms except six-shooters, and
> they were driving a buggy or buckboard. They drove as hard
> as they could until they came to the siding where a boxcar
> was standing, into which they climbed. The Indians kept
> them there for sometime, riding around the car but keeping
> carefully out of shot. Seeing that they would be unabled to
> do their intended victims any harm so long as they chose to
> remain in the car, they finally rode off, and Tucker and his
> companion made their escape to Deming.[97]

Tactically—and smartly—Josanie had subdivided his broncos into small but operationally hard-hitting platoons. Thus proportioned, these Apaches literally terrorized southwestern New Mexico and southeastern Arizona Territories, looting and burning and killing and gleefully gang raping Andrew Yeater's wife.[98] Traveling in excess of 1200 miles, stealing and wearing out as many as 250 horses, Josanie's month-long foray had also netted Apaches—with the loss of but one man—near 40 lifeless bodies on the backtrack.[99] Gus Chenowth had not ratcheted their body-count upward, but he came damn close. At some point during their four-week havoc-wreaking incursion and while yet in the Bootheel, Josanie's indefatigable raiders espied in the distance a single mule-drawn wagon, a yellow wagon, driven by a lone white-headed and aging occupant.[100] Apaches were exploiters of opportunity and here, right before them, was a golden opportunity. Providentially Gus Chenowth saw them, too. Running from danger was not in his psyche, never had been! Obediently the mules answered to the leather lines' unexpected tug and an authoritative "Whoa." Standing upright in the wagon, Gus raised one hand high—extending it toward the Heavens, chanting prayers he trusted would be heard. Just in case though, his other fist clutched a heavy octagon-barreled Sharps' buffalo gun: A long-range rifle that could in the colloquial speak of Southwesterners: "Keep the wolf away from the door." Apache wouldn't be afforded the chance to toy with this boy. Did they really want to invoke the wrath of this guy's God? Or risk the fire-belching roaring and test the tearing thumps from his big .50 caliber? No, trading Apache lives for a couple of mules or simply to fetch a trophy scalp would not have been an equitable bargain.[101] Gus went on his way, the Apaches went their way.[102] Both had passed the test of good sense.

Another fellow, a quite well known fellow, would not exhibit good sense—or good manners. The year following Josanie's murderous—but admittedly daring—raid and his slippage across the borderline into Old Mexico, the curtain was drawing to a close for San Carlos Reservation's boundary jumping bronco Apaches. Geronimo and his holdouts will be of particular interest for the narrative in hand. Though perhaps it flies in the face of popular cultural correctness, there's a truth vis-à-vis Mr. Geronimo: Many, if not most, nineteenth-century Apaches didn't like him. Unfortunately the old warrior's omen was that of a raven, "one who always brings trouble and lives always on death."[103] In this case, however, the immediate dissatisfaction for the Chenowth tribe was not with Geronimo but with a haughty and rude—in their minds—U.S. Army man.

This piece of oral history may not be welded tight with the conclusiveness of papers archived at some historical repository— but testing its veracity is not a wise choice—not while visiting with Chenowth descendants. It's concrete and immovable. Subsequent to Geronimo's bending to an irreversible surrender in a spot not too far south of the Cienega Ranch, Skeleton Canyon, the unarmed Apaches and military escort were making their way north. The ultimate destination was Bowie Station just inside the Arizona Territorial border. According to one writer—although not source specific—General Nelson Miles and Geronimo, along with a few other soldiers and Chiricahuas, were traveling in advance of the main body of beleaguered Apache prisoners and their company of brass-buttoned guards.[104] The less troublesome geography though, necessitated a northbound journey just inside the New Mexico Territorial line—right through the eastern edge of the Cienega Ranch. Thirsting horses were in want of a drink and rest: Men, white and Apache, wanted a quick break. At Chenowth headquarters was that ever precious commodity—Water. And, too, a special treat: Watermelons. Gus Chenowth was absent when Geronimo's renegades and Nelson Miles and his soldiers made their abrupt September 1886 show at the Cienega Ranch. Their visit would be memorable for Mary Chenowth.[105]

Miles wanted, more-or-less ordered, that Mrs. Chenowth prepare a quick meal for him and the small cadre of officers. Enlisted men and Apaches could find calories in the watermelon patch. Impatiently and recklessly the soldiers tromped and tore through the melons, satisfying their lust but fanatically destroying as much or more than they were consuming. The Apaches, on the other hand, gorged on the luscious red watermelon meat, but were careful not to dislodge any vines or waste a deliciously dripping bite. After the stopover, Mary Chenowth mentioned that times in the Bootheel were hard—and she had many mouths to feed—could General Miles spare any coins for his and his men's noonday repast? He begrudgingly coughed up 50¢ and accented his brand of thank you with a stinging criticism of Mary as a cook, adding that the fare was lousy. As far as the watermelons devoured or destroyed—he'd pay not a penny. Not one goddamned red cent![106]

Purportedly, and again there is not a sound basis for challenge, before departing Geronimo removed money from a leather pouch stitched to his belt, and placed the coins in Mary's callused hand, proffering thanks—a genuine heartfelt thanks, she thought. Gus Chenowth returned home to Mary's fresh news—and the little grievance about Miles' ill-mannered behavior. Family lore asserts that he immediately saddled a fast horse with lots of bottom (staying power) and chased after Geronimo and Miles.[107] He overhauled them, too! Then, accordingly Gus contemptuously upbraided Miles, issuing him the what-for in speech not suited for a pulpit—or anywhere else. By the best guesstimate, the flabbergasted general wisely let Gus vent, smartly shrugged off any protest, and continued with his plan for delivering Geronimo and the Apache prisoners for their date with destiny—a train trip to Florida.[108]

Subsequent to the Apache problem diminishing and the ranks of pale-skinned ne'er-do-wells somewhat thinned, one might mistakenly surmise the Bootheel was in for a spell of tranquility. After all: Russian Bill and Sandy King had been suspended from an overhead beam in a Shakespeare Hotel; Billy the Kid Grounds had been killed at Chandler's Milk Ranch; the McLaury brothers, Frank and Tom, plus nineteen-year-old Billy Clanton had been gunned down near Tombstone's OK Corral; Zwing Hunt had escaped the Cochise County Jail only to meet his Maker in the Chiricahua Mountains; Billy Leonard and Harry "The Kid" Head, were pushing up daisies after being bushwhacked by Bill and Ike Heslet; then it was time for the Heslet brothers to suffer the turn-around is but unfair play, ghastly giving up the ghost in a streaming hail of gunfire; John Ringo had finalized a suicide on the banks of Turkey Creek; one way or the other—upright or laid out—Curly Bill had forevermore departed the neighborhood; Morgan Earp, Frank Stilwell, and Florentino Cruz had been viciously assassinated, gangland style; and Wyatt B. S. Earp, John Henry "Doc" Holliday and their dubious affiliates had scampered out of the region like so many humiliated rats, running hard ahead of lawfully drawn Pima County murder warrants.[109] Well, the ever rascally Warren Earp did make an impressive show four years later—about the time a dispirited Geronimo had surrendered. An astute U.S. Army officer, Captain Gustavus Cheyney Doane, pathetically sizing-up the Earp clan's youngest brother as "the most contemptible character I ever saw, [Warren] Earp of Colton, a murderer who was driven from Tombstone. . . ."[110]

The vacuum of Bootheel nefariousness and banditry would soon be backfilled. Perhaps most notably by the High Fives: Will "Black Jack" Christian and his older brother Bob, Code Young, Bob Hayes, and George West Musgrave.[111] Also riding to the bugle of Bootheel regional criminality were such well-known misfits as Edwin "Shoot-'em-up Dick" Cullen, Will Carver, Dave Atkins and the Ketchum brothers, Samuel W. "Sam" and Thomas Edward "Tom," also sometimes referred to—mistakenly—as "Black Jack."[112] For damn certain Tom Ketchum could be as mean as a Bengal tiger with a toothache, but his treacherous and murderous temperament didn't faze Gus Chenowth one iota. The part-time parson and full-time tough cookie penned and had the note sent to bad ass Tom Ketchum: Steal one head from the Cienega Ranch remuda or cattle herd and daylight would shine through the .50 caliber hole in his midsection.[113] Turning the other cheek was just fine for Jesus, but in the lonesome Bootheel turning up the heat for a *mal hombre* was more sensible—provided one had enough sand to cover the ground he stood on. Gus Chenowth had sand.

Particularizing the interpersonal relationships Gus had with this or that Southwestern owlhoot or lawman is likely a task unachievable. On the other hand one sad story touching Chenowth plays in the theater of Wild West drama. The sheriff of Grant County, Baylor Shannon, and his posse comprised of Frank M. Galloway, Steve Birchfield, and Frank McGlinchy were on the hunt after bandits. In the wild and woolly San Simon Valley when it was time to make camp the lawmen, fearing that they could be ambushed, opted to post a guard—taking turns standing watch. After midnight a noise awakened Sheriff Shannon. He nudged his pallet companions, Birchfield and McGlinchy. The three bleary-eyed lawdogs scented something was amiss, detecting movement about fifty feet from camp—coming toward them. Naturally the verbal challenge was hurled. There was no response. The sheriff gave the command: "Shoot—Shoot!" The shadowy form dropped to the ground, dead. Then it dawned on the uptight trio, Frank Galloway was missing in action. Shock washed across the law-men's awareness: They had killed their own man, who with his coat collar pulled up around his ears, had been answering Nature's call. Friendly fire had finished Frank—though he surely would have said it wasn't too friendly. Thoroughly humiliated and embarrassed and grief-stricken the posse did manage to transport Galloway's body to the Cienega Ranch. From there with the help of Gus and one of his wagons the dead deputy was removed to Lordsburg, then to Deming for burial.[114]

By any measure the Bootheel was wild country, only inhabited by the hearty. The Chenowth brood fit well. Gus and Mary—absent any meaningful argument—with willpower, stamina, and guts had carved their niche in southwestern New Mexico Territory's rugged ranch country. Survival in an unforgiving land cried for everyone to pitch in, do their fair share. So, it might be demonstrable that Chenowth boys familiarized themselves with cow work, but the girls did, too! In fact, while she might not have reached the status of a genuine tophand, Loyola Agnes "Ola" was at home horseback and quite handy with a catch-rope. A drugstore cowgirl she was not.

The next major episode in his life would be a real heartbreaker— not only for Gus and Mary, but other Grant County families as well; it's not an upbeat or pretty story. Their second oldest surviving boy, Howard Pinckney, they could be proud of—on the one hand. He had beneficially attended the New Mexico State Normal School at Silver City, earning solid educational credentials, which was not too customary for ranch-raised boys of the time. Classroom schooling could be damned, though: Howard Chenowth wanted to make his mark and money horseback, cowboying for the oversized Diamond A Ranch—an outfit with an extensive variety of divisions and cow-camps scattered throughout southwestern New Mexico Territory.[115]

Genetics and environment and everyday life's experiences build the person. Howard was born of tough stock in a tough place living a tough life. In the wee morning hours of 28 August 1904 he would have a tough time at Silver City. The evening before, accompanied by a Diamond A foreman, Pat Nunn, and fellow cowboy Martin "Mart" Kennedy, formerly of Abilene, Texas, Howard had ridden into Silver City for a hard-earned holiday of honky-tonking and hurrahing.

As the night wore down, the blood/alcohol level in Howard's veins spiked—appreciably so. By midnight he was mind-numbingly drunk: Totally reckless and stupidly smashed. Later events will prove Howard wasn't bullet proof, but for the moment he felt himself ten feet tall, especially atop his favorite Diamond A horse Bonito, which he foolishly tried to ride into Silver City's Palace Saloon.[116] For the short go such tomfoolery was forestalled though soberness did not follow. The clock struck midnight and Howard and Mart were mindless and yet thoroughly drunk. The partying was ongoing. For that night, hurrahing not hangovers was on the cowboy's agenda. At somewhere near 2 a.m. Pat Nunn, who had earlier separated from Howard and Mart, had something on his agenda too: Getting back to the Apache Tejo cow-camp. His order to the cowboys was step into stirrups and strike for camp, a charge forthright and easily understood. And, one easily defied. Mr. Mart was in no mood to quit the fun. His bad attitude was instantly decipherable: Work and Mr. Nunn could go to hell. Chenowth was betwixt and between.

In but a heartbeat it went haywire. Foreman Pat Nunn, according to a guy in the know, was "reckless and just full of the devil."[117] There were few men in the southwestern New Mexico world that could berate Pat Nunn with a string of curse words and in-your-face insubordination, and Mart Kennedy wasn't one of them. After peeling his gunbelt and pitching it to the sidewalk, Pat Nunn jumped off his horse with every intention of dispensing a big dose of comeuppance. Mart soon found himself on the tail end of an old-fashioned ass whipping. At this point Howard was but a spectator, but that changed when he heard Mart cry for help or simply decided no man could abuse his good friend. Howard—quick as a cat—picked up Pat's six-shooter, a Colt's .45, (SN 221976), and purposefully popped a cap.[118] The bullet punched through Nunn's corduroy vest and smashed into his brand new pocket watch. Chenowth's second shot grazed Pat's forehead, "tearing away his eyebrows." The third bullet, well, it just went wild—somewhere.[119] Pat Nunn, fearing Chenowth's next shot would cash his ticket, ducked into the Club House Saloon.

Rushing to the distinct sounds of gunfire was Grant County Deputy Sheriff Elmore Murray. Unhesitatingly he tried to disarm Howard, but to no avail. His grappling with the gun-wielding Howard was made even more problematic when Mart jumped into the affray. It was a three-way tussle, a life and death struggle. Also hastening to the hysteria unfolding on Silver City streets was forty-five-year-old Perfecto Rodriquez, an unarmed ex-Deputy U.S. Marshal and local lawman. Perfecto may or may not have heard Mart's bid to Howard: "Shoot the sons-of-bitches," but he probably didn't hear the six-shooter's exploding report or feel any pain.[120] Howard's fourth shot had ripped into his heart and Perfecto Rodriquez was slammed to the street, his death instantaneous.[121] Naturally such hubbub also attracted the attention of Silver City's town marshal, William H. Kilburn, a son-in-law of the well-known New Mexico Territorial lawman Harvey H. Whitehill. Chenowth's fifth shot, the last round in the Colt's cylinder, plowed into Kilburn's neck, knocking him to the dirt, paralyzed.[122] Thus disentangled from their adversaries Howard and Mart fled up Texas Street and into the womb of darkness for awhile—a little while.

Testifying to the drunkenness of Kennedy is brain-dead easy: Within the hour Mart ambled and stumbled into the Palace Saloon: He just wanted one more drink. The arrest was effortless. The apprehension of Chenowth was not effortless. Howard was spotted hiding behind boxes on the porch of Samuel Lindauer's store. At first Howard ignored the pleas to surrender—Now! Good sense finally won out—almost. Howard came out from behind the crates, but failed to heed orders to drop the six-shooter. So, a single charge of No. 6 birdshot from the right barrel of John Collier's shotgun dropped Chenowth and—correspondingly—Pat Nunn's empty Colt's .45 to the porch's floor. Subsequent to examination at the town's hospital and a determination that the wounds would not kill the wild-eyed shooter, Howard was lodged in the Grant County Jail.[123] At the Preliminary Hearing the justice of the peace found there was sufficient Probable Cause, and ordered that Howard be confined without bail, pending action of the grand jury.[124]

Although a writer for the *Silver City Independent*, acting as a psychic, haughtily penned that Howard's "actions seemed to indicate that he did not even know where he was," the journalist's piece did not undermine the prosecutor's case. The die had almost been cast with the uncalled-for death of Perfecto Rodriquez, but when it was announced that Marshal Kilburn had, too, given up the ghost due to Howard's doings, the outcome was a foregone finale: Conviction for murder.[125] Twenty-three-year-old Howard Chenowth luckily skated across the scaffold, but he did catch hard time—fifty years. He would, however, remain in the Grant County Jail pending his appeal to the New Mexico Territorial Supreme Court—but not for too long.

Gus Chenowth perhaps figured that if the Lord God Almighty owned plenty of forgiveness, well, he too could forgive—but not forget. He would not—despite any man's law—desert his boy to desolately endure fifty years of his life behind tall prison walls. Details on the frontend are sketchy, almost certainly purposefully, but details on the backend are not. Purportedly Gus Chenowth told his oldest boys they'd have to liberate Howard from the law's clutches, and if they thought that too challenging, he'd just take the matter into his hands and do the job himself. The family was tight—and tough! Gus could look forward to his Christmas present being delivered to the Cienega Ranch—his boys would play Santa Claus.[126]

After reading the boldfaced type in Silver City's *Enterprise*—**Daring Rescue of Howard Chenowth**—Gus did not have to look hard for answers. All he had to do was mosey out to that big haystack at the Cienega Ranch, the one with the hollowed out secret room below, and ask Howard. The Christmas Day jailbreak had come off absent a hitch. Outside some of Howard's siblings—there are reports sisters were involved—held getaway horses. Inside the dungeon one of his brothers, mostly likely Hale, had stuck a six-shooter in jailer Frank Watson's and trustee B. F. Gooch's faces saying "Throw up your hands boys, I mean business. . . . I want Howard. . . ." At the entrance to Chenowth's austere steel cage the purpose of the audacious mission uncorked: "Howard, I've come after you." Matter-of-factly, according to newspaper citations, Howard replied: "Well, if you have come after me, I guess I'll have to go." And he, and they, went.[127]

Generally it was thought that Howard had—by a relay of fast horses—slipped across the line into Old Mexico.[128] How much due diligence Sheriff Charles A. Farnsworth burned up hunting for the escapee would fall into the realm of guesswork, but there's little doubt all the lawmen were familiar with the Cienega Ranch and Howard's family. Who among them wanted to test Gus Chenowth's gumption and grit and gunplay handiness? Was the Cienega Ranch off-limits? There's not even a hint any of those lawmen entertained an idea that Gus would rat out his boy. If God wanted them to know where to find Howard, He'd tell them! Gus wouldn't—and didn't. After lying low several months, when lawmen were focused on other newsy and exciting events Howard chose to abandon his haystack lair forevermore. Gus bid his son farewell, knowing in his heart of hearts that he would probably never see Howard again.

Were one to follow Howard's footprints after vamoosing from
the Grant County jailhouse and subsequent to shedding claustro-
phobic confinement of an underground hideaway at the Cienega
Ranch, the journey would wind down in Brazil. There, under
the assumed name Charles Martin, fugitive Howard Chenowth
would do what he knew best, cowboy and ramrod on Brazilian
cattle empires dwarfing those typically found in America.[129]
Howard may have been a fugitive from New Mexico Territory
justice—one with a $600 price on his head—but he was cap-
tured in South America by one Miss Yulé Butendorp, a beauty of
German extraction living with her ranching family, folks heavily
invested in the Brazilian cattle industry. The couple was joined
together in matrimony, complying with civil laws of the *Estado
de Matto Grosso*.[130] From this union seven children would issue:
Daisy, Amos, Douglas, Ola, Ula, Frances, and Ruby.[131] Although
Howard would be devastated by the death of Yulé during childbirth, he would eventually be handed a governor's pardon—some
say after payment of a whopping bribe—and return to New
Mexico Territory, his Portuguese-speaking children in tow, grandchildren Gus would never see.

Spring was breaking open throughout New Mexico's Bootheel,
but life's book was closing for John Augustus Chenowth. At age
78 the pioneering warrior knew his allotted time on earth was
drawing near. Prudently he executed a Last Will and Testament on
the second day of April 1913.[132] Within the month, on the twenty-
fifth Gus Chenowth—due to the infirmities of old age—quietly
slipped to the other side at the Cienega Ranch.[133] Gus was buried
onsite. Mary Chenowth devoted her life to the children and grandchildren, never remarrying or removing from Arizona. Thirty
years after saying goodbye to Gus, Mary succumbed to natural
causes on July 27, 1943; she was 92.[134]

Taking measure of the man in John Augustus Chenowth's
case is easy. He owned the heart of a lion, the ferociousness of a
man-eating tiger, the stubbornness of a cross-eyed mule, and the
faithfulness of Old Shep. He danced to no man's fiddle. Gus knew
the Bible chapter and verse, and those ancient scriptures could be
unraveled to suit expediency and convenience if called for. In the
context of exploring issues of Old West criminal justice in New
Mexico's rough Bootheel from the viewpoint of Gus there was
God's Law, Man's Law, and Chenowth's Law.

John Augustus "Gus" Chenowth, a plucky southwestern preacher capable of sermonizing or shooting, and his wife Mary Murray Chenowth, a true pioneering lady: Emblematic of the species that really "Won the West." *Courtesy Rhetta Smith.*

Cienega Ranch headquarters in the rugged Bootheel region of southwestern New Mexico, the hazardous and bloody playground of bronco Apaches, Mexican bandits, and blue-eyed killers and cow thieves. *Courtesy Rhetta Smith.*

Jimmy "Sweetheart of the San Simon" Hughes. Living and roaming the Bootheel and into southeastern Arizona Territory, Jimmy earned a big reputation—not a good one though. *Courtesy David Johnson.*

John Augustus Chenowth by vocation and avocation was fascinated with wagons. Here, at the Cienega Ranch, Gus poses with but one of his early day conveyances. *Courtesy Charles Randolph Chenowth.*

John Peters Ringo. He too roamed the Bootheel of New Mexico and the streets of Tombstone, Cochise County, Arizona Territory. John Ringo's authenticated man-killing tally didn't match his hard reputation, but, then neither did the factual count of his speciously puffed adversaries. *Courtesy of David Johnson.*

Joseph Graves Olney aka Joe Hill of Hoo Doo War fame. A bona fide six-shooting tough cookie from Texas. He claimed new stomping grounds in southwestern New Mexico and southeastern Arizona. *Courtesy David Johnson.*

Even the Chenowth girls were top-hands. Here, Ola has tagged a fat calf and is dragging it to the Cienega Ranch branding fire. *Courtesy Rhetta Smith.*

The notorious Geronimo, subsequent to his final surrender to U.S
Army personnel, during a stopover at the Chenowth's Cienega Ranch,
he actually thanked and paid for the Apache prisoners' partaking of
a visit to Mary Chenowth's watermelon patch. According to family
lore, a haughty General Nelson Miles did not, and was rude and
condescending. *Courtesy Nita Stewart Haley Memorial Library and J. Evetts
Haley History Center.*

Gus Chenowth and sons, plus one. From L to R: Howard, Charles, Hale, John Augustus, Earl, and little Barbara Kennedy. *Courtesy Charles Randolph Chenowth.*

Howard Chenowth, a student at the Normal School in Silver City, New Mexico Territory, and later a Diamond A cowboy. During a drunken nighttime spree downtown, he killed two peace officers, was arrested, broke jail, and disappeared—resurfacing as Charles Martin in Brazil. *Courtesy Rhetta Smith.*

Charles A. Chenowth, oldest of the surviving Chenowth boys, for a time worked at the San Bernardino Ranch, along the Mexican border east of Douglas, Arizona, owned and operated by the legendary Southwestern frontiersman, cattleman and lawman, John Horton Slaughter. Here, Charles is standing behind the bearded John Slaughter, bareheaded, beside the cowboy hat wearing Lewis Jorgensen. *Courtesy Charles Randolph Chenowth.*

Archaic gravesite of John Augustus "Gus" Chenowth at the Cienega Ranch Cemetery in the remote borderland—the Bootheel—of southwestern New Mexico: Both the country and the man were tough. *Courtesy Jan Devereaux.*

I'm Shot All to Pieces, Everything Quiet

9

James Dallas Dunaway was born into a violent world: Texas during the tumultuous 1870s. Comanche and Kiowa and Apache were raiding for reward and revenge, Mexican bandits were breeching the Rio Grande slaying and stealing, all the while busy blue-eyed feudists and merciless desperadoes were fanning the flames of lawlessness with acts of mayhem and murder. Texas was a mess.

The disorder was no deterrent to William E. Dunaway. Subsequent to his mother dying, William left his Little Rock, Arkansas, home as but a distant memory, traveling to Texas with the Richard Loomis King family who were migrating to the Lone Star State from Mobile, Alabama. They settled in Travis County, south and a touch west of Austin, the county seat. In due time, William married Richard King's sixteen-year-old daughter, Mary Elizabeth "Betty." William successfully acquired a "blackland farm" and operated a cotton gin originally owned by his mother-in-law, Nancy Bradshaw King. The little community of Manchaca was home to the happy couple, and the birthplace of their first-born child, James Dallas Dunaway, who had initially seen light of day on February 12, 1874.[1]

Prior to crossing into the onset of his teenage years, James Dallas, accompanied by his parents and three younger brothers, Arthur Hugh "Chick," William Ernest, and Dollie Fred, relocated to Llano, Llano County in the bluebonnet-studded Texas Hill Country. There William began trading in cattle and later took employment as a Llano County deputy sheriff. At one point William assumed the duties of jailer. The family moved into the living quarters at the county lockup in use at the time.[2] Although it's not quantifiable with hard proofs, a dab of common sense coupled with James Dunaway's latter-day work history would suggest that this is about the time he became infatuated with the idea of someday becoming a Texas lawman.

Just how much William Dunaway and his boys knew or did not know about the hard luck befalling some of Llano County's lawmen is nebulous. The county's first sheriff, Samuel Lee Lockhart, had been stabbed to death by a disgruntled gambler wielding a butcher knife. Somewhat later, probably after the William Dunaway family had relocated to Llano County, Deputy Sheriff James B. O'Bannon was mortally gunned down with his own revolver, after prisoner C. C. Davis had wrestled it away from him during a jailhouse fracas. Beyond doubt the Dunaways were residing in Llano County when Deputy Thomas H. Nowlin was shot and killed just across the county line in neighboring San Saba County while attempting to serve an arrest warrant. And, too, they were Llano County citizens when an ex-sheriff of Llano County, Matthew Caldwell Roberts, passionately engaged his brother-in-law, also an ex-sheriff of Llano County, Benjamin Franklin "Ben" Beeson, in a downtown Llano gunfight. Ben Beeson died leaking blood onto the town's dirt street, while Matt Roberts survived but suffered at least one life-threatening bullet wound.[3]

Llano County was pretty, and pretty tough, too! So was Mr. James Dallas "Jim" Dunaway. Perhaps he was, in the final breakdown, a little too tough. Nonetheless, while yet in this twenties he pinned on the law-enforcing badge, becoming Llano's city marshal.[4]

Exactly where, why, or how he picked up the nickname is indistinct but someone or several folks hung the tag "Toots" around his neck. Perhaps he was a real ringtail-tooter, a euphemism characterizing fellows who'd battle a grizzly bear with switch—or guys who'd just as soon go to a fight as a frolic. From time to time he may have had to deal with hard-core *mal hombres* but as city marshal misbehaving boys caused him much headache and heartburn—and a most unwanted dowsing with urine from the jailhouse toilet. That nasty soaking soured his disposition, maybe. At least one youngster thought as much, uncharitably writing years later that he clearly thought "that 'Toots' was the black sheep of the family. He used to always like to draw his gun when he was sure he could get the 'drop' on the other fellow."[5]

Good man or mean man or simply a misunderstood man, either way, Jim Dunaway had pinned a lawman's badge to his vest.

He had also pinned on a boutonniere, walking Miss Annie Speegle down the aisle and across the threshold, *circa* 1894. From this union four children would be born, and mentioning them now is not inappropriate: Alva Ray, Clive Speegle, Fred, and James Dallas, Jr. Later Jim Dunaway would marry for a second time, to Hallie Dunlap (*circa* 1905). From this joining together two kiddos would issue, Dan and Halline. But this is not a recap of the children's stories. The narrative belongs to their father, a career-minded law enforcer.[6]

Jim Dunaway for whatever reason opted to forgo being city marshal and become a Ranger. Although he enlisted with the Ranger Force at Llano on 6 July 1903, the actual oath of office was administered on the eighth day of July, in faraway West Texas at Fort Hancock. The new recruit had held up his right hand before an El Paso County justice of the peace and was sworn in as a private in the Ranger Force, officially assigned to Company B, then commanded by Captain William Jesse "Bill" McDonald.[7]

Already an experienced lawman, Jim Dunaway didn't shy away from making arrests. Before the month was out Dunaway and two other Rangers arrested three fellows for shooting up the town of Fort Hancock, taking them before the local magistrate for adjudication.[8] The following month in the process of tracking a suspected mule thief he single-handedly arrested John McCain while the suspect was in the act of "robbing" (more likely burglarizing) a "T&P Caboose."[9] During September 1903 Private Dunaway assisted Captain McDonald on an investigation at Marfa, Presidio County. Mr. L. N. Holbert, the county attorney, according to McDonald "had been taken from the hotel by a mob and seriously beaten." Subsequent to their investigation, Texas Rangers Dunaway and McDonald had proficiently identified the perpetrators, but, in the end, the victim fearing reprisals for prosecution prevailed on the district attorney to drop the filing of criminal charges. A weak-kneed complainant was a cross lawmen had to bear from time to time—then or now. For the next two months Private Jim Dunaway was assigned to "quarantine duty" at Eagle Pass, Maverick County, where he made an occasional misdemeanor arrest.[10] After returning to the headquarters camp, Dunaway arrested an alleged thief in El Paso County before 1903 closed.[11]

As the new year of 1904 kicked off, Ranger Privates Jim Dunaway and C. T. Ryan found themselves working the Big Bend Country. Before the month was out they had arrested three fellows for unlawfully carrying handguns, locking them in the jail at Marfa, Presidio County. Private Dunaway then arrested an armed robbery suspect, turning him over to El Paso County authorities for detention and disposition.[12] Then, well-nigh unbelievable considering the far-flung jurisdictional territory he had been working in West Texas, Private Dunaway was ordered to deep East Texas for temporary duty, yet a Company B assignment—the wheels had come off in Trinity County and thereabouts. So thought the Adjutant General, and so knew Captain Bill McDonald. Of a strip of ground known locally as Kittrell's Cut-Off, the company captain had this to say, not hesitantly declaring it "was probably one of the most lawless places you could find anywhere . . . Many murders have been committed there and no one ever convicted for them. . . . If a whole community has no use for law and order it's not worth while to try to enforce such things. You've got to stand over a place like that with a gun to make it behave, and when you catch a man, no matter what the evidence is against him, they'll turn him loose. In Groveton . . . they had only two law-respecting officers—the district clerk and the county attorney . . . and the county attorney they killed."[13] Women and children flat stayed away from town on Saturdays.[14] What Captain Bill McDonald failed to mention was that part of East Texas owned a protracted and systemic cauldron of lawlessness: Definitely long before his appearance in Trinity County. In fact, that piney-woods section was home turf for a yahoo with near as much name recognition as the Texas Rangers themselves: John Wesley "Little Arkansas" Hardin.[15]

And much later, into the early twentieth-century, even spiffily decked out Trinity County lawyers carrying smoke-belching six-shooters was no anomaly. East Texas dispute resolutions outside the courtroom were commonplace. One personal squabble at Groveton between a pair of attorney brothers on one side and a Trinity County constable, a husband and father of six, on the other, ended up netting—after the fireworks—a dead Precinct 1 lawman and a grieving chap filing legal briefs and arguing litigated cases before the bench by himself.[16]

Though it demands a short chronological leap and then a return to the natural order of storytelling, characterizing law enforcing actions and criminal justice matters in Trinity County is relevant—and in a perverted way, somewhat entertaining: The lackluster performance of one sheriff, who had made no investigation into a mysterious Trinity County homicide, was brought to light after the victim's mother, a year later, notified authorities regarding the official findings of attending physicians at her daughter's deathbed: On the Death Certificate was the notation, "This may be murder." Texas Ranger R. D. Holliday, assigned to Livingston (Polk County), made an investigation, breaking the case wide open after discovering that the disinterred corpse was "loaded with strychnine," and the supposed grieving widower had "taken out a huge life insurance policy on his spouse." Another Trinity County sheriff, after the nighttime escape of two teenagers from his jail, much to the embarrassment of county commissioners, told a Houston, Texas newspaperman: "the only way I could keep anybody in my jail here at Groveton is to feed 'em well and beg 'em to stay."[17] Returning to the narrative at hand, Private Jim Dunaway arrived in Trinity County sharp-eyed and bushy-tailed on 29 February 1904.[18]

Numerous were the unsolved murders racked up in the heavily wooded counties of Trinity, Walker, San Jacinto, and their adjacent neighbors. One was a particularly gruesome whodunit. Near Groveton an elderly lady, Mary Jane Touchstone, had been foully murdered for her money—or supposed money that she had secreted. The victim had been beaten with a club, had her throat cut, and then pitched off the front porch of her residence making a meal for feral hogs—a less than ingenious ploy that was supposed to make her death seem accidental—as if she had taken a fall, knocked herself unconscious, evidence of foul-play devoured by the swine; slyly converted into fertilizer. It was passerby Jim Ray, not pigs that discovered the body, first. The clues were plain. It was a homicide.[19]

Assisted by Ranger M. G. "Blaze" Delling, Captain McDonald quite productively identified a suspect, Ab Angle, ultimately eliciting a confession. In the specialized speak of lawmen—then and today—when Angle "let his milk down" he named his coconspirators: Relatives. Captain McDonald and Ranger Delling rounded up, besides Ab Angle, J. Jenkins, Hill Hutto, Wash and Joe Tullis, as well as one of their female relatives Martha Tullis.[20] The criminal case was slated to be heard by a grand jury in Trinity County.

While that spate of law enforcing was taking place, keeping his fellow Rangers in East Texas busy, Private Dunaway was exhibiting the stubbornness of a mule, the industriousness of a workhorse. He arrested a fellow at Groveton for unlawfully carrying a pistol; and he also snagged two fellows for conspiring to lastingly silence the only eyewitness to a double homicide—by murdering him. "The accused men admitted the whole truth." Not surprising to the Rangers, but nevertheless disheartening: "One of these men was made constable, deputy sheriff and jailer as soon as he was released from jail." Not to be discouraged, Private Dunaway then arrested another idiotic brute for rape and burglary. Then, par for the course it might seem, Ranger Dunaway latched on to another fellow for unlawfully carrying a six-shooter and "jugged" him. But, alas, the local sheriff came to the defendant's rescue, promptly releasing him and "pretending he was an assistant of his."[21]

Subsequent to the Trinity County grand jury hearing testimony regarding the murderous death of Mrs. Touchstone after indictment warrants issued for Wash and Joe and Martha Tullis, and Hill Hutto. Texas Rangers Jim Dunaway and T. C. Taylor made the apprehensions, placing the suspected defendants in the Trinity County Jail at Groveton. Before the month was out Private Dunaway participated in the arrests of A. A. Smith for Carrying a Pistol, Fred Stokes for Drunk & Disorderly, as well as another ne'er-do-well alleged to have stolen a horse.[22] The following month, April 1904, before being summoned back to District Court at Llano to testify in an old case, Private Dunaway did manage to safely arrest Robin Smith for attempting to murder the aforementioned A. A. Smith. Perhaps A. A. had had a good reason to be sporting a six-shooter.[23]

Certainly prisoners Burton and Stafford, ensconced in the Henderson County Jail at Athens and charged with Rape were most happy to see Ranger Privates Jim Dunaway, Blaze Delling, and H. B. Smith. Sheriff W. O. Williams, afraid that the prisoners would be taken from the jail and lynched, had sought assistance. Arrival of this trio of Rangers quieted the crowd of agitators and the threat of potential "mob violence" was averted.[24] Shortly thereafter Privates Dunaway and Smith rounded up three murder suspects in Trinity County and at Lovelady, Houston County, jailing all three, and for good measure latched onto White Williams, an untrustworthy guy alleged to have committed an act of perjury.[25]

Lacking irrefutable forensic evidence linking the murder defendants to the scene of the crime, the prosecutor in the Touchstone homicide case was wholly dependent on the incriminations of Ab Angle, surely an untenable position when seeking imposition of nonpartisan criminal justice. It seems that Ab feared his kinfolk more than he feared the absolute freedom gained by snitching them into prison. Angle retracted his confession. The district attorney's case collapsed. The good guys don't always win. There was, however, a touch of comeuppance for the frightened retractor; Ab's original and formalized confession had been taken after the administering of an oath. Legally he had painted himself into a corner. Recanting the earlier admission meant that he had knowingly fibbed and sworn falsely to lawmen the first time around, a clear-cut felony violation. Defendants in the murder case "walked." Ab Angle danced into the state penitentiary at Huntsville, to the tune of three years for perjuring himself.[26]

Not to belabor the point, but a quick review of Company B's Monthly Returns reveals that Private Jim Dunaway was—along with several of his *amigos*—immersed in a whirlwind of law enforcing activity in East Texas. During October 1904, either acting alone or assisting a fellow Ranger, Jim Dunaway arrested multiple alleged suspects for Shooting into a Train, Assault to Murder, Carrying a Pistol, and Violating Local Option Laws. The following month after a short stint lending a hand to the sheriff of Fort Bend County at Richmond with district court security, Private Dunaway was back in harness in Trinity County. There he made arrests for Swindling, Assault and Abusive Language, Murder, Affray, Bribery and Malfeasance in Office, and Intimidating a Witness. One of those arrests was of H. H. Dailey, a local constable and deputy sheriff. In Trinity County especially, Jim Dunaway was making good friends and bad enemies.[27]

Quite interestingly in light of all the hoopla habitually awarded Ranger captains, if the last Monthly Return for 1904 is spot on, Private Dunaway was single-handedly responsible for all of the Company B arrests during December. One of those apprehensions in San Jacinto County near Oakhurst was rather chancy, at least so infers Captain Bill McDonald:

and on the 21st [Dunaway] arrested Gus Palmer and Bob Cleveland for burning the houses & was forced to take charge of several parties who purposed to Kill Dunaway for investigating the burning of the houses & he disarmed them taking several shot guns, Winchesters & pistols from them & having to buck some of the main leaders of this gang of desperadoes, one of the parties charged with arson is the constable of that precinct.[28]

With his family yet in Llano, Private Dunaway celebrated the holidays by arresting a fellow in Trinity County on Christmas Eve Day for Drunkenness and Disturbing the Peace. Christmas Day found Dunaway arresting a nitwit apparently having too much eggnog: He had been carrying a pistol "& shooting same off in passenger train."[29] Yes, if James Dallas Dunaway had aspirations of a working-life as a lawman there was plenty of work—markedly for a Ranger in East Texas. With little relief in sight, at some point in time and exactness is elusive, Private Jim Dunaway's wife and children relocated to the little town of Trinity, southwest of Groveton.[30]

A lazy lawman does not generate any acclaim or any complaint. An active lawman generates both. Private Dunaway, if he was anything, was active. Subsequent to a homicide investigation Captain McDonald arrested two murder suspects at Madisonville, Madison County. One of the alleged bad boys, Red Harle "was turned out of the jail & aided to escape" by M. B. Seay, who had made threats against Rangers. For three days there was quite an uproar, and during the acrimonious dustup Captain McDonald and Private Dunaway disarmed "several parties & unloaded some shot guns that had special loaded shells to Kill the rangers." Unfortunately as the index of heated rhetoric went up, the degree of rational thinking spiraled down, at least for the hot-tempered Seay. During the process of being taken into custody for Carrying a Pistol and Aiding a Prisoner to Escape, the foolhardy Seay "attempted to shoot Dunaway. . . . " Such pigheaded insolence was a big mistake. Instead of shooting the miscreant, which would have seemed somewhat justifiable, Private Dunaway figuratively bent the barrel of his six-shooter on Seay's cranium—and then locked him in the Madison County jailhouse. Though it may sound askance today, the next move on the part of Seay was not all that unusual then: He filed a formal Complaint with a local justice of the peace against Dunaway, charging him with

Aggravated Assault. Captain McDonald had no choice—and was in fact obligated—to arrest Dunaway, who quickly guaranteed his future presence at any court hearings. Ranger Jim Dunaway was promptly released from custody, though in all probability any detention time was more technical than physical. Thereafter the lively—and potentially dangerous—brouhaha temporarily faded but not the back-burner brewing of bad-blood between a few East Texans and the Rangers.[31]

Part of the big news for Private Jim Dunaway for February 1905, besides the fact bootleggers were thumbing their noses at the sheriff in Trinity County, was that the Company B headquarters shifted from Fort Hancock to Sierra Blanca, then El Paso County, now Hudspeth County. The pending criminal charges did not prevent Private Dunaway from doing his job. He accompanied the Company B commander first to Madisonville to attend court, and then to Groveton for an appearance in district court where, according to Captain McDonald they "were important witnesses in several felony cases." Afterward, Private Dunaway made a sojourn into Houston and San Augustine Counties in an attempt to locate crucial witnesses who "had been run out of Trinity County."[32]

Private Dunaway was in store for very welcome news during March 1905. The nonchalant wording in the Company B Monthly Return borders on comic if it were not too, so dead damn serious: "Pvt. Dunaway with pvt. Smith went to Houston & met Capt. McDonald & went to Madisonville to attend the trial of himself, charged with Aggravated Assault on one Bood Seay, had no trial as the co. attorney dismissed the case. . . . ."[33] Hardly had he time to catch his law-enforcing breath before Dunaway was forced into action, arresting William Perkins and Will Ervin for Assault to Murder, locking them in the Trinity County Jail at Groveton.[34] James Dallas Dunaway may have been one tough Ranger, but lawmen are human: He was bedridden with a case of the Mumps for part of June 1905.[35] By the end of the month he had recovered and was fit for duty—in South Texas.[36] Headquarters for Company B had once again been repositioned. It was formally relocated to Alice, then Nueces County, now Jim Wells County, about forty-five miles west of Corpus Christi.[37]

Once again Ranger Dunaway found himself engaged in a type of caretaker work along the Texas/Mexico border, rather than the proactive law enforcement work he had been doing in densely populated East Texas: For several months he had been tasked with guarding the quarantine line, not returning to the Alice headquarters station until 19 October 1905.[38] Though it was not the typical arrest scenario, during November, Privates Jim Dunaway and L. E. Flach took W. R. and Tom Selman into custody for Killing Deer Out of Season, turning the boys over to the sheriff of La Salle County, W. T. Hill, at Cotulla.[39] The arrest of poachers may not have seemed overly electrifying but there were big doings on Private Dunaway's upcoming calendar.

On the first day of March 1906 Jim Dunaway's resignation from Company B became effective. Separating himself from the Rangers was not a wholesale career change. The $40 per month state salary was undervaluing his talents, so he thought:

> The reason I ask to resign is because I expect to make the race for City Marshal of Llano, Texas, my former home County, as you know I resigned the City Marshal office to join your Company on July 1, 1903 [sic July 8]. . . . I believe it is to my advantage, considering the difference in the salary that I ask you to accept this resignation and allow me to make the race for City Marshal.[40]

His career as a Texas Ranger, however, was far from finished. The effort to regain the position for the city marshal spot at Llano had not panned out. On 16 April 1906 Dunaway enlisted in Company A, Ranger Force, then commanded by Captain James Abijah Brooks, and at that time officially headquartered at Laredo, Webb County, but increasingly spending law enforcing time in and around Colorado City, Mitchell County, west of Abilene. The following month, no doubt as preplanned, Jim Dunaway was promoted to the position of 1st Sergeant, Company A.[41]

Sergeant Dunaway was many things it seems; a back-down man was not one of them, though. All of the causative contributors to a swelling squabble may be partially buried in the dustbins of history, but one end result is not: a bloodied and sore head. Inside city limits at Odessa—a pretty tough spot in its own right—several Company A Rangers became entangled in somewhat of an imbroglio. Due to the resignation of Sheriff Gene E. Graham, a man holding an interim appointment was filling the vacancy pending the next scheduled election.[42] And for whatever the reason, justified or not, the provisional sheriff, T. G. "Gee" McMeans, an ex-Ranger who would later be killed in a gunfight with the fêted Frank Hamer, interjected himself into the mischief or the merriment—or was pulled in. Sergeant J. D. Dunaway took offense and a grisly scuffle between he and McMeans ensued— for a little while anyway. Jerking out his Colt's revolver Sergeant Dunaway put it to use as a threshing machine—a steel club— bludgeoning Sheriff McMeans or as a newsman reported: "hammered McMeans over the head with his six shooter."[43] Ranger Private Nathanial Pendergrass "Doc" Thomas grappled with his boss trying to defuse the hurtful mess and public relations disaster; while Gee McMeans intelligently retired from the badge-wearers' battlefield. Sergeant Dunaway was not appreciative of the interference, threatening to summarily discharge Private Thomas from the Ranger Force. Ector County Judge Branch Isbell jumped into the subsequent verbal mêlée, telegraphing Governor Lanham of the trouble between McMeans and Dunaway and if action was not taken quick a killing would be imminent.[44] Private Thomas even jumped the chain-of-command and wired the adjutant general: "Please order sergeant Dunaway from Odessa at once. . . ."[45] Adjutant General Hulen's two-telegram response was not subject to but one meaning, instructing Sergeant Dunaway:

> Proceed to Colorado at once. Have detachment follow. Ship such equipage as cannot be transported overland with horses. . . . [A second telegram] Take your men, horses, camp equipage, etc., now at Odessa to Colorado City. Leave Odessa as soon as practicable.[46]

One would guess Dunaway was wholly at fault, but ambiguity creeps to the surface after noting the remarks of Odessa's prominent building contractor W. T. Malone, who asserted that there had been a cleverly designed plot to murder Sergeant Dunaway. According to Malone, the telegram to the adjutant general from Ranger Thomas had "been dictated by the Saloon Keeper (the backbone of this lawless element). . . . Also, I can truthfully say that the boys [Rangers] have conducted themselves as gentlemen while here. . . ."[47] Later County Judge Isbell and a committee of Odessa's citizens would extol the work of Ranger Thomas: "His actions throughout the whole proceedings were characterized by judgment and a loyalty to his duty as an officer of the law. He did all in his power to promote peace, and was we believe the coolest and most fearless man in the crowd. He coolly and fearlessly, without favoring citizens, county or state officers, did that which was best under the circumstances, and acted as few men would have done."[48]

Nevertheless, even J. A. Brooks was of a mind that Sergeant Dunaway "had gotten matters in bad shape up there," hoping that he would "have no serious trouble in quieting everything up there," once the captain arrived at Odessa.[49] In the end cooler heads and wiser counsel prevailed. Captain Brooks after making an appearance, instructed Sergeant Dunaway that he had made a command decision and had already—with no compromise—preapproved him a Leave of Absence—an extended Leave of Absence. Sergeant Dunaway, faced with no alternative, scooted for the comforts of hearth and home.[50] At least for awhile, Captain Brooks was mulling over the idea of reducing Sergeant Dunaway in ranks, busting him back to a private, but such did not materialize.[51] James Dallas Dunaway's forgiving nature—if there was one—was on hiatus. Thereafter Sergeant Dunaway and Doc Thomas were "bitter enemies." Even after Doc had been mortally gunned down in an irrational dispute with a Potter County deputy sheriff at Amarillo, Dunaway made "some very unkind remarks about Thomas since he was killed."[52] Sympathy for a foe was as foreign for Ranger Jim Dunaway as the need to splint his backbone: He could be an agreeable and lifelong friend or a very dangerous begrudging enemy.

Sergeant Dunaway, perhaps after some well deserved or well needed rest and relaxation, returned to duty as Company A's top noncom. Along with Private Ivan Murchison, Sergeant Dunaway made the Ranger presence felt in Kent County, along the Salt Fork of the Brazos, arresting several misbehavers charged with stealing cows, horses, and for carrying six-shooters. The prisoners, as they were snagged, were politely turned over to Sheriff Roy at Clairemont, the county seat.[53] Sergeant Dunaway also snagged something else, although but fleetingly. Captain J. A. Brooks was away from Company A headquarters, scouting in the Lower Rio Grande Valley. While thus occupied he had formalized his decision, tendering his resignation from the Ranger Force. From

November 16, 1906, until December 31 Dunaway filled the vacuum as the acting Company A commander. The dustup with Sheriff Gee McMeans, in the long run, seems not to have hampered his standing with the front office—at this time anyway. When Francis Noel "Frank" Johnson was named captain of Company A, quite naturally Dunaway relinquished his short-term status as company commander.[54]

While Sergeant Dunaway was showing the Ranger flag in West Texas, thunderstorm clouds in Trinity County were building. When the tornado touched down Sergeant Dunaway would be caught in the whirlwinds of devastation and death. Many state-paid lawmen disdained the mobility required of service in the Ranger Force, the frequent duty taking them away from home and family: A little service in the Ranger Force could go a long way. In numerous Texas counties the sheriffs were ex-Rangers: Service with the state having been but a steppingstone for the more lucrative and politically attractive job. Most of the time, then, there was an amicable and cooperative working relationship between the local sheriff and Rangers assigned to cover his county. While that may have been the norm, it did not hold one hundred percent of the time. Sometimes not all was nice. Texas Ranger Jim Dunaway had not gotten along well with the sheriff of Trinity County, John F. Standley. By proxy Sergeant Dunaway didn't get along too well with Sheriff Standley's cronies and political backers—and never had. Aside from Sergeant Dunaway, another Texas Ranger noncom had been "instructed to work in cooperation" with Sheriff Standley, "if possible."[55]

It seems that Trinity County, for whatever reason, was a hotbed for bootleggers and gamblers. The principal and steadfast legal team representing the parasitical sporting crowd and who could be counted on to "defend bootleggers in any violation" were downtown Groveton lawyers Kenley, Campbell, and Poston. Not too surprisingly—for those in the know—was the fact these legal beagles were also top-dog contributors and "ardent supporters" of Sheriff Standley.[56] Assuredly the Trinity County Attorney, H. L. Robb, was not enamored with the sheriff's performance, writing to Ranger Captain Bill McDonald: "Of course I don't know whether Standley is acting in good faith or not, I rather suspect that he is not. He has done so many irregular things since he has been in office that I would not be surprised at anything he would do. Being so completely under the influence of that Kinley [*sic*] & Stevenson gang. . . ."[57]

Innuendo is cheap. That said, a Texas Ranger sergeant contemporary to the times, remarked in official correspondence to the adjutant general that Sheriff John F. Standley "didn't take much interest in depressing bootlegging. . . ."[58] Or, the murder of an undercover operative secretly hired to prospect for prosecutable proofs, evidence enough to sustain convictions and slam the jailhouse door behind bootleggers and their attendant riffraff. Detective F. R. Meyer, originally from Brazoria County, had been fatally bushwhacked and it seemed to both interested and disinterested observers that if anything was going to be done about it, the Rangers would do it, not Sheriff Standley. Sergeant Herff Alexander Carnes and Private Milam H. Wright, Company D, were dispatched to Trinity County to manage the homicide investigation.[59]

Coinciding with the Rangers arrival at Groveton on October 11, 1906, the county attorney H. L. Robb initiated a "court of inquiry" regarding the murder of Detective Meyer. In the hot political climate Ranger Carnes noted and was not bashful about repeating the grave doubts he held concerning the above-board cooperation of the sheriff. After hearing that A. M. Campbell of the above cited attorney alliance was championing the inquiry was "nothing but a sweat box" and "knowing that Mr. Stanley [*sic*] and this firm were closely connected in this way, the court concluded not to divulge any evidence in regards to these cases to Mr. Stanley. We always found it convenient to examine witnesses when Mr. Stanley was absent. [Ranger Private] M. H. Wright and I from then on done most of the summonsing of witnesses, even went outside of the county after witnesses."[60]

According to Sergeant Carnes the citizens of Trinity County and the town of Groveton in particular, organized a Law and Order League "for the purpose of suppressing bootlegging and crime." According to Texas Ranger Carnes the majority population was wholly "dissatisfied" with Sheriff Standley, a Democrat. The Law and Order League nominated their hand-picked man, G. H. Kirkwood, a previous Trinity County sheriff, to run against Standley in the November 1906 election as an Independent. When the polls closed and the ballots were counted Trinity County had a new but experienced sheriff, one Ranger Sergeant Carnes characterized as "very efficient" and in but a short time Kirkwood had "succeeded in bringing back most all fugitives from that county and has almost suppressed bootlegging and gambling."[61]

Sergeant Dunaway had a reputation too, a hard one. W. S. Randolph, "an old physician" at Oakhurst, was perplexed and pissed off. He wrote the governor: "I write you in the interest of humanity & peace to send Some rangers to this place, as soon as possible as everything is in a State of ferment & there is imminent danger of further murders being perpetrated. You can not act too quickly. I think Dunaway & one or two others would be the best ones you could send as he (Dunaway) has the situation and understands it better than anyone else as he has been here twice & would accomplish more good than anyone else could as they fear him. . . ."[62]

Upon completion of the investigative stage of their homicide investigation Sergeant Carnes and Private Wright arrested H .O. Parks and Virgil Winslow, charging them with assassinating Meyer, and made prisoners of John Winslow, Paul Meadows, and Earnest Seviney for acting in the role of accomplices.[63] Then, as expected, legal maneuverings of the defense team kicked in: motions for Habeas Corpus hearings, bond reduction requests, and efforts calculated to work for the defendants' advantage—a change of venue. The tactics—all legal and what a good defense attorney would do—guaranteed any trials would not take place until the following year, 1907. Sergeant Dunaway, for whatever reason, was closing out 1906 at home in Trinity County when he got the call to accompany Private Milam Wright to Glidden, Colorado County, the day after Christmas, "looking out for the interest of the G.H.&S.A. Ry. in time of a strike."[64] After making an investigation at Glidden, Sergeant Dunaway matter-of-factly determined that there would be no need for a Texas Ranger presence "as all of the strikers here had gone to Houston and San Antonio," further advising Adjutant General Hulen that the whole dustup was, "Just the Engineers and Firemen fussing among themselves."[65]

Subsequent to completing the assignment at Glidden, James Dallas Dunaway, yet Company A's 1st Sergeant, and Company D's Private Milam Wright on 16 February 1907 via Beaumont traveled to Bessmay, Jasper County, to interview what was supposed to be an important witness, but as it turned out the fellow's supposed testimony was clarified as having no value—worthless. It was Dunaway's last Company A assignment; he transferred into his old unit, Company B, now commanded by Captain Tom M. Ross, and headquartered at Alice.[66]

By way of his familiarity with events and personalities in Trinity, Walker, and San Jacinto Counties, it was but reasonable to pair Dunaway, now Company B's sergeant, with Company D's Private Milam Wright on another touchy investigation. They were to keep the peace at Oakhurst, San Jacinto County, and, too, determine the identity of just who was posting "threatening letters to parties residing there." Whether he was in fact connected with the threatening mail is indeterminate, but while on this scout the two Rangers arrested an alleged murderer, "a negro, W. H. Hargrove" near Palestine, Anderson County, returning him to Oakhurst.[67] Ranger Wright departed East Texas heading to his Company D headquarters at Austin. Sergeant Dunaway departed for Trinity County.

Ranger Sergeant James Dallas Dunaway owned status as a fellow having no shortage of guts, a newspaper correspondent penning that he "had been in many fights—and is one of the rangers relied upon for his bravery."[68] One high-ranking Texas Ranger official commented, ". . . . I served on the border with Jim Dunaway and knew him well. He had one of his thumbs shot off in a night battle with a band of smugglers on the Rio Grande."[69] Although this gunplay is not source cited, it's most likely—at least in part—true. Likewise, an additional claim that Dunaway may have killed a borderlander of Mexican heritage has thus far eluded conformation. Certainly the Texas Ranger owned plenty of pluck. Too, as previously spotlighted, ostensibly Dunaway also owned a nitroglycerine temper, one that would detonate at the slightest jostle.

Before the month of April 1907 was halfway expired Sergeant Dunaway caught a tiger by the tail, lawyer R. O. Kenley, the old political pal of Sheriff Standley. The attorney was a wordsmith not a fighter, so after being struck—or allegedly struck—by Dunaway he squawked rather than fought. His bewailing complaint was loud enough to be heard at Austin—by the governor.[70] An entry in the Company D Monthly Return is somewhat explanatory: "April 13—Capt. Hughes has started to Trinity and Groveton to investigate charges made against Sergt. J. D. Dunaway for striking R. O. Kenley—went via Palestine. Went to Groveton—returned to Austin on 17th and brought Sgt. Dunaway with me. Out 4 days.

Traveled 532 miles." This time, so it seems, Sergeant Jim Dunaway had stepped in it. After an audience with the bigwigs at Austin the chastisement message was clear, or should have been: Dunaway was to stay out of Groveton and stay away from the lawyer.[71]

Furthermore, according to R. O. Kenley, after the assaultive incident Sergeant Dunaway had threatened to kill him if he ever whined about the ass-whipping.[72] The pigheaded barrister had squealed, that was now not hush-hush. A Ranger's ears had perked, a teeth-gnashing wolf was on the prowl, heading for Groveton. Meanwhile at ever-hectic Groveton attorney R. O. Kenley was figuratively—and maybe literally—shaking in his fancy hand-stitched boots. He was scared to death of J. D. Dunaway.

The two had had previous difficulties to be sure. Kenley's aver that Dunaway had accosted him on a previous occasions is more than believable, knowing the Texas Ranger's proclivity for aggressively settling scores and forcefully tending to personal business absent any hesitation or postponement. Nervously pacing the floor in his upstairs office at Groveton that afternoon of April 26, 1907, lawyer R. O. Kenley checked the chamber of his shotgun, making sure it was loaded with buckshot, not piddling birdshot. Jim Dunaway was not a man to shoot at and miss or fail to put down.

On the street below, at about 1:30 p.m. Ranger Sergeant Dunaway was chatting with Trinity County's ex-county attorney, H. L. Robb near H. J. Mangum's store. The range was short, the muzzle blasts deafening. Dunaway and Robb were slammed to the ground. Six balls of 00 had punched into Dunaway's back and right side, two into Robb's head. Both men lay bleeding in the street, gasping for air, clinging to life. The curtain of blue smoke emanating from the upstairs office window pinpointed the shooter's or shooters' location, a hard fact that not even lawyer Kenley would deny. In his mind he had made a preemptive strike, kill before being killed by a run amok Texas Ranger named Jim Dunaway. What about poor Mr. Robb? He was but collateral damage, an accident: So said R. O. Kenley as he and his brother-in-law, R. E. Minton were posting their individual bail bonds.[73] Whether he had acted as the lone triggerman or with the aid of coconspirators was yet up for grabs, but the bushwhacking attorney would stand the heat all by himself, taking the whole blame, trying mightily to beat the rap. The fact he had not been the intended target was of not the least comfort for the unconscious H. L. Robb; he died.[74]

While being hustled to a cot and while awaiting medical attention, Sergeant James Dallas Dunaway had the presence of mind to understand Texas Ranger headquarters would need to be in the know. He asked for a pen and a scrap of paper, composing words for a telegram to Austin: "I am shot all to pieces. Everything quiet."[75]

Captain Hughes, Sergeant Carnes and Private Wright rushed to Groveton, not thoroughly of a mind that attorney Kenley had acted alone, noting in Company D's Monthly Return, "started to Groveton to assist in keeping the peace and to work in the case of R. O. Kenley and others shooting Sgt. Dunaway and H. L. Robb. . . ."[76] A newsman covering the story penned: "Three men were seen by different parties at the window of Kenley's office during the shooting. . . ."[77] Assuredly the Texas adjutant general didn't believe the letter writing attorney had acted independently, had bitten from the hard plug by himself: "Kenley, the lawyer who shot them from a window of his office, along with his brother-in-law, who was present and no doubt did part of the shooting, are now under a two thousand dollar bond."[78] Interestingly, though it had not been thought so during the initial examination, it became apparent to his attending physician that Robb's injuries had been inflicted by buckshot, but not just buckshot: The death-wound was "thought to be a rifle ball."[79] Although the newspaper coverage is spotty, examining the Company D Monthly Return for April 1907 does reveal that Sergeant Carnes and Private Wright did arrest R. O. Kenley, his brother Carrol H. Kenley, R. E. Minton, and Ollie Freeman, charging them with Murder and placing them in Sheriff Kirkwood's Trinity County lockup.[80]

While recuperating Dunaway, too, knew he was in somewhat of a pickle, already having been admonished for his volatile relationships with the ex-sheriff of Trinity County and lawyer cohort R. O. Kenley. Taking pen in hand, Jim Dunaway wanted to make double damn sure the adjutant general was aware of a salient tidbit of information, and it seems the sergeant too thought there was more than one shooter. With but minimal editing herein, Sergeant Dunaway wrote:

> Sir, thought drop you a few Lines and Let you know how am getting along. All of my Wounds are healed up on my Body except the one where was shot clear through and it will be

Closed and out of danger of Blood poison infecting it any way. But my Left leg where was shot With a larger Bore Gun it is in a Bad Condition yet. It is healing slowly and of Course it is still running, and all of the dead flesh is not sluffed out yet But can Walk short distances on it and will if can hold out to make out full Report Last of Month. Will send same to you. Genl. I send you By M. Wright the papers showing you Just how was shot and don't want Kenly or any of his attys to see it, for they contend all of his evidence Will be I started toward his office with My hand on my Gun and of Course if that be a fact I would have the shots in My front and not in My Back and side, so don't Let them see it as would be a great help to them to make of their Medicine for Court. Hoping to see you soon.[81]

Sergeant J. D. Dunaway had pegged R. O. Kenley's likely defense strategy tight. Even in faraway Arizona Territory, at Bisbee, it was being reported the shotgun wielding lawyer was contending that "Dunaway had made threats against him and was coming towards his office in a suspicious manner just previous to the shooting."[82]

In regards to the Groveton collision and of Sergeant Jim Dunaway being shot, Texas Ranger officialdom was near myopically zeroed on two issues: Matters relating to his healthiness and protecting him from any other would-be executioners. Doctor F. L. Barnes who was treating Dunaway at the Trinity infirmary updated the adjutant general proffering that his patient would eventually recover, although he did have "a stormy time since about the 4th day after being shot on account of hemorrhage from wounds in his lungs."[83] Dunaway's brother Chick, a restaurant and pool hall proprietor in Llano, upon hearing of the shooting, rushed to Jim's bedside in Trinity. Gauging the circumstances and challenges, Chick penned a quick note to AG Newton explaining his reasoning for needing help: ". . . . Have been told by Parties from Groveton & also this Place that there was a chance for those Parties, James' enemies to make an attempt to assassinate him Before he were able to be up & as I am Strictly a Stranger here will ask you to Place one Man here each night. . . . If I were acquainted with James' enemies & could attend to same myself & not request such of you. . . ."[84] The response was quick. Acting Attorney General Phelps transmitted a Western-Union telegram to Chick Dunaway: "Two Rangers will report at Trinity—Letter follows." Sergeant Herff Carnes and Private Parker Weston managed the trip to Trinity and began coordinating with Doctor Barnes about medical issues and railroad executives regarding transportation matters. Sergeant Dunaway and his wife Hallie were to be removed—with the strictest of secrecy—from Trinity to Llano via a brief stopover at Houston and a hospital checkup at Austin.[85] At long last Jim Dunaway begin licking his wounds and stoking the fires of retribution at his hometown.

Back at Trinity another fellow, merchant S. E. Barnes, was dead set about getting a message to Governor T. M. Campbell, recommending that "you will have him [Dunaway] removed from this section of the state and keep him away thereafter. Another trip on his part to Groveton will inevitably lead to further bloodshed there. . . . He certainly cannot be a prudent man for it does not seem possible that a sane man in his position would ever have gone to Groveton under the circumstances he did the day he was shot there and Robb killed. . . . We can only judge the future by the past. . . ."[86] Texas Ranger headquarters had plans for Sergeant James Dallas Dunaway and the Texas criminal justice system had plans for one lawyer named R. O. Kenley.

Although it looks as if it were a never ending saga, the hot-tempered wrangle between Jim Dunaway and R. O. Kenley, there seems to be a hard bottom line. He hadn't been shooting at or intending to injure H. L. Robb, Kenley argued: His death was but an unfortunate mishap—an accidental outcome. On the other hand he was trying to kill Sergeant Dunaway, of that he'd freely admit—but he had good reason, self-defense. On a change of venue Houston was the site selected for the Assault to Murder trial. Harris County Sheriff Archie R. Anderson was deeply troubled that such high-profile drama had a chance of suddenly erupting into more bloodshed. All witnesses and spectators were to be searched. Astonishingly the *Fort Worth Star Telegram* and the *Bellville News Democrat* accented the sheriff's trepidation, candidly acknowledging at the Harris County courthouse doorway "about 100 pistols were taken from parties entering the court house here before the trial began."[87]

Not unexpectedly Dunaway was a necessary component of the prosecutor's case. Such an Affirmative Defense as self-defense obligated Kenley to testify—and he did. The jury believed him. They deliberated just thirty minutes and acquitted him.[88]

The book was closed on the *State of Texas vs. R. O. Kenley*, but the last chapter was yet written in the thriller, *Ranger Dunaway vs. Lawyer Kenley*, not if the anecdotal tale offered by William Warren Sterling is taken at face value. Sterling says he picked up the story straight from the horse's mouth, an eyewitness: Frank Hamer. Subsequent to the trial Dunaway and Kenley came face to face at a downtown Houston drug store lunch-counter. In but a heartbeat Ranger Dunaway doubled his fist and force-fed Kenley a knuckle sandwich, knocking him to the floor. Purportedly, Kenley regained his footing and then verbally assaulted Dunaway as if that would have any sting. The Ranger sergeant didn't whack him again, nor did he go for his pistol—there may have been just too many nonaligned witnesses for a sure-enough head-thumping or a pitiless killing. The Texas Ranger sergeant may not have procured his pound of flesh, but sniveling Kenley, an admitted backshooter was spitting blood, choking on the shame of being a wimp and being whipped—at least such must have been in Sergeant J. D. Dunaway's mind. The proprietor of the drugstore was awestruck—a touch of genuine hero worship, perhaps dubiously bestowed. Again creditability depends upon accommodating W. W. Sterling who obtained it second-hand through Frank Hamer: "The owner of the pharmacy changed its name to the Ranger Drug Store, and it went by that title for many years."[89]

Sergeant Dunaway had recuperated enough to be back in the saddle again, and had been faithfully living up to scouting assignments for Company B in South Texas under Captain Tom Ross at Alice.[90] Subsequent to the acquittal of R. O. Kenley, a new duty station was in store for Sergeant Dunaway. On July 3, 1908, Captain Ross was notified in writing by Assistant Adjutant General Phelps that although he should yet carry Sergeant J. D. Dunaway and Private Sam McKenzie on his roster, the Rangers were to report for duty at Comstock, Val Verde County, where they would be under the direct supervision of Company D's captain, John R. Hughes. This was indeed a bizarre administrative redeployment, even for the Texas Rangers. Moreover when incorporating the second half of the message: Captain Ross was given backfilling authority due to the fact that Dunaway's and McKenzie's "stay may be for some time. . . ." Which was a benign and understated way of saying the boys weren't coming back soon, but could now build their Texas Ranger résumés in far West

Texas. Too, rather oddly, Jim Dunaway would continue to figuratively wear the stripes of a Company B Ranger sergeant.[91]

In less than a week after receiving orders, Dunaway and McKenzie made their appearance at Comstock. Their tenure there was short lived. Captain Hughes ordered them to the rough and tumble mining town of Shafter, Presidio County.[92] Tracing Sergeant Dunaway's footprints as he was enforcing the law in far West Texas—with an occasional trip to South Texas—is doable but unnecessary for taking real measure of the man. That he was capable and tough may be gleaned from a single incident—another one.

During late October 1908 S. A. Wright was alleged to have murdered a "Mexican" near the Sunset Mining Camp in southern Presidio County. An inquest and an arrest were called for. Riding out of Shafter to investigate and officiate were Sergeant Dunaway, Ranger Privates Alex Ross and Sam McKenzie, as well as a local justice of the peace. The arrest was executed absent trouble; transporting the prisoner back to Marfa, the county seat, and lodging him with Sheriff Milton B. Chastain proved dicey: Lynch mob mentality had raised its ugly head and "about 35 armed Mexicans from the settlement on the Rio Grande arrived and demanded the prisoner. The Rangers refused to give him up—and it looked for awhile like there was going to be war between the Mexicans and the Rangers, but finally the Mexicans backed off and the Rangers took their prisoner to Shafter and put him in jail. He was later taken to Marfa jail."[93]

During the first quarter of 1909 Sergeant Dunaway once again was reluctantly hitched to some unpleasant duty for a go-gettin' Texas Ranger: Quarantine Guard on the Rio Grande, this time at Del Rio, Val Verde County.[94] Predictably J. D. Dunaway was not happy. Perhaps by now it is also not unpredictable that a local sheriff was not any too happy with Ranger Dunaway either. Sheriff Charles C. Hartley made his ire known—in writing—to Captain John R. Hughes. The good sheriff was ticked because, according to info he was getting from his deputies, Sergeant Dunaway had authorized a citizen, Marcellus Lowe, "to carry a pistol and go with him to different places in Del Rio." Understandably the sheriff didn't appreciate being kept in the dark about such an illegality and was doubly troubled when Dunaway told him "that it was nobody's business who he had to carry a pistol." Sheriff Hartley, after praising other Rangers, ended informing Captain Hughes:

"Now, I fear that he and I cannot work together as we should, and I am going to ask it of you, if you can use him anywhere else satisfactorily and will move him away from here you will do me a personal favor."[95] Hughes did not dilly-dally.

In a letter to Adjutant General Newton three days after Sheriff's Hartley's complaint Captain Hughes made his feelings about Dunaway known, ordering him to report to his home at Llano and await further orders from his Company B boss, Captain Tom Ross. Furthermore he had an ear full for AG Newton, saying, among other things: "You will note in Sheriff Hartley's letter that he says he would like for me to move Dunaway away from Del Rio if I had some other place that I could use him. I have no other place that I can use him. . . . Sergt. Dunaway will have to return to El Paso in about two months as witness in a cattle case but it will not be necessary for him to be a member of the Ranger Force at the time. I had to send Dunaway away from here to prevent serious trouble and can't afford to bring him back here again. It is my opinion that he will be better off out of the Ranger Service than in it."[96] Captain Hughes punctuated the seriousness with an additional appeal to the adjutant general, requesting that a railroad pass be awaiting Sergeant Dunaway at Austin, from Austin to Llano—one way![97] Dunaway tried to plead his case—in vain. AG Newton updated Captain Hughes: "Sergeant Dunaway called at the office on his way to Llano, and I conversed with him over his case, and the impossibility of placing him where he would be of service."[98] Captain Ross was benevolent, simply marking on the Company B Monthly Return for May 1909 that Sergeant J. D. Dunaway had "resigned on May 20" not that the separation from the Ranger Force had been involuntary.[99]

A full-scale biography would stipulate that meticulously tracking James Dallas Dunaway's movements after separating from the Ranger service—this time—was mandatory. Such is not the case in this narrative's format, even if it could have been accomplished with precision. Suffice to say that Dunaway drifted into and out of several law enforcing jobs, and drifted into and out of Mexico doing security and private detective work, handily honing his bilingual language skills. At one point he was chief special agent for the Santa Fe Railroad at Houston and at other times a commissioned deputy sheriff.[100] It is in that latter role—as a deputy sheriff—that Dunaway's story will be revisited.

At some stage during late 1914 J. D. Dunaway landed himself a deputy's sheriff's position at Rocksprings, Edwards County, working for L. A. Clark, yet in his twenties and the youngest sheriff in the county's rich history. That the well-seasoned J. D. Dunaway and the neophyte sheriff began their working relationship amicably is probable. That it quickly soured is provable. All too soon, according to Sheriff Clark, he found that Deputy Dunaway "was a trouble maker, instead of a peace officer." Furthermore, if he really was quantifying the general public's feelings accurately, they too had found Jim Dunaway "wants to force himself on the people of this county, the majority of whom I find, after close investigation, do not want him." Politicians listen to their constituents: Sheriffs are politicians. Sheriff Clark fired Deputy Dunaway, finding it necessary to "deprive him of his commission as an officer. . . ."[101]

The timing was fortuitous. Due to the ongoing intrigues of the Mexican Revolution and the January 1915 discovery of the genocidal *Plan de San Diego* wherein all Anglo males older than sixteen were to be summarily executed subsequent to the ruthless invasion and conquering of several Southwestern states by Mexican nationals and their deluded *Tejano* allies, Lone Star officialdom and the general population were aghast and astir.[102] State forces were to be beefed up; a decidedly golden opportunity for James Dallas Dunaway to once more throw his name into the hopper and become a Texas Ranger. During February 1915 the ever zealous Dunaway deftly orchestrated a written petition from his fellow citizens in Llano County, one championing him as "an honest, reliable man, and that in every position he has ever held he made a good, efficient officer and did his duty fearlessly under all circumstances."[103] True, Dunaway was always fearless, but not necessarily always nice. News sometimes travels fast, and this is one of those instances. Upon hearing of Dunaway's petition, Sheriff Clark at Rocksprings, in no uncertain terms telegraphed Governor James E. Ferguson: "Kindly do not appoint J. D. Dunaway a Ranger. Letter and petitions will follow."[104]

As noted, politicians listen to their constituents and Governor Ferguson was a politician. Though he would be removed from office, at the time under study Ferguson knew—or believed—that twenty leading citizens from Llano County had more voting clout than one young sheriff from Edwards County. At the governor's behest, the adjutant general messaged Captain John Jesse "J. J." Sanders, Company A, Ranger Force:

> The Governor has indicated that if this man is insubordinate and personally objectionable to you that he does not intend to force him on you, but his recommendations are so strong that the Governor wishes at least to give them serious consideration.[105]

Captain J.J. Sanders was not shy. He replied, that while an Edwards County deputy Dunaway "had become so trouble-some that the citizens demanded that he [Sheriff Clark] revoke his deputy-ship, which he did . . . therefore I, nor any of my men would like to work with him."[106] Such a less than ringing endorsement wouldn't be a persnickety little detail for a headstrong and hell-bent chief executive. At Del Rio on the 29th day of March 1915 James Dallas Dunaway, at age forty-one, swore his allegiance to the State of Texas, once again, becoming a private in the Ranger Force. The governor kept his word and didn't "force" Dunaway on Sanders, but assigned him to Company C, then headquartered at Austin and commanded by Captain E. H. Smith.[107]

Though his headquarters may have been Austin on the official paperwork, and his boss may have been Captain Smith in the staffing model, as a practical matter Private J. D. Dunaway reported to Val Verde County Sheriff John W. Almond at Del Rio, who was serving one of his several rounds in office.[108] Claude B. Hudspeth, a powerhouse Texas state senator and a man with no little ranching interests, had exercised his political muscle making sure Rangers were looking into the wholesale theft of sheep and goats taking place in Val Verde, Kinney, and Edwards Counties.[109] Working in tandem with Dunaway was another private from Llano County and a future Texas Ranger captain, Willie Lee Barler. Another Company C Ranger—rehired with Dunaway—was Francis Augustus Hamer. Just like Privates Dunaway and Barler, Frank was tasked with running down sheep and goat thieves— and in Hamer's case hog thieves, too, although he was normally working northeast of Val Verde County in Kimble (Junction) and Gillespie (Fredericksburg) Counties.[110] Also working under the direct supervision of Sheriff Almond, but financially funded by the section's sheep and goat raisers, was Nat B. "Kiowa" Jones, a former paid Ranger but now designated as a Special Ranger assigned to Company C.[111] That Private Dunaway was the least bit reticent about working the territory overseen by one of his chief critics, Sheriff Clark—who he most likely considered but a young whippersnapper—is belied in a written Scout Report of Kiowa Jones, who made the trip from Sonora, Sutton County, "to Rocksprings to see Dunaway."[112] And, too, by correspondence from AG Hutchings to Dunaway at his Rocksprings address.[113]

The game of Musical Chairs was nothing new for those in position to rearrange the seating and clear the deck for Ranger commanders. Governor Ferguson was busy. The reshuffling would affect Private Dunaway. Earlier in the year John R. Hughes left the Ranger Force, knowing his commission as a captain would not be renewed by "Farmer Jim" Ferguson. Whether Hughes was sacked or quit is but a matter of semantics. Hughes removal had, in real terms, paved the way for J. J. Sanders to assume command of Company A, and James Monroe Fox to accept the captaincy of Company B, headquartered at Marfa, Presidio County. Now, Ferguson and Henry Hutchings, the adjutant general, could redeploy Private Dunaway without "forcing" him on Captain Sanders. On the 1st day of June 1915 Dunaway transferred into Company B.[114]

Seven days prior to Private Dunaway transferring into the unit, Texas Ranger Private Eugene Hulen and Mounted U.S. Customs Inspector Joe Sitter had been murdered by Mexican bandits inside one of Presidio County's hidden canyons near the *Río Bravo*. Seven days after Dunaway's Company B enlistment, Private Robert Lee Burdett, also a borderland Texas Ranger was vilely murdered by Mexicans along the Rio Grande, at the little hamlet of Fabens, only a few miles downriver from El Paso. The following month, July 1915, in the Lower Rio Grande Valley an armed band of Mexican interlopers and *Tejano* sidekicks kicked off their *Plan de San Diego*, breeching the international line; marauding and stealing and murdering north of Brownsville. Before the following month had elapsed the well-known Mexican Revolution character—who was also a U.S. Government fugitive—Pascual Orozco Jr. and four of his comrades would open fire on ranchmen, and the following day die in a blistering gunfight near High-Lonesome Peak in the craggy Van Horn Mountains of Culberson County at the hands of a posse manned by a sheriff, deputy sheriffs, cowmen, and two ex-Texas Rangers, one of whom was then employed as a U.S. Mounted Customs Inspector.[115]

Customarily historians deal with the key activities of dead people. Texas Rangers, deputy sheriffs, and the U.S. Custom's river riders profiled herein were living in real time, day by day. So, acknowledging that the early deaths of Hulen and Sitter and Burdett and Orozco's gang had little or nothing to do with any grand scheme of genocide, no matter how harebrained it might have been—like the *Plan de San Diego*—is but fair.[116] But, at the time, did officers on the ground know that?[117] Likewise it's but just to own up to hard truth: Bona fide border area lawmen in West Texas and the Lower Rio Grande Valley really owned a deficiency of foresight: Were they judging the extant possibilities and probabilities of their futures by the past? If so, it surely looked bleak, depressing and dangerous and deadly. What happened to their law enforcing colleagues could very well happen to them— at any time. Historians are privileged with access to a rear-view mirror. Texas Rangers did not/do not make use of Tarot cards or crystal balls.

An independent interpretation by two prominent scholars seems spot on, even if somewhat discomforting: "The principal targets of the Plan de San Diego's announced war without quarter—Anglo males over sixteen—were too obtuse to realize that their deaths would be both legitimate and necessary . . . and they obstinately refused to be massacred. In fact, their attitude was that since the Mexicans were so anxious to wage a war without quarter they would show them what a war without quarter was all about. What ensued was what Anglos in South Texas called the 'Bandit War,' a savage struggle involving a lot of racial profiling, with bullets raining on the just and the unjust alike."[118]

Following up in a later work, *The Plan de San Diego: Tejano Rebellion, Mexican Intrigue*, the distinguished and award-winning authors peel the fat off of tasteless political correctness. Maintaining their roles as conscientious historians, they opt for cutting straight to the bone by adhering to truths and employing commonsense. Is it really incredulous that borderland folks living in real time would center on the *Plan de San Diego's* component of ethnic cleansing, rather than searching for the sociological undercurrents and motives of disillusioned and deluded radicals and shameful bandits? The scholars rightly retort: "Imagine that."[119] In the same vein of trimming cooked up gristle from the red meat of premium cuts, the authors serve up another tidbit to chew on regarding the plan's sanguine instigators and boots-on-the-ground followers: "The *sediciosos* were a lot better at writing than at fighting."[120]

Breaking free from concocted shackles of one dimensional political correctness reveals historical truths—and the search for truth is what historic study purports to be—that no subgroup owned exclusivity when it came to racism and stereotyping and stupidity. Along the Rio Grande there was enough to go around.[121]

Hardly had the buzz died down over the killing of Orozco south of Van Horn, when Dunaway and another Company B Ranger, Walter Rushin, scouted west of there, into the neighborhood of Sierra Blanca. They were in hot pursuit of a highjacker, a Post Office robber. On the seventeenth day of September 1915 the pair of Rangers located and safely arrested their man, hauling him back to El Paso County in handcuffs, and turning the hapless prisoner over to the well-known sheriff, Peyton J. Edwards.[122] Had he a crystal ball, James Dallas Dunaway may have very well—in the final rundown—opted to stay in El Paso.

Fredericksburg, Texas, is a quaint German town, picturesque and pleasant: Nice place to visit. In the first week of October 1915, Ranger Dunaway was there, not visiting and not any too nice. A Gillespie County grand jury was then sitting, hearing witnesses. The case-hardened and hard-boiled J. D. Dunaway was on tap to testify.

Also there as a witness was a nineteen-year-old known locally as Taliaferro. He knew something about the mysterious disappearance of some sheep and goats. Taliaferro was sitting outside in front of a merchentile. Although there's but a single version to cite, purportedly—and it seems believable—when Ranger Dunaway walked by the minding-his-own-business fellow, he said, not courteously: "You little son-of-a-bitch, don't look at me so mean." According to a happenstance bystander, "The young man sprung to his feet and remarked to Dunaway, 'I cannot take this off of any man.'" By way of honor Taliaferro may have been right, but, too, he was hotheaded. There on Fredericksburg's sidewalk stood two spring-loaded fellows with hair-trigger temperaments and *mucho machismo*. Odds-on Taliaferro didn't know he'd be tangling with a Grizzly bear, but he felt froggy—and he jumped! The fisticuffs—if there were any—were short lived. Taliaferro fell to the sidewalk, his skull fractured, presumably the result of connecting with the blue-steel barrel of Jim Dunaway's Colt's revolver.[123]

A Fredericksburg's attorney, Thomas J. Martin, may have instigated the Indictment against Dunaway, but for damn sure he made his displeasure known to Governor James E. Ferguson: the unmitigated gall of an undisciplined Texas Ranger whipping a witness! And, particularly about Private Dunaway he puffed and predicted: "if this man is not removed from the service that in a course of time his actions will result in a killing of some good man."[124] Governor Ferguson's uncoiled response was rattlesnake quick, instructing his adjutant general: "Please look into this matter, and if you find the facts as stated by him [Martin], remove Dunaway from the service."[125]

In the highly charged political climate it did not take long for the shoe to drop. Texas Ranger Dunaway was booted out of the service without a second thought. The adjutant general notified lawyer Martin: "J. D. Dunaway will cease to be a Texas Ranger on October 31."[126] With no options Dunaway handed over his railroad passes and commission to Captain Fox, after making arrangements to have his horse shipped home.[127] Dunaway was a Ranger no more.

The fundamental theme of this narrative was to emphasize the sometimes laudable and sometimes rocky law enforcing career of Dunaway while a Texas Ranger. Although he would try to reenter the Texas Rangers during 1918, he was politely informed that his application would be placed in the suspension file "for consideration at such time as there is a necessity for increasing the Ranger Force."[128] The Texas Rangers either rightly or wrongly had washed their hands of James Dallas Dunaway. That said, to prematurely register an idea that his Texas/Mexico borderlands law enforcing career was defunct would be folly. To follow his day by day footprints as a U.S. Government agent will now be left for a womb to tomb biographer, should someone wish to tackle a worthwhile book-length project. For this treatment, suffice to say, subsequent to his impotent attempt at regaining Ranger status, Mr. Jim Dunaway was intermittently employed as an Immigration Officer and as a Spanish language interpreter for the U.S. District Courts.[129]

Enforcing the law is hard work—typically a young man's game. After twenty-one years the grind and gunshot wounds took their toll. Although but fifty years of age Dunaway became increasingly weak. He was placed under a physician's care at Llano on December 21, 1923, but subsequently died of "heart failure" on February 21, 1924.[130]

Having a go at judging Dunaway's law enforcing career in nutshell is problematical. For this study only his days as a Texas Ranger were explored—purposely. For those periods of time while he was enlisted in the Ranger Force two core themes seem to emerge. Texas Ranger Dunaway, if circumstances spun "Western" in but a heartbeat, could—and would—stay hitched. Were one fighting a real battle in real time, Ranger James Dallas Dunaway's steadfast presence would be highly valued, much appreciated, and rather reassuring. There is, though, that flip side. As more than one captain—and adjutant generals—learned, trying to supervise Dunaway could prove nightmarish. Jim Dunaway's personal honesty and integrity and sense of duty were never questioned or in doubt: His temperament was. He was not a man to brook insult. Regrettably, sometimes even good lawmen have to—at least to a point—take a spoonful of guff and swallow some pride. Ranger James Dallas Dunaway had no appetite for such gibberish. His boiling point was low—way too low for the place and changing times, even in Texas. Though in some quarters agenda-driven folks choose to ignore the truth, Texas Rangers were really—despite the bumps—marching towards professionalism. Likewise there is that other hard to accept reality, the Wild West era had faded, passing James Dallas Dunaway by.

Captain William Jesse McDonald. As a legendary Texas Ranger he supervised and worked closely with Ranger James Dallas Dunaway, and on at least one occasion was even legally obligated to arrest him. *Courtesy Armstrong Research Center, Texas Ranger Hall of Fame & Museum.*

Seated from L to R: Texas Ranger Captain J. A. Brooks, John Morgan Brooks, and Special Ranger J. D. Harkey. Standing from L to R: Rangers Ivan Murchinson, Nathan Pendergrass Thomas, and James Dallas Dunaway. Texas Ranger Dunaway threatened to kill Ranger Thomas for his interfering with the pistol whipping he was issuing to provisional Ector County Sheriff Gee McMeans, a fellow later fatally cut down by the fêted Frank Hamer. From *Captain J. A. Brooks, Texas Ranger* by Paul N. Spellman and published with permission from the University of North Texas Press.

Texas Rangers in camp near Colorado City, Mitchell County. Ranger J.D. Dunaway was ordered out of Odessa, Ector County, and instructed to report to the Texas Ranger's Colorado City camp without delay. As identified in photograph, from L to R: 1-R.B. Baker; 2-N.P. Thomas; 3-Ivan Murchison; 4-T.B. White; 5-Parker Weston; 6-Captain Frank Johnson; 7-Billie McCauley; 8-Oscar J. Rountree. *Courtesy Armstrong Research Center, Texas Ranger Hall of Fame & Museum.*

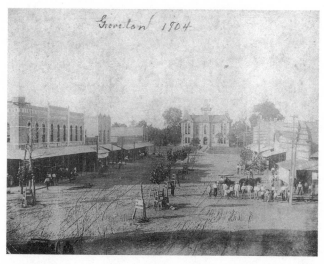

Groveton, Trinity County, Texas. While a Texas Ranger, J. D. Dunaway would be ambushed and severely wounded by a shotgun wielding and thoroughly disgruntled bushwhacking lawyer, shooting down from an upstairs office window. *Courtesy Trinity County Historical Commission.*

Herff Alexander Carnes, left, and Edgar Thomas Neal. Ranger Carnes would play a leading role during the investigation of dubious and illegal doings in Trinity County, and would also provide protective security for the critically wounded Ranger Dunaway after he was ambushed on the street at Groveton, Texas. Courtesy Armstrong Research Center, Texas Ranger Hall of Fame & Museum.

The legendary Frank Hamer, posted to the county adjacent to James Dallas Dunaway's bailiwick, may have had a nasty meeting with Bonnie and Clyde on the distant horizon, but in the short term, working territory at Junction, Kimble County, cattle rustlers, sheep and goat thieves, and a pig stealer occupied part of his time. L to R: Frank Hamer with palm over the Winchester's muzzle, and Texas Ranger amigo Robert Marmaduke "Duke" Hudson. *Armstrong Research Center, Texas Ranger Hall of Fame & Museum.*

An intermixed grouping of Texas lawmen: The notorious and controversial Texas Ranger Captain Henry Lee Ransom seated on left, James Dallas Dunaway seated behind him. *Courtesy Armstrong Research Center, Texas Ranger Hall of Fame & Museum.*

Captain John Reynolds Hughes, seated far right, in a letter to Texas Ranger headquarters coughed up his personal estimation of the hair-trigger temper of James Dallas Dunaway: "It is my opinion that he will be better off out of the Ranger Service than in it." The Rangers are, standing L to R: Herff Alexander Carnes, Sam McKenzie, and Arthur Beech. Seated L to R: Tom Ross, Albert Mace, and Captain Hughes. Note their cartridge belts are filled with rifle ammunition. Despite hyped Hollywood legend about pistol packing Wild West lawmen, a rifle was the preferred weapon of choice when the situation turned "Western." *Courtesy Armstrong Research Center, Texas Ranger Hall of Fame & Museum.*

CHAPTER 10

Most Feared Gangster of the Time

Brushing aside much of the popularized poppycock and some of the anemic theoretical attempts at turning bloodletting feuds into grandiose statewide conspiracies, there is yet room and reason to sharply focus the historic spotlight on an authentic example of Wild West organized crime, one firmly rooted in the Southwest with tentacles snaking through state and territorial lines and slithering across an international boundary.

Overcoming evil—substantial evil—is often the journalistic device employed when inflating a storyline—be it fiction or nonfiction. Jugging a needy pickpocket, where's the pizzazz in that? Triumphing over a worthy antagonist is what makes the story work—and sell. In the literary effort to create worthy meat for the ferocious Lion of Tombstone to devour, a scraggly looking fellow, Newman Haynes "Old Man" Clanton, is sometimes speciously puffed into the exalted position of an organized crime luminary. The whipsawing is a lame and a twentieth-century attempt at revising nineteenth-century truths. Factually: "Today we think of Old Man Clanton as if he is as well known as Satan himself . . . but at the time of the events the press couldn't or didn't want to even bother to give him a name."[1] In point of fact, at the time, newspapermen didn't even seem to suppose Clanton worthy of owning a first name.[2] In regards to this counterfeiting, a modern-era journalist hammers out the legitimate coin of truth:

> Old Man Clanton is portrayed time and again as a Cowboy Kingpin or Sagebrush Godfather, said to be the power behind all the illegal cowboy activity in Cochise County [Arizona]. But was he really? Consider this: Newman Haynes Clanton

was never charged with any crime, and he was quoted and
portrayed in contemporary newspapers as a solid citizen. . . .[3]

Likewise, chiseling slivers of factuality and amalgamating them
with hypothetical shards of wishful thinking does fabricate an end
product worthy of beer-table debate: The one about dressing family feuds in the see-through clothing of a political and ideologically motivated cabal. In truth, though, the authenticated historical
merit is somewhat hamstrung—due to a scarcity of sustaining
evidence: Nevertheless, one side is championing for believability with unfathomable and somewhat bizarre conjecture, the other
side advocating for securing the more traditional tale. So, as it
should be, thoughtful readers may peruse two divergent tomes,
assembling their own well-versed decision: Was the Taylor/Sutton
Feud or Sutton/Taylor Feud really the deadliest blood feud in
Texas, or was it the feud that wasn't?[4]

On the other hand, sustaining facts that the Southwest border country was home turf for a legitimate—well, illegitimate—
organized crime boss is easy. Perhaps, though, it's but fitting to
first carve out a working definition—a generic definition—of
what many criminologists would, at least loosely, consider components for an organized crime syndicate, or in today's terminology, a criminal cartel.

Generally speaking the fundamentals for qualifying as an
organized crime combine would include violations of the law on a
large scale; pursuit of profit through criminal means; the traits of
formal organization, with a division of labor and tightly structured
groups answering through an identifiable chain-of-command;
realization of and an acceptance of punishment for violating the
illicit outfit's policies and/or rules of conduct; businesslike coor-
dination between various sub-components; and a personally perceived feeling of immunity from arrest and prosecution by law
enforcers and district attorneys, predominately through the means
of financial corruption, blackmail, slippery underhanded political
payoffs—or due to an abject fear of being whacked for not looking the other way.[5]

Not surprisingly most nineteenth-century horseback gangsters
roaming the Southwest were anything but organized. Particularly
in Texas and the twin territories of New Mexico and Arizona the
owlhoots were for the most part wholly disorganized, nominally

acting as a vicious pack of teeth-gnashing wolves, subservient only to the most dangerous and depraved and dominant psychotic personality present at any given time. There was, however, an exception: John Kinney. His ascension to the throne of being a top dog crime boss, however, was not an overnight climb.

John Kinney was a Yankee. His 1853 Massachusetts birthplace was at or in close proximity to South Hadley, Hampshire County.[6] By way of a westward migration the widow Mary Ellen Kinney found herself and brood at Chicago, broke and hungry, near her wits' end. Stepping to the forefront and lying regarding his age, John offered himself as the figurative sacrificial lamb. As a raw recruit he joined the U.S. Army, turning over to his mother the enlistment bonus so the destitute family could continue moving west, first to Indian Territory, later backtracking to Iowa. While the family moved west, during April 1868 John Kinney marched east to the U.S. Army's Cavalry School at Carlisle, Pennsylvania. Subsequent to extra training at Fort Harker, Kansas, Private John Kinney was a full-fledged cavalryman, assigned to Troop K, 3rd U.S. Cavalry, posted—among other places—at southern New Mexico Territory's Fort Selden.[7]

Sited in Doña Ana County near banks of the Rio Grande, eighteen miles north and a touch west of Las Cruces, forlorn Fort Selden was—if not a hellhole—close to it. "Although strategic in location, Fort Selden was isolated. It was 500 miles from the nearest railroad in Colorado, and 250 miles from the nearest telegraph in Santa Fe."[8] Appearance-wise Fort Selden was drab, a systematic collection of structures manufactured from sun-dried adobe bricks and hard-packed dirt floors, surrounding the ever obligatory parade ground and flagpole. Slapped together during 1865, Fort Selden was thought to be strategically located for a multitude of military errands: "its purpose was to be a base camp for scouting missions sent out to reconnoiter fifteen thousand square miles of rugged, arid, and hostile territory. Their [the soldiers'] tasks were to protect settlers from Indians, chase rustlers, capture outlaws, escort the mail, protect travelers and wagon trains, and provide natural disaster relief."[9] It was a tall order. Most especially since more fighting occurred in and around the post between soldiers and soldiers, soldiers and civilians, than did in the field chasing Apaches or blue-eyed desert desperadoes. Fort Selden and the nearby civilian hovels known as Leasburg were planted on damn tough real-estate and inhabited by damn tough pale-faced warriors and damn profane painted princesses.

There were not garden clubs and knitting circles and church socials at cantankerous Leasburg. The iniquitous emporiums of pay-as-you-go sin at Leasburg were "inhabited principally by liquor sellers, gamblers and prostitutes of the lower class."[10] A paymaster running behind schedule was never a problem. Whores and barkeeps and tinhorn gamblers at Leasburg were willing—more than willing—to trade sexual favors and whiskey and settle gaming debts with Uncle Sam's property. According to one U.S. Army officer—just at Leasburg—the government was losing between $50 and $60 per day, due to the "illegal exchanges" between Fort Selden's soldiers and Leasburg's pirating riffraff. Atrociousness of the boldly illicit traffic is underscored: "Some whiskey dealers brazenly bartered their wares within the limits of a post, leaving in their wake intoxicated soldiers without weapons and clothing. The enormity of the problem is suggested by Captain James R. Kemble's request in 1867 for fifty-five revolvers to replace those lost by his company during the previous year. General James H. Carleton, then commanding the district of New Mexico, marveled that a company of eighty-eight men was left with only thirty-three pistols. It was obvious that the men had sold their weapons, for each revolver would command a much higher price on the local market than its original twelve-dollar purchase price. . . ."[11]

If one were lucky enough to not be one of the seven or eight soldiers foully murdered at Leasburg, twiddling one's thumbs on post was not too safe either. Inside the post commander's office two lieutenants jumped tacky and pulled their service revolvers, vowing to kill each other. They succeeded—miserably so—both officers crumpled to the dirt floor, bleeding and sledgehammer dead.[12]

For Fort Selden the statistical calculation was not any too benign: More soldiers perished as a result of outright lawlessness—twice as many—than did in the fort's entire combat history.[13] Emphatically, it must not be misconstrued, while John Kinney was with the military stationed at Fort Selden, it wasn't just soldiers that were being killed in Leasburg's barrooms and bordellos or murdering each other at post headquarters in Doña Ana County.

At nearby La Mesilla the Democrats and Republicans were at each other's throats—literally. During the sunshiny day of August 27, 1871, the whiskey level in bloodstreams went up, tolerance for differing political ideology went down. On the town's quaint little plaza, the Democrats and Republicans traded good sense for stupidity. Six-shooters came out. When the fireworks finally quieted, between seven and fifteen reposed New Mexicans were dead, and as many as fifty—or as few as thirty—were suffering serious gunshot wounds and/or bashed heads and bloodied noses. Unfortunately the galloping U.S. Army from nearby Fort Selden had arrived too late to put the quietus on rioting and prevent the senseless killings.[14] John Kinney had found a home to his liking, not in the military, but in this stretch of rough and tumble southern New Mexico Territory, a killing ground. He was a rough and tumble *mal hombre*.

Discarding his sergeant's stripes, John Kinney mustered out of the 3rd Cavalry on April 13, 1873, purportedly at Fort McPherson, Nebraska.[15] Discharging documents reveal the mustering out official noted that Sergeant Kinney had been considered a "brave soldier, a sober and honest man."[16] Such an optimistic evaluation of Kinney was premature, if pushed forward a few years. Or, he just had the blue-coated pencil-pushing discharging officer fooled. John Kinney quickly returned to New Mexico Territory, taking up residence in his old army stomping grounds, Doña Ana County. And it was there he began building his reputation, not as a nice guy but as a first-rate cow thief, hoodlum, and gangster: One with a proven knack for leadership—a Godfather in the making.

However, prior to ascending the stairway to Kingpin status, all creditable racketeers have to "make their bones." Kill somebody. John Kinney's chance—the first recorded chance—came on the night of 1 January 1876, or the wee morning hours just past midnight. John Kinney and his cowboying and cow stealing pals Jessie Evans, Jimmy McDaniels, and Charles "Pony Diehl" Ray locked up in a fisticuffs mêlée with troopers from Lieutenant Colonel Thomas Casimer Devin's 8th Cavalry at a Las Cruces *baile*. Private Matt Lynch, due to internal injuries sustained in the battle royal, would die four days later. But in the short term, it may be reported that John Kinney had unpredictably and all at once bought into a genuine ass whipping—and was carried out of the place by his cronies—bleeding and bruised, mad as a goddamn hornet![17]

Perhaps the old Texas saw was clichéd, but for this setting it was ringing true for John Kinney and his cohorts: "If God wanted men to fight like cats and dogs, He'd given 'em claws and paws." Returning to the dancehall, but *bravely* remaining outside, Kinney, Evans, McDaniels, and Pony Diehl unlimbered their Colt's .45s poking the barrels through open windows and into the darkened doorway. The crescendo was deafening. Privates Benedict Alig, Hugh McBride, and Sam Spencer felt the lead bullets tearing into their torsos, but luckily, lived to tell about it. The innocent bystander, an unnamed "Mexican," and Private John Reovir probably didn't hear or feel a thing—they just hit the floor, cold-anvil dead.[18]

Due to Doña Ana County's lackluster law enforcing apparatus, John Kinney and his dubious crew had little to fear, at least in the short go—a fact well noted by Lieutenant Colonel Devin who in an official report of the incident to the Secretary of War via the chain-of-command, chided local authorities with "supineness," being mentally and morally inactive—do nothings! Devin was not wrong. John Kinney was on the make, knowing he was not really ten foot tall, but thinking he was bullet proof—literally and figuratively and legally.

And it did not matter to ne'er-do-well Kinney how he made his money—fair means or foul. He established a *rancho* on the west bank of the Rio Grande about three miles from La Mesilla in what was generally characterized as the Mesilla Valley. All too soon it became widely known as "the headquarters for all the evildoers in the country."[19] If John Kinney had ever owned a good reputation as a soldier stationed in southern New Mexico Territory, it was a thing of the past. His standing in the Mesilla Valley was rotting quickly. Many thought him of lower repute than the cow thieves, killers, and general misfits hanging out at his ranch. He was even catching notice as far away as Santa Fe, the editor of the territory's leading newspaper, the *Daily New Mexican*, describing him as "leader of the New Mexico rustlers, and the man who has proven such a terror to the cattle interests of the territory." John Kinney, according to the no nonsense newsman, was the "major general" of all New Mexico cow-stealers. Furthermore, unabashedly and publicly the evocative scribe was broadcasting in the broadsheet, absent even a hint of trepidation, that John Kinney was "a braggart, talks loud, drinks hard, lacks prudence, has killed two men, brags of killing others; is bold but lacks nerve."[20] Kinney was soon to mark his notch-stick again.

For an anthological format it's not necessary to reel out and dissect the plethora of motives sometimes shrouding John Kinney's next dustup—a desperate La Mesilla gunplay. There is a hard bottom line—a funeral. On 2 November 1877 John Kinney was at Leandro Urieta's home at La Mesilla. In the front yard he was engaged in an intense conversation with Charles Bull and Ysabel Barela. Previously, somehow and by someone, John Kinney had been forewarned that Ysabel Barela was hellbent on killing him—settling his hash—with "a brand new Winchester." He who hesitates may die. John Kinney jerked out his blue-steel six-shooter, shoved the muzzle into Barela's blathering face and touched the trigger, "blowing away his lower jaw and inflicting a fatal wound."[21] A Johnny-on-the-spot newspaperman tweaked the gory little story: "Kinney drew a pistol which he pointed at Bull, who sprung to one side."[22]

Incensed at the reporters' inaccurate reporting, Kinney parried: "He [Barela] was under the influence of whiskey, while I was just as sober as a man could be. The man that says I put my pistol in Charley Bull's face is telling what is not so."[23] What was so: Was that the ever pugnacious John Kinney didn't deny killing Ysabel Barela. However he did hotfoot across the county line, opting for a leave-of-absence at Silver City, Grant County, New Mexico Territory.

Meanwhile back in Doña Ana County, it seems the widespread law enforcing apathy was bumping hard against public indignation and public pressure—John Kinney's goose was in need of a cooking. The county grand jury fired up the pot, returning criminal indictments.[24]

The fact Kinney was at Silver City was no secret. The fact that his hard-as-nails reputation had accompanied him to the picturesque city "Built to Last" was no mystery either. It was just the spot for a fellow of Kinney's ilk, "a town with all its hair on, its population a mixture of the most fearless and most desperate men on the frontier."[25] As thus far drawn from specifics and by implication, John Kinney was amassing a following: cutthroats and thieves, murderers and misfits, and a string of ethically challenged guys capable of winking at the law when it best suited their pocketbooks. All too soon it was recognized throughout the southwest

borderlands, "the gunfighter proving ground" that "blistering cauldron where so many Wild West gunmen made their reputations"
that John Kinney was—among other things—a "hired gun." His
six-gun talent was for sale, and that was not hush-hush cloak-and-
dagger hooey. What is frankly troubling though, and it will likely
never be explained, was during his sojourn in and around Silver
City, John Kinney forged a peculiar and seemingly unbreakable bond with the powerhouse county sheriff, Harvey Howard
Whitehill, and his fearless man-killing deputy Dan Tucker.[26]

Hardly had Kinney relocated to Grant County—progressively
laying the foundation for a criminal network, an organized crime
empire—and strategizing about how best to cope with Indictments
returned in Doña Ana County, than the desperate call went out for
his six-shooter skills and those of his henchmen. Some Texas fellows were in trouble: Bad trouble!

As so often is the case with biographical profiles, for the
moment John Kinney's story must be chronologically sidetracked
for a stage setting. The summarization will be quick. Scrupulously
adhering to facts—as troubling as it sometimes is—in some ways
historically knocks sideways inane rationalizations for misbehavior, mayhem, and murder. Professed under a guise of righting
wrongs of the past, the malignant excuse making is at this late date
quite widespread. Too, so is the manipulative awarding of a free
pass for ignoring constitutionally enacted statutes then in place.
For the most part crafty apologists and the inherent lameness of
their pretexts is a modern-era phenomenon. Comprehending and
condoning are not synonyms.

That said, the reality check is this: Geographically El Paso
County was a part of Texas, and by legislative tenet the citizens
were obligated to obey those laws promulgated at the statehouse.
Therein lay the rub. Far-flung El Paso County, from a genuine
no-nonsense perspective, was metaphorically comparable to "an
island in a sea of sand . . . hundreds of miles and decades in time
from most ports of civilization."[27] Demographically it might
as well have been an appendage of Mexico. Although the Rio
Grande served as an international line defining sovereignty, in that
context at El Paso, for most residents, the river was absolutely
meaningless. The *Mexicanos*, persons of Mexican decent and citizens of either nation, living along both banks of the *Río Bravo*
numbered roughly 12,000.[28] "Only about eighty non-Mexicans

lived in the valley. Although of varied national origin, they were usually lumped together as 'Americans.' Some five thousand Mexicans farmed the valley, and another seven thousand made up the Mexican city of Paso del Norte, at the mouth of the pass."[29] For those common and everyday folks, members of long established and extended family groups, they crossed the *Río Bravo* at their laid-back pleasure: There were many fiestas and fandangos and funerals to attend—and sometimes a good fight.[30]

Primarily *Mexicanos* along the Rio Grande on the Texas side were not Johnny-come-lately Americans. Those of middle and/or an advanced age were plainly Mexican Nationals by birth, but now by sheer happenstance and a not accidently orchestrated 1840s war with Mexico they were now citizens in a foreign land, but had not geographically budged an inch. Not in body. Certainly not mind:

> There was one other quirk of the Mexican mind which no Missouri lawyer could ever accept, and that was a fine, frank disrespect for written codes of law. Among those humble *peones* and proud *ricos* flourished a set of democratic ideas which went beyond anything an American had been able to subscribe to since 1776. They knew that power originates in the people and they reasoned that what the people agree on must be right regardless of the law books. "They were the people, and the people were the law."[31]

Many citizens in El Paso County's Rio Grande Valley, "as a mass were opposed to the American method of government, and any new or progressive laws which [are] in opposition to their accustomed views or feeling are [were] opposed to the extent of great disorders."[32] Remembering at the time under review for John Kinney's narrative that there was no railway connection to El Paso of any type whatsoever gives way to a salient point: "In short, El Paso County was beyond reach of state protection, and it lay on the border of a nation whose authority was weak and uncertain: and the policy of the Federal government was expressed in definite language, but weak in execution."[33]

Perhaps one of the best of such cross-cultural examples applicable to El Paso County was the Texas school law requiring kiddos between eight and eighteen to attend classes, boys and girls. *Mexicanos* on the Texas side were aghast. What good Catholic parent would even consider forcing an Americanized secular education on their children? No Bibles in the classroom? Blasphemy! Oh, yes, sending their innocent and chaste daughters over the age of fourteen years to school with boys, well, that was unthinkable, unfathomable—and unenforceable! Busybody lawmakers at Austin could just rethink the whole damn thing—that public school nonsense. Father Antonio Borrajo—"who hated everything American and particularly the compulsory school law" forbid his parishioners sending their kids to school: "the priest triumphed and the school law became a dead letter in El Paso County."[34]

Further complicating the melding of differing cultures was language. Although it may now register as fussy and tasteless, Texas State law was implicit—and El Paso County was in Texas. The sheriff, Charles Kerber (real name Friedrick Sperfechter), was in somewhat of a legal pickle: "In the event many [felony] indictments were found by the grand jury, it would be impossible, under the laws of the State, to find enough qualified petit jurors to try the cases, because the law requires the petit jurors should speak the English language. After indictments were found the only way to try these cases would be by change of venue to another county."[35]

Adding to the palatable cultural discord and mutual racism revealed by specific *Mexicano* and Anglo profiteers and hotheads, another ingredient was poured into the festering wound—Salt. Intrigues by parties wishing to profit from the saline lakes some 100-odd miles east of El Paso, for this retelling, must be pared down to the nub: Sly intrigues had been ongoing for years.[36]

The bottom line is this: Adhering to Texas' land laws, the salt lakes were *legally* acquired by George B. Zimpelman, with his lawyer son-in-law Charles H. Howard acting as on-the-ground agent. By any man's measure Howard was "a man not a mouse" and he was, too, pig-headed, ham-fisted and an all-around firebrand.[37] American capitalism okayed profiting from the ground one held title to, be it fat steers grazing on the topside, gold and silver buried on the bottom side, apples and oranges seasonally falling from above or the deliciously juicy wine-making grapes hand-picked from manicured vineyards. The land yielded. The American reaped its bounty. Philosophically certain *Mexicanos* had a differing take. By heritage and tradition thinking certain commodities should be free for the taking—and profiting from in distant marketplaces after fulfilling the local community's needs: Salt was one of those properties. Rather succinctly a historian shortstopped real world reality: "Even if the Mexicans and *teja-nos* did not have the legal right to the salt, they felt they had the moral right."[38] Louis Cardis, an Italian, like Charles Howard had an outsized ego and was politically powerful in El Paso County. Louis Cardis was the *Mexicanos'* upfront English-speaking voice for perceived and/or real patterns of injustice and insensitivity—and backroom guarantor of their own thoughtless prejudices.[39]

Absent telling the whole story in exacting detail, which others have masterfully done, cutting to the chase reveals that Charles Howard shotgunned to death Louis Cardis in what may or may not have been a justified preemptive strike. Self-defense if you will, get the other guy before he gets you.[40] A trial jury would never decide the merits of such an argument—or its lack of merit.

The wheels had plainly come off in El Paso County—at least so thought the state's perplexed chief executive. The Frontier Battalion's commander, Major John B. Jones, by order of the governor and adjutant general, was sent to investigate and extinguish the flames of raging disgruntlement. Thereafter a hastily formed detachment of Texas Rangers was fashioned from local stock—several of them confirmed killers and cow stealers and multifaceted menaces: one being the aforementioned six-shootin' and murderous pal of John Kinney, Jim McDaniels.[41] The hastily mustered Company C detachment was placed under direct command of an untested neophyte lawman, John Barnard Tays, now a spanking-new Texas Ranger lieutenant and forevermore the blood brother of the town's esteemed Episcopal clergyman, Joseph W. Tays. The selection was, according to at least one prominent historian, "not a proud moment in the career of Major Jones . . . Jones must also bear some responsibility for the character of Tays detachment."[42] El Paso County's stage was set for a hurricane of idiocy!

For pressing feisty John Kinney into such a sociological mess the crux of the matter is simple. A riotous mob formed, murdered a Texas Ranger and a storekeeper, forcing other Rangers to surrender—sans their Colt's six-shooters and Winchesters and cartridges and pride. Purportedly, from across the *Río Bravo*, the ever vociferous and vitriolic priest, Father Borrajo, was fanning the flames of bedlam: "Shoot the Gringos and I will absolve you."[43] Whether those words were actually spoken or not is inconsequential, for sure the priest did not want to curb any chaos.[44] Then nitwits from the run amok crowd summarily executed Howard, another Ranger, and one more hapless fellow, callously dumping them into an abandoned well after savagely mutilating their dead bodies.[45] Subsequently a hysterical rampage of looting stores and stealing property overrode any spectrum of sane rationality and good sense.[46] Just grievances may have washed away in the frenzy of bloodletting, pilfering, and pirating.[47]

Unquestionably outmanned, Sheriff Kerber had turned to the governor of Texas with a plea that he be allowed to raise a posse from nearby New Mexico Territory. The telegram had been answered in the affirmative, the request granted. Kerber swanked:

> I expect 50 citizens from Silver City, and then I will drive the scoundrels ahead of me like sheep. . . . I have no courts, no justice; nearly all were in the row, and I have to take it all in my hands. I know Texas will uphold me if no other State does. You will find I will not allow the greasers to pass unpunished.[48]

Hardly were Sheriff Charles Kerber's remarks the singular ones harboring a clear-cut bigoted racial pedigree. *Mexicano* Cipriano Alderete was just as dogmatic:

> We have marked everything down from the time when the rooster trod the hen until she laid the last egg. Everything is going to be paid for now, and we do not care what happens here after we have evened the score. You can take all these old houses. What are they worth? We will go across the river or somewhere else.[49]

Before returning to the timeline and picking up John Kinney's part in the story, it's helpful to pause and reflect on another hard truth, one often—lamentably—but conveniently brushed aside. For most histories of the area and time period, the native Spanish-speaking population figures along both banks of the Rio Grande/ *Río Bravo*, as earlier noted are given as 5000 on the American side, 7000 on the Mexican side. Studying the best available primary source estimates, the so-called El Paso Salt War mob measured at the top end about 500 fanatical looters and rioters—and a few murderers. If these demographic numbers are realistically correct, and there's no compelling reason to depreciate them too far upward or downward, the true quantifiable correlation is fixed—and is enlightening. A statistical accounting, then, does indicate that near 95 percent of the whole *Mexicano* population of El Paso's Rio Grande Valley voluntarily and thoughtfully opted to sit out any participation, whatsoever, in demonstrating, extorting, rioting, kidnapping, looting, murder, and/or frantic extralegal executions and pointless mutilations. Frankly, the nonpartisan comparative analysis is uncomplicated: If the evident bad behavior was really some type of groundswell people's movement—as is often alleged—in the Grand Scheme it roped in but few people.

It seems—all too frequently—the actual emphasis on the much ballyhooed El Paso Troubles has been to promote a blame game: Journalistically or sociologically rushing to defend one set of miscreants, while altogether condemning and rebuking and excoriating the other. Unfortunately such hurried carelessness or calculating cleverness has very real but unintended consequences: The champions have been overlooked. Should not the 95 percent of *Mexicanos* choosing not to have had a hand in blatant criminality and murder be roundly applauded? For the vast majority of the majority population it is abundantly clear: they were purposefully and mightily setting good examples for their children, not only were they obeying the law, but respecting the actual spirit of statutory law.[50] Should they not be fairly and fittingly extolled? Casting nets too wide is folly. Blanket indictments are threadbare. In the usual sense the so-called Salt War really wasn't a war. Critical forces of personality, greed, and uncontrolled egos had trumped sanity and soberness.[51] Demographic accountability plainly reveals the bloody rampage was not a *populist* movement and, in accord with those numbers, not any too popular. A rhetorical question is not out of place: Was it the Insurgency that wasn't?

A minority population subset of murderous and looting and duplicitous *Mexicanos* would soon learn they hadn't cornered the market on meanness. From Silver City the aforementioned Dan Tucker captained a hard-riding posse answering Sheriff Kerber's call, John Kinney among the rabble known generically as the Silver City Rangers.[52] The speedily enlisted recruits were "hard faced and battle scarred . . . they nearly all had reputations."[53] Not unrealistically it's been scholarly proffered: "Sheriff Kerber had been promised the aid of 50 men from Silver City. On December 21 [1877], 30 men from Silver City arrived; judging by their performance it is well that 50 did not come. . . . Many of them were men of evil reputation, and hard character. . . ."[54] A snippet in the *Galveston Daily News* was prophetic, maybe not twenty-first century politically correct, but prophetic nevertheless: "The blood shed by the Mexican butchers at San Elizario will hardly be suffered to go unavenged for the flimsy technical reason that it was a purely local squabble over a salt pond."[55]

Now the boot was on the other foot and the sheriff, a detachment of real Texas Rangers, and some yahoos from New Mexico Territory standing-in as pseudo Rangers, wanted to kick ass! The legalities could be dammed! Their settling of scores cannot be made light of, excused, condoned—or historically erased. Collectively their behavior was atrocious and murderous—and wholly indefensible by any civilized standard, anywhere. They, too, had morphed into a mob. Prisoners were gunned down while *purportedly* escaping, and sexual assaults were perpetrated at gunpoint. *Mexicanos* were threatened, violently thumped on the head, shot inside and outside their homes, and personal property purloined by this hard set of death dealing desperadoes and first-class ruffians. Several of the New Mexico ne'er-do-wells were not subserviently content to unassumingly confine their retaliatory misdeeds to Texas; they exported the madness to Mexico. Many were the upright *Mexicanos* and Anglo Texans truly glad to see the unruly crowd from New Mexico Territory—finally—disband and go home. And home some of them went to what was apparently a rousing reception:

> A considerable number of the Silver City contingent to the El Paso army of occupation retuned to town last Saturday. They expressed themselves as well satisfied with their lark. No expense, plenty of fun and a measure of experience which may be turned to advantage in future campaigns.[56]

Their historic legacy is appalling! Their crimes were inexcusable; their unbridled racism rancid. For a time it seems certain folks along both banks of the Rio Grande were bending to craziness. Equating the El Paso Troubles with the American Revolution's Boston Tea Party is a stretch that won't stand scrutiny: Kinney's choosing to remain in El Paso was no tea sippin' matter either: He opened the Exchange Saloon.[57]

Gospel hymns, punctuated by fire and brimstone sermons from the pulpit draw reverent folks. Whiskey and whores and wagering and a wanton disregard of self-restraint drags its own crowd. The Exchange Saloon was not a sanctuary in the churchy sense, but it was sanctuary for a pool of depraved cutthroats and ne'er-do-wells, cow stealers and homicidal psychotics—and pond scum. John Kinney was the Kingpin—Ringleader—Top Dog at "a hangout for the most parasitical."[58]

Kinney's physical tenure as an El Paso barroom proprietor would be somewhat short-lived. Conversely, the heavy hands of his disreputable outfit would be much longer felt in that town. The city, sometimes mockingly dubbed "Hell Paso," would not be able to shake John Kinney's influence for several years. Without delay Kinney concocted his brand of criminal cologne—and it categorically reeked with an aroma of wickedness. All too soon John Kinney's name and gang of horseback buccaneers became "household" words at wild and woolly El Paso. According to one reflective resident, who was actually there at the time, it was but "a common occurrence to see these men go through the town shooting at those who opposed them."[59]

Gist of the putrid stink emanating from the crime boss' saloon can be distinguished—quickly. Shortly after opening the Exchange, John Kinney and another fellow engaged in a six-shooter imbroglio. "Buckskin Joe" Haytema managed to get off a lucky shot, injuring Kinney's left hand, but afterwards had to flee the barroom with an empty revolver, right fast ahead of John's loaded Colt's .45 and his fully charged and stinging rounds of vocal contempt.[60] John Kinney's mean deportment ratcheted up another notch. Skinning John Kinney's story to the bone—even with a dull knife—leaves the nitty-gritty intact. Kinney, due to energy of his persona and, for the time and place, unrivaled managerial skills in the Southwestern world of crookdom, had carved his niche. John Kinney would very shortly and very rightly claim owneriship of "the Southwest's most organized criminal enterprise."[61] He either sponsored or associated with cow thieves, killers, and U.S. Army payroll robbers.[62] He also spent no little effort in devious schemes focused on intimidating would-be voters.[63] Pinning on a shiny badge as one of Sheriff Charles Kerber's deputies only added to his overall effectiveness as a mob boss—and amplified the price for acquiring John Kinney's strong-arm talents and the six-shooter services of his hired-guns.[64] Extra firepower was needed in Lincoln County. Two factions were crusading for economic dominance—with bullets. John Kinney was for sale.

Corralled in this format, trying to break down underpinnings of the Lincoln County War story would be journalistically suicidal—an unorganized stampede of foolishness and imprudence. Simply stated, it can be accurately reported that Kinney and a passel of his good-for-nothings reported for duty under the auspices of Sheriff George Warden Peppin of the Murphy/Dolan federation.[65] Purportedly John Kinney, not uncharacteristically it would seem, bragged to an affiliate of the rival lineup, the McSween/Tunstall bloc, why he had temporaily left El Paso on the back trail. According to the witness, Kinney remarked that he had come to Lincoln County for "collaterial" and when pressed John sardonically described "collaterial" as "cattle and horses and things."[66] The sassy gunfighting guy from El Paso was at Lincoln when the Five-Days Battle erupted. Ostensibly, he was one of the casualties, at least so said Frank Coe:

> The Kid [Kid Antrim aka Billy the Kid] led the way out with a six-shooter in each hand. We came running through fire and bullets. Bob Beckwith charged for the door and the Kid shot him right between the eyes and he fell almost in the burning door. The men of the other side were all full of whiskey or they would not have made such a charge. There were four or five of the Beckwiths and they were all killed during the war. They began to scatter when the Kid came out. A noted bully, John Kinney, who they had got on the Rio Grande, was right up close to the door. He was behind an adobe wall about two feet and a half high. He raised up just as the Kid shot Beckweith, and the Kid let him have it. The Kid shot his mustache off. Kinney told me later that the bullet just cut his lip. He dropped back like he was dead. The Kid thought he had killed him, jumped the fence, and ran on. Kinney said that he might have killed the Kid as he ran off, but was afraid to rise up, as he was afraid the next man coming out of the door would get him. . . .[67]

Hemorrhaging John Kinney did rise up, at least so said the seriously wounded Yginio Salizar: "After the battle in Lincoln I was left for dead but was taken to other side of [the] mountain. I was shot first in the side and next in the back. There is a bullet there yet. The other time was shot in hand. I don't know who shot me. John Kinney took my gun away from me after I was shot down and kicked me. I was conscious, but just laid there."[68]

Histories of the Lincoln County War are abundant, some quite good, others partisan and garbled and due to substantive inaccuracies are dreadfully misleading. Caution is the byword. Even brigand John Kinney's deeds have sometimes been underwritten by hurried sloppiness. John Kinney's real crime doings during the classic siege and killing of several fellows, including Alexander McSween and the burning of his home, register as thoroughly reprehensible—good fodder for latter day writers though. Leopards do not change their spots, Kinney was a predator. True, Billy the Kid, blazing six-shooters in hand, did manage his getaway for awhile—a little while—but he and John Kinney would shortly meet again. Kinney wasn't any too nice, but in this instance he wasn't an imbecile, a clueless fool. Ahead of lawfully drawn felony Indictments as payback for his abysmal—and illegal— performance in Lincoln County, John Kinney and his not playacting gangsters returned to the neighborhood of El Paso.[69]

Their arrival did not go unnoticed. Presently the Ranger lieutenant, James A. Tays, who had replaced his brother, would report: "Every thing is quiet at present & Kinney has made his appearance again with quite strong party but they are operating on the Mexican Side of the River."[70] Followed up by another missive the overworked lieutenant lamentably updated Ranger headquarters about the fact that Kinney's band was "on the steal" but due to the "River and the State Line" being so very close, the overconfident outlaws were continually crossing and "defying" them. Too, it seemed that John Kinney and his nasty crew had found some easy marks, at least according to Ranger Tays: "Kenneys [sic] band are back in Franklin & the Jews are scared badly as the roughs along with Kenney are making threats on their Stores."[71] Malice and aforethought were not always drawn: Negligence is plentiful.

Where men—even good men—are handling guns there's room for slip-ups and stupidity. Such was the case while Frontier Battalion boys were waiting for a slick chance to effectively waylay noted cow thief and master-class thugster Kinney on Texas ground. Private Henry Crist had enlisted with the Rangers during September 1878.[72] The following month, he was dead! The distraught but diligent Lieutenant Tays updated Major John B. Jones: "I am sorry to inform you that on the night of the 13th Henry Crist one of my last Enlisted men was Accidently Shot by a Pistol falling from the holster of another man[.] The Bullet passed through the haunches cutting the Bowels [.] The Man lived Eleven Hours[.] I am of the opinion that it was purely accidental but very much to be regretted."[73]

Apparently—at least in his mind—banking plenty of political firepower at the local level, John Kinney slipped into New Mexico Territory and—in the end—surrendered to Doña Ana County lawmen absent a gunplay, answering for the earlier gunning down of Ysabel Barella at La Mesilla. Granted a Change of Venue, a not inappropriate transfer it proved to be, the trial jury at Silver City returned its verdict: Not Guilty. Subsequent to charges from Lincoln County falling into an abyss—the recurring lackadaisical policing and prosecuting—the by no means dormant criminal career of Sir John Kinney, as he was now being referred to, skyrocketed.

If the newspaper report is credible, during another six-shooter dustup John Kinney shot and perhaps killed a "Mexican" near his old stomping grounds, Fort Selden. Another motion for a Change of Venue was asked for and granted. Again, at Silver City, the verdict was Not Guilty.[74] John Kinney, so it seems, had friends in high places at Grant County's shiretown: And not just a few in adjacent Doña Ana County, as well as in Lincoln County. Kinney's gun was yet for sale. The sheriff wanted to make a buy.

It seems Kid Antrim had been snared at Stinking Springs and returned to La Mesilla in chains to strand trial for ambushing the Lincoln County Sheriff, William Brady. The murder had not been a standup showdown on Main Street but a coldhearted bushwhacking: Carried out while secreted behind an adobe wall. The Kid would have his day in court, although the outcome was fairly foreseeable from the get-go. Charitably—in making a good story better—it's been written that Kid Antrim was a little darling of the native Spanish speaking populace, a superstar of sorts. Perhaps, in part, it's right. Likewise it's as well true that twelve jurymen heard the prosecutor's arguments, weighed the evidence, and rendered a verdict of Guilty. And, too, it's also bona fide fact every one of those fellows—all tried and true—were Hispanic, not an Anglo in the jury box. Not one. One of those jurors, Felipe C. Lopez, and his brother Florencio, were actually in the Doña Ana County courtroom when Kid Antrim was hobbled before Judge Warren Bristol's judicial bench for sentencing. The Kid had been decked out in a black suit of clothes and black shoes, all courtesy the gentleness and generosity from the Sisters of Mercy, Catholic nuns from the Loretto Academy and Convent of Las Cruces. Eeriness enveloped the two Lopez brothers: They could sense Antrim was *vestido de muerto* [dressed for death]. He was! The execution was slated for conclusion near the crime scene, Lincoln, Lincoln County, New Mexico Territory.[75]

Fine-tuning the mechanics of transporting the convicted murderer from La Mesilla to Lincoln was a nightmare, logistically. Though, truthfully Antrim had few solid friends left in his camp at the time, still by any lawman's measure the felony prisoner could be classified an "Escape Risk." Sensible protocol for the journey would demand due diligence. John was diligent and dangerous. Kinney provisionally sold his time and the services of his six-shooter—if need be—to the sheriff. The deal was straightforward: Should there be an attempt at escape or rescue, Kid Antrim would be the very first guy gunned down—no dilly dallying, no excuses—and no silly second thoughts. John Kinney, accompanied by Dave Woods, Bob Olinger, Billy Matthews, D. M. Reade, Tom Williams, and W. A. Lockhart—all heavily armed—profitably moved Kid Antrim to Lincoln on April 21, 1881.[76] As Wild West annals confirm, from there Kid Antrim, a Death-Row inmate, hardheartedly assassinated two deputies, escaped the makeshift jailhouse, topped a horse, and spurred wildly toward earthly death at Fort Sumner and eternal life in history books—and on the silver screen. Crime boss John Kinney—who was not anywhere near Fort Sumner when the Kid gave up the ghost—just went back to work.[77] He was a busy man.

Sandwiched between the several stints John Kinney acted as a mercenary, he had fashioned a network of enterprising nonconformists, hard cohorts loath for conforming to any manmade law. Lower level minions were soldiers, answering to Kinney, but never bending to legit authority. The Southwest was booming with economic prospects for hardworking honest men—and crooks. One and all were tied by common cord—they liked beefsteak and pot roast and succulent ribs. Zealous restaurateurs, frugal husbands, and penny conscious housewives hungered for beef—at bargain basement prices. Red meat put the fire in men's bellies, muscles on kids' bones.[78]

John Kinney cornered the wholesale meat business with style—by wholesale cattle stealing. For kitchen tables or café tables there was a glut of high quality beef—all thanks to John Kinney. That he built an illicit empire is unarguable. That he was an astute businessman is unchallenged. Smartly, John Kinney oversaw the livestock business from hoof to mouth—the steer's hoof, the consumer's mouth. Whether it be herds of walking beeves or carload lots of hanging carcasses was of no import for John Kinney. Cow stealing cowboys, bloodied slaughter house employees, and knife wielding butchers owed an allegiance to John Kinney, undisputed King of the Rustlers. Tasty meat on the table at cheap prices, well, most anybody would like that—no questions asked.

Kinney's business model was uncomplicated. Platoons of cow thieves, under a command structure of sub-lieutenants, worked specifically defined territories, coordinating closely with their bad brethern in adjacent fiefdoms: All ruled by Sir John Kinney. One of those subordinates was the aforementioned Pony Diehl, a nitwit misfit whom a newspaperman identified "as black a picture of an unhung villain as we can find in a year's search."[79] John Kinney's underlings would steal cattle in their assigned domain and hustle the herd for a handoff to associates, who shortly thereafter passed them off again. The set up was childlike but it worked. A herd of fat cattle purloined in southern New Mexico Territory or Mexico was pushed north—and vice versa. Cattle stolen in Texas were fast pressed west—and vice versa.

Wheeling and dealing John Kinney, incisively recognizing that already huge profits could be made greater by bypassing middlemen, shaped the second tier of his lucrative transnational plan. He established himself as the most important discount purveyor of hanging beef carcasses for Las Cruces/La Mesilla and El Paso/ *El Paso del Norte* (now Ciduad Juárez).[80] Some fifty-odd miles north of Las Cruces was the railroad stop of Rincon. And it was here, with unchallenged access to an open secret railway siding, Kinney founded headquarters for his dressed beef setup. In but short order he was—reportedly—shipping 84 quarters of beef to El Paso every day.[81] Simply crunching those numbers is helpful: Solely for the El Paso marketplace—on an annual basis—Kinney was shipping from an inventory of more than 7,500 head of dead cow creatures. That the general public was but winking at illegalities, the hypocritical populace "that didn't give a hoot in hell where the meat came from as long as it was cheap," is evidenced by the fact that Rincon, in the everyday speak of southwestern New Mexicans, was known as Kinneyville.[82] Not slowly Kinney expanded his distribution network, shipping beef by rail north to Socorro and Albuquerque, New Mexico Territory, and south to Chihuahua and Palomas, Mexico.[83]

If walking beeves and slaughtered cattle—although stolen— were but the only two legs propping up John Kinney's stool of an organized criminal empire it would unmistakably topple. Kinney was in critical need of a third leg for solid support and John screwed it in place: Fear! Incontestable evidence has thus far shown, and will continue to reveal as the narrative unfolds, that John Kinney was indeed the "Real McCoy" in the realm of real fighting with real guns. There is, too, an analogous dynamic. Embellishing his man-killing scorecard, aside from an inane ego boost, had the practical advantage of putting the "fear of God" in would-be enemies—and/or commercial competitors. So, whether or not he had actually killed fourteen men as he bragged doesn't matter: Some folks thought he had.[84] Truthfully, it was believable. Quantifiably it's not demonstrable, not anywhere near watertight.

Though relatively short in physical stature, the debauched John Kinney was a human dynamo at physically settling or becoming involved in disputes. Two yet to be mentioned examples will suffice. In the first instance, at Rincon, inside Pete Carl's saloon, John Kinney became embroiled in a six-shooter dispute with one Pat Kelly. Kinney would have forfeited his life that day, had it not been for Pete Carl's intervention: "He knocked Kelly's arm up just as he fired." Kinney was a scrapper. Near the same time Kinney supposed that one of his henchmen, Frank Emmons, had insulted or was paying way too much attention to his wife, Juana. John Kinney pistol whipped him unmercifully. According to eyewitnesses the blows "sounded like an ax hitting an oak tree." Afterwards, for sure, Frank Emmons was not a pretty picture: He had "deep cuts all over his skull and his face was bruised and blackened in every feature, his lips and ear cut open, his jaw broke, and several teeth and a piece of jaw bone knocked out."[85]

The crime chieftain wasn't near through: "John Kinney ordered a Mexican to dig a grave saying that he would supply the corpse in a few days. While the empty grave yawned and the neighbours speculated on who he might have in mind, Kinney himself patrolled the village with a Winchester under his arm, defying the authorities to arrest him. The latter avowed their complete willingness to oblige. . . ."[86] There is no worthwhile evidence that John Kinney ever cold-bloodedly killed Frank Emmons, but there is an offshoot truth: Area lawmen—either through bullying or bribery—were in his pocket. During her twilight years a New Mexican lady wittingly summed up the situation, declaring that John Kinney "was the most feared gangster of the time." Then she wryly added hardcore reality: "That up against his rifles the bean-shooter civil law was powerless."[87]

Cheap beef was good for the consumer, bad for the cattleman. If the newspaper reports are accepted at face value and, taking into account the huge geographical stage Kinney dominated, it's not far-fetched though it's somewhat mind-boggling, his gang stole near 10,000 head of cattle in a single month, January 1883.[88] What is not far-fetched is that area ranchers were mad. For Governor Lionel Sheldon's eyes sixty-six New Mexico Territorial cowmen signed a petition highlighting their misery and misfortune. Aggravated ranchmen wanted to double down, making sure the governor was up to snuff: These cow thieves were not itinerant waddies gone wrong. They were saddle-toughened career criminals, strategically stationed throughout the desert Southwest, receiving orders from and answering to the big boss through a chain-of-command. Collectively the fed-up ranchers had made fire and lit the fuse, now it was time to see if the territory's chief executive owned any dynamite or just dribbling dialogue. He detonated, orally. The bombast was real: Sheldon guaranteed he "would make New Mexico safe for honest and industrious people" or barring that, he would "depopulate the whole damn territory."[89]

The governor's dynamic ignition wasn't confined to talk. He called out the territorial militia and his orders to Major Albert Jennings Fountain were not fuzzy:

> The bands you are in pursuit of are in combinations and constitute armed marauders or banditti. They are armed against society, and their acts and crimes are numerous and are calculated to set at defiance all law and government. They must be treated not as individual criminals, but as foes of

the public. While I wish them arrested, tried, convicted and punished by the courts, you must treat the case as the manifestation requires and as public security demands. As I have before written, I put great confidence in you and in your officers and men, and I assure you that it will be a case presenting extraordinary features which will cause me to treat your command or any member thereof otherwise than as you recommend.[90]

The unfeigned phantom behind "As the manifestation requires and as public security demands" does not necessitate any theoretical and/or wrinkled-brow academician's classroom construal. There really was a nitty-gritty and easily read bottom line. It was this: Put the damn kibosh on this mess right now. If need be kill the sons-of-bitches! Executive clemency will be forthcoming.

Armed with a *carte blanche* Albert Jennings Fountain, not immune to a dash of ambition and an occasional dab of "swashbuckling," and not nary for a split-second chancing "opportunity for fame and glory to slip away unused" dispatched his legions.[91] Sir John Kinney was in need of a potent dose it was supposed: Fountain would give him a choice—Castor Oil or Strychnine.

John Kinney was the top dog, and he sniffed trouble in the air. With his tail tucked between his legs he secretly—he thought— scampered into Grant County to chew the fat with ex-sheriff Harvey Howard Whitehill, the first lawmen to have arrested the then juvenile delinquent, but later full-grown murderer, Kid Antrim. Were there warrants for his arrest in Grant County? That's what John Kinney wanted to know. There were in Doña Ana County, so he'd been clued. Whitehill didn't know of any— as of yet. John Kinney was on the dodge, but he was flush with cash, his wife and brother having promptly and purposely—under orders—deflated Kinney's hefty El Paso bank accounts.[92] John Kinney trotted off into the night.

Meanwhile divergent companies of the 2d Cavalry Battalion, New Mexico Territorial Volunteer Militia were nosing around, too. Major Fountain had called out the Mesilla Guards, the Las Cruces Rifles, and the seasoned Shakespeare Guards.[93] Captain J. F. Black, a much-admired frontiersman was deployed the furthest west, scouring the daunting Gila River country along the New Mexico/Arizona borderline with his Shakespeare Guards, subsequent to a hard-charging but unproductive campaign in Lincoln County.[94] Commanding the Las Cruces Rifles was a whirlwind of a combat man, Captain Eugene Van Patten, veteran of fighting Yankees and Apaches, and future Doña Ana County sheriff. For this undertaking he was to clean out the nasty nest in and around Rincon and at Kinney's Cottonwood Ranch near Lake Valley, roughly forty-five miles east of Silver City. Major Fountain would ride with Captain Van Patten's company. The steadfast headman for the Mesilla Guards was Captain Francisco Salazar, who would begin his dragnet fifteen miles south of Las Cruces/La Mesilla, principally focused on La Mesa, the seedy lair for Kinney's lieutenant Doroteo "Tiger" Sains (Saenz), an evil killer known locally as "the fastest gun on the river."[95]

Tiger Sains proved to be pretty fast at diving through windows, too. On 20 February 1883 he, his brother Mario and Faustino López, without delay and little fanfare crawled through one in the backroom of a scandalous La Mesa *cantina*, while other pinned down desperadoes in a front room were engaging Captain Salazar's militiamen in a scorching gunfight. Although Tiger, the posse's prime target, made a clean getaway, Eugenio Pedraza didn't. He gulped his last breath, which a local journalist declared was "a relief to every stockman in southern New Mexico." Salazar's men did manage to take three breathing prisoners, José Enriques, Severo Apodaca, and most luckily—but not knowing it then—Margarito Sierra. There was, however, the buzz of loose talk that in the case of a doomed Pedraza the border country convention of *la ley de fuga* had been triggered, the owlhoot gunned down *purportedly* during a foolhardy try at jumping custody. From political and ideologically centered postures various newsmen were gingerly entertaining questions about process, not necessarily overawed by results—no matter how dramatic.[96]

On their northern sweep to Rincon and the country between there and Lake Valley, Fountain and Van Patten didn't provoke or suffer any gunplay. They did latch onto a quartet of hard-cases, Mariano Cubero, Leonardo Maese, Gaspar Montenegro, and Juan Bernal. Others, too, were snared in the wide loop being cast, but their names—at least for now—are lost to history. What was not buried in obscurity was Major Fountain's aggressiveness in searching houses and barns and boxcars of the trains he forcefully stopped. Broadsheet editors made two notes: His policies were dubious at best, unsavory and unconstitutional at worst, and Kinney was yet to be caged.[97]

Fountain caught a break. Due to level-headed preplanning Tiger Sains was no stranger to Texas Ranger Captain George Wythe Baylor of El Paso. At Concordia, Texas, he was captured and then turned over to Fountain for transport back to Doña Ana County.[98] The geographical gap between El Paso and Las Cruces was short, travel time—on a train—trifling. Tiger Sains didn't want to travel by train, so he jumped off and ran into the brush for awhile—a little while. Sain's jaunt—silhouetted against the night's sky—ended with loud reports of Fountain's pistol. Not unexpectedly some scribes were a wee bit skeptical. Was Tiger making a break for liberty? Or, was he shoved off the train and shot? Major Fountain stuck to scenario one—vehemently!

In regards to the Tiger Sains killing, Major Fountain reeled in another fortuitous break, particularly after it was made public that the murderous outlaw had been keeping score of his homicides—at least some of them—in a tattered and blood stained personal diary. Mindlessly and self-incriminatingly "the fastest gun on the river" had tallied:

> Con pistol en la matto
> Yo mato Americanos
> Tres mato.[99]

If truth be told, the translation to English speaks volumes and in the minds of many folks passing judgment from an armchair, it somewhat mitigated any assertions that Tiger Sains bled to death atop the desert sand as result of *la ley de fuga* administered by the quick work of Major Fountain: "With gun in hand I have killed Americans. Three I have killed."[100]

John Kinney didn't catch a break. During that sneaky nighttime detour into Silver City, and later the next day, and unbeknownst to him, he had been spotted by an embittered enemy or given up by a supposed friend. At any rate, Frank Cartwright, Superintendent for the Sierra Grande Company at Lake Valley, owned very valuable and critical criminal intelligence. At Silver City the highly sought fugitive had been stocking up on supplies, and not just a little revolver and rifle ammunition.[101] Superintendent Cartright telegraphed Major Fountain. Upon receipt of the news Fountain sent hard-riding couriers to find Captain Black and react. Black's mandate from the major was plainspoken: Capture John Kinney "at any hazard." Newshounds, ever drooling for a good story—an appetizing story—gobbled up this one:

> Capt. J. F. Black, of Shakespeare, is making the Gila very uncongenial for the followers of his highness—Sir John Kinney—and deserves great credit for the same. Mr. Black is not a tenderfoot as the rustler will observe after he comes in contact with him a few times.[102]

Armed with the freshly relayed data, Captain Black and the Shakespeare Guards quickly picked up John Kinney's southwestern bound trail—it was easy work: the outlaws were driving a stolen herd of 36 horses and mules. Scooting across New Mexico Territory's southwestern border, Kinney and his wife plus a brother, had forted-up at York's Ranch near Ash Springs, seven miles south of Clifton, Arizona Territory. Pesky little details about chasing across a manmade boundary line made not a whit of difference to Captain Black: York's ranch was encircled. There, according to El Paso's *Lone Star*, commonsense overhauled Kinney: "Notwithstanding all his brag and bluster, he quietly surrendered and begged like a Mormon elder for his captors to spare his life."[103] Making darn sure not to let persnickety legalities quickly ruin a good thing, Captain Black right fast hustled his prisoners back into New Mexico Territory, locking them in a sidetracked boxcar at Lordsburg. John's wife and brother posted a cash bond and were released. The Sagebrush Godfather, due to intercession of Governor Lionel Sheldon, was not turned loose. Kinney was glumly whining "that he would as soon be sent to Hell as taken back to Las Cruces." Such static was but background noise for Fountain's ears. He rushed to Lordsburg, latched onto the gang of rustler's "major general" and subsequent to the speedy train trip east ensconced him in Doña Ana County's steel-barred hotel. For the short-term John Kinney was up the creek without a paddle and, for the long-term, he would just be up-the-river.[104]

John Kinney's abrupt undoing at trial could be laid at the doorstep of that former colleague in crime, Margarito Sierra, who had "flipped." Cutting a deal, he agreed to tell the truth. Fighting for his ever-lovin' liberty in the "free world" John Kinney would never consent to such foolishness as confessing—to anybody for anything. He'd gamble with a jury. The game's stakes were high, the deliberations short—eight minutes. John's drag from the pot was a nickel—five years to do.

For the most part cattlemen—it may be logically guessed— where quite ecstatic to see the King of the Rustlers cuffed and carried to the penitentiary at Lansing, Kansas, where New Mexico Territory's felonious inmates were incarcerated prior to the grand opening of their very own prison at Santa Fe in 1885. On the second day of May 1883 prison officials issued Sir John Kinney a new wardrobe as well as a new identification number: He was now simply known as #2923, a convict from Doña Ana County doing time for Larceny of Cattle.[105] Those less directly affected by king-pin Kinney's incarceration may have had more ambivalent feelings than victimized Southwestern cattlemen if another snippet in El Paso's widely circulated *Lone Star* is emblematic of the general public's fickleness:

> When Kinney was in his glory, beef at Rincon was six-cents
> a pound: now it is twenty-five and scarce at that.[106]

What was not scarce was the commendation and condemnation being laid at the feet or hurled at the head of Major Fountain. The crime boss may have been dethroned—out of the saddle— but that did not dampen the major's enthusiasm for breaking the back of Kinney's onetime empire. Fountain's raids continued, more known and suspected outlaws were arrested—and more known and suspected outlaws were mortally cut down in the act—or *alleged* act—of fleeing custody. Newspaper editors had a field day, the underpinnings of their pieces not atypically in line with their favored brand of politics or their own affiliations with political parties and party bosses.[107] Personal perspectives are pervasive—even if not persuasive.

Polishing this phase of Albert Jennings Fountain's story is best left to his biographers and Wild West writers: But what of John Kinney? With the king's scepter removed from his left hand and the six-shooter from his right, Kinney was high-ranking no more, just a convict doing hard time. Institutionalized in a

faraway place, prisoner Kinney had forfeited any influential footing he may have owned—and measuring at but 5-foot 6 in height,
he was not standing on high ground in the face of brawny convicts who were snarling man-eaters in their own right. However
he did have a fighter in his corner. High-powered and capable
lawyer William T. "Poker Bill" Thornton would handle Kinney's
battles by proxy—not from behind high walls, but in front of
an appellate court's bench. Thornton scored a knockout. On the
nineteenth day of February 1886 the prison gate swung open
and John Kinney stepped out; his motion for a new trial having
been granted. While confined Kinney had been a model prisoner.
Now, even he realized he'd best walk the straight and narrow
path—until the final disposition. Though the lower court quietly dismissed the case, on paper the judge covered his fanny by
awarding the Third Judicial District Court a safety valve, "with
leave to reinstate."[108] Perhaps Sir John Kinney did have friends in
high places. ¿Quién sabe?

As proffered at the beginning of this piece, there is a work-
able definition of organized crime. That Kinney was the touchable
headman of one such outfit is—or should—suffer no argument.
Paid gunman and criminal godfather Kinney ruled with an iron
fist and lead bullets, thinking he was above the law—and for
awhile maybe he was—controlling underlings and corrupting a
number of western Texas' and southern New Mexico Territory's
look-the-other-way politicians and policemen. John Kinney was
no counterfeit crook or pretend crime boss. Those unflattering
characterizations—crook and crime boss—are legit. Gold-plated!
Kinney's undoing would not be the handiwork of some steely-
eyed gunfighter sheriff or town marshal. For that assignment it
would take special finances and calling up the territorial militia:
Catching the big fish is not easy.

Although there is plenty of meat for a sub story about John
Kinney dueling with the U.S. Government over pension matters
regarding military service during the Indian Wars and in 1898
Cuba during the Spanish American War, within the pledged context of this anthology it's time appropriate to bring John Kinney's
wickedly distended tale to a close. His criminality—at least his
known criminality—was done. Reading his mind is impossible.
Had he undergone genuine rehabilitation? Had a leopard really
shed its spots? Only John Kinney and his God know for sure.

Historians can cite with certainty, however, that suffering Bright's disease John Kinney, with his boots off, on the twenty-fifth day of August 1919, died. At Prescott, Arizona, where he had been living a reasonably exemplary life—so the obituary claimed—he was peacefully interred. Perhaps the writer for Prescott's *Courier* didn't know the full story, or didn't want to know the full story, when he eulogized: "All who knew him were his friends."[109]

Transportation into and out of old El Paso County in days prior to the railroad was always problematic. Pictured here is a mud-wagon type stagecoach of the Butterfield and Overland Mail Stagecoach Co. near the wild and woolly town sometimes dubbed "Hell Paso." In this delightful period daguerreotype, driver David McLaughlin is perched in the jockey box—stovepipe hat—deftly handling the "leather ribbons." *Courtesy Nita Stewart Haley Memorial Library and J. Evetts Haley History Center.*

Many Old West aficionados and collectors credit this image of a standing 19th-century character as the notorious criminal kingpin John Kinney. Perhaps it is! However the provenance for such a conclusive claim, thus far, has not been tacked down satisfactorily. Was this fellow branded as John Kinney purely for the sake of a duplicitous and/or an unchallengeable expediency? The photo's reverse side caption is simply "New Mexico Rustlers." Seated are also two as of yet unidentified New Mexico Territory rustlers, reputed rustlers. Conceivably, they *might* have been fellow murderers Charles Ray "Pony Diehl" and Jimmy McDaniels— two of Kinney's henchmen. *¿Quién sabe? Courtesy New Mexico History Museum.*

Thomas Jefferson Bull, a southern New Mexico Territory powerhouse politician and future sheriff of Doña Ana County. He was present when outlaw John Kinney unceremoniously tapped out the running lights of Ysabel Barela, shooting him in the face. *Courtesy Doña Ana County Sheriff's Office Museum.*

As a continuation of the La Mesilla gunplay wherein John Kinney killed Ysabel Barela, the Doña Ana County Sheriff Mariano Barela, pictured above, ended up shooting and mortally wounding an allegedly drunken coconspirator, Learndo Urieta. *Courtesy Doña Ana County Sheriff's Office Museum.*

Rincon, New Mexico. This was one tough spot and a headquarters for cow stealing mogul John Kinney. Throughout the Southwest this railway stop was popularly—though infamously—known as Kinneyville. *Courtesy Nita Stewart Haley Memorial Library and J. Evetts Haley History Center.*

William "Will" Huntington and wife Lucy as photographed during the era that they were at Rincon, New Mexico, feeding railroad workers. In a charming typescript Lucy characterized Rincon: "Were many outlaws there at the time going up and down the streets shooting their guns. We never knew when a bullet might come into our car." A photograph of Will has sometimes been misidentified as Sheriff George Peppin of Lincoln County War fame. *Courtesy Lewis A. Ketring, Jr.*

One of the ever hard-working Lopez brothers, Agustin T. Lopez, and his bride, the stunningly attractive Maria Val on their wedding day. Agustin earned an enviable reputation throughout the Mesilla Valley as a businessman, deputy sheriff, and in Hollywood as a silent screen star, before advent of the "talkies." *Courtesy Augustin V. Lopez.*

These cowboys, working for the well respected Lopez family of the Mesilla Valley, had gathered a herd of horses. Not all horseback cavaliers working the ranges of southern New Mexico were of questionable character. Some, such as the Lopez brothers and their diligent crew, were favorably known in the valley. *Courtesy Augustin V. Lopez.*

Guadalupe Ascarate, Doña Ana County Sheriff, at the time Sir John Kinney was in his 1883 outlaw prime. The sheriff and Albert Jennings Fountain were not on necessarily congenial terms, especially following the arrests of alleged desperadoes and the ill-fated gunning down of several "escaping" prisoners. Rancorous and backbiting political battles in the early Southwest were common, ferocious and comical. *Courtesy the Doña Ana County Sheriff's Office Museum.*

Captain Eugene Van Patten, Commander of the Las Cruces Rifles, New Mexico Territorial Militia and a future sheriff on Doña Ana County. *Courtesy Doña Ana County Sheriff's Office Museum.*

Florencio Lopez, an Indian fighter, Doña Ana County deputy sheriff, and resolute Southern New Mexico Territory militiaman. His brother, Felipe C. Lopez, was one of the jurors at La Mesilla convicting Henry Antrim, aka Billy the Kid, of cold-bloodily murdering Lincoln County Sheriff William Brady. Both Florencio and Felipe were in the Doña Ana County courtroom and witnessed Antrim vestido de muerto—dressed for death—when he was sentenced to be hanged. *Courtesy Doña Ana County Sheriff's Office Museum.*

John Kinney, the Godfather. Note, this very widely distributed photograph is actually a cutout of John Kinney's face transposed over the face of Harvey Alexander "Kid Curry" Logan as pictured in the near classic Fort Worth image of Butch Cassidy and the Sundance Kid. The tricky deception is amateurish, the motive inexplicable. *Courtesy Nita Stewart Haley Memorial Library & J. Evetts Haley History Center.*

Agustin T. Lopez atop his gallant steed on a Hollywood set. Lopez and John Kinney both survived gunplay during an earlier time in southern New Mexico. Perhaps in this publicity shot Lopez was about to let the Colt's hammer drop on an imaginary John Kinney, one of the Mesilla Valley's real *mal hombres* from an earlier day. *Courtesy Augustin V. Lopez.*

An aging John Kinney with nieces and nephew during a 1910 visit to Iowa. *Courtesy Lewis A. Ketring, Jr.*

A Lewis A. Ketring photograph of John Kinney's gravesite in the Odd Fellows Cemetery, Prescott, AZ. *Courtesy Nita Stewart Haley Memorial Library & J. Evetts Haley History Center.*

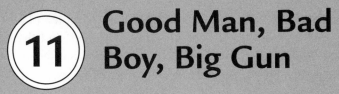

CHAPTER 11

Good Man, Bad Boy, Big Gun

Forbearance regarding a law enforcer's mindset is sometimes not easy. Armchair critics are ever-present. A lawman's split-second street-level decision may be loftily debated and argued the next day in barrooms and living rooms and classrooms—or years later as challenging legal questions wind their way toward final adjudication by slow-grinding appellate courts. The clock does not stop down in the trenches, allowing for communities' peacekeepers to hurriedly call for timeouts, pondering their next best course of action when circumstances turn "Western." There is a fine line between overreaction and inaction. Lawmen executing a careless misstep on that perilous tightrope run the risk of meeting tragedy face first—or condemnation from afar, by spectators in the grandstands averse to chancing risks. Elbert Norton Hanks was a risk taker.

Little did he know it then, but when Elbert Norton Hanks was born on the sixteenth day of December 1868 in Alabama, the Lone Star State was, perhaps, closing out the worst year for Indian raids in her long and illustrious history.[1] As he was marching toward maturity, if Elbert Hanks ever dreamed about heading west to the wild and woolly frontier and becoming an Indian fighting cavalryman or spur-jingling cowboy, the imaginings go unrecorded. He moved west to be sure, just not too far: Cotton Plant, northeastern Mississippi. Conjuring up a notion that Elbert Norton Hanks was a corn-fed farm boy is not farfetched. That he developed a knack for handling livestock—horses and mules—will be clear.

The richness of Mr. E. N. Hanks having enjoyed agricultural roots is not what will move his story forward within the framework at hand. Unmistakably, he had tenderly cultivated and nurtured a budding romance that had flowered. That is water-tight. As is another fact, by the early 1890s Elbert Norton and his Mississippi-born wife Alice Elizabeth (Brock) Hanks, and their toddling son Walter, piled into a mule-drawn wagon and headed for the setting sun and promises Texas held.

They did not make the trip alone, though. Traveling with them in another wagon were Alice Elizabeth's sister and her husband. It was an arduous journey by any man's or woman's reckoning. The daily grind of camping and jumping into and out of an animal drawn contraption was wearisome. Crossing the Mississippi River on a ferry was scary. Dawning of the twentieth-century may have been on time's distant horizon, but for everyday working folks getting from A to Z with all one's worldly trappings was yet a hard chore. Rich men could hire it done: Poor men just did it! How much preplanning had gone into the migration is unspecified, but their final destination is not: Streetman, in Freestone County but near straddling the Navarro County line, seventy-odd miles south of Dallas. In life's big book the relocation to Streetman was but a stopover, a chapter—and a short one at that. The Elbert Norton Hanks family moved across the Freestone County boundary and into Navarro County, settling at the little community of Powell, eight miles east of Corsicana, the county seat.

Powell was at the cusp of bigness. With coming of a railway connection—the Cotton Belt Railroad—and the exploratory, but somewhat surprising discovery of oil before the close of the century, Powell was booming, literally and figuratively.[2] With such a hurried influx of hungry speculators and wage working roust-abouts, motivated businessmen stepped into that vacuum between want and have. Business houses burgeoned. Money changed hands—feverishly. Prior to days of improved roadways and rou-tine motorized travel between towns the hiring of buggies, wag-ons, carriages, saddle horses, and even sleighs was necessary for those not opting to walk. Pleasure excursions to the countryside for a grand picnic or moonlight courting rituals obliged the rent-ing of suitable conveyances. So, as a practical matter, especially in Texas, any town with population numbers soaring—or even sputtering—had one, or in some cases two or more livery stables.[3] Elbert Norton Hanks opened a livery stable at Powell and, it would seem, he was sitting on top of the Lone Star world.[4]

Before the century clock had turned the Hanks' household grew by two. The apple of Elbert's eye, daughter Maggie had made her native Texan appearance (1894). Three years later treasured son Ray Hayes (1897) added to the family's happiness. Something else—besides a blossoming family—was growing, too: An inexplicable restlessness in Elbert Norton Hanks. He moved into Corsicana, supplementing the livery stable business as a teamster hauling local freight. Shortly he abandoned that line of work and bought into or bought outright a downtown grocery store. Playing the role of a plunging entrepreneur, a capitalist merchant, was a dream come true for the hardscrabble Alabama boy—for the moment.[5]

Although it steeps somewhat of a romance novel there is a sidebar story—an anecdotal story—to family doings of the Hanks family. Whether he was a good friend or barely an acquaintance of Elbert Norton Hanks is obscure, but after the death of his wife Mr. Roberts was having more than a tough time raising his teenage son William. The lost sleep was due to a financial shortfall, not disciplinary or behavioral problems with the boy—in fact Will was a pleasant lad and a hard worker. He was such a good boy in fact, that when the elder Roberts made known his intention to presently leave Corsicana seeking more lucrative employment elsewhere, Elbert Norton Hanks stepped in offering youthful William Roberts a real job and a real home. The charitable pitch was accepted. Mr. Hanks now had a third son and a store clerk—of sorts. Passionate fires grow hot. Perhaps not necessarily surprising to anyone but Elbert Norton Hanks, a raging inferno was consuming his domicile. Seventeen-year-old Maggie Hanks and Will Roberts were mad about each other, madly in love. Dousing love's flames with common sense was surely not an unthinkable parental proposition, just impossible. In the middle of the night Will and Maggie eloped. Grocer Elbert Norton Hanks had been figuratively stabbed, betrayed, he figured. Ecstatically, in the long run, Elbert Norton's stone-cold attitude about his backstabbing son-in-law and impertinent daughter melted away with each burp of his first grandson, Kelton. All was forgiven.[6]

There was little forgiveness on the streets of Corsicana, and never had been, however. Blood washing into the crumbly chinks between bricks on the city's main avenues and amid splits in the plank boardwalks, or mopped from barrooms' hardwood floors was not an everyday occurrence—but it was not uncommon.

One fellow early on, Jesse J. Rascoe, had made his mark as a ringtail-tooter, an authentic man-killing *mal hombre*. His first reported Corsicana killings are short on hard substantiation, but it is generally rumored and has been passed down through subsequent generations that during 1865 after his mother had been inadvertently or purposely pushed off a walkway by a black Union soldier, Jesse retaliated—absent a hint of worry—by bushwhacking several of Uncle Sam's boys in blue. Taking into account Jesse Rascoe's unmitigated hatred for "carpetbaggers and blue belly black soldiers" an administrative move by Reconstruction Governor Edmund J. Davis can but be classified as weird: He made an interim appointmetnt for Jesse Rascoe to serve a few months as the sheriff of Navarro County.[7]

Hardcore evidence abounds for Rascoe's next gunplay. On the seventh day of August 1874 a black chap found himself in a dispute with an ever incorrigible Jesse, grabbing "a jug and a piece of iron with which to defend himself." Essentially, carrying a jug to a gunfight is not an operative or wise tactic. Rascoe whipped out his Colt's revolver and triggered a hot .45 round into Aaron Gibbins' head. Mr. Gibbins was dead and Mr. Rascoe fled. Three days later, with the pursuit yet in high gear, Jesse J. Rascoe mortally gunned down posseman Johnson Thompson before he jumped across Louisiana's state line, a man on the dodge. Eventually fugitive Rascoe was apprehended—not anytime soon—and returned to Corsicana. A jury set him free for killing Gibbins—and he made bond for the pending charges regarding Thompson's death. Four days after Christmas 1877, while at liberty on bond, the irascible Jesse Rascoe gunned to death Harry Lackey in Smith's Saloon on Corsicana's Beaton Street. After smartly dodging city policemen's bullets, Jesse Rascoe, once more, took an immediate hiatus in Louisiana. Later, after another apprehension—wherein Jesse was wounded—he was locked away in the Navarro County jail. Though Jesse Rascoe's ongoing story borders on a Ripley's Believe It Or Not, a jailbreak and gunbattle ensued after inmates had pilfered several pistols. Ultimately four of the five prisoners were run to ground, wounded and recaptured—Rascoe made good his getaway, again. Renegade Rascoe rode from Corsicana through Mexico and into Arizona's and New Mexico's history books, but that makes for another extraordinary Wild West tale.[8]

Jesse Rascoe was not Corsicana's one and only firebrand. The culmination of one humorless row ended when Navarro County's officialdom went to war—with each other.[9]

> Last Saturday night a difficulty occurred in this place between Wm. Smithey, Deputy Sheriff, and W. B. Johnston, District Clerk, in which Smithey was shot in the mouth with a derringer, the ball lodging near the neck bone after passing under the tongue . . . . On Wednesday Johnston stood his examination before Justice A. H. Sherrill, who after hearing all the evidence discharged him on the ground of self-defense.[10]

For real Wild West theater one would think Corsicana's district clerk, Bill Johnston, had simply slipped one by the Grim Reaper. Had the devil been disguised as a deputy wearing the tin-star or had he been a champion of blind justice who'd come in second, which in a gunfight is last place? Lady Luck was riding on Johnston's coattails, of that there cannot be too much doubt:

> In about ten minutes after his acquittal he shot and killed H. R. Morrell, and was again arrested and tried next moring before the same authority and again acquitted without being required to give bond in either case . . . . In the meantime Johnston left and went to Austin and was elected Sergeant-At-Arms for the Senate . . . .[11]

Texas politics and politicos have always sparked their own brands of paradoxical entertainment. Too, a round or two of fisticuffs was just fine for muscled-up sports wearing short boxing trunks and pounding heads, in a ring, behind the ropes. On Corsicana's mean streets, though, big Colt's six-shooters and little S&W hideout pistols—and spent bullets—trumped KOs or a referee's call.

During another episode of Corsicana bedlam city policeman W. H. Wallace and a prominent livery stable owner, Mr. E. Bennett, argued over the princely sum of $1.00 regarding the "hire of a horse." Policeman Wallace killed citizen Bennett and was himself arrested, but during a failed escape attempt was mortally gunned down without too much fanfare.[12] Another bullet-spitting brouhaha left a Corsicana policeman of but five days dead. Charley D. Maddux died on the sidewalk while the alleged rapists he had just tried to arrest raced away in the futile quest of finding a policeless panorama.[13]

Navarro County Sheriff Robert H. Cubley's namesake son "Little Bob," an as of late deputy sheriff, engaged in what the *San Antonio Daily Light* drolly dubbed a "three cornered fight" with man-killing city policeman Rufe Highnote and civilian Calvin M. White: "Little Bob" finishing in last place—on the mortician's table.[14] Subsequent to a wild saloon fracas, Navarro County Constable J. N. Craig found himself wholly upside down, dead, all due to the defendant "shooting him with a pistol and then and there with malice aforethought cutting him, the said John N. Craig with a knife."[15] Even discounting the dreadful murder of the aforementioned (Chapter 4) Gideon Christian Taylor, Superintendent of the Navarro County Poor Farm, it's not unreasonable to assert that wearing a polished badge in and around Corsicana was risky business.

Fourteen-year-old Boyd White wasn't necessarily a chance taker—he was a nondescript survivor in what could then be a hard and cruel world for an educationally challenged and economically disadvantaged black teenager. Texas during the early 1900s was not a place ahead of the times with regards to even identifying—much less solving—any tricky and uncomfortable sociological questions. Corsicana was but a microcosm. Times would change, but not real fast. Boyd White, born during the Spanish American War, was simply a product of heritage and era. His nickname was "Boy" and whether that's an appellation Boyd ginned up for himself or was a generic derogatory tag thrust upon him is unknown. Nevertheless, that's what he answered to. Topping the scales at 135 lbs. and stretching mightily to break the five-foot, four-inch mark, Boyd White was short on towering physical stature—but not shortchanged with owning a tough mental attitude. Nor should it come as any big surprise, he could not read nor write or lay legitimate claim to ever having gone to one day of school. Boyd White was wholly illiterate, not only about blackboard lessons but simple genealogical features, too: Such as where his parents were from. What little he had or tried to have he worked for as a common laborer—the honest income anyway. For good or bad, native Texans are independent: A birthright it seems to an outsider. Presumably, and there is a smidgen of evidence to support it, White was not a hard drinker or a heavy smoker—but he was a scrapper, scars on his left cheek and on his left hand would attest to that, adding to the episodes of his waging war when it suited him. A defiant streak was real. Boyd White was wrapped tight.[16]

Despite the recognized dangers persistently hanging above the heads of Corsicana's—indeed all of Navarro County's lawmen—Elbert Norton Hanks was somehow growing restless. Profit from the grocery store was maintaining his livelihood. He was, after all, acceptably providing for his family; a solid middle-class standard of living. And that family had grown. Alice Hanks had given birth to a precious baby boy, Joe Bailey.[17] What more could a man want than a loving family and a successful—reasonably successful—business, as well as the heartfelt esteem of neighbors? Yet, for Elbert something was missing.

Though in certain respects it's really inexplicable, some folks—men and women—are drawn, psychologically pulled, toward finalizing a decision about becoming a peace officer. For those not so afflicted, taking that career fork may seem like pure insanity: The hours are long, the pay is low, and peril is ever present. Elbert Norton Hanks wasn't crazy. He did, however, crave more fulfillment than selling tomatoes and canned goods. Elbert became a Corsicana policeman.

Of course following patrolman Elbert Hanks as he walked his downtown beat, particularizing his routine day by day activities, is unworkable. As expected he carried a revolver, but he had other non-lethal items in his personal arsenal: Handcuffs, knuckles, and a one-wrist come-along.[18] On the Continuum of Force policeman Hanks was steadfast in belief that his gun was a course of last resort. Intermittently a slobbering drunk or highly agitated fellow would slip off the half-cock notch and would have to be physically restrained, but Officer Elbert Norton Hanks had staked out a methodology of which he took personal pride, in fact it morphed into a trademark method of his policing: He took special pleasure in talking someone into jail, using his brain rather than brawn. In his mind—and practically speaking, too—it made much more sense than thumping heads and wrestling them into the jailhouse bleeding and bruised and hurting. Elbert Norton Hanks knew he was a man. He didn't have to prove that to himself—or anyone else. Elbert Norton Hanks wanted to be a good policeman.

Although the precise date is lost to history, Patrolman Hanks traded his city badge for a county badge, becoming a deputy constable for Navarro County. Fees from the service of civil papers boosted his income, but it did not purge any criminal workload.[19] He was a peace officer and as such was expected to enforce the law—all of the time, regardless. Even if an alleged violator was yet short of measuring up to the maturity mark. Say, a teenager like Boyd White.

Had Boyd White been levelheaded and burdened with the realities of adulthood he might have stayed put—content to work off time at the Navarro County Poor Farm for his as of yet undisclosed infraction of the law, a misdemeanor to be sure. He didn't! Fourteen-year-old Boyd earned new status—an escapee.[20] Perhaps he thought himself a big shot, not buckling to authority. He was now on the lam, hiding like a rat.

Trying to exactly determine what Constable Elbert Hanks was intent on accomplishing the twenty-fifth night of June 1912 is superseded by fact, what really happened: At about ten o'clock he spotted Boyd White. Problematically, Boyd White, walking along city railroad tracks, saw Constable Hanks, too. Boyd ran. Hanks chased after him.

Boyd's familiarity with or relationship to a black business owner is indefinite, but, panting heavily he burst into a local café, Constable Hanks close on his heels. Purportedly the startled owner—quickly deciphering what was transpiring—told Boyd White to duck out the backdoor. Whether it was aiding and abetting is vague; perhaps he was simply trying to avoid trouble inside the eatery. Just as fuzzy is whether or not Boyd White grabbed a loaded pistol from under the counter, or whether or not he was handed the revolver. As Boyd rushed for the backdoor he had it in hand. Unbeknownst to Boyd White—and maybe the restaurant proprietor—the door leading from the dark storeroom to the outside world was locked—locked securely. Boyd was trapped. Constable Hanks dashed though the front door and not seeing White, quite naturally advanced toward the storeroom and its passageway to the alley. As an unswerving lawman he had little choice but to press on. After all, he was just chasing after a wayward boy, an escapee to be sure, but a mere child nonetheless. Hanks stepped inside—and couldn't see a damn thing—it was dark, pitch black. That's eerie, anytime. With his revolver in one hand, Elbert Norton Hanks reached into his pocket, fishing for a wooden match. Boyd White crouched behind a wooden crate. Quickly Hanks struck a match on his pants—now a lost art—and abruptly the room was dimly illuminated. The sudden flash of blue and orange fire fleetingly blinded the disoriented constable, but not the young desperado with spiders in his mind. The chance—maybe the only chance—for a clean getaway was now at hand. Boyd White pulled the trigger. The fiery match was extinguished—purposefully or accidentally? The unnerved kid fired a second shot. The first sound Boyd heard was rather evident, conclusive guesswork, but a steel object hitting hardwood had to be Hanks' unholstered gun tumbling from his hand. The next noise was irrefutable, the unchecked body of a man crashing to the ground. Elbert Norton Hanks hadn't heard gunshot number two. He was stone dead on the storeroom floor, the bullet having torn its channel through his chest. Boyd White had murdered a Texas lawman, not a prudent move. Sympathy would be in short supply for such cowardice. Though technically but a boy he was a murderous man-killer. Boyd White bolted for freedom.[21]

In a panic White, "accompanied by another boy of his color," fled to the little Navarro County farming community of Rice, about ten miles due north of Corsicana. His jump up the road was understandable but not too smart. Boyd White's uncle, Don Norris, lived at Rice. Whether such useful intelligence was common knowledge or learned through the post-incident investigative work is really moot: Deputy Sheriff Warren Bradley had the information. Before sunrise he was at Rice and shortly thereafter had one scared—and maybe unrepentant—juvenile in custody. And, too, for good measure he arrested two more fellows with Boyd, taking the handcuffed trio back to Corsicana, lodging them in jail. There was little—really no—doubt as to just who had killed the popular constable. Corsicana's white community was outraged—a few hotheads were threatening a lynch rope climax for the sordid and senseless installment. Sheriff M. S. Clayton was not about to be bamboozled into making a choice between surrendering the fourteen-year-old prisoner or heroically standing in the gap, maybe forced into shooting some quarrelsome nitwits. Before any insanity could gain impetus for an operational foothold, he had deputies spirit Boyd White to Big D and the relative safety of Sheriff Ben Brandenburg's iron-bar hotel, the Dallas County jail. A clip in the *Dallas Morning News* spotlighted Corsicana's near brush with stupidity:

Considerable excitement prevailed here this evening, when more than 300 men gathered around the jail and demanded

the prisoner whom they believed had been brought here. The
Sheriff stood in the door of the jail and assured the mob that
the Negro was taken to Dallas. Satisfied with this explanation, the gathering quietly dispersed.[22]

Family and friends and colleagues gathered around at Corsicana's
Oakwood Cemetery and peacefully laid Elbert Norton Hanks
to rest. Absent a fortune teller's crystal ball she had no way of
knowing, but Alice Hanks would survive her murdered husband
by forty-three years, always a devoted mother and loving grand-
mother. Too, during those early years Alice was heartbroken that
her son Joe Bailey, who was a "High 5th-Grader," had to drop out
of school in order to lend his mother a helping hand, contributing
to her cheerless efforts at maintaining a livelihood.[23] Unmistakably
the graspable period of immediate grieving had to play itself out.

Just as certainly the wheels of justice had to turn. The Navarro
County Grand Jury was to sit for its regular October term, scarcely
three months away. Prior to the grand jury actually hearing felony
cases and taking sworn testimony, a conscientious district attorney
would want to make sure a few legal matters were screwed down
tight—namely in defendant White's situation a written confession.
Subsequent to being brought down from his upstairs cell in the
Dallas County jail and while adhering to proper protocols, Boyd
White was interviewed in the presence of a witness, O. N. Early.

It might prove mindboggling to readers raised on an over-
simplified diet of Wild West drama and hip-pocket justice, but
even a hundred or more years ago legal protections expressly
guaranteed by the U.S. Constitution were applicable. Without a
doubt the interviewing attorney orchestrated—penned the written
confession—making certain Bill of Rights safeguards were not
omitted, but that is not improper. Matching wits with Boyd White
was not the purpose at hand; predicting the winner of that type
contest would have been a no-brainer. Elements of the crime
needed to be covered in the voluntary confession and they were.
After going over the hurriedly prepared statement, Boyd White
confirmed its validity by making his "X" mark. Incarcerated murder defendant Boyd White admitted.

My name is Boyd A. White. I have been warned by E. L.
Wilkinson asst. co. atty. The person to whom this statement

is made that I do not have to make any statement at all, second that any statement made by me may be used in evidence against me and not for me on my trial for the offense concerning which this statement is made. I make the following voluntary statement in writing. My name is Boyd White, they call me "Boy." I killed Mr. Hanks. I couldn't get out the door without passing by him and I thought he would shoot me so I shot him first. I saw Mr. Hanks coming down the TX & B.V. RR track. I started to go around the house but Hessie Carlisle told me to go through the house and out through the kitchen. I ran in at the front door of the restaurant. Mr. Hanks followed me in at the same door. I ran through the restaurant and reached up and took Hessie Carlisle's pistol off the shelf back of the lunch counter and then went on into the room back of the restaurant. I tried to get out of the kitchen but the back door was fastened. I then returned to the cleaning room and saw Mr. Hanks coming into the room from the restaurant. He walked in about 3 steps and struck a match on his pants. I saw his pistol in his right hand. I was leaning against the right side of the door that leads from the dining room to the kitchen. I saw that I couldn't get by Mr. Hanks so I raised the pistol and shot at Mr. Hanks. He either dropped the match or it went out. I heard him walking as if he were stumbling. I shot once more in his direction. I heard him holler, "Oh!' and heard his gun drop on the floor. I dropped the pistol on the floor and ran out the backdoor which leads up the stairway.[24]

The return of a formal Indictment following presentation of the criminal case to a Navarro County Grand Jury was but a foregone conclusion. Its simplicity speaks for itself, charging that Boyd White "willfully and with his malice aforethought Kill and Murder E. N.Hanks by Shooting him, the said E. N. Hanks with a gun."[25] On November 4, 1912, Navarro County Sheriff Clayton boarded a train, traveled to Dallas and served the Capias Warrant on Boyd White.[26]

Certainly the return of an Indictment had been predictable as would be the jury's verdict at trial. There was, however, a bothersome little detail: Boyd White's age. The Texas system of criminal justice—then and now—allows for the trial jury finding a defendant guilty to deliberate a second time, setting the punishment within prescribed legal guidelines. The jury hearing Boyd White's case had a weighty matter to settle. Though the stricture would eventually fall by the wayside of enlightened thinking, during 1912 such a radical philosophy was foreign to Texas' inimitable brand of jurisprudence. Since the defendant was under the age of sixteen years, should they assess his punishment at less than five years confinement Boyd White would be sent to the State Institute for the Training of Juveniles. On the other hand, if the jury meted out a sentence above five years, the defendant would be sent to the state penitentiary.[27]

There was no sympathy for fourteen-year-old Boyd White. Not a shred! A. H. Kerr, foreman of the jury, returned their findings to the court: "guilty of murder in the first degree and do assess his punishment by confinement in the State Penitentiary for life."[28] There would be no appeal. On 19 December 1912 convicted murderer Boyd White was processed through intake in the Texas State Prison at Huntsville, given identification #34118, issued prison garb, and the next day transferred to the Harlem Unit in Fort Bend County, a few miles east of Richmond.[29]

Any psychological analysis and/or behavioral judgments made from a time this far removed would be less than precise—and in a historical context wholly meaningless. Boyd White had committed a grown man's crime, and he could now do time with grown men. That was the law. He had a damn tough row to hoe, literally and figuratively. Hearing his excuses or weighing his justifications is, of course, impossible. Enumerating all of his disciplinary infractions whilst at the Harlem Unit or AWOL from the Harlem Unit or attempting to escape from the Harlem Unit is doable. He was not a model prisoner. When Boyd White had entered prison a notation about the expiration date of his sentence—when he could look for release—was succinct and cold: "Death."[30] He had little to lose.

Almost from the get-go inmate White was a problem child. Reviewing his Conduct Register Transcription Form is revealing and, perhaps, somewhat disquieting. The infractions of prison rules or overt acts of criminal behavior are too numerous to particularize in detail. In an abbreviated format it may be mentioned that inmate #34118 was put in chains or placed in solitary confinement for such boneheaded breaches as Escape (on the run for fourteen days), Attempted Escape, Disobedience (ten times), Impudence, Fighting (seven times), and Burning a Cotton Pile. Circumspectly it may also be revealed that his last recorded difficulty was in 1922, when he was twenty-four years old. Ten taxing years of prison life apparently had whipped him. Boyd White could now go along and get along. There was no bona fide gain—tilting with windmills—or prison guards. He had learned a lesson, maybe not *the* lesson for a wholehearted rehabilitation or *the* morals of a sincere repentance, but, nevertheless, he had taken to heart practical implications of his vulnerability. By the time he was twenty-seven he had earned status as a "Trusty" and Boyd White found day by day existence at the Harlem Unit much easier.[31] Legal deliverance, not blameless forgiveness, would come shortly—relatively speaking—for a convict, a "Lifer."

One of the hallmarks of Texas Governor Miriam A. Ferguson's administration—rightly or wrongly—was the granting of pardons. She came through for Boyd White. On 17 January 1927 the Proclamation of Pardon was signed, sealed, and three days later delivered to the Harlem Unit. After fifteen years as a hard-time convict, Boyd White walked out into the "free world."[32]

Real-time lawmen are not ten-foot tall and bullet proof, despite contrary messaging that movie moguls and scriptwriters and novelists fallaciously broadcast and pen. Good guys can go under. Elbert Norton Hanks stood tall—till he ran after a little boy with a big gun.

Alice Elizabeth and Elbert Norton Hanks. *Courtesy Kathy Katelin*.

The Hanks family, Elbert and Alice with children L to R: Walter, Ray Hayes [in toddler's dress], and Maggie. *Courtesy Robert W. Haltom.*

In 1885 Corsicana had 20 Saloons ...

At the time policeman Elbert Norton Hanks was patrolling his beat on Corsicana's mean streets, customers in want of finding a spot suitable for sampling a quick nip of straight whiskey were not to be disappointed. *Courtesy Navarro County Historical Society.*

A delightful peek inside Elbert Norton Hanks' downtown Corsicana grocery store. Elbert Norton and wife Alice Elizabeth are behind the counter, while brothers Hayes and "Ben" Hanks are standing beside the apple bin. Interestingly, considering the budding romance to be and an impending elopement, William Roberts, the lad Mr. Hanks "took in" is standing behind his future wife, fifteen year old Maggie Hanks. It would take the birth of a precious grandson to permanently cool Elbert Norton Hanks' temper regarding the perceived backstabbing. *Courtesy Robert W. Haltom.*

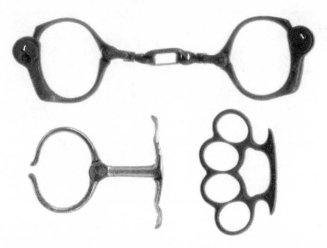

Non lethal law enforcement tools of the trade belonging to Elbert Norton Hanks: Brass knuckles, handcuffs, and a one-wrist come-along. Hanks believed the duty pistol was an instrument of last resort. *Courtesy Robert W. Haltom.*

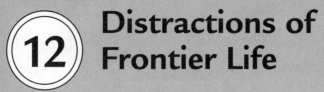

Distractions of Frontier Life

Since *Bad Company and Burnt Powder* started off with a true six-shooter tale involving a young Texas Ranger, perhaps the same would be fitting for the last episode of the narrative. More especially would it be apropos given that the subject of this sketch is the younger brother of the Ranger spotlighted in the first chapter. Though Cal Aten's enlistment with Company D predated his, make no mistake, little brother Edwin Dunlap "Eddie" Aten would cleave unto himself several noteworthy and spine-tingling adventures while carrying a Colt's .45 for the State of Texas.

Perhaps the briefest of genealogical data would be a helpful refresher. Eddie Aten's birthplace was not in Texas, but in Abingdon, Illinois. Born on the fifth day of September 1870, the last child of Reverend Austin C. and Kate Aten, Eddie moved with his sizeable family to the vicinity of Round Rock, Texas, just short of his sixth birthday.[1] Cashing in on a touch of literary license it would not be unreasonable to suppose that Eddie, just like any other youngster, would have been all ears when older brothers Frank and Ira returned to the farm that Saturday afternoon in 1878. They had a story to tell: One about that young wounded outlaw squirming and moaning in agony, confined to a cot inside a tin shop serving as the makeshift hospital. Most likely seventeen year old Frank bragged, puffing his chest about actually standing at Sam Bass' beside, while their daddy said a few comforting prayers about last minute salvation. Ira, fifteen years old, would have chimed in: Making sure eager beavers Cal and Eddie knew he, too, had even laid eyes on the notorious desperado: Albeit from the outside whilst looking though a window.

There shouldn't be any room for argument, Eddie had his full share of routine chores to knock off: Most farm boys did. It may be said with clarity, however, that from time to time Cal and Eddie, along with their cousin Elmer and even the little petrified cousin Virgie, sneakily crept toward the granary, knotty hardwood weapons in hand. Subsequent to the nervous whispers and that mandatory period of gutting-up, the would-be big-game hunters would suddenly jump into the grain bin. Then it was a helter-skelter battle royal seeing just who would win the game of clubbing scampering rats. It took some sand to do that, they supposed. Sometimes at the big barn overhead beams served as the "tightrope" and the older kids showed off their balancing talents while the little ones looked up in awe. And, too, there were those times everyone went swimming—with the slithering snakes, bravely postulating when on dry land that they had been Cottonmouths, but secretly hoping while in the water that they weren't. And one could bet his last dollar those squirming boys and girls wiggled their way through Sunday sermons. The good Reverend A. C. Aten was no piker, merely dribbling out a few blistering words from the pulpit. No, not according to Virgie's remembrance: "He believed in giving us enough to last a week. We often brought our dinners."[2]

It was in and around northern Travis and southern Williamson Counties that Eddie moved from a youngster's mischief to post adolescent maturity—maybe? Sometimes it's rumored a preacher's kiddos are easily bent toward wildness. If that rings true, young Eddie Aten fit the mold, at least so indicates a sketchy anecdotal profile: "The stern religious upbringing practiced by his father, an old fashioned 'fire and brimstone' minister, conflicted with the distractions of frontier life in Texas that appealed to the unruly youth. It soon became apparent to all that life on the family farm was neither to his liking nor suited to his temperament."[3]

Eddie's older brother Ira, now both an ex-Ranger and an ex-Fort Bend County Sheriff, had forsaken—temporarily—the life of a paid lawman, relocating to the far-flung Texas Panhandle. Ira had purchased land in Castro County near the little hamlet of Dimmitt, which would shortly become the county seat. Purportedly, at age twenty-one Eddie just couldn't seem to let go of a few reckless habits. Though it may bear the weight of legitimate argument, either at the urgings of his parents or at the invitation of Ira—or both—Eddie became a genuine Castro County resident. Ira had already been on the lookout for finding Eddie a suitable piece of land.[4] A spot he could legally claim. One he could pay for by tapping into Texas' liberal land policy and the financially smart time-payment plan. Eddie, along with Ira, even earned extra money laboriously hauling lumber from Amarillo when it came time to construct Castro County's elegantly trimmed two story wooden courthouse: Eddie pocketed $59.51.[5] At this juncture older brothers Ira and Cal had already tasted their fair share of excitement. Eddie had not. There must be more to life than cajoling mules from a wagon seat or hoeing weeds or digging postholes. Just idly sitting on the front porch after a day's work and watching the sun go down was boring.

Though an alleged incident is less than well documented with a paper trail, the overall gist echoes true. The second half is provably square on target. Because Eddie was inclined to hang out in saloons in his spare time, it's purported he developed a proclivity for playing Poker. Gambling and drinking were not uncommon forms of diversion in the day, but such pursuits were wrought with risk. Sometimes patrons with tarantula juice in their bloodstream and fight on their brain could slip off of the half-cock notch. Purportedly Eddie slipped, and ". . . .matters climaxed when he shot a man in a difference over a card game."[6] Accurateness of an assertion that while in the Panhandle he settled someone's hash with a six-shooter might be iffy.[7] The cold hard fact that Ira did is not.

During a personal dispute Ira and the Tennessee bred McClelland brothers, Hugh and Andrew, had dueled on what is now Dimmitt's courthouse square. It had been a legit gunfight by definition. Known locally and historically as the shoot-out on Jones Street, Ira had blasted away at Hugh and Andrew and they at him. Decidedly atypical for a real gunfight, Andrew had had Colt's revolvers in each hand and was dexterously alternating fire, shooting first one then the other. It was pretty fancy gun handling for witnesses to watch, but his bullets were not flying true. Andrew, wholly ignoring the prudent advice for participation in a gunplay "take your time, quick," had simply been shooting too fast for accuracy. Cool and collected, according to one eyewitness, Ira was "shooting like shooting squirrels out of a tree." After smooth knocking the fight out of Hugh with a well-placed bullet, Ira had calmly directed his smoking Colt's .45's front sight to his next target's midsection, touched the trigger and a somewhat dexterous Andrew "fell like a beef." After nursing their wounds and hurt pride the McClelland brothers scooted out of Dimmitt, returning to the Volunteer State. Ira Aten voluntarily surrendered to the sheriff. Afterward he stood trial and was acquitted, but two wavering jurors later admonished, saying he "was a little hasty in shooting two men for only calling you [him] a liar, but we were not willing to send you to prison for it."[8]

Eddie Aten was well aware of the several gunfights brother Ira had engaged in over the years, and knew of bother Cal's part in the shooting wherein the two Odle boys had given up the ghost in Edwards County that Christmas Day of 1889. It would not be wild speculation to suggest that, at some point, he had even handled the engraved Colt's .45 the young outlaw bequeathed Cal. Absent a smidgen of primary source proof, it is not tasteless to question whether or not Eddie Aten really did shoot someone because they were arguing over who was free to rake the Poker table's pot. On the other hand, even from this claim two hard facts may be drawn: There would be gunplay in his future and big brother Ira's influence and friendships with Texas Ranger hierarchy would pave the way for Eddie to relocate and reset his moral compass.

At the top edge of the Big Bend Country and east of Alpine, now county seat for Brewster County the largest county in Texas, was the municipality of Marathon then in Buchel County which was never officially organized and eventually abolished.[9] Outside of town Captain Frank Jones, commander of the Frontier Battalion's Company D, maintained his company headquarters at a spot the Rangers had christened Camp Cleveland.[10] On 16 September 1892 Eddie Aten, twenty-two, reported for duty at Camp Cleveland, swore an oath of obedience and fidelity to the State of Texas, becoming the third Ranger from the clan of Aten to sign on with Company D.[11] Even if he had been somewhat of a wayward youth, those escapades would register as but paltry kid's play when stacked against what the coming calendar had in store.

Trailing Private Aten's historical footprints during the earliest stages of his Ranger career would be tricky—and less than absolutely trustworthy. Each Ranger company commander was mandated to submit an activity report at the end of the month, the Monthly Return. Typically the name of a rookie Ranger is not straight away singled out. Until developing a measure of seniority and a functional touch of on-the-job tutoring, the new Ranger's name is dumped into an abyss of anonymity. Customarily it's only the headman of a Ranger "scout" that is identified by name, then generically followed with something akin to "and five men" or "assisted by three men." As the newness wears off and the ability to independently handle assignments grows, so, too, does the likelihood of earning citation by name in the Monthly Return. Ranger Eddie Aten will be no exception, and there would be that customary learning curve. In due time, Eddie Aten will ride tall in the saddle through several high-profile enforcement actions—meriting many mentions by name. And while speaking of Ranger reports, their brevity often warrants a chuckle. Private Eddie Aten was yet a rookie in West Texas when Sergeant Daniel Lynch "D.L." Musgrave shot it out with a crazed yahoo just west of the Pecos River and notified headquarters at Austin:

> This morning we were fired on by Chas. Small a noted desperate character and he was killed by me.[12]

Less than a month after enlistment a seemingly unrelated event would loom large in Eddie Aten's life as a Texas Ranger. Captain Frank Jones, after the death of his first wife, was about to give marriage another chance. He had fallen in love with a divorcee, one with two out-and-out connections to the Texas Rangers. Her father, George W. Baylor was an old-school Ranger commander, and afterward a not retiring or bashful El Paso County political voice and newsman. That link in the chain welding Helen to the Rangers could not be broken. The other one could. Earlier Helen had married James B. Gillett who would spend six years in the Texas Rangers, a stint as city marshal for El Paso, and then become the sheriff of Brewster County. Later in life he would compose a somewhat classic autobiography about his—and others—Ranger experiences. The electorate knew Gillett as a tolerable law enforcing man, wife Helen knew him as a philandering whorehouse client. The suit for divorce had been specific. Her ex-husband to-be had been adulterously misbehaving in Madam Roland's bordello. In someway one might sympathize with Mr. Gillett. That is, if a characterization of his wife is repeated naked and unvarnished: "Helen, [was] a high-spirited romanticist. . . .Helen was an 'uptown' kind of girl, singing at church programs and musicals, and getting her name in the social columns of the newspaper. She was known to read love stories in bed until almost noon and leave the bed unmade most of the time."[13] Regardless, the divorce was granted. By the time Frank Jones met Helen Baylor she was single, attractive, and available—they both would give marriage a new try.

Though the heartstring joining together was "as dubious as loading a pistol with buckshot" the couple married at the Ysleta home of George Baylor on October 3, 1892, where the bride would reside.[14] Captain Jones would honeymoon with his wife at Ysleta as time and demands of the job permitted.

Newlywed Helen Jones' father was adamant that a complement of Texas Rangers be stationed nearer the geographical population center and much closer to the scene of incessant criminality. He messaged Adjutant General Woodford Mabry on February 15, 1893 pinpointing some hard borderland reality, that murders were on the upswing and "that the theft of cattle is [was] nearly an everyday matter." Noting that thus far the local authorities had been unable to capture the killers of Ranger Sergeant Charley Fusselman a couple of years earlier, George Baylor voiced his unbridled opinion, imploring that if his no nonsense solution was implemented the trouble would be put right: "A squad of Rangers with their pack mules & 20 days rations would have Kept on their trail without regard to State or national boundaries & captured or Killed the murderers, and this, that element know and the presence of the Rangers would soon give us peace & security."[15] El Paso County Sheriff Frank B. Simmons seconded the motion, as did the sitting grand jury, petitioning the adjutant general to send in the Rangers: "This frontier extends in a settled portion of the County for over a hundred miles, and it is impossible for the regular Civil Officers to prevent their [outlaws] depredations and it is imperative that this frontier shall be guarded by a regular force."[16]

Captain Frank Jones was not speechless either: "I have just returned from El Paso County where I went to further investigate reported lawlessness and am more convinced that a Company of Rangers is more needed there than at any point in Tex."[17] Yet responsible for the whole of far West Texas, the Company D base camp was still at Camp Cleveland near Marathon. With his father-in-law and wife at living at Ysleta, coupled with a legitimate crime problem and the very real potential for a raging political firestorm due to inaction, it should come as no great surprise that company headquarters would be repositioned to El Paso County, where watchfulness would be the byword. Private Eddie Aten redeployed with his captain and seven other Ranger privates on the 13th day of June 1893. After a march of 250 miles and ten days travel Ysleta became the new field headquarters for Company D.[18]

A particular thorn—or thorns—in the side of area lawmen were illicit activities that could be laid at the doorstep of the Olguín family, not lovingly known throughout El Paso County and points beyond as the "Bosque Gang."[19] Due to his age of ninety plus years Clato Olguín had willingly relinquished his patriarchal position as the godfather of an indisputable crime family. Clato's sons, Jesús María, Antonío, and Pedro, now captained the outfit's pervasive criminal enterprises. Acting as dutiful gangland lieutenants were Jesús María's sons, Severío, Sebastián, and Pecilliano. One and all, according to George Baylor, were a "hard set."[20]

Contrary to popular belief the Olguíns were not in fact Mexican nationals, but native Texans, "born and raised at San Elizario and were voters in that place until they became fugitives from Texas."[21] Jesús María and Severío were under grand jury indictment for felonies and/or had outstanding warrants as result of Complaints sworn to and filed before a justice of the peace.[22] Earlier and on the Texas side of the Rio Grande, Jesús María, Sebastían, Severío and "an unknown Mexican" had with arms resisted arrest by El Paso County Deputy Ed Bryant and two unidentified helpmates: Assault to Murder charges followed.[23] Antonío had previously been convicted of rape, sent to the Texas penitentiary at Huntsville, but after a victorious prison break was at the moment parking his fanny on the Mexican side of the zigzagging Rio Grande.[24] According to one report, the Olguíns weren't confining their unchecked badness to Texas' side of the river: "On or about June 25 several of Olguíns 'got on a drunk' in the village of Guadalupe in Mexico and killed one man and wounded three others, one of whom was expected to die."[25] The Olguíns were *mal hombres* in everyone's book—in real time!

Although based at Ysleta on a fixed basis for less than a full week, the ever gutsy Captain Frank Jones fashioned a tactical team with but one purpose—apprehend those damn Olguín thugs, the mean ones, those wanted by the law. Riding with the captain were Corporal Carl Kirchner and four Ranger privates,

Eddie Aten, T. F. Tucker, John Woodard "Wood" Saunders, and Robert Edward "Ed" Bryant, a former Texas Ranger and dually commissioned El Paso County deputy sheriff who had just reenlisted with Company D three days before.[26] Advantaging himself of the Rangers supposed firepower, a young man by the name of Lujan attached himself to the party. He was in search of several wandering—likely stolen—horses. By almost any Western man's reckoning this single-minded assortment of Texas Rangers were the right stuff—determined, daring, and dangerous. On the evening of June 29, 1893 the detachment pitched camp near "the old River, East bank, 7 miles below Tres Jacales, Mex."[27]

Complicating an already shaky situation was geography. The Olguín crew for the most part inhabited—or in George Baylor's words "infested an island that has been a sort of neutral ground."[28] The so-called neutral ground was known locally as Pirate Island, a quite apt name it would seem. The Rio Grande of course was the definable line separating Mexico and Texas, except in this stretch of El Paso County that line was often indistinguishable. The ever erratic waters of the Rio Grande had carved a collateral channel. Not unexpectedly then, the dry land between the ancient Rio Grande and the newly cut channel was disputed ground. The island of shifting sands was narrow but several miles long, decorated with dense growths of tangled underbrush. The line separating two countries in this instance—running down the middle of Pirate Island—was but imaginary: ". . . .the Mexican side of this old channel that is recognized as the line but there are no marks of any international survey to show where the line is."[29] Not up for any wrangling about boundaries, however, was the motherland status of Tres Jacales, a tiny river front settlement of borderlanders. Tres Jacales was Mexico's territory—pure and simple, not even a shadow of doubt: Virtuously disposed Mexican citizens wouldn't live there, Mexican soldiers seldom patrolled there, and Texans didn't want it.

During the early morning hours of June 30th Rangers worked their way through the labyrinth of trees, bushes, shrubs, reeds, cacti, and cattails, at length spotting themselves on Pirate Island, not too far from Clato Olguín's *rancho*, decidedly on the Texas side. Riding up to Clato's abode the suspicious Rangers were not greeted with overtures of politeness but with surliness, perhaps in comeback for their tough talk and battle-ready deportment, perhaps not. These Rangers were not proselytizing missionaries, but were gritty paid gunman on a life and death mission. Their decisions—rightly or wrongly—were made in real time. Armchair critics far removed would have plenty of safe space and *mucho* time to moralize, commending or condemning. Benign judgments come real easy, after-the-fact. The upshot of Frank Jones and men "rounding up the Ranch" was measurable: Zilch. The wanted men had been forewarned, having "crossed over to the Mexican side to the house of Antonío Olguín."[30] Mulling over their next move the Rangers took leave of a quick break and wolfed down breakfast. Dejected, well attuned to the fact they'd been outfoxed, the Rangers tightened chinches, stepped into the stirrups, pointing their horses' heads toward Ysleta. They'd leave Pirate Island on the back trial, empty-handed, and make fight another day. So they thought! George Baylor picks up the story:

> After getting breakfast the Capt. Started up the River on the main road which crosses backward and forward from one side to Mexico Several times, the River being very crooked and being overgrown with this chaparral it is difficult to determine when one is [in] Texas or Mexico. About 3 Miles above the Olguin Ranch while in the advance Capt. Jones who was in the advance with Pvt. Tucker saw two Mexicans coming down the road towards them who on seeing the Rangers wheeled and ran back & the Rangers immediately gave chase & Kept up the road: After a run of three or [four] hundred yards—Corporal Kirchner—Pvts. Saunders and Aten passed Capt Jones & Pvt. Tucker and ran on the Mexicans, one of them Jesus M. Olguin fell from his horse and turned square off to the left of the road, he being near Antonio Olguin's house & double back again across the road & ran into the house. The other turned off to the right of the road & threw up his hands. There were 4 houses in this settlement which is on the main road & some 200 yards from the Texas line. . . .the second house on the right was occupied by 5 or 6 Mexicans and as Corporal Kirchner passed he being ahead, a volley was fired from the door at him. One bullet Struck the magazine of his Winchester bending it so he could only fire one shot & then reload. Saunders came next & a Second Volley was fired at him. Aten come close behind & a third volley was fired at him, which he returned by a shot from his six-shooter, this being first shot by the Rangers. . . .[31]

Despite his tender age and relatively greenhorn status as a Texas Ranger, it would seem Eddie upheld his end of Aten tradition: His backbone didn't need a splint. Eddie exhibited guts during the gunplay. So, too, did Captain Jones. Almost instantly after dismounting in front of the house from which gunfire was emanating the captain caught a bullet in the thigh, sledgehammering him to the ground and dislodging the hold on his Winchester saddle-gun. Shaking off near unbearable pain the captain readjusted to a semi-upright position, his wounded leg extended in front of him. He began returning fire with his Colt's six-shooter. Private Tucker slid out of the saddle, rushing to the captain's side. Yet horseback the other Rangers had overrun the position held by Jones and Tucker and were now engaged in checking their spider-minded horses' momentum, hurriedly executing an abrupt one-eighty. Captain Jones took another bullet, this one slamming into his chest. Tucker heard the thump and saw dust fly, shrieking a logical inquiry to his boss. With labored voice Jones retorted "Boys, I'm shot all to pieces. I am Killed."[32] And he was.

Corporal Carl Kirchner, by virtue of circumstance the man now in command, moves the nightmarish narrative: "We continued to fire on them until they retreated & hid in the building. Just then a friendly mexican who was with us in search of stolen horses told me we were in mexico in the outskirts of Tres Jacales a small mexican town & the people had sent for the mexican soldiers who would be there in 15 minutes. My first decision was to stay with our dead Captain & Kill or capture the mexicans but after waiting about 45 minutes I saw from the appearance of everything we would be over-powered & murdered so we retreated to this side & thence to San Elizario where I found it impossible to get a single white man to assist me. . . ."[33]

Fighting with Colt's .45s and Winchesters for this Pirate Island episode was cooked. Wrangling with Mexican officialdom regarding the return of Captain Jones' body and personal property was broiling: As were matters of international diplomacy. The Texas/Mexico border country is land of the *mordida*—the bite—the bribe. Though it can not stand as unequivocal, it doesn't take too much reading between the lines to fathom that a little sweetener was added to the recipe for returning the dead captain's body back across the Rio Grande. The July 7, 1893 letter from El Paso County Sheriff Frank Simmons to Texas Governor James S. Hogg is helpful with understanding borderland truths—as disturbing as they sometimes might be: "I have been to quite an expense in getting the body of Capt. Frank Jones, Company D State Rangers from Mexico. Will the state help me pay these expenses? My office pays but little, [and] it will be quite a hardship on me if I have to pay all this expense. Hope this will receive a favorable consideration at your hands. . . ."[34] At Washington, D.C. the Minister of Mexico, M. Romero, filed an official protest that armed Texas Rangers had "invaded" Mexico.[35]

In the real worlds of governmental bureaucracy and big business stinky stuff invariably rolls downhill. Based at Fort Bliss, 2nd Lieutenant H. N. Royden, 23rd Infantry, U.S. Army, was at the bottom end of Federal Hill. Under orders from General Wheaton the young officer was assigned to make an official investigation into the alleged south of the border invasion. Stopping by the Texas Ranger camp at Ysleta, Lieutenant Royden registered his need for an escort, someone to shepherd him to Pirate Island. John Reynolds Hughes, formerly Company D's 1st Sergeant had been promoted to captain, filling the heartrending leadership vacuum. Captain Hughes amiably bent to the soldier's request: "I sent R. E. Bryant and E. D. Aten, two members of my company who were with Capt. Jones when he was killed. I sent them with Lieut. Royden as guides [and] they inspected the ground thoroughly. . . ."[36]

There is a sidebar story associated with the aftermath of Frank Jones' killing, one sometimes dismissed prematurely as being but apocryphal. Ernest St. Leon, an ex-Ranger, was more than a little distraught about the captain's death. St. Leon was a man of action. He was standing off-stage but ready to assume a starring role if given the okay. The message Ernest St. Leon sent Adjutant General Mabry is transparent:

> Referring to the murder of our Brave and beloved Captain by outlaws—I would respectfully ask and request to be sent out: provided his murderers are not apprehended within the next week . . . . but for God's sake General if those men succeed in escaping from officers now in pursuit I beg of you to send me out and there I will stay until I either bring them to Justice or go the same way as poor Frank.[37]

Many are the stories of allegedly guilty "Mexicans" committing suicide while kicking their heels underneath a live oak—at the end of a rope. Others were shot—assassinated. Though this sketch is about the life and adventures of Eddie Aten and not St. Leon, an intriguing item does warrant notice. For a period of about six months Ernest would be paid for his services as a Texas Ranger while working in the shadows—off the books, so to speak. Distilling fact from folklore in this instance has been addressed in treatments distinct from this narrative.[38] In this regard, what Private Eddie Aten knew or did not know is lost.

And, perhaps at this point it's worth mentioning a fact welded tight. Captain John Hughes and Eddie Aten would forge a friendship unbreakable. As Rangers, Hughes had already worked with brothers Ira and Cal Aten and, in fact, had been with both men during the times of scary gunplay. Only the Grim Reaper could break the bond between John Hughes and the three Aten brothers, but not even he was powerful enough to fracture their fond memories and mutual affection. History is witness to that.

Subsequent to the murder of Captain Jones it seems the Rangers of Company D were spinning in a whirlwind of enforcement actions. Private Eddie Aten was swept into the storm. He, along with Private J. V. "Jim" Latham, accompanied well-known Deputy U.S. Marshal George A. Scarborough on a scout to Hueco Tanks looking for fugitive John Brooks. On that very same day one of his Company D cohorts, Private J. W. Fulgham, was forced into a chilling gunplay while scouting in Reeves County along the Pecos River. Ranger Fulgham earned the blue ribbon, the desperado the red—second place in the gunfight. Gravediggers put feet to the shovels.[39] The Texas criminal justice system put Ranger Fulgham's feet to the fire, but it only took a trial jury twelve minutes to cool his heels with an acquittal.[40]

After returning to Ysleta Private Aten seemingly executed an abrupt turnabout, returning to Hueco Tanks looking for a herd of stolen cattle which had escaped Ranger notice. Then, along with Captain Hughes, and Privates Jim Latham, F. W. McMahan, Wood Saunders, Will Schmidt, Joseph Russell "Joe" Sitter, and the renowned New Mexico Territory deputy sheriff, Ben Williams from Doña Anna County (Las Cruces), Ed Aten scouted for a band of robbers thought to be haunting West Texas. Their targets were tracked down, but robbers they proved not to be, just a band of peaceful Pueblo Indians on an antelope hunting excursion.[41]

The following month someone else was hunting at Ysleta— hunting for trouble. Shortly after Thanksgiving it seems Jose

Apodaca went on a tear. Ranger Privates Aten and McMahan were expending a few hours of downtime at an area billiard hall. Captain Hughes had okayed such a recreational retreat, noting that such a spot was a good place to also "learn the news." Aten's and McMahan's friendly game was interrupted by the earsplitting screams of a woman, one definitely in distress. Jerking out their Colt's .45s, both Rangers rushed outside. There they spotted a frightened female trying to climb out of a buggy, shrieking "He's trying to murder us!" On the buggy's floorboard was another form, one of a bloodied and seemingly dead woman. Standing over her was Jose Apodaca, rifle in hand, feverishly clubbing the woman sprawled at his feet. When challenged by Rangers Aten and McMahan, the maddened maniac miscalculated. He may have thought pointing his weapon at the Rangers would be intimidating. It was idiocy. Both Texas Rangers fired their pistols. Apodaca dropped as if pole axed, wounded but not incurably. Though it was but routine legal business, the two Rangers were required to post bond and await action of an El Paso County grand jury. They were, in the end, exonerated.[42]

The following year there can be no doubt that Eddie Aten was saddened upon learning that one of his fellow Company D Rangers had been foully murdered by an ex-Company D Ranger. The notoriously desperate and drunken Baz Outlaw had gunned down Private Joseph McKidrict at the El Paso sporting house operated by Madame Tillie Howard. Outlaw, in turn, had been killed by a man of equally unsavory reputation, John Selman—who would later slay the likewise nastily disposed John Wesley Hardin.[43] Alligators were eating alligators at El Paso.

Eddie Aten was not working El Paso proper, though. Proving himself as a most capable lawman Eddie Aten had been promoted to the rank of corporal and was stationed above El Paso, just below the New Mexico Territory borderline at Vinton, Texas.[44] Such an assignment may have seemed appropriate—on paper—but Corporal Aten was all over the place for the months of June and July 1894: First, on the fifteenth day of June he and an unnamed Ranger latched on to Richard Haywood, a fugitive from New Mexico Territory wanted for Highway Robbery, turning him over to a deputy sheriff from Doña Anna County.[45] Next, they were at Fort Hancock looking for stolen horses and while there arrested Pedro Apodaca for Assault to Murder. By the middle of the month he was heading for Central Texas.[46]

Big trouble was brewing at Temple. Taking Privates Will Schmidt, Jim Latham, and Ed Palmer with him, Corporal Aten left El Paso County for a near two week Bell County assignment; joining Captain Hughes who had rushed ahead at the behest of headquarters. So, too, had the commander of Company F, Captain James Abijah Brooks, as well as men from other Ranger companies.[47] Devil-may-care striking railroad employees—according to management's viewpoint—were threatening violence. A dozen and half unsmiling Texas Rangers bristling with Winchesters riding the rails and patrolling the railway yards had its desired outcome: There was little real trouble. The cogent preventive enforcement tactic had worked, except for Jack Gifford. He was arrested by Captain Hughes for Assault and Battery, purportedly directing his anger and thrown punches at "scabs" who were replacing union men. The prisoner was released to the custody of Temple's city marshal. There is another upshot that may be attributed to the Temple trip. A photo op. Texas Rangers were not camera shy. Eighteen hard-boiled Texas Rangers, rifles in hand and boxcars behind them, posed for the professional shutterbug before disbursing and heading back to their respective camps. Corporal Eddie Aten and his men, when all was said and done, by the time they retuned to El Paso County had racked up an astounding 2278 miles of railroad travel.[48]

After the short-lived brouhaha at Temple, it is rock solid that Corporal Eddie Aten was granted a furlough. Pinpointing his activities while on vacation is—or could be—maddening. Did he return home to visit with family? Or was this the timeframe when he married Miss Elena Benavidez, the daughter of a "wealthy wine maker" in El Paso County?[49] With clarity it may be reported he was back in harness on the 5th day of August 1894.[50] From that point forward it seems that most of Corporal Aten's duties were for awhile more-or-less routine. That is, if any police work qualifies as routine.

The following year Corporal Aten was involved in a rather high-profile West Texas murder investigation. At the UX Ranch in picturesque Jeff Davis County, Selverio Mangose had been murdered while gathering cattle. Selverio and the little bunch of cattle he had amassed became separated from his cowboying pals. The motive is elusive, but it seems that prominent sheepman W. J. Patterson fortuitously stumbled upon Selverio and just "walked up and shot him."[51] Corporal Aten and Private Joe Sitter were dispatched to Jeff Davis County. On the dodge Patterson had slipped into New Mexico Territory, but was tracked down and apprehended by the Rangers.[52] Corporal Aten's innate grit and investigative skills did not go unnoticed. Captain Hughes knew Eddie had honed himself into a topnotch lawman.

On 24 June 1895 the Company D 1st Sergeant, Carl Kirchner, voluntarily discharged so that he could enter into the "saloon business" at Ysleta. The next day Eddie Aten shed his corporal's stripes, becoming the company's top noncom.[53] Again, following Sergeant Aten's workaday footprints is not too taxing. Enumerating the scouts and arrests he made is retrievable. Especially since most of his travel from point to point, from one supervisory assignment to the next, was now for the most part accomplished while looking out the window of a Pullman coach making good time on Texas' spider-web network of rail lines. The next major law enforcing task on Sergeant Aten's near agenda would wear thin any of the pleasures or passions for riding the rails. Big doing were on tap. Right out of the governor's office.

Part of the Texas Ranger mystique is mythos. That the majority of Texas Rangers were honorable and brave is unarguable—excepting to a cadre of dogmatic detractors emotionally and/or culturally driven by inane preprogrammed interpretations. That said there are core truths: Though it sounds good, in reality the One Riot, One Ranger statement is clichéd staleness overblown. Another pronouncement is trite, the one puffing that a lone Ranger would charge Hell with a bucket of water. Rather cleverly an esteemed historian with *mucho* Ranger studies under his belt appropriately postulated that sometimes commonsense and professionalism calls for more buckets—and more Rangers.[54] Circumspectly carving the fact from the fiction also cuts to the core of another Texas Ranger fable: That the Rangers prevented a prizefight from taking place at El Paso during February 1896. Is it a remarkable true story? Yes. Were the Texas Rangers a part of that story? Yes. Did Sergeant Aten meaningfully participate in the story? Yes. Did steely-eyed Winchester toting and six-shooter wearing Texas Rangers really put the kibosh on a boxing match taking place in Texas? No. Nevertheless, they were there and their presence is historically significant in an overall assessment of the Texas Rangers' law enforcing worth and institutional flexibility.

It takes but a moment and quick recap to separate wheat from chaff. Big time boxing promoter Dan Albert Stuart from Dallas was pushing hard for a main-event match between two celebrated pugilists, Gentleman Jim Corbett and Fighting Bob Fitzsimmons. In due course Corbett bowed out and was hastily replaced by Peter Maher.[55] There was a fly in the ointment. A moralizing Texas Legislature had by law made boxing within the state unlawful, a felony. Often in the rewritings it's scrubbed out of the story, but a salient fact must not be thrown out with the historic bathwater: Once the state lawmakers made it illegal, Dan Stuart was not going to have the fight take place on Lone Star ground: "I will proceed under the law as it is and hunt other fields outside Texas! You see I am now, and have been, law-abiding. Yes, sir, the contest will not come off in Texas."[56] Even the redoubtable Captain John R. Hughes, Sergeant Eddie Aten's boss, grasped that the hoopla about the fight taking place in Texas was just that, hoopla: "I have not tried to conceal the fact that I would prevent the fight from taking place in Texas but have always expressed myself that I did not think they would try it on Texas soil."[57]

Stubbornly clinging to a notion that he would not be forced to backtrack on his proposition to promote the fight, Dan Stuart moved headquarters for the circus—a Fistic Carnival—to El Paso. Contrary to mythmaker's shenanigans, the purpose of relocating to El Paso was not to stage the fight there, but due to El Paso's proximity to other viable venues: Old Mexico and/or Arizona and New Mexico Territories.[58] Hopping across the border to Juárez would be near effortless. Hopping aboard a westbound train and exiting Texas could be pulled off in a jiffy—promptly and without difficulty. Cunning Dan Stuart could—and did—keep busy-body moralists guessing. Fearing the worst—that he might be outfoxed—the governor, Charles A. Culberson, summoned Rangers to guarantee he wasn't to be legally or politically or morally or laughingly embarrassed. Captain Hughes began to formulate plans as where he could best deploy the manpower buildup: "I will be at El Paso when the men from the other companies arrive there and will station them where they will do the most good."[59] Texas Rangers follow orders. The adjutant general, company captains, and their heavily-armed subordinates converged at El Paso. Company D's 1st Sergeant was there already, a specific task would be delegated for Eddie Aten. He was to unflinchingly stick with flatcars carrying materials for building the boxing ring and grandstands. When those cars were offloaded he was to report the location with haste—that's where the fight would be taking place.[60] Captain Hughes was sure he had the right man for the right job:

> The secret of where the fight will take place has been guarded with great care and there are very few who know where it will take place. I think it will be impossible to make the fight a success without making some preparations a few days beforehand and I don't think they can make any preparations and keep me from finding it out.[61]

Often in Texas Ranger histories with an excoriating bent, actuality is clouded by the fog of bias. In most cases on-the-ground everyday Rangers were far removed from the plotting of policy makers—for the good or for the bad. Their job was not easy, but it was not knotty due to wondering what an armchair-thinker might say someday. Using today's lexis, the political doings were above Sergeant Aten's pay-grade. The chief executive of Texas had a clear message:

> We are not Concerned except as to Territory claimed by Texas . . . watch matters closely night & day.[62]

Ranger Sergeant Aten had been handed a real message, too: Don't lose sight of that equipment. Eddie was living in real time, with a real job ahead of him. Aten was not a man to be bulldozed: Not by anyone, big and stout or lean and mean. In the dead of night, as the fireman began stoking the locomotive's firebox, starting the process for cranking up and moving out, Sergeant Aten jumped aboard, climbing into the engine's cab. His mission was clear-cut, his determination was steadfast. No room for any mealy-mouthed palavering. There was not an inch of middle ground to give. The engineer was not any too happy. In no uncertain terms he voiced a fierce threat for Sergeant Aten: "You're not going to ride on this engine. If you try it, I'll knock you off with the shovel." There is the old saw about taking a knife to a gunfight. It's applicable for shovels, too! In but an instant he became "the scaredest engineer in Texas when Aten eased the muzzle of a .45 up against his stomach and told him what to do next."[63] The train, westbound, summarily left the El Paso railway yards. The supposed destination was a sham from the get go. Sixteen miles northwest of town at Strauss, New Mexico Territory the engineer reversed course, and when passing back through El Paso proper did not slow down. Before him, though Sergeant Aten didn't know it at the time, lay 389 miles of desolate West Texas.[64]

Stops along the way had not been attention grabbers. That changed at Langtry, Val Verde County, just west of the Pecos River.[65] It was the stomping grounds of that ever waggish jurist, Judge Roy Bean, proprietor of the iniquitous Jersey Lilly Saloon. Real time reality engulfed, washed over Sergeant Aten. Jim Bates, president of the Dallas Athletic Club was overseeing the handiwork of forty-two Mexican laborers who had been standing by, ready to meet the train and unload boxing ring equipment. Sergeant Aten was sharp, but it did not take a wily detective to figure this one out. This was the place! Sergeant Eddie Aten's identity as a Texas Ranger was not secret. While he was preparing a message for the telegraph operator to transmit, no one doubted its contents or its addressee. In fact, if the gossipy tidbits be true and there's not reason to discredit them, numerous were the attempts at bribing Eddie Aten to forgo spilling the beans. He spurned their overtures and offers of cash. Aten may have been rough-cut around a few edges, but he was not crooked.[66] His spine was steel, his loyalty concrete, his ethics unbendable.

The rest is history. The sporting crowd finally arrived on 21 February 1896 and crossed a plank walkway to a sandbar in the middle of the Rio Grande where the fight would come to fruition. From overlooking cliffs the Rangers watched the bout below—which was outside their law enforcing jurisdiction—without having to up $20 for a ringside seat, half a month's pay.[67] The show was grand but it was short. Lasting but one minute and forty-three seconds before Fighting Bob Fitzsimmons decked Peter Maher for the ten count.[68] The fun was done.

So while Sergeant Eddie Aten had been head down, exhaustively doing his job in the wilds of woolly Val Verde County, his Texas Rangers buddies—and all the big bosses—before coming to Langtry, had lined up on the El Paso County Courthouse steps, squarely in front of photographer J. C. Burge's rickety tripod and still-camera.[69] The captured image has captured imaginations worldwide. In this specific case Eddie Aten was shortchanged. He missed immortalization in one of the most published and more widely distributed Texas Ranger photographs of all time.

Although it's not quantifiable with hard facts and absolute figures, two substantial dynamics resulted from Governor Culberson sending Texas Rangers to El Paso: One, any would-be criminals or skeptic citizens were now plainly aware that when necessary—or thought to be necessary—Texas Rangers from multiple companies could converge on very short notice anywhere in the state. Secondly, those Texas Rangers, regardless of where their personal sympathies lay regarding the prizefight, would stand at the forefront—gun in hand—ready to enforce and defend Texas law as directed.[70] They would obey orders! Practically speaking, however, just in regards to the prizefight which was never destined to violate the state's criminal statutes, it's been duly annotated by an accomplished scholar that imprudently bringing so many Texas Rangers to El Paso unnecessarily had been "an overkill that should have been avoided."[71]

Pinpointing with precision when Sergeant Aten was actually posted at Pecos, Texas, is hazy. State health officials had drawn a quarantine line owing to the discovery of diseased cattle and Company D Rangers were detailed to the Reeves County region to ensure strict compliance. During March 1896 Sergeant Aten was the man placed in charge of the Pecos detachment.[72] Certainly he was still there as of the late summer of 1896.[73]

Perhaps spotlighting just one arrest will satisfactorily reflect the mettle and levelheadedness of Sergeant Eddie Aten. Without delving into its origins, a feud of long standing had festered in Pecos, Reeves County. At half past one o'clock on 3 October 1896 hell popped inside the Johnson & Heard Saloon. Barney Kemp Riggs, a certifiable man-killer, and John Madison Denson were standing at the polished mahogany bar, cautiously eyeing each other. Also with a boot on the burnished brass-rail was William H. "Bill" Earhart, a pal of Denson, an enemy of Riggs. Though unspoken, tension as well as billowing blue cigarette and cigar smoke filled the air—disturbingly so. The bubble of restraint inside Bill Earhart finally burst and out jumped his six-shooter. Barney Riggs got there first, his .45 belching a bullet and plummeting Bill to the grimy barroom floor—dead. Barney's next shot missed, but a turn of the Colt's cylinder put another round under the hammer and when it dropped, so too dropped Mr. J. M. Denson—dead. Not unwisely, not knowing who was now friend or foe, Barney extracted spent brass and reloaded with hot rounds.

Now loaded for bear, Barney sought the safety of darkness in an unlighted room, and waited. Sergeant Aten was in town. As would be expected of a good Ranger, he had hotfooted to the echoes of gunfire. Sergeant Eddie Aten didn't rush in headlong like a headstrong rookie, however. He was cucumber cool. Outside, Sergeant Aten pumped eyewitnesses for hard data; learning just what and just how all hell had broken loose at Pecos.[74] With what he deemed a reasonable update Aten boldly stepped into the Johnson & Heard Saloon, calmly announcing his presence and warning Barney Riggs it was time to stand down, time for a pow-wow not a resumption of gunplay. While standing on the fuse connected to volatility, Ranger Sergeant Aten was somewhat startled when Reeves County Sheriff Daniel Murphy dashed inside the taproom, desirous of making an arrest—right quick. Eddie Aten circumspectly defused the sheriff's well-intentioned desire to kick ass and take names. The Ranger's job was to prevent anymore carnage—not let an act of bone-headed irrationality open the floodgates of bloodshed. Using his legal Discretion and sound Judgment, Aten allowed that it would be okay for Tom, Barney's brother, to visit with him awhile in the darkened room with no windows. Sergeant Aten was tuned into reality—if Barney Riggs bolted out, gun in hand, he would drop him deader than a cold-steel anvil or sure die while trying to. On the other hand, he had plenty of time for tempers to cool, passions to deflate. In the end, Sergeant Eddie Aten's smarts paid its dividend. Barney Riggs surrendered head held high, not humiliated or shamed. Eddie Aten escorted his prisoner to the Reeves County lockup.[75]

Barney K. Riggs may have been ill over the legal mess he was embroiled in, but Sergeant Eddie Aten was just sick. At Pecos or somewhere nearby he had contracted Typhoid Fever and was bedridden.[76] Captain Hughes was desirous of repositioning the detachment at Pecos, but as of four days before Christmas 1896 his 1st Sergeant was yet incapacitated and unable travel.[77] Aten was not playing possum or whining or malingering; he was damn sick. Captain Hughes was somewhat worried, notifying Quartermaster W. H. Owen on January 17, 1897 that Sergeant Aten "came near dying [and] he is not yet able for duty."[78] Company D's commander was getting sick and tired, too. He was engaged in a bitter dispute over charges submitted relating to Aten's nursing care and temporary accommodations at Pecos, claiming that Eddie was only being kept alive by a trifling diet of "beef juice and whisky" but billed exorbitantly for the fare and sleeping quarters.[79] Captain Hughes even pitched in the hint of a wicked conspiracy directed by a notorious West Texas troublemaker and murderer for hire: "You will notice that he writes on letter head of J. B. Miller who is a bitter enemy of Rangers and the sheriff at Pecos and in fact all officers. I think Miller has influenced him to do this."[80] While James B. "Killing Jim" Miller may have been a vicious foe of the Texas Rangers he certainly had naught to do with the outfit's budgetary shortfall. Captain Hughes was ordered by headquarters to provisionally drop five names from the company's Muster & Payroll as of February 10, 1897. Since Sergeant Aten was unable to button down normal duties, he was one of the Rangers cut.[81] Replenished were the Rangers coffers and recuperated was Eddie Aten. As of March 1, 1897 he was reinstated as Company D's 1st Sergeant.[82] And by the eighteenth day of the month he seemed fit as a fiddle, well enough to lead a two-man scout onto the ever perilous Pirate Island looking for a band of horse thieves. The Rangers didn't recover any horses or horse stealers, but did arrest two fellows for hog theft.[83] Sergeant Aten was back in the saddle again, as a single man.

Unfortunately the all too frequent caveat must be inserted: The precise timeframe is nebulous at best, the hard facts remain unchanged. Somewhere along the way Eddie and Elena lost a child, a daughter "when only a few years of age." Begging the question was it an accident or due to natural causes is understandable, but unanswerable. Likewise it would be but feathery puff to fill in another blank. Whatever was the reason or excuse or anguish, Eddie and Elena separated shortly after the youngster's death.[84]

The next few months were a tornado of goings-on for Sergeant Aten. He chased after train robbers and scouted the Rio Grande after cow thieves. For fourteen days he rode trains with another Ranger, hoping someone would be foolish enough to give high-jacking a try. He arrested a rapist and disturbers of the peace. He was deployed to head a detachment based at Marathon, and from there, on just one scout with Mounted U.S. Customs Inspectors, he was out 29 days, traveling some 600 horseback miles.[85]

When the morning's orb cast her spears of sunlight into Marathon on New Year's Day 1898, Sergeant Aten was yet there, the hurricane of commotion had not dissipated. The arrests were numerable, ranging from Carrying a Pistol to Murder. Aside from the bothersome yahoos crying for arrest, Sergeant Aten was not immune to another niggling problem that occasionally nipped at good Rangers' heels: Political paybacks. When Private N. A. Singleton resigned so that he could head for the "Yaqui gold fields in Mexico," Captain Hughes was ordered to backfill with someone he or Sergeant Aten did not know, O. B. Settle, "who has political influence [and] is a particular friend of Gov. Jester." Unfortunately for the boys of Company D in general and its command structure in particular, Private Settle was "not liked by the stockmen amongst whom he has to work . . . . and for assisting a man who was indicted for Murder to beat his case in District Court at Alpine, Brewster Co . . . . [and] was doing the Ranger Service more harm than good."[86]

The hard life was beginning to take its toll on Sergeant Aten. A grueling scout with four men to the very spot where the Rio Grande makes its big bend, investigating "the rumor of armed Mexicans being at the settlements" was acutely taxing for the sergeant, a fellow yet trying to shake off the lingering side-effects of Typhoid Fever.[87] Two days after Independence Day 1898, after having served in the Rangers for near half a dozen years, the last three as Company D's top noncom, Sergeant Eddie Aten said *adios* to his law enforcing *amigos*, having his name officially dropped from the outfit's Muster & Payroll. Eddie Aten had high hopes for greener and healthier and much more profitable pastures.[88] Captain Hughes promptly promoted forty-year-old T. T. Cook, a veteran Ranger to fill the slot.[89]

According to one source, as a civilian Eddie Aten from time to time performed "undercover work for Captain Hughes and on occasion went into Mexico on assignment."[90] The validity of such postulation will not be challenged herein. It is quite likely true. Although it's now and again tough for theoretical thinkers to fathom, the absence of a convenient paper trail to peruse when tracking enforcement activities along the border is commonplace, no anomaly. Sometimes in the honorable hearts and minds of no nonsense on-the-ground go-getters, some borderlands doings were best left unsaid—on paper.[91] Does that mean it didn't happen?

Apparently unable to resist once more being a Texas Ranger, on the 13th day of April 1901 Eddie Aten reupped, accepting the position of a private in his old unit, Company D, Frontier Battalion, yet headquartered at Ysleta, and still commanded by Captain John R. Hughes.[92]

Private Aten's enlistment coincided with two El Paso County happenings. The Company D headquarters was being relocated from Ysleta to Fort Hancock and the President of the United States was scheduled to make an appearance at El Paso. Of course, the first order of business was to protect President William McKinley, moving the Texas Ranger camp was put on interim hold. In fact, according to Captain Hughes, not only were the Rangers to help with keeping order, they were asked to participate in the grand parade also.[93] On 5 May 1898 Captain John Hughes, Lieutenant John J. Brooks, along with Company D Privates, E. B. Jones, O. Carrilla, and Eddie Aten reported for duty at El Paso. The record is silent about them taking part in the parade, but if he did so, Private Aten would have been sitting tall in the saddle, riding his $60 horse, a five-year-old gray gelding, branded <K.[94] After spending the night in El Paso the boys returned to Ysleta for the short go, but were finished relocating company headquarters to Fort Hancock by the time June's Monthly Return was due at Austin.

It is quite interesting to note that the Monthly Return for June 1901 enumerates but a single arrest: Private Eddie Aten is credited with arresting Refucio Rodriquez for Assault and Battery, then turning him over to the Justice of Peace for El Paso County's Precinct 6.[95] This solitary arrest by a Ranger from enlisted ranks is intriguing on its face. It came at a time when the Frontier Battalion was betwixt and between. Due to interpretative manipulations there had been a binding decision that the enabling legislation creating the Frontier Battalion allowed for custodial arrests only at the hands of commissioned officers—captains and lieutenants— not by privates and sergeants. Therefore, until such inarticulate legalese was fixed by state legislators any arrests made by enlisted Ranger personnel could be classified as unlawful, exposing them to criminal prosecution: False Imprisonment. As a stopgap measure—until made right on Austin's Congress Avenue—only Texas Ranger captains and lieutenants could legitimately make physical arrests. Had Private Eddie Aten been asleep? In due course the predicament was disentangled and the Ranger Force created with a birthday of 3 July 1901. The Frontier Battalion, after a run of a quarter century, officially ceased to exist five days later. In truth the Texas Rangers had hardly skipped a beat.[96] Nor had Eddie Aten it seems; he was yet a Texas Ranger.

Perhaps hypnotizing himself with wishful thinking and won over to the notion it was time to advantage himself with a surefire cash cow, Eddie Aten resigned from Company D once more, to take effect November 30, 1901.[97] He opened a saloon and gambling hall at El Paso, but all so soon the cow's milk went dry and the easy money but trickled. While thus engaged in that saloon business and before the swinging-doors swung for the last time, there is a compelling corresponding tale—a real dandy if true. Though it must be registered as anecdotal oral history, it is said that one of Aten's belligerently besotted patrons took a shot at Eddie, but missed. Eddie grabbed his 1886 Winchester propped behind the bar and humorlessly drove a spiraling bullet through one of the assailant's lungs. Purportedly, when the wounded man regained mobility he looked up a stunned Aten and thanked him: The gunshot had cured his Asthma![98]

Predictably, with yet no family burdens chaining itchy feet, Eddie hotfooted southeast to Shafter, Presidio County, not too far north of the Rio Grande. There he went to work tending bar and dealing Faro for his old friend and former Texas Ranger colleague Ike Herrin. Eventually Aten bought out Herrin's interest, becoming the barroom's sole proprietor.[99] Dissimilar to his brothers Ira and Cal, who seemed happiest when on the farm or ranch, Eddie was more inclined towards city life. The lure of El Paso was dazzling. Shafter was dreary. The choice was easy.

Returning to El Paso during 1906, Eddie Aten landed employment as a Special Officer with the railroad. He had, at long last found a home—geographically and vocationally. Nine years later he found a wife. On the 20th day of February 1915 Eddie married a widow from Las Cruces, New Mexico, Gertrude Backus Aiello. No children from this union would issue.[100] Ironically, so it now seems, 1915 was the same year Captain John Reynolds Hughes was callously "cashiered." The swearing in of a second-rate governor foreshadowed the shoving out of a first-rate Ranger. Governor James E. Ferguson had no place for John R. Hughes on the payroll—partisan politics trumped principle.[101]

The soon to be impeached Texas governor, however, could not impeach the bond of friendship between Hughes and the Aten brothers, Ira, Cal, and Eddie. Ira, now a big time businessman and agriculturalist in southern California routinely passed through El Paso, visiting and reminiscing with John and Eddie who maintained their homes there. On the way home he would overnight with his brother Cal at the Lelia Lake ranch in the Texas Panhandle. Likewise, Hughes would journey regularly to Ira's El Centro, California estate for extended vacations. One of Ira Aten's Lone Star State tours is especially noteworthy. Texas was celebrating its centennial during 1936. Ira could not resist. In the course of this trip old-time Rangers Jim Gilson, John Hughes, and Ira Aten all ganged up in El Paso at Eddie's and Gertrude's congenial home for a confab—a gabfest. Quite logically during the retelling and reliving of breathtaking adventures from bygone days the Pirate Island gunfight was revived and correspondingly the death of Captain Frank Jones was reawakened. The captain's Colt's six-shooter and handcuffs had not been returned by Mexican authorities after his merciless murder, but his Winchester and pocket watch had.[102] Subsequently, because he was held in such esteem by the Jones' family, John Hughes had been given Frank's timepiece as a small token of friendship. Now, during the 1936 visit, it was time to pass the heirloom to an actual combatant, a bona fide veteran of that shoot-out, Eddie Aten. Poignantly Hughes handed Eddie the watch to retain as a keepsake.[103]

Following a forty-plus year career as a Special Officer for the railroad, Aten retired in 1947, at age seventy-seven. Eddie Aten had graduated from the school of hard-knocks and hard living. He had survived gunfights and traded shots with fools. The good Aten name was yet sterling, not tarnished by him. History would know plenty of Wild West brothers who had tainted the family name while strutting boardwalks of Tombstone or making gunplay's in wild and woolly Texas during the Reconstruction era. But all things must go, even the good guys. Eddie Aten passed to the other side at El Paso on January 31, 1953 and was buried in the city's Rest Lawn Cemetery. The old warrior had seen it all.[104]

Edwin Dunlap Aten's parents, the Reverend Austin Cunningham Aten
and wife, Katherine Eveline. *Courtesy Armstrong Research Center, Texas
Ranger Hall of Fame & Museum.*

A delightful photographic image of the Aten children from an antique family album. Front row L to R: Austin Ira, a Texas Ranger to be; Thomas Quinn; and Franklin Lincoln. Back row L to R: Edwin Dunlap "Eddie" a Texas Ranger to be but here yet clothed in the dress of a toddler; Clara Isabell "Belle"; Calvin Grant "Cal" a Texas Ranger to be; and Margaret Angelina Elizabeth "Angie." *Courtesy Doug Turner.*

Ira Aten, horseback. At the urging of his parents and the invitation of older brother Ira, Eddie relocated to the Texas Panhandle, settling near Dimmitt, Castro County. Apparently the locale was too tame for Eddie, who wished to follow in his brothers' footsteps as Texas Rangers. *Courtesy Armstrong Research Center, Texas Ranger Hall of Fame & Museum.*

Carl Kirchner. *Courtesy Armstrong Research Center, Texas Ranger Hall of Fame &*
Museum.

Wood Saunders, *Courtesy Nita Stewart Haley Memorial Library and J. Evetts Haley History Center.*

Texas Rangers from multiple companies, including Eddie Aten, converged on Temple, Bell County, in an effort to prevent misbehavior during a strike of railroad employees: Standing L to R: Captain J.A. Brooks, Captain John R. Hughes, John Nix, Eddie Aten, Ed "Big Ed" Connell, T. M. Ross, Lee Queen, A. A. Neeley, G. J. Cook, and Dan Coleman. Sitting L to R: Jack Harrell, Will Schmidt, C. B. Fullereton, G. N. Norton, Ed Palmer, Joe Natus, J. V. Latham, and E. E. Coleman. *Courtesy Armstrong Research Center, Texas Ranger Hall of Fame & Museum.*

George A. Scarborough. As a Deputy U.S. Marshal he made several "scouts" with Texas Ranger Eddie Aten throughout West Texas—and into southern New Mexico Territory. Though his actual law enforcing record is rich, Scarborough is probably best known as the man who killed the man [John Selman], who killed the man [John Wesley Hardin.] Scarborough would later be killed by murderous desperadoes during a shoot-out along the New Mexico/Arizona borderline. *Courtesy Nita Stewart Haley Memorial Library and J. Evetts Haley History Center.*

These gritty Winchester Warriors gathered for one of the most publicized Texas Ranger photographs. They had been assigned to interdict an illegal prizefight, thought possibly—but wrongly—to take place in Texas. While these lawmen stood for the shutterbug, Texas Ranger Sergeant Eddie Aten was in the field keeping an eagle eye on the necessary materials for constructing the grandstands and boxing ring. *Courtesy Armstrong Research Center, Texas Ranger Hall of Fame & Museum.*

Barney Kemp Riggs, seated in center, a noted Southwestern ex-convict and man killer. After killing two men at Pecos, Reeves County, he reloaded his Colt's six-shooter and holed up in a darkened backroom at the Johnson & Heard Saloon. Exercising his legally awarded Discretion and employing his typical good Judgment, Texas Ranger Sergeant Eddie Aten defused the volatile situation, calmly talking Barney Riggs into surrendering. *Courtesy Ellis Lindsey.*

Four old-time Texas Rangers visit a headstone memorializing the 1893 death of Captain Frank Jones on Pirate Island. Standing L to R: Eddie Aten, Ira Aten, and Ed Bryant. Kneeling: John R. Hughes. Ex-Rangers Eddie Aten and Ed Bryant were veterans of the disastrous gunplay. *Courtesy Armstrong Research Center, Texas Ranger Hall of Fame & Museum.*

During a 1936 visit at Eddie Aten's home in El Paso these four ex-Texas Rangers gather for a confab. Standing L to R: Ira Aten and Jim Gilson. Seated L to R: Eddie Aten and John R. Hughes. *Courtesy Jeri and Gary Boyce Radder.*

The 1936 visit pictured in the foregoing photograph is when John R. Hughes presented Eddie Aten with the pocket watch recovered from the body of Captain Frank Jones. Hughes has been given the timepiece by the Jones' family, and he passed it along as a gesture of esteem to an actual participant of the gunfight. *Courtesy Louise and Donald M. Yena Collection.*

Endnotes

Chapter 1

1. Bob Alexander, *Rawhide Ranger, Ira Aten: Enforcing Law on the Texas Frontier*, 13; Robert W. Stephens, *Texas Ranger Sketches,* 15; Federal Census, 1870, Indian Point, Knox County, Illinois.
2. Ibid.; Charles H. Harris III, Frances E. Harris, and Louis R. Sadler, *Texas Ranger Biographies: Those Who Served, 1910-1921*, 11.
3. For an all-embracing examination of outlaw Sam Bass the reader must access Rick Miller's *Sam Bass and Gang.*
4. Rick Miller, *Texas Ranger John B. Jones: and the Frontier Battalion, 1874-1881,* 206-207.
5. Alexander, *Rawhide Ranger, Ira Aten*, 1-9.
6. Transcript of Ira Aten interview, El Centro, California, by Evetts Haley, Earl Vandale, and Hervey Chesley, July 1941. Hereafter Aten-1941. Nita Stewart Haley Memorial Library & History Center (HML&HC), Midland, Texas.
7. Monthly Return, Company D, Frontier Battalion, April 1888. Texas State Library and Archives (TSA).
8. For a comprehensive comparison between Ira Aten as a legitimate nineteenth-century lawman, and Wyatt Earp, as a twentieth-century literary and Hollywood creation, see Bob Alexander, "Square Deals and Real McCoys," *Wild West History Association Journal*, June 2011, 32-52; also, William B. Shillingberg, *Tombstone, A.T., A History of Early, Mining, Milling, and Mayhem*: "Only after his death would Wyatt Earp become a respected, larger-than-life heroic symbol. But even that would not last, and today this mythical view of the man appears tarnished to objective researchers not blinded by hero worship," 139; and, Don Chaput *The Earp Papers: In a Brother's Image*: "Much has been written about the West, and in particular the Earp brothers. Through dozens of television productions, hundreds of books and magazine articles, each generation of the entertainment world decides to interpret the Earps anew. But these efforts are concerned with legend, with literary and show business mystique not with history," xii-xiv; Frederick Nolan, *The Wild West: History, Myth and the Making of America* simply pigeonholes Wyatt Earp as an "almost forgotten

relic of the old frontier," until reborn for the twentieth-century mass media marketplace. See page 139. The recently released (2013) and authentically revealing *Wyatt Earp: A Vigilante Life* by Andrew C. Isenberg explores in detail Earp's convoluted attempts at twentieth-century self-promotion: "Though Wyatt, who died in 1929, did not live to see it, Hollywood's embrace of him as a paragon of law and order was the realization of his last and undoubtedly his greatest confidence game, his surest revenge, and his most complete reinvention." See page 9.

9. Sergeant Ira Aten, Company D, Frontier Battalion to Captain L. P. Sieker, Quartermaster, Frontier Battalion, April 29, 1888. "The 25¢ is for my younger brother being sworn in." TSA.

10. Alexander, *Rawhide Ranger, Ira Aten*, 146.

11. Handwritten Memoir of Calvin Grant Aten, Courtesy Robert W. Stephens.

12. Sheriff H. W. Baylor, Uvalde County, Texas, to Adjutant General W. W. King, Austin, Texas, April 6, 1888, TSA.

13. Andrés Sáenz (Andrés Tijerina, ed.), *Early Tejano Ranching*, xiv.

14. Memoir of Calvin G. Aten. The Jones family's contribution to Texas law enforcing is also spotlighted in *Lawmen on the Texas Frontier: Rangers and Sheriffs* by Candice DuCoin. Frank Jones referred to brother Gerry as "Dood."

15. Luke Gournay *Texas Boundaries: Evolution of the State's Counties*, 83; Betty Dooley Awbrey and Claude Dooley, *Why Stop? A Guide to Texas Historical Roadside Markers*, 535.

16. Handwritten Memoir of Calvin Grant Aten. Here Cal Aten is making reference to a comic strip character.

17. Ibid. Although Cal Aten unquestionably knew of what he spoke, Ed Blackburn, Jr., *Wanted: Historic County Jails of Texas* makes no reference to Zapata County having a jail prior to 1900—which does seem peculiar in light of the county's long history.

18. Ibid.

19. Ibid.

20. Ibid.; Sammy Tise, *Texas County Sheriffs*, 559.

21. Ibid.; Captain Jones riding away from the scene is clear indication that he was not anticipating Private Aten doing any serious damage with his carbine.

22. Ibid.

23. Captain Frank Jones to AG King, December 9, 1887, TSA.

24. Paul N. Spellman, *Captain John Rogers, Texas Ranger*, 68. For a cautious and thinking reader, one not beguiled by bizarre, tortuous play-like psychosexual analysis, a full-length biography of Garza may be found by circumspectly surveying Elliott Young's *Catarino Garza's Revolution on the Texas-Mexican Border*.

25. Captain Jones to AG King, May 19, 1888, TSA.

26. Monthly Return, Company D, Frontier Battalion, May 1888, TSA.
27. Monthly Return, Company D, Frontier Battalion, June 1888, TSA.
28. Captain Jones to AG King, July 31, 1888, TSA.
29. Captain Jones to Captain Sieker, August 31, 1888, TSA.
30. Captain Jones to AG King, September 24, 1888. "The wires have been cut and there is no telegraphic communication with Starr Co. Sebree is in the U.S. post under protection of the Commander. I am informed that 60 armed Mexicans demanded that Sebree be delivered to them, and had to be threatened with Gatling guns to induce them to leave. . . ." TSA.
31. *Laredo Times*, September 28, 1888.
32. Telegram, from AG King to Captain Jones, Realitos, Duval County, Texas, September 22, 1888. "Call in all near detachments to join you at Rio Grande City and proceed without delay to that point with such men as you have with you. Take your entire camp." TSA.
33. Captain Jones to AG King, September 30, 1888, TSA.
34. Monthly Return, Company D, Frontier Battalion, October 1888, TSA; Bob Alexander, *Winchester Warriors: Texas Rangers of Company D, 1874-1901*, 221-222; Blackburn, *Wanted*, 305-306.
35. Robert W. Stephens, *Walter Durbin: Texas Ranger and Sheriff*, 69.
36. Monthly Return, Company D, Frontier Battalion, November 1888, TSA; Paul N. Spellman, *Captain J.A. Brooks, Texas Ranger*, 69: "From October 1888 until the following October, Company F camped outside Rio Grande City, concentrating on horse and cattle rustlers crossing from Texas into Mexico."
37. Monthly Return, Company D, Frontier Battalion, January 1889, TSA; Tise, *Texas County Sheriffs*, 503; Blackburn, *Wanted*, 333-334.
38. Monthly Return, Company D, Frontier Battalion, April 1889, TSA; Undoubtedly, if the "s" were left off of the word "Privates" it could be interpreted that Private Hughes and (Sergeant) Aten made the trip to Burnet regarding the Dick Duncan murder case; however, such was/is not the case. For a rather comprehensive look at this intriguing murder investigation, the reader is referred to Alexander's *Rawhide Ranger, Ira Aten*, Chapter 10, "Would as soon go to a fight as a frolic." See pages 170-188.
39. Monthly Return, Company D, Frontier Battalion, June 1889, TSA; Robert W. Stephens, *Bullets and Buckshot in Texas*, 36; Chuck Parsons, *Captain John R. Hughes: Lone Star Ranger*, 50.
40. Monthly Return, Company D, Frontier Battalion, May 1889, TSA.
41. Captain Jones to Adjutant General Woodford Heywood Mabry, December 20, 1892. "If you have no objection I would like to visit Austin about the 6th of January on some business connected with my candidacy of the Marshal's office. I am very anxious to meet some parties who will be in Austin when the Legislature convenes." In TSA.

42. There are numerous accounts of the Jaybird/Woodpecker Feud. Some suggested reading would include C. L. Sonnichsen's *I'll Die Before I'll Run: The Story of the Great Feuds of Texas*, 232-281 and Pauline Yelderman's *The Jay Birds of Fort Bend County*, though the latter is—as the title suggests—to some extent partisan; Ira Aten's particularized involvement in the Jaybird/Woodpecker Feud is covered thoroughly in his biography *Rawhide Ranger, Ira Aten* by Alexander.

43. Aten-1941, HML&HC.

44. Monthly Return, Company D, Frontier Battalion, August 1889, TSA.

45. *Galveston Daily News*, August 27, 1889; Alexander, *Rawhide Ranger, Ira Aten*, 208.

46. Appended List of Persons Arrested, submitted with Monthly Return, Company D, Frontier Battalion, August 1889, TSA.

47. Monthly Return, Company D, Frontier Battalion. November 1889, TSA.

48. Stephens, *Bullets and Buckshot in Texas*, 52.

49. Herein reporting about the Odle brothers' criminal activity is a synthesis of material contained in Stephens' *Buckshot and Bullets in Texas*, Parsons' *Captain John R. Hughes*, and Alexander's *Winchester Warriors* and *Rawhide Ranger, Ira Aten*.

50. Aten-1941, 64-65. HML&HC; Monthly Return, Company D, Frontier Battalion, April 1887.

51. Stephens, *Bullets and Buckshot in Texas*. 53.

52. Monthly Return, Company D, Frontier Battalion, September 1889, TSA.

53. Alexander, *Winchester Warriors*. 253.

54. Copy of Walter Durbin's autobiographical manuscript in author's possession. Courtesy, Robert W. Stephens.

55. Alonzo Van Oden (Ann Jensen, ed.), *Texas Ranger's Diary and Scrapbook*, 40.

56. Ibid., 10.

57. *El Paso Times*, April 6, 1894.

58. All sources concur that the civilian posse and the Rangers were prepositioned near Bullhead Mountain with their plan to apprehend or ambush Will and Alvin Odle. The main variance between versions is whether or not the outlaws were to be there for criminal purposes or merely celebrating the holiday season with associates. It is a matter of little consequence in the overall story.

59. Calvin Grant Aten to Austin Ira Aten, December 12, 1936.

60. Stephens, *Bullets and Buckshot in Texas*, 54.

61. Cal Aten to Ira Aten, December 12, 1936.

62. Handwritten Memoir of Calvin Grant Aten. A section of the memoir about Alvin Odle's revolver is repeated in full on page 222 of Alexander's *Rawhide Ranger, Ira Aten*. The engraved Colt .45 is currently on extended loan and display at the official repository for the Rangers in the Texas Ranger Hall of Fame & Museum, Waco, Texas.

63. John R. Hughes to AG King, December 25, 1889, TSA.
64. Captain Jones to Captain Sieker, December 29, 1889, TSA.
65. Captain Jones to Captain Sieker, December 31, 1889, TSA.
66. Sheriff Ira Aten to Cal Aten, April 20, 1890.
67. Private Calvin G. Aten to Captain L. P. Sieker, April 22, 1890, TSA.
68. Sheriff Ira Aten to Cal Aten, April 10, 1890.
69. Ira Aten to Captain Sieker, September 17, 1888, TSA.
70. Cal Aten to Captain Sieker, April 22, 1890, TSA.
71. Ibid.
72. Ira Aten to Cal Aten, June 28, 1890.
73. Monthly Return, Company D, Frontier Battalion, August 1890, TSA.
74. Stephens, *Texas Ranger Sketches*, 16.
75. Enlistment, Oath of Service, and Description Ranger Force, C. G Aten, June 1, 1918, TSA; Descriptive List, C. G. Aten, June 1, 1918, TSA; Harris, Harris, and Sadler, *Texas Ranger Biographies*, 11.
76. Alexander, *Rawhide Ranger, Ira Aten*, 317.
77. Handwritten Memoir of Calvin Grant Aten.
78. Numerous interviews with one of Cal Aten's great-grandchildren, Joseph Trobaugh II, the person inheriting the specifically identified Colt revolver and the handwritten note: Items now on loan to TRHF&M by Mr. Trobaugh.
79. Handwritten Memoir of Calvin Grant Aten.
80. Ira Aten to Imogen Aten, November 25, 1936. Courtesy Panhandle Plains Historical Museum (PPHM), Canyon, Texas.
81. Handwritten Memoir of Calvin Grant Aten.
82. Stephens, *Texas Ranger Sketches*, 16; *Clarendon News*, April 6, 1939; Ira Aten to Sister and Brothers, April 20, 1939, TRHF&M; Harris, Harris, and Sadler, *Texas Ranger Biographies*, 11.

Chapter 2

1. For a comprehensive biography of Hittson, see Vernon R. Maddux, *John Hittson, Cattle King on the Texas and Colorado Frontier*. The chapter herein is an edited and revised treatment of Bob Alexander's "Comanchero Nightmare: John N. Hittson" which appeared in the April-June 2004 edtion of the *National Association for Outlaw and Lawman History Quarterly*.
2. J. Evetts Haley, "The Comanchero Trade," *The Southwestern Historical Quarterly* 38, no. 3. (January 1935): 157.
3. For an overall capsule discussion of cultural dissimilarities between the Amerindians and Eurasians, see, T. R. Fehrenbach, *Comanches, The Destruction of a People*, 3–29.
4. Historic material regarding Amerindians' attainment of the horse and metal implements, and the resultant impact the acquisitions had on their culture abounds. An interested reader may want to review

Frank Gilbert Roe, *The Indian and the Horse*; Frank Raymond Secoy, *Changing Military Patterns of the Great Plains Indians*: "the implementation of any of the military technique patterns in the Plains except for that of the Pre-horse—Pre-gun period, was only possible through trading and raiding relations," 94; and Bernard Mishkin, *Rank and Warfare Among the Plains Indians*, "In stressing the individual psychological elements in warfare, students of Plains culture have not totally neglected to note the presence of an economic factor," 3. Also see, Elizabeth A. H. Johns, *Storms Brewed in Other Men's Worlds: The Confrontation of Indians, Spanish, and French in the Southwest, 1540-1795*.

5. Haley, 157; and Charles L. Kenner, *The Comanchero Frontier: A History of New Mexican-Plains Indian Relations*; also, Carl Coke Rister, "Harmful Practices of Indian Traders of the Southwest, 1865-1876," *New Mexico Historical Review* 6, no. 3 (July 1931).

6. Josiah Gregg, *The Commerce of the Prairies*, 219. Also see, Jerry Sullivan, "Devils In Sombreros—The Comancheros," *True West*, October 1970. "The next mention of the Comancheros was in 1839, by the man who named them, Josiah Gregg," 17.

7. Sullivan, 16-19, 52-54. Although in a climate of political correctness sometimes the Comanches' and Kiowas' barter in human captives is downplayed, nevertheless, the practice existed. The author cites several examples: Santana's remarks that "Stealing white women is a more lucrative business than stealing horses"; the liberation of Refugio Picaros, purchased from the Comanches by Jose Francisco Lucero for four knives, one plug of tobacco, two *fanegas* of corn, four blankets, and six yards of red cloth; Guadanlans Galope, twelve years old, ransomed by Vincente Romero for one mare, one rifle, one shirt, one pair of drawers, one buffalo robe, some bullets and thirty small packages of powder; ten-year-old Teodoro Martel was bought from the Comanches by trader Powler Sandoval; Rosalie Tavaris, after her husband and daughter had been killed by Comanches was bartered to Sandoval for two blankets, ten yards of blue cotton, ten yards of calico, ten yards of cotton shirting, two handkerchiefs, four plugs of tobacco, one bag of corn, and one knife. In the *San Antonio Express* of January 18, 1869, John S. Friend pleads for "Indian agents or traders or any person having an opportunity" to rescue his eight-year-old son Lee Temple Friend and a neighbor's seven-year-old daughter, Malinda Caudle, who had been "taken from my house by Indians. . ." Upon recovery of the children the liberator would be "liberally remunerated." The heartrending appeal is repeated in whole by Kenner, *A History of New Mexican-Plains Indian Relations*. For a recently published account of Texas Indian captives, see the outstandingly researched and skillfully written volume, *The Captured* by Scott Zesch. And the interested reader would be remiss in not accessing the

exhaustive work of Gregory and Susan Michno in *A Fate Worse Than Death: Indian Captivities in the West, 1830-1885.*

8. Ibid., 19.

9. Edgar C. McMechen, "John Hittson, Cattle King," *The Colorado Magazine* 11, no. 6 (September 1934): 165. Also see, Maddux, 11, who identifies John Hittson's mother as "Mary Ann Beck Hart." And see, "Hittson, John," *The Handbook of Texas* alphabetical citations: "Polly [Beck] Hittson." All citations are in concurrence regarding John Hittson's date of birth.

10. Ibid.

11. Ibid.; and Maddux, *John Hittson, Cattle King*, 12.

12. Ibid. Several of the landmark bends in the Brazos River country were named after the Hittsons, the loop around Pleasant Valley is known as Hittson's Bend, and just south of that another turn in the watercourse is called John Hittson's Bend. Maddux, *John Hittson, Cattle King*, 12.

13. Gournay, *Texas Boundaries, Evolution of the State's Counties*, 71.

14. Awbrey and Dooley, *Why Stop?* 372.

15. Maddux, *John Hittson, Cattle King*, 12. Also Tise, *Texas County Sheriffs*, page 402: "John Hittson was elected the first sheriff on August 8, 1856; re-elected April 27, 1857 (when the county was organized), August 2, 1858 and served until August 6, 1860."

16. Ibid., 5: "Hittson failed at his first job—frontier sheriff of Palo Pinto County. Against a powerful vigilante movement he found himself incapable of carrying out his duties."

17. Charles Robinson, III, *The Frontier World of Fort Griffin*, 109.

18. Maddux, *John Hittson, Cattle King*, 5; William E. Burrows, *Vigilante!—The Story of Americans . . . Then And Now . . . Guarding Each Other*, page 22, asserts that in Shackelford County, Texas, there were nineteen (19) executions administered by vigilantes.

19. Ibid.; For additional discussion of the Old Law Mob see Ty Cashion, *A Texas Frontier: The Clear Fork Country and Fort Griffin, 1849-1887*. Interestingly, the author reports that John Hittson's brother William denounced certain actions of the Old Law Mob. See page 49. And also see the adroitly written and admirably researched biography of one of the principals of this Old West saga, *Bravo of the Brazos, John Larn of Fort Griffin, Texas*, by Robert K. DeArment.

20. "Hittson, John," *The Handbook of Texas*; and see Maddux, *John Hittson, Cattle King*. Maddux reports that John Hittson joined his brother, William, "and together they built two picket houses for their families," after John left the Palo Pinto Sheriff's office in 1861. See page 59. Also see Frances Mayhugh Holden, *Lambshead Before Interwoven, A Texas Range Chronicle, 1848-1878*, 92. The ruins of Camp Cooper are located on the Throckmorton County ranch of Julia Putnam's family.

21. Ibid. "[Hittson] owned approximately 500 head of livestock in 1860."

22. Maddux, *John Hittson, Cattle King*, 59. And see, "Hittson, John," *The Handbook of Texas:* "During the Civil War the Hittson brothers moved westward to settle at Camp Cooper, an abandoned federal camp"; Clifford R. Caldwell, *Robert Kelsey Wylie: Forgotten Cattle King of Texas,* 61: "Having successfully avoided service in the Confederate military, Hittson is said to have been tireless in his quest to gather unbranded 'Maverick' cattle from the range"; for in-depth discussion of Confederate conscription policies, see David Paul Smith, *Frontier Defense in the Civil War, Texas' Rangers and Rebels.*

23. McMechen, "John Hittson, Cattle King," 165; M. L. "Mel" Johnson, who worked for John Hittson, mentions that John's brand was JON. See M. L. Johnson, "Trailing West," *Frontier Times*, January 1969, 20. Also, Maddux, *John Hittson, Cattle King,* 172: "The Hittsons farmed the land until the Civil War when the whole family turned to cow hunting." Worthy of note, indeed, is the simple question, "whose cows?"

24. "Hittson, John," *The Handbook of Texas:* "Branding ownerless cattle and marketing them in Mexico, John Hittson became the wealthiest man in the region by 1865."

25. Awbrey and Dooley, *Why Stop?* 402. The Callahan County headquarters for the Hittson Ranch would have been located approximately four miles east of what is now Putman, Texas.

26. "Hittson, John," *The Handbook of Texas.*

27. The J. R. Webb Papers, Richardson Library, Hardin-Simmons University, Abilene, Texas; and McMechen, "John Hittson, Cattle King," 167: "Hittson himself rode home after the battle, soaked with blood from an arrow wound in his hip." Also, J. Marvin Hunter, ed., "Callahan County Pioneer Passes Away," *Frontier Times*, July 1947. "The Hitson [*sic*] Creek was named for John Hitson [*sic*], who had a fight on the creek with the Indians. In this fight Hitson was pinned in his saddle by an arrow and he rode into camp in that condition." See page 460. Depending on the source citation, Hittson suffered over his lifetime as many as eight battle scars from marauding Indians' arrows. And, *Colorado Chieftain*, October 17, 1872: "[Hittson] carries eight arrow wounds . . ." Accurately determining the number of Comanches or Kiowas he personally "dispatched" is an unworkable exercise.

28. Maddux, *John Hittson, Cattle King*, 61. This location was a civilian installation built for mutual protection and should not be confused with Fort Davis in far West Texas, a US Army post. For geographical orientation regarding the civilian bastion of Fort Davis, and the military's Fort Griffin, see Lester W. Galbreath's *Fort Griffin and the Clear Fork Country.*

29. Ibid., 60-61. And 65, n. 24 for a more or less complete listing of the inhabitants making Fort Jefferson Davis their home. Also see, Holden, *Lambshead Before Interwoven*, 121; and, Leon Claire Metz,

John Selman: Texas Gunfighter; also Metz's *Encyclopedia of Lawmen, Outlaws, and Gunfighters*, 216.

30. McMechen, "John Hittson, Cattle King," 164.
31. "Hittson, John," *The Handbook of Texas*; Clayton W. Williams, "That Topographical Ghost—Horsehead Crossing," *Old West* (Winter 1974): 51; and, James S. Brisbin, *The Beef Bonanza: or, How to Get Rich on the Plains*, 70: "Among the great drivers North are John Hittson, who brings up from Texas to the Plattes every year 7,000 to 8,000 head."
32. McMechen, "John Hittson, Cattle King," 169.
33. Charles Kenner, "A Texas Rancher In Colorado: The Last Years of John Hittson," *West Texas Historical Association Yearbook* 42 (October 1966): 28.
34. Maddux, *John Hittson, Cattle King*, 4.
35. Ibid. Also see Kenner, "A Texas Rancher in Colorado," 37: "One reason for Hittson's relative eclipse was apparently due to his old nemesis, alcohol."
36. Kenner, "A Texas Rancher in Colorado," 29.
37. Ibid.
38. Charles Kenner, "The Great New Mexico Cattle Raid—1872," *New Mexico Historical Review* 37, no. 4 (October 1962): 257; also, Richardson, Rupert Norval, *Comanche Barrier to South Plains Settlement*, 157.
39. J. Evetts Haley, *The XIT Ranch of Texas, and the Early Days of the Llano Estacado*, 27.
40. Gournay, *Texas Boundaries*, 81. Although created from the colossal Bexar Land District in 1858, Runnels County was not organized until 1880.
41. Kenner, *A History of New Mexican-Plains Indian Relations*, quoting from Jess Hittson's November 2, 1899, testimony in Indian Depredation Case Number 6501, page 169; Maddux, *John Hittson, Cattle King*, asserts that it was the elder Hittson that branded the bovine with the message and places the date as July 4, 1868. See page 136. Either way, it's a delightful piece of Texas folklore.
42. *Rocky Mountain News*, April 29, 1873.
43. Philip J. Rasch, "The Hittson Raid," The New York Posse of the Westerners, *Brand Book* 10, no. 4 (1963): 78. "He [Hittson] is said to have obtained some sort of authority from the Governor of Texas, although it has not been possible to locate such a paper in the archives of that state"; Maddux, *John Hittson, Cattle King*, 154. There was no mention of Hittson in the governor's papers. Edmund J. Davis was the Governor of Texas at the time.
44. Ibid.; also, Haley, "The Comanchero Trade," 171: "Finally John Hittson, Texas cowman, decided that even though the meek might inherit the earth they would never possess its livestock rode out to help himself in a truly Texian way. He, too, armed himself with

powers of attorney from various cowmen, but his faith was firmer in the persuasive power of Judge Colt. . . ."

45. J. Evetts Haley, *Charles Goodnight, Cowman and Plainsman*, 195.

46. Rasch, "The Hittson Raid," places enlistments of Hittson's posse as "three parties consisting of eighty men each," which certainly, based on other primary and secondary source material is an overaggressive estimate, although the figure was used in a contemporary newspaper and is the probable source for Rasch's inflated numbers; Kenner, "The Great New Mexico Cattle Raid," places the overall strength of the battle group as "three parties—about thirty men each." See page 246.

47. DeArment, *Bravo of the Brazos*, 27. And, for additional information on Clay Allison, see Chuck Parsons, *Clay Allison, Portrait of a Shootist*; also see, Sharon Cunningham, "The Allison Clan—A Visit," *Western-Outlaw Lawman History Association Journal*, Winter 2003 and Spring 2004. This excellently researched two-part piece is must reading for serious Allison students. Interestingly the author rightly and legitimately questions whether or not Allison participated in a Charles Goodnight cattle-drive. Since it has been written that Allison, for a time, settled near Hittson Bend on the Brazos River in Palo Pinto County, conceivably he was employed by John Hittson rather than Goodnight. For years beginning in the 1860s, Hittson annually drove cattle to New Mexico and/or Colorado via the Goodnight-Loving trail. Also, focusing on Allison in New Mexico, see Sharon Cunningham, "Clay Allison: 'Good-Natured Holy Terror,'" *Wild West*, October 2013, 40-45; and J. S. Peters, "Riders for the Grant," WOLA *Journal*, Summer 2002 for well-investigated data touching on several of the personalities mentioned in this text, Allison, "Chunk" Colbert, and the Wilson brothers, etc; also see, Morgan Nelson "'First among the first," James Patterson, 1833-1892," *Wild West History Association Journal*, October 2009.

48. Ibid.

49. Joseph G. McCoy, Ralph P. Bieber, ed., *Historic Sketches of the Cattle Trade of the West and Southwest*, 133-134. The complete biographical profile and story of Hugh Martin Childress, Jr. may be found in Bob Alexander, *Lawmen, Outlaws, and S.O.Bs.* Volume 2, 232-249. Also, there are mentions of Hugh Martin Childress, Jr. in Randolph W. Farmer's *"Curly Bill": Horse Thief, Cattle Dealer, Murderer, Lawman, 1858-1909.* Check index.

50. Kenner, *A History of New Mexican-Plains Indian Relations*, 193; Chris Emmett, *Fort Union and the Winning of the Southwest*, 360.

51. Ibid.

52. DeArment, *Bravo of the Brazos*, 29.

53. Ibid.

54. Fabiola Cabeza de Baca, *We Fed Them Cactus*. This truly interesting little volume is particularly germane to the topic at hand, as it contains

remembrances, although understandably self-serving, from an actual Comanchero. "The Comanches would meet us at our camps along the buffalo country. There we exchanged our goods for cattle and horses that the Indians had driven from the unfenced land of the cattle kings. We gained very little from the trade, as the Americans to whom we sold the cattle paid us low prices for them. It was merely getting rid of them for whatever we could get," 45-50.

55. Haley, "The Comanchero Trade," 17.
56. Kenner, "The Great New Mexico Cattle Raid—1872."
57. Miguel Otero, *My Life on the Frontier 1864-1882*, 62.
58. Ibid. Maddux, *John Hittson, Cattle King*, based on the speaker's physical description is convinced Hittson made the explicit speech. See page 169. Don Bullis, *New Mexico Historical Biographies*, 345.
59. Ernest Wallace, "Colonel Ranald S. Mackenzie's Expedition of 1872 Across The South Plains," *The West Texas Historical Association Year Book* 38 (October 1965): 15.
60. Information regarding the Texans' actions at Loma Parda are a synthesis of Rasch, "The Hittson Raid," 78; Kenner, "The Great New Mexico Cattle Raid—1872," 172-173; and logically, Maddux, Hittson's biographer is relied on throughout. Also see Don Bullis, *New Mexico's Finest: Peace Officers Killed in the Line of Duty, 1847-2010*, 276.
61. Ibid.
62. Santa Fe *New Mexican*, October 1, 1872.
63. Robert Juylan, *The Place Names of New Mexico*, 207; F. Stanley, *The Loma Parda Story*, 11: "Meantime another trade was gathering momentum at Loma Parda. Comancheros took knives, guns, bread, tortillas, mirrors, hatchets, ammunition to the Palo Duro country in the Texas Panahndle and returned with beeves and horses stolen by the Plains Indians from the Texans for the purposes of trade."
64. Daniel C. B. Rathbun and David V. Alexander, *New Mexico Frontier Military Place Names*, 108.
65. Santa Fe *New Mexican*, October 1, 1872.
66. Ibid. The edition of December 27, 1872, mentions the arrest; an edition of December 30, 1872, notes the prisoner "be tried for the killing of Seaman at Poma Parda [*sic*] last summer," and an item appearing in the issue of January 2, 1873, highlights the escape from the San Miguel County jail at Las Vegas. The prisoner is consistently identified at Martin Childers, which may be exactly corrected to Hugh Martin "Mart" Childress, Jr., an undisputed member of the Hittson crowd.
67. *Rocky Mountain News*, January 5, 1873, picking up a story from the *New York Evening Post*.
68. Ibid.
69. Cabeza de Baca, *We Fed Them Cactus*, 47-49.
70. Kenner, "The Great New Mexico Cattle Raid—1872," 258.

71. Maddux, *John Hittson, Cattle King*, 187-188.
72. Ibid., 191; Also, Lawrence Clayton and Joan Halford Farmer, eds., *Tracks Along the Clear Fork: Stories from Shackelford and Throckmorton Counties*. Mentions of John and William Hittson throughout.

Chapter 3

1. Gournay, *Texas Boundaries*, 43.
2. Glenna Fourman Brundidge, ed., *Brazos County History: Rich Past, Bright Future*, 21.
3. John Gorman, "Reconstruction Violence in the Lower Brazos River Valley," 395, in Kenneth W. Howell, ed., *Still the Arena of Civil War: Violence and Turmoil in Reconstruction Texas, 1865-1874*.
4. Awbrey and Dooley, *Why Stop?* 67.
5. *The Bryan Eagle*, December 26, 1889.
6. Tise, *Texas County Sheriffs*, 62; interview by author with Phyllis Poehlmann, March 30, 2011; *West Kerr Current*, April 22, 2010. In a letter to the author of December 30, 2010, Phyllis Poehlmann notes that Willy Millican's middle name was "Ashley," rather than the sometimes written "Ashby."
7. Carl H. Moneyhon, "The Democratic Party, the Ku Klux Klan, and the Politics of Fear," 255-258, in Howell, ed., *Still the Arena of Civil War*.
8. Ibid.; and Carl H. Moneyhon, *Texas After the Civil War: The Struggle of Reconstruction*, 95.
9. Ibid.; also see, Carl H. Moneyhon, *Edmund J. Davis: Civil War General, Republican Leader, Reconstruction Governor*, 118.
10. Tise, *Texas County Sheriffs*, 62.
11. Ronald G. DeLord, ed., *The Ultimate Sacrifice: Trials and Triumphs of the Texas Peace Officer, 1823-2000*, 44; Ross J. Cox, *The Texas Rangers and the San Saba Mob*, Vol. 1, 3. Author Cox deftly explores mob mentality as he unwinds the myths and misinformation swirling around actions of the notorious San Saba Mob. For another analytical exploration of facts, not overblown and undocumented folklore about this phenomenon, the reader is referred to David Johnson's first-rate treatment of another extralegal episode of bloody Texas history, *The Mason County "Hoo Doo" War, 1874-1902*. Both authors significantly expand the baseline of data as earlier recorded in C. L. "Doc" Sonnichsen's, *I'll Die Before I'll Run: The Story of the Great Feuds of Texas* and *Ten Texas Feuds*.
12. Brundidge, *Rich Past, Bright Future*, 98.
13. Barry A. Crouch and Donaly E. Brice, *The Governor's Hounds: The Texas State Police, 1870-1873*. Quoting a letter from Dr. Gill to his sister and mother, page 10.
14. Brundridge, *Rich Past, Bright Future*, 98; DeLord, *The Ultimate Sacrifice*, 44.

15. Ibid.; Clifford R. Caldwell, *An Anthology of Old West Tales: Selected Works of Clifford R. Caldwell*, 159.

16. Ibid.

17. Clifford R. Caldwell and Ron DeLord, *Texas Lawmen, 1835-1899: The Good and the Bad*, 31-32; Brundidge, *Rich Past, Bright Future*, 98.

18. *Cleburne Chronicle*, April 12, 1873. Quoted in Brundidge, *Rich Past, Bright Future*, 270.

19. Katy Stokes, *Paisano: Story of a Cowboy and a Camp Meeting*, 16-60.

20. *Houston Post*, November 8, 1935.

21. Poehlmann interview as cited.

22. Caldwell, *An Anthology of Old West Tales,* 160-161.

23. Affidavit and related case file from the National Law Enforcement Memorial Foundation (M. R. Millican), courtesy Ronald G. DeLord. Additional thanks must be extended to Bill Page, Texas A&M University, for his outstanding and cooperative research efforts regarding the death of M. R. Millican, as contained in the NLEMF files furnished for this chapter; *The Bryan Eagle*, December 26, 1889 and January 9, 1890; *Dallas Morning News*, January 14, 1890.

24. Brundidge, *Rich Past, Bright Future*, 276.

25. Millican Family History files as maintained by Phyllis Poehlmann and cordially photocopied for this author; Caldwell and DeLord, *Texas Lawmen, 1835-1899*, 31; *Bryan Eagle*, June 26, 1890; The U.S Federal Census of 1880 enumerates Millican as a Brazos County resident, with an occupation as a "guard."

26. Ibid.; DeLord, *The Ultimate Sacrifice*, 62: "Pet's brother Will, told the Curds to leave town and not come back or he would kill them. When Zeke later returned, Will Millican killed him in front of one of the saloons on Main Street."

27. Oath, W. A. Millican, Ranger Force, April 25, 1905, Madison County, Texas, TSA; Monthly Return, Company B, Ranger Force, April 1905: Col. & Q.M. General L. P. Sieker, Austin, Texas to Captain W. J. McDonald, Sierra Blanca, Texas, June 2, 1905, TSA.

28. The Company B headquarters had been shifted from Fort Hancock to Sierra Blanca. See, Monthly Returns, Company B, Ranger Force and Letterhead with Texas State Seal:

29. Captain W. J. McDonald Company B, Ranger Force, to Adjutant General John A. Hulen, May 28, 1905: "I wish you would order transportation for privates Dunaway & Millican from Sierra Blanca. . .," TSA.

30. Harold J. Weiss, Jr., *Yours to Command: The Life and Legend of Texas Ranger Captain Bill McDonald*, 226.

31. Austin's *Daily State Journal*, October 11, 1872.

32. Enlistment, Oath of Service, and Description Ranger Force, W. A. Millican, July 21, 1905, TSA.

33. Monthly Returns, Company B, Ranger Force, April 1905 through June 1906, TSA.
34. Captain W. J. McDonald, Company B, Ranger Force, to Col. A. E. Devine, Assistant QM General, October 3, 1905: "Privates Flach & Millican are both laid up with fever"; Telegram, Captain McDonald to Adjutant General John A. Hulen: "Edna, Tex, Oct. 4, 1905. Privates Flach and Millican down sick. . . ."; Monthly Return, Company B, Ranger Force, January 1906, TSA.
35. Monthly Return, Company B, Ranger Force, January 1906 and March 1906, TSA.
36. Monthly Return, Company B, Ranger Force, May 1906, TSA.
37. W. A. Millican to Reverend L. R. Millican, March 22, 1906, Courtesy Phyllis Poehlmann.
38. Ranger Private W. A. Millican to Ranger Captain Bill McDonald, June 1, 1906; Captain W. J. McDonald, to AG Hulen, June 17, 1906, TSA.
39. *The Bryan Eagle*, December 26, 1889.
40. U.S. Federal Census, 1880, Brazos County, Texas; Millican Family Genealogical summaries, courtesy Phyllis Poehlmann; *The Examiner*, April 24, 2003, byline Joy Stephenson, "The People Who Made Millican."
41. Ibid.; Caldwell, *An Anthology of Old West Tales*, 161.
42. G. W. Dunlap to W. A. Millican, July 25, 1899, Courtesy Phyllis Poehlmann.
43. Varying accounts place W. A. Millican's DOD as either November 15, 1906 or November 16, 1906; Clifford R. Caldwell and Ron DeLord, *Texas Lawmen: More of the Good and the Bad, 1900-1940,* opt for November 15, 1906. See page 419.

Chapter 4

1. Gournay, *Texas Boundaries*, 51; For an enlightening glimpse into Navarro's thought processes, see *Defending Mexican Valor in Texas: José Antonio Navarro's Historical Writings, 1853-1857*, David R. McDonald and Timothy M. Matovina, eds.
2. Tise, *Texas County Sheriffs,* 389.
3. James Buckner Barry (James K. Greer, ed.), *Buck Barry: Texas Ranger and Frontiersman*, 64.
4. Blackburn, *Wanted*. 251-252.
5. Navarro County Historical Society (Nancy Marcus Land, ed.; Ethel Bennett Stokes, contributor), *Navarro County History: Public Buildings, Historical Events, and Early Businesses,* Vol. 5, 47-50. A historical peek at the community of Petty's Chapel is found in *Navarro County History*, Wyvonne Putman, ed., 169-170.
6. Blackburn, *Wanted*, 252.

7. *Dallas Morning News*, September 25, 1894.
8. Many of the specific details and exact quotations are taken directly from appellate case No. 934, *Tom Murphy vs. The State of Texas*, April 15, 1896, Court of Criminal Appeals. Hereafter simply cited as Appellate Case-934.
9. Weldon I. Hudson, *Navarro County, Texas Marriage Records, 1847-1881*, 59.
10. Caldwell and DeLord, *Texas Lawmen, 1835-1899: The Good and the Bad*, Vol. 1, 78.
11. Fred Tarpley, *1001 Texas Place Names*, 55 and 136.
12. Occasionally it is written that Tom Murphy purchased the revolver instead of his brother Jim, no doubt based on a faulty newspaper report. Wording in Appellate Case-934 is not indistinct: "It was in evidence, that the 38-caliber Winchester cartridges fitted a 44-caliber Colt's pistol. The witness, Kauffman, who was a pawnbroker, testified, that on Saturday, the day before the homicide, he had sold Jim Murphy a Colt's 44-caliber pistol and a box of No. 38 Winchester cartridges. " From the same document, "and the same [pistol] was identified by the witness, Kaufman [pawnbroker], as the same he had sold to Jim Murphy on Saturday." Since identical facts are repeated twice in Appellate Case-934 the likelihood of any typographical error is diminished; September 8, 2012, interview by author with Clifford R. Caldwell, researcher, writer, and authority on antique firearms. Mr. Caldwell stated that the .38-40 caliber cartridges would fit into the cylinder of a .44-40 caliber revolver and could be safely fired. He further advised that although this practice would not produce the optimum result in accuracy, it was not an uncommon practice during closing years of the nineteenth-century.
13. Appellate Case-934.
14. Ibid.
15. *Dallas Morning News*, September 24, 1894. This newspaper story reverses Tom and Jim Murphy's ages, stating that Tom is the older to the two, which is in conflict with the numerous court documents cited herein.
16. Appellate Case-934.
17. Ibid.
18. *The State of Texas vs. Jim and Tom Murphy*, Navarro County District Court, Cause No. 4426: Murder. For a list of witnesses, the Murphy boys' brother-in-law is identified as "Meador." For Appellate Case-934 he is "Meadows."
19. The map was prepared by Surveyor C. W. Carr on 2 July 1895, TSA. The crime scene map specifically identifies the brother-in-law's residence as the "Meador" house.
20. *Dallas Morning News*, September 24, 1894.
21. Appellate Case-934.

22. *Dallas Morning News*, September 25, 1894.
23. Ibid.
24. Historical Society, *Navarro County History*, Vol. 5, 48.
25. *Dallas Morning News*, September 25, 1894.
26. Ibid., "where Jim Murphy said it would be found, and is a white-handled Colt's .45-caliber [*sic*] six-shooter. A pawnbroker identified it as the one he had sold to Jim Murphy last Saturday."
27. *The State of Texas vs. Jim Murphy and Tom Murphy.*
28. Indictment, Navarro County Grand Jury, October 1894 term, J. A. Townsend, Foreman.
29. Appellate Case-934.
30. Ibid.
31. Ibid.
32. Ibid. The Texas Criminal Court of Appeals dealt with the issue in great length, ultimately determining that "The court erred in holding the little negro, Jimmie Griggs, a competent witness."
33. Ibid. At the time—well ahead of improved forensics in general and ballistics' technology in particular—the conclusive connection of specific firearms to specific crimes was less than exact.
34. Ibid.
35. Ibid.
36. Ibid. From reading the appellate decision it appears the higher court was quite perturbed with the trial judge allowing this to be a part of his instructions to the Jury. It was a wholly baseless claim on the part of the prosecutor that Gid Taylor was trying to disarm Tom Murphy. If he was, nothing indicating that was entered into the record, where it needed to be before a jury could so be instructed.
37. *The State of Texas vs. Jim Murphy and Tom Murphy.*
38. E.O. Call to Governor Culberson, April 9, 1898, TSA.
39. Appellate Case-934.
40. Certified copies of the Motion for a Change of Venue regarding *The State of Texas vs. Jim and Tom Murphy*, and Judgment sustaining the motion, TSA.
41. Notes in the Affidavit and Personnel File For Texas Peace Officers Killed in the Line of Duty (Gideon C. Taylor), CLEAT; Awbrey and Dooley, *Why Stop?* 426-427.
42. Convict Register, Texas Department of Criminal Justice. No. 15429, Tom Murphy, July 12, 1897, TSA.
43. Ibid."Punished 11/23/98 2 nights d/c [detention cell] cursing fellow convict," TSA.
44. Call to Governor Charles A. Culberson, April 9, 1898, TSA.
45. Petition, twelve jurors convicting Tom Murphy in Henderson County; Petition, twelve jurors finding Jim Murphy not guilty; Sheriff K. Richardson to Governor Culberson, January 5, 1898; J. T. Deen, District Clerk to Governor J. D. Sayers, January 21, 1899; County Judge

W. F. Freeman to Governor Culberson, January 1, 1897; County Clerk
Ben F. Warren to Governor Culberson, December 30, 1897; Tax Col-
lector L. N. Forster to Governor Sayers, January 19, 1899; District
Judge W. H. Gill to Governor Culberson, January 4, 1898; District
Attorney John S. Jones to Governor Culberson, January 15, 1898;
Paul Jones to Governor Culberson, January 15, 1898; A. B. Watkins
to Governor Culberson, January 6, 1897; Ex-Sheriff John F. Cook to
Governor Culberson, January 3, 1897; Dr. J. C. Hodge to Governor
Sayers, January 18, 1898; W. T. Carroll to Governor Culberson,
January 14, 1898; and Petition to Governor Culberson in behalf of
Tom Murphy with in excess of 350 signatories, TSA.

46. J. D. Roberts to Governor Sayers, March 18, 1897. Interesting, too, are
Robert's further remarks which are not becoming to Gideon Christian
Taylor: "As to the deceased Taylor was his special friend but yet he
was rather over bearing, and believe he perhaps was the cause of his
own death." In TSA.

47. T. H. Barron to Governor Culberson, January 8, 1898, TSA.

48. Petition from near 1000 citizens of Navarro County to Governor
Culberson, TSA.

49. Board of Pardon Advisors, State of Texas, Cause No. 18564, Thomas
Murphy, Recommendation to the Governor, September 20, 1899,
TSA.

50. Texas Department of State, Executive Clemency, Reasons For and
Pardon, *The State of Texas vs. Thomas Murphy*, September 23, 1889,
TSA.

Chapter 5

1. Leon Metz, *John Wesley Hardin: Dark Angel of Texas*, 17; Lewis
Nordyke, *John Wesley Hardin, Texas Gunman: The Complete and
Fabulous Story of One of the Old West's Most Notorious Outlaws*, 44;
Richard C. Marohn, *The Last Gunfighter: John Wesley Hardin*, 21;
Chuck Parsons and Norman Wayne Brown, *A Lawless Breed: John
Wesley Hardin, Texas Reconstruction, and Violence in the Wild West*,
25-26; Putman, *Navarro County History*, 114. Though it punctures
the typically overinflated balloon regarding an icon of Texas shoot-
'em-up history, the unadulterated truth in the case of John Wesley
Hardin is more-often-than-not purposefully glossed over or naively
underplayed by writers idealistically finding the fact somewhat inconvenient and not worthy of accenting. To be sure John Wesley Hardin
was a man-killer, one with an unenviable but quantifiable scorecard
of dead bodies. Troubling as it might be for his overall image, the
majority, the vast majority, of those cuts on his notch-stick were made
when he was but an impetuous and hotheaded teenager. In fact, his
last absolutely authenticated killing occurred on his twenty-first or

twenty-second birthday. Accurately portraying Hardin for what he actually was, an utterly fearless and wholly reckless and outright compassionless delinquent with a whopping deficiency of good judgement may be a vexing reality. He hardly fit the mold Hollywood writers have cast. Aside from his man-killing tally, it's interesting to note that John Wesley Hardin spent considerably more years both running and hiding from the law or locked away by the law, than he did as an innocent child or halfway responsible adult: The arithmetic is absolute.

2. United States Census 1860, Navarro County, Texas; Lewis Publishing Company, 1893, *Memorial and Biographical History of Navarro, Henderson, Anderson, Limestone, Freestone and Leon Counties,* 515.

3. Putman, *Navarro County History,* 193.

4. For an excellent treatment of the Cynthia Ann Parker narrative, see, Jo Ella Powell Exley, *Frontier Blood: The Saga of the Parker Family.* Interestingly Paul H. Carlson and Tom Crum in *Myth, Memory and Massacre: The Pease River Capture of Cynthia Ann Parker,* endeavor to debunk certain relevant factors concerning the return of Cynthia Ann Parker to Anglo "civilization." The reader must cautiously judge the merit of their factual arguments and accept or reject their sociological commentary. Also, S. C. Gwynne, *Empire of the Summer Moon: Quanah Parker and the Rise and Fall of the Comanches, the Most Powerful Indian Tribe in American History.*

5. Charles Kenner, "Guardians in Blue: The United States Cavalry and the Growth of the Texas Range Cattle Industry," *Journal of the West,* January 1995, 48

6. Ibid.

7. *San Antonio Daily Herald,* June 16, 1876.

8. J. Frank Dobie, *Cow People,* 18.

9. Interview by author with Teddy Weaver, Weaver Ranch, Wortham, Texas, December 15, 2010. Mr. Weaver, a relative of Alf Rushing, is also a wellspring of data about historical affairs of northern Freestone and southern Navarro Counties.

10. Texas Death Records reflect a DOB of September 17, 1859, while his headstone in the Richland, Navarro County, Texas, cemetery utilizes September 17, 1856. The U.S. Census of 1860 enumerates Alf as a four-year-old male, living with his parents. Though important from a genealogical perspective, the discrepancy does not materially affect the story at hand, though the 1856 aver seems the strongest.

11. Weaver interview as cited; U.S. Census of 1870, Navarro County, Texas, Spring Hill Post Office; *Certificate of Death* for Josephine (Rushing) Newman, Sweetwater, Nolan County, Texas.

12. John Wesley Hardin, *The Life of John Wesley Hardin, As Written by Himself,* 15-16.

13. Richard C. Marohn, *The Last Gunfighter: John Wesley Hardin,* 21.

14. Physical description from unidentified newspaper clip; James B. Gillett, *Fugitives From Justice: The Notebook of Texas Ranger James B. Gillett*, 99.
15. Peter Watts, *A Dictionary of the Old West*. Definition #1 "Who knows?" #2. *¿Quién Sabe?*—"The Texan's term for a Mexican cattle-brand which was so complicated that at the sight of it a man would scratch his head and say: 'Who knows.'" See page 258.
16. Rufus Hardy, Navarro County District Attorney to Texas Governor John Ireland, August 21, 1885, TSA; Gillett, *Fugitives From Justice*, 99; Tise, *Texas County Sheriffs*, 389.
17. Ibid.
18. Gillett, *Fugitives From Justice*, 100; Lewis Publishing, *Memorial and Biographical History*, 515.
19. *Dallas Weekly Herald*, March 10, 1877.
20. Ibid., July 28, 1877.
21. Ibid., December 8, 1877.
22. *Galveston Daily News*, December 12, 1877.
23. Thomas Rynning, *Gun Notches: A Saga of a Frontier Lawman, Captain Thomas H. Rynning as Told to Al Cohn and Joe Chisholm*. Rynning, in writing of military saddles furnished the Rough Riders said: "Most of the boys could ride anything in reason, for we were recruited mainly from Arizona, New Mexico, and Oklahoma. But instead of good old reliable caques and hulls like they'd been raised on, they hadn't anything between the ends of their backbones and those buck-jumping broncs but those dinky little army saddles. A man might as well be bareback when a pony is spreading himself as on one of those postage stamps." See page 144.
24. Indictment, Freestone County Criminal Case No. 1088, *The State of Texas vs. Alf Rushing, Harve Scruggs and Frank Carter*; Chuck Parsons, and Donaly E. Brice, *Texas Ranger N. O. Reynolds: The Intrepid*, 167-168.
25. *Galveston Daily News*, December 12, 1877; Clifford R. Caldwell and Ron DeLord, *Texas Lawmen, 1835-1899: The Good and the Bad*, 242; Ronald G. DeLord, ed., *Thirteenth Biennial Texas Peace Officers' Memorial Services* (Program), May 1-2, 2011, Texas State Capitol, 76.
26. Ibid.; *Fort Worth Daily Democrat*, December 11, 1877.
27. Ibid.; Freestone County, Texas—Criminal Docket 1867-1887. #1088: *The State of Texas vs. Frank Carter, Alf Rushing, Harv Scruggs*, Charge: Murder, 803
28. Weaver interview as cited and additional February, 26, 2011 interview with Teddy Weaver and Shirley Weaver.
29. Major Jones to AG Steele, September 25, 1878, TSA.
30. Virginia J. Bounds and Imogene C. Barham, compilers, *Limestone County Texas Cemetery Survey*, Vol. 1, Part 1.

31. Telegram, Mayor Seely to Major Jones, December 28, 1877, Courtesy Rick Miller.

32. Freestone County Sheriff J. P. Robinson to Texas Adjutant William H. Steele, December 28, 1877, TSA.

33. Putman, *Navarro County History*, 162.

34. Hardin, *The Life of John Wesley Hardin, As Written by Himself*, 101; Marohn, *The Last Gunfighter*, 88-89; Chuck Parsons, *The Sutton-Taylor Feud: The Deadliest Blood Feud in Texas*, 162-163.

35. Major John B. Jones, Frontier Battalion, to Mayor W. M. Seely, Wortham, Texas, December 31, 1877, TSA.

36. Jerry Sinise, *George Washington Arrington: Civil War Spy, Texas Ranger, Sheriff and Rancher*, 21-22; Robert M. Utley, *Lone Star Justice: The First Century of the Texas Rangers*, 117: "He [Arrington] was John C. Orrick then, but when he came to Texas in 1870 he changed his name in a move to erase a tainted postwar past." Jan Devereaux, *Pistols, Petticoats and Poker: The Real Lottie Deno, No Lies or Alibis*, 123: "Like so many of the gals and guys populating the western frontiers, even Sergeant Arrington had assumed an alias. He had left his birth name and an unsavory incident in Alabama behind."

37. Sinise, *George Washington Arrington*, 22: "Rushing wasn't found, and as far as can be determined, he never was captured by Arrington." Parsons and Brice, in *Texas Ranger N. O. Reynolds: The Intrepid* state Arrington did arrest Rushing (page 183) but the aver was slightly misconstrued, the *Monthly Return* having the margin notation "attempt" to arrest, rather than "arrested." During a December 20, 2010, interview Donaly Brice, one of the authors and a preeminent researcher and writer, confirmed that after reviewing primary source documents there is no indication that Arrington or other members of his "scout" ever arrested Alf Rushing.

38. Enumeration of "Arrests and Attempts" by Company C, Frontier Battalion, TSA.

39. *Luling Signal*, January 17, 1878, Newspaper clip courtesy Chuck Parsons; *Galveston Daily News*, January 10, 1878. Newspaper citation courtesy Rick Miller.

40. C. H. Graves, Attorney, Fairfield, Texas to Governor of Texas R. B. Hubbard, June 1, 1878, TSA.

41. Major John B. Jones to Adjutant General William Steele, September, 25, 1878, TSA.

42. Affidavit for Police Officers Killed in the Line of Duty: Charles Powers, Wortham City Marshal, DOD 9-23-1878, Courtesy Ron DeLord, CLEAT; *Galveston Daily News*, September 24, 1878; *Austin Daily Statesman*, September 28, 1878; Letter of Uel L. Davis, Jr., Chairman, Freestone County Historical Commission, courtesy DeLord; *The National Police Gazette*, October 5, 1878; Freestone County District Court Indictment No. 1120, October 12, 1878, *The State of Texas vs.*

Marcus Seely; Caldwell and DeLord, *Texas Lawmen, 1835-1899,* 242; Weaver Interviews as cited; also, Rick Miller's *Bounty Hunter,* 188. Miller also details another controversial shooting involving Seely and Jack Duncan subsequent to the killing of Frank Polk.

43. Frederick Nolan, *Bad Blood: The Life and Times of the Horrell Brothers,* 16.
44. Major John B. Jones to AG William Steele, September 25, 1878, TSA; Alexander, *Winchester Warriors: Texas Rangers of Company D, 1874-1901,* 1-2.
45. *Galveston Daily News,* December 13, 1877.
46. Deputy Sheriff I. R. Moore, Boone County, Arkansas, to Texas Governor O. M. Roberts, June 3, 1880, TSA.
47. *Galveston Daily News,* January 30, 1878.
48. Ibid.; B. H. Gardner, County Attorney, Freestone County, Texas, to Texas Governor O. M. Roberts, June 17, 1880, TSA.
49. Gardner to Roberts, June 11, 1880, TSA; Unidentified newspaper clips, each highlighting the wanted status of Alf Rushing and George Harris.
50. Texas Department of State: Extradition Service No. 605, *The State of Texas vs. Alf Rushing,* Murder, "June 6, 1885: Requisition on Cherokee Nation. Reward of $200. Jack Duncan, Agt. And Mailed B. F. Gardner, Co. Atty. At Fairfield," TSA. For those in want of more data on the fascinating frontier character Jack Duncan, the reader is referred to the expansively researched and adroitly written *Bounty Hunter* by Miller, Duncan's biographer.
51. Cal Polk Memoir, "Life of Cal Polk," Copy of typescript courtesy Chuck Parsons. This interesting memoir may also be accessed by reviewing the Fall 2011 edition of the *Plum Creek Almanac,* edited and annotated by Chuck Parsons.
52. Ibid.; for mention of another owlhoot working for the JJ see Harry E. Chrisman, *Lost Trails of the Cimarron,* 78.
53. Haley, *The XIT Ranch of Texas,* 42: "To the east of Buffalo Springs, the North Palo Duro loops south into Texas from what was then called No Man's Land, and then swings back to join the Beaver."
54. Ibid.
55. Weaver interview as cited.
56. Robert K. DeArment, *Alias Frank Canton,* 71.
57. Ibid.; *Dallas Morning News,* December 18, 1885. "Alf Rushin [*sic*], a refugee from justice, charged with killing Jack Barfield, Marshal of this town [Wortham], was recently captured and jailed at Buffalo, Wyoming. Large amounts were offered for his arrest."
58. Frank M. Canton, Sheriff Johnson County, Buffalo, Wyoming, to Mrs. Josie Newman, Sweetwater, Nolan County, Texas, January 2, 1885.
59. *Indian Journal,* January 4, 1886.
60. *The Dallas Morning News,* January 28, 1886.

61. Freestone County Attorney R. M. Edwards, to Texas Governor C. A. Culberson, July 13, 1898, TSA.

62. Executive Office Application for Requisition No. 516; Capias Warrant for the Arrest of Alf Rushing, July 13, 1898; R. M. Edwards, Freestone County Attorney, to Texas Governor C. A. Culberson, July 13, 1898, TSA.

63. Sid J. Boykin to J. Evetts Haley, June 23, 1927. In this letter Boykin adds the names of George Jefferson, Frank Lloyd, and Bill Benson to the Causey brothers and has the purchase price for Jim Newman closing at $600 rather than $60 as earmarked in the following citation; Haley, *The XIT Ranch of Texas*, 46; J. W. Williams, *The Big Ranch Country*, 79: "Newman, in accordance with the open range custom of his day, had not bothered to become owner of the land and, of course, was forced to move on when the Capital Syndicate purchased it as a part of their famous XIT Ranch." Miles Gilbert, Leo Remiger, and Sharon Cunningham, *Encyclopedia of Buffalo Hunters and Skinners*, Vol. 1, 105.

64. Ibid.; George A. Wallis, "Cattle Kings," *New Mexico Magazine*, June 1936, 46.

65. L. F. D. Notes by Hervey Chesley, June 5, 1939 in the HML&HC: "Doak Goode—took up and built a house there. He and Newman had a shooting scrape about that thing [and] Newman won out. That was the DZ." Jean M. Burroughs, ed., *Roosevelt County History and Heritage*, 29; Rollie Burns [W. C. Holden, ed.] *Rollie Burns: Or, An Account of the Ranching Industry on the South Plains*, 100; Jim Gober [James R. Gober and B. Byron Price, eds.], *Cowboy Justice: Tale of a Texas Lawman*, 67.

66. Burroughs, *Roosevelt County History*, 31; J. Evetts Haley, *George W. Littlefield, Texan*, 161: "below the rolling sandhills covered with rusty-red sage grass, was the Portales Spring, over whose cool waters Jim Newman and Doak Goode were waging warlike dispute."

67. Weaver interviews as beforehand cited; Burroughs, *Roosevelt County History and Heritage*, 31-32; F. Stanley, *The Milnesand New Mexico Story*, 4: "and what became the Milnesand community was part of the vast DZ ranch which was about the biggest spread in these parts before homestead laws and railroads bought the townsite companies." F. Stanley, *The Rogers New Mexico Story*, 3: "Rogers was once part of the vast DZ ranch. The south camp of the outfit was near Milnesand and the north beyond Arch below the Salt Lake." Richard C. Hopping, *A Sheriff-Ranger in Chuckwagon Days*, 107-118, quote on page 111: "He liked Coke [Hopping], and soon made the proposition that Coke take over the foremanship of the H-Bars which was jointly owned by Tom Trammel and his brother-in-law, Jim Newman, of Sweetwater, Texas." And "Across the line in New Mexico were other big outfits: Jim Newman and Bill Curtis with the DZ . . . .," 172; May Price

Mosley, *"Little Texas" Beginnings In Southeastern New Mexico,* 17: "Later well-known drift fences were the DZ drift fence between the DZ range (a large ranch to the north owned by Jim Newman with headquarters at Salt, or Portales Lake) and the LFD range. . . ." James F. Hinkle, *Early Days of a Cowboy on the Pecos,* 18.

68. George B. Root to J. Evetts Haley, November 25, 1927, HML&HC; Boykin to Haley as cited.

69. J. Frank Yearwood to J. Evetts Haley, December 9, 1927, HML&HC.

70. David Farmer, ed., *History of the Cattlemen of Texas,* 297; Tise, *Texas County Sheriffs,* 393.

71. U.S. Census, 1920 and 1930, Sweetwater, Nolan County, Texas. Although no conclusiveness appends it is interesting to note that an "Alf Rushing" was a witness in a murder case in Yazoo County, Mississippi. Though the offense occurred in 1915 an arrest was not made until 1919, with trial taking place the following year. Since the Alf Rushing of this saga was enumerated in the 1920 census in Nolan County, Texas, and was by all accounts a "Westerner" it seems unlikely our Alf Rushing and the Alf Rushing at the Mississippi murder trial are one in the same. Data concerning this murder case was graciously furnished by the ever tireless and amicable researcher Sherrie Parks, Sweetwater, Texas.

72. Weaver interviews as cited.

Chapter 6

1. This chapter highlighting the adventures and misadventures of Ruben (or Reuben) Flanoah "Noah" Wilkerson is in large part an edited and revised treatment of this author's previously published article in the January-June 2005 ("Double Issue") NOLA *Quarterly.* Subsequently (2009) writers Ed Walker, Helen Wilkerson, and Marilyn Read published *Guilty. . . .But Not As Charged* and somewhat bizarrely commented on page 11, "The story of Noah Wilkerson needs to be told." Later, page 225, the authors imprecisely imply, "Until quite recently the story of Noah Wilkerson has survived only in the memories of his family or of someone who heard accounts of his misfortune from an old-timer." Such an unequivocal declaration is misleading in light of previously published material. Quite candidly—and dutifully—the three authors, two of which are related to Noah Wilkerson, admit on page 226 that, "We have written the story from Noah's point of view." Indeed, *Guilty. . . . But Not As Charged* is a rather charitable recounting of the life and death of a Western bad man on the run—a fugitive. The endnotes cited herein for this chapter—one and all—were published in the 2005 story and hopefully proved to be and continue to be valuable resources for persons expanding on or repeating the dubious outlaw saga of Noah Wilkerson. Biographical data concerning the life

of George Washington Clayton is abundant. For this chapter a synthesis of source materials was utilized, including but not limited to the following: *A History of North and West Texas*, by B. B. Paddock; *Clayton Family History*, by Lawrence Leonard; personal interviews with descendants, Ed Walker, Brownwood, Texas; J. C. Wilkerson, Winters, Texas; Pat Watkins, Ballinger, Texas; Randy Fancher, Mustang, Oklahoma; and interviews with Talpa, Texas, cattle rancher E. Dale Herring and the late local Ballinger area historian David Allbright. Depending on the source, both written and oral, Dorinthia (Clayton) Wilkerson's first name is sometimes cited or spoken deleting the second "i." The most frequently used "Dorinthia," for this story, will be used throughout. In some genealogical references "Reddin" is listed as "Redden," although the specificity used in identifying the correct "Amanda," in this instance, is indisputable.

2. Both Paddock and Leonard write that George Washington Clayton saw service during the Civil War in the 4th Mississippi Cavalry under command of Colonel James Gordon. While it is true that Gordon commanded both the Second and Fourth Mississippi Cavalries, it seems that it is much more probable that Clayton served in the 2nd rather than the 4th. John F. Walters, *Military Units and Histories*; also see, H. Grady Howell, Jr., *For Dixie Land I'll Take My Stand!—A Muster Listing of All Known Mississippi Confederate Soldiers, Sailors and Marines*. In this comprehensive multi-volume listing, there is not a Clayton enumerated as serving with the 4th, but there is a G. W. Clayton serving with the 2nd. See page 506. Likewise an inspection of microfilm General Index Records at the Confederate Research Center (CRC), Hill College, Hillsboro, Texas, fails to identify a Clayton in the 4th Mississippi Cavalry but does indicate the service of a G. W. Clayton in the 2nd.

3. Leonard, *Clayton Family History*, 9.

4. Ibid. Data on Emmett Anderson Clayton's birthday and life differ among family members interviewed.

5. Gournay, *Texas Boundaries—Evolution of the State's Counties,* 81.

6. Glen Smith, "Some Early Runnels County History, 1858-1885," *West Texas Historical Association Year Book* 42 (1966). Awbrey and Dooley, *Why Stop?* Also, Charlsie Poe, *Runnels Is My County.*

7. Ibid., 113. For a first-hand account of this skirmish with Comanches, see, M. L. Johnson, "Battle With Indians in Runnels County," *Frontier Times,* January 1946. "Late in the afternoon they withdrew and, after a short consultation bundled their herd of horses and rounded up all of our 700 head of cattle and drove them off, leaving about twenty Indians to stand guard over us until nearly dark, when the whole band disappeared in the distance. It seems unreasonable to say that these Indians did not kill a single one of us, although several members of our party were severely wounded. Ten or twelve Indians and about as many horses were killed and a number of Indians were wounded.

Years after this fight Jess Hittson sued the Government for the loss of his horses and cattle. . . .the case enabled Mr. Hittson to recover $14,900, which was paid over to the Hittson estate in 1909." 61-65.

8. Ibid. "They [Texas Rangers] skinned him [Indian] (as they had some of the other Indians killed at Valley Creek), and one of the men in the company made some beautiful quirts out of the hide, trimmed with ornaments from Indian hair." 116.

9. Ibid. "Captain Maltby reportedly paid twenty-five dollars for a quirt made from 'Old Jape's' hide. He is also said to have bought the Indian's scalp when he left the Ranger service." For an overall glance at Ranger activities in the vicinity see, R. R. Havin, "Activities of Company E, Frontier Battalion, Texas Rangers, 1874-1880." *West Texas Historical Association Yearbook.* Volume XI. [1935]. 62-72.

10. For a biographical sketch of John M. Formwalt, see, Stephens, *Bullets and Buckshot in Texas,* 216-219. Also, Stephens' *Mannen Clements— Texas Gunfighter.* 68-74.

11. Smith, "Some Early Runnels County History, 1858-1885." "In fact, the sheriff [Formwalt] allegedly shot up the town more often than anyone else, but he had a rationale which elevated his actions above common horseplay. Formwalt, it is said, would amble by the saloons casually announcing that closing time had come. After completing this preliminary task he would walk to the end of the street, roll a cigarette, smoke it, and if by that time there were still saloon lights burning, he extinguished them with a large slug of lead." 118.

12. F. S. Millard, *A Cowpuncher of the Pecos.* The incident happened in Ballinger, Texas, after the county seat was moved there from Runnels City. See page 44.

13. Ibid.

14. John Formwalt shot Riley B. Midgett on November 23, 1883, and the man suffered his bullet wounds until December 7 when he died. See Stephens, *Bullets and Buckshot in Texas,* 216-217; also see Smith, "Some Early Runnels County History, 1858-1885," 120

15. *Runnels County Record,* February 10, 1883.

16. Leonard, *Clayton Family History,* 9. And under Family Record Group—George Washington Clayton, 1.

17. *Runnels County Record,* September 13, 1884.

18. In certain genealogical reports, Noah's birthday is given as February 14, 1861. Other reports indicate he was born in 1860, a discrepancy for this story making little difference. He did, apparently, tell a 1900 census enumerator that he was 40 years old when tallied on June 13. His headstone, however, indicates February 13, 1861, which is no doubt the date furnished by his wife at the time of his death.

19. John Carson, "Wyoming's Mysterious Badman," *Frontier Times,* Winter 1961, 17: "a young Texas cowboy named Wilkerson." And, interviews with Wilkerson's descendants as cited.

20. Ed Walker, Brownwood, Texas, to author, September 8, 2003.
21. Interview with J. C. Wilkerson, grandson of Noah Wilkerson, Winters, Texas, April 2004; also, Pat Watkins, Noah's granddaughter, during an April 2004 interview at Ballinger, Texas, supported the assertion that, indeed, Noah was a man many feared.
22. George Washington Clayton's displeasure with the fact Dorinthia and Noah were to be married is unanimously confirmed by family members and the fact the couple eloped is also indicative of George Washington Clayton's poor regard for Noah Wilkerson.
23. Leonard, *Clayton Family History,* Family Record Group—George Washington Clayton, 1. Ed Walker to author, September 8, 2003. And, interview with Randy Fancher, Mustang, Oklahoma, May 3, 2004.
24. Ed Walker to the author, September 8, 2003. Dorinthia's and Noah's children were: Arthur Ewing, October 18, 1881; Mertie, September 5, 1883; Beulah, December 8, 1887; Luther Reuben, September 14, 1889; Leonard Eugene, August 20, 1891; Nora, December 28, 1893; Chester Alexander, July 5, 1896; Dewey Clarence, November 12, 1898; and Loyd F., March 18, 1901.
25. Leonard, *Clayton Family History,* 10.
26. *The State of Texas vs. Noah Wilkerson,* Runnels County Criminal Case Number 123, Testimony of Ben R. and George Wilson.
27. Ibid.
28. Ibid.
29. Ibid.
30. Indictment, *The State of Texas vs. Noah Wilkerson*: Offense: Assault, with Intent to Murder: A True Bill filed October 1, 1886, Runnels County District Court.
31. Stephens, *Bullets and Buckshot in Texas* and *Mannen Clements— Texas Gunfighter.*
32. Verdict Form, *The State of Texas vs. Noah Wilkerson,* Runnels County Criminal Case Number 123, dated October 22, 1888.
33. Only reported crimes may be measured. Crimes that actually occur but are not reported are classified as "Dark Crimes" or the "Dark Figure." For varying reasons a victim may not report crime to authorities; personal embarrassment in the case of a sexual offense; loss of face in losing a fight in a nightclub parking lot; not wanting insurance premiums to rise; not wishing to cause an undue hardship for a partisan supporter; and a host of other factors. When a lawnmower is stolen from a garage, and the victimized owner fails to report it to law enforcement because the level of his insurance deductible exceeds the value of the lawnmower, it is but one modern-era example. The offense becomes a "Dark Crime," but the reality that a lawnmower was stolen is not erased from factuality. For a discussion of "Dark Crime" see, John E. Conklin, *Criminology,* 77-78; and Richard H. Anson and Gerald D. Robin, *Introduction to the Criminal Justice System,* 24-25, 598: "Almost

one in five assault victims didn't report their attacks because they believed the offenders, even if caught, would not be punished!"

34. First quotation from the *Saratoga* (Wyoming) *Semi-Weekly Republican*, November 21, 1900.

35. Ed Walker to the author, September 8, 2003. And, interviews with J. C. Wilkerson, April 2004.

36. Unpublished paper presented to the Coleman County Historical Commission by (and signed by) Chester Wilkerson, Noah's son. The date of the presentation is unknown, but E. Dale Herring, who graciously furnished a copy to the author June 28, 2003, said that it was "probably thirty or forty years ago." Most family oral history supports this version of the fight. And, unpublished typescript prepared by Noah Wilkerson's grandson, J. C. Wilkerson.

37. *Rawlins* (Wyoming) *Semi-Weekly Republican*, November 21, 1900. There seems little doubt that the newspaperman picked up these allegations from Runnels County Sheriff R. P. Kirk who was, at the time, in Wyoming personally investigating the Wilkerson case.

38. *The State of Texas vs. Noah Wilkerson*, Criminal Case Number 1306, Coleman, Coleman County, Texas. Also see, *The State of Texas vs. Noah Wilkerson*, Criminal Case Number 401, Runnels County, Texas; Affidavit of District Attorney: "pending against him in Coleman County . . . It grew out of a difficulty Wilkerson had with Mr. Gray. Gray charged Wilkerson with beating him with a pistol. Wilkerson swore he had no pistol. . . ."

39. Ibid.

40. Inquest Findings, Justice of the Peace Weeks: "that deceased [Slate] came to his death by a gunshot wound, likely a .44 caliber pistole [*sic*] (six-shooter) at the hands of party or parties unknown at this time."

41. Court of Criminal Appeals, *Noah Wilkerson vs. The State of Texas* Runnels County District Court, Number 401 [1899]. For physical information regarding "Tump" Eldred, see Convict Record Ledger, Data Transcription, TSA. Also see, Runnels County Criminal District Court Docket Book, Criminal Case Number 232, The *State of Texas vs. Tump Eldred*, Murder, based on a Complaint filed by Sheriff R. P. Kirk on August 25, 1898.

42. Preliminary Hearing, *The State of Texas vs. Noah Wilkerson*, Runnels County Justice of the Peace Court, Case Number 234, September 7, 1898.

43. Minutes of the Runnels County District Court, October 19, 1900, *The State of Texas vs. Tump Eldred*. In return for Tump's testimony and a resultant guilty plea, his first-degree murder charge was reduced to murder in the second degree, and he received a twenty-five year prison sentence.

44. *The State of Texas vs. Noah Wilkerson*, Runnels County Criminal District Court Case Number 401.

45. Ibid., The testimony.
46. Ibid., The verdict.
47. *The State of Texas vs. Noah Wilkerson*, Coleman County District Court, Criminal Case Number 1306: The verdict.
48. Interestingly, the 1900 Census for Coleman County, Texas, enumerates Noah Wilkerson's location: "Prisoner." That same census for Ballinger, Texas, lists Tump Eldred as a Runnels County prisoner.
49. Ed Walker to the author, based on correspondence with Helen Wilkerson to Ed Walker, July 20, 2003.
50. Reportedly, at least according to Chester Wilkerson in the presentation to the Coleman County Historical Commission and interviews with family members, it is suggested that a "kinsman," frequently identified as Noah's brother Zan, slipped into the area quietly, bringing the hacksaw with him, and departed the very next day, so as not to draw attention. Other theories point toward another of Noah's brothers, Berry Edward, as also, in some way participating in planning or executing the jailbreak. ¿*Quién sabe*? Certainly none of the accounts are historically conclusive; Noah had help, but from just who is speculative. Logically, it is believed the metal cutting saw was furnished to Dorinthia so that she could not have been identified as purchasing one locally. The assertion that Dorinthia and Noah had a "quick interlude" at the Coleman County Jail is suggested by family members, based on the birthday of the couple's last child, Loyd. Unquestionably, any student of the Old West will handily recognize the systemic laxity frequently associated with county jail administration. A local jail or penitentiary absent escapes was an out of the ordinary exception, not the norm. Visitation protocols were, likewise, lax.
51. Ibid.
52. Ibid. And, family interviews by author as enumerated. Also, Donaly E. Brice to author August 19, 2003, TSA: "on the 19th day of June 1900 R. F. (Noah) Wilkerson did escape, he being a convict under conviction for murder." There is a letter in family members' possession that indicates that Noah was traveling with a man called "Joe Taylor" as late as October 1900. It should be remembered that William "Bill" Taylor escaped jail with Wilkerson. Whether the two Taylors were one and the same person is indeterminate as of this writing.
53. Governor's Proclamation of Reward: $500 for the capture of Noah Wilkerson, TSA.
54. Joe Erimmer, Parachute, Colorado, to D. (Dorinthia) S. Wilkerson, Ballinger, Texas, December 29, 1900. "I first met him [Noah Wilkerson] about October 10, 1900 and he came to this place shortly after that time . . . I had not expected he was wanted by the authorities. . . . Wilkerson traveled under an assumed name [that he gave me] and it was Lee Escue."

55. Inventory of Noah Wilkerson's personal property at the time of his death in Wyoming, Wyoming State Archives (WSA), Cheyenne, Wyoming. And, personal inspection of the weapons by author during interviews with Pat Watkins and J. C. Wilkerson.

56. Apparently the genesis of this story is from Sheriff Kirk's own mouth, as it was carried in the *Rawlins Semi-Weekly Republican* on November 21, 1900, during a time-frame the sheriff was in Wyoming. In possession of Wilkerson's relatives is an unidentified news clip which appears to be a Texas paper picking up the story from an unidentified Cheyenne, Wyoming, newspaper.

57. Copies of appropriate excerpts from the diary were furnished to the author by J. C. Wilkerson, Noah's grandson, Winters, Texas, hereafter cited as Wilkerson's Journal.

58. Wilkerson's Journal. For a brief sketch of the once booming Liberty, New Mexico, see F. Stanley, *The Liberty Story*, 4: "Liberty was a gathering place for comancheros, traders, sheepherders, Comanches, Kiowa-Apaches, Kiowas, rustlers, horse thieves. . . . Rustlers felt safe here from law and order. . . . Trail drivers and cowboys often came by for hard liquor and a night on the town. . . . It was a wild frontier hamlet. . . ." Also see, Julyan, *The Place Names of New Mexico*, 203.

59. Ibid. Here, in marking his diary from memory after several days, Wilkerson inadvertently confuses which town he came to first, after crossing into Colorado. It was Trinidad, then Walsenburg, rather than vice versa, as he recorded.

60. Ibid.

61. Ibid.: "lots of peaches and apples here . . . Oct. 16 and 17, cut peaches . . ." And, Joe Erimmer to D. S. Wilkerson as cited.

62. Joe Erimmer to D. S. Wilkerson.

63. Sylvia Beeler, "Reminiscences of Early Day Pioneers," *The Snake River Press*, October 16, 1980. And see, Mae Urbanek, *Wyoming Place Names*.

64. For some mentions of Meldrum and his killings, see Carson as previously cited; John Carson, "The Middle Years of Bob Meldrum," and Andrew Martin, "I Knew Bob Meldrum," both in the Spring 1970 edition of *Old West*; Larry K. Brown, "The Art of Murder—Robert D. Meldrum: Lawman, Killer, Artist," *Casper Star-Tribune*, March 30, 1997; and the prolific work of Chip Carlson as subsequently cited.

65. Chip Carlson, *Tom Horn—Blood on the Moon*, 100-104.

66. Ibid.; Chip Carlson, *Tom Horn: "Killing men is my specialty . . .,"* 59-65. For an assertion that Meldrum was a Pinkerton man, see Chip Carlson, *Joe Lefors—"I slickered Tom Horn . . ."* "Other prominent figures in turn-of-the-century annals who were Pinkerton operatives, their ciphers, and professionals, as shown in the company's files, were R. D. Meldrum, deputy sheriff in Dixon, *'Cigar'. . . .*" 156.

67. Deposition of Robert D. "Bob" Meldrum, Inquest into the death of Noah Wilkerson, Carbon County Justice of the Peace M. A. Groshart's court, November 15, 1900, Courtesy, Carl Hallberg, Reference Archivist WSA; and, Rans Baker, Historian, Carbon County Museum, Rawlins, Wyoming, to author, August 9, 2003.

68. *Rawlins Semi-Weekly Republican*, November 24, 1900. "Before leaving, Sheriff Kirk made arrangements to pay Deputy Sheriff Meldrum the $200 reward which he had offered for the capture of Wilkerson."

69. Deposition of Robert Meldrum: "stayed with him all day, ate dinner with him. We were together till just about five o'clock when I became positive that that was the man . . ." Also see, *Rawlins Semi-Weekly Republican*, November 17, 1900. "Deputy Sheriff Meldrum had several conversations with the man [Wilkerson], but did not disclose the fact that he was an officer. He [Wilkerson] talked quite freely to the officer.

70. Deposition of Charles E. Ayer, November 15, 1900, WSA.

71. Ibid. And see, Meldrum's Deposition although he said, "did not know precise words used."

72. Ibid.

73. Deposition of Robert Meldrum. Supported by the Deposition of Ayer.

74. *Rawlins Semi-Weekly Republican*, November 21, 1900.

75. Depositions of Meldrum and Ayer. And see, *Saratoga Sun*, November 22, 1900: "shot him in the mouth, from which wound he expired almost instantly."

76. Inquest Ruling, Death of Noah Wilkerson, Carbon County, Wyoming, November 15, 1900, WSA.

77. Carlson, *Tom Horn, "Killing men is my specialty . . ."* 59

78. Ibid. And see, Wyoming Penitentiary identification card and photograph: inmate Meldrum, Robert D., No. 2370. WSA; Also, Brown, "The Art of Murder."

79. Ibid. "For reasons best understood by Bob Meldrum, he wrote to the Carbon County Sheriff in Rawlins that he wanted to turn himself in, but only to Wyoming officers—possibly fearing he would suffer the same fate as the Wilkinson [*sic*] he had murdered in 1899 [1900]."

80. The Savage rifle was listed by serial number at the time of the Inquest and the handgun was described as a ".41 Colt's revolver, in .45 frame 7-inch barrel, all chambers loaded," in WSA. Checking the Colt's serial number in *Colt—An American Legend* by R. L. Wilson, indicates the firearm was manufactured during 1897, a time appropriate for this story.

81. Affidavit of R. P. Kirk Sheriff, November 22, 1900, at Carbon County, Wyoming. And, Release and Receipt of Property, signed by David Craig, District Court Judge, Rawlins, Wyoming, and R. P. Kirk, Sheriff of Runnels County, State of Texas, WSA. And see, *Rawlins Semi-Weekly Republican*, November 24, 1900: "received word from the governor of Texas to take the body back to that state. Sheriff Kirk

also received a telegram from the wife of the deceased requesting that the body be taken back. Sheriff Kirk left Thursday night for home with the remains."

82. *Ballinger Banner-Leader*, February 16, 1901: "he [Kirk] was able to secure only expense money, the governor saying he was not authorized to pay a reward for the man dead."

Chapter 7

1. Genealogical data about Philip C. Baird was graciously furnished to the Mason County Historical Commission, Mason, Texas, by his granddaughter Maryland K. Campbell.

2. Notations concerning Baird's physical description are taken from his Descriptive List, the document used to identify him as a Texas Ranger, TSA.

3. Monthly Return, Company D, Frontier Battalion, September 1882, TSA; Alexander, *Winchester Warriors,* 176-177.

4. Monthly Return, Company D, Frontier Battalion, September 1882, TSA; Certification of Captain L. P. Sieker, for enlistment and issuance of property to P. C. Baird, November 30, 1882, TSA.

5. Alexander, *Winchester Warriors,* 176; Lieutenant L. P. Sieker to Adjutant General W. H. King, January 13, 1882, TSA.

6. Ibid., 303.

7. Monthly Return, Company D, Frontier Battalion, November 1882, TSA. The arrest for Masturbation, no doubt, would equate some way with today's charge of Public Lewdness.

8. Monthly Return, Company D, Frontier Battalion, March 1883, TSA.

9. Monthly Return, Company D, Frontier Battalion, April 1883, TSA.

10. Captain Sieker to AG King, June 4, 1883, TSA.

11. Captain Sieker to AG King, June 21, 1883, TSA; Captain Sieker to John O. Johnson, Frontier Battalion Quartermaster, June 21, 1883, TSA.

12. Monthly Return, Company D, Frontier Battalion, October 1883, TSA.

13. Captain Sieker to AG King, December 5, 1883, TSA.

14. Corporal P. C. Baird to AG King, December 15, 1883, TSA.

15. Ibid.

16. Samuel Stanley, "The Fence Cutter's War," *Real West*, August 1985, 21.

17. Joanne S. Liu, *Barbed Wire: The Fence That Changed the West*, 46; Wayne Gard, "The Fence Cutters," *Southwestern Historical Quarterly,* July 1947, 2.

18. Ruth Whitehead, "That Bloody Fence Cutting War," *The West*, December 1969, 20.

19. *San Saba News*, August 17, 1939: "60 Years Ago They Didn't Want Any Barb Wire Fences Here." News clip courtesy Lynn Blankenship, San Saba, Texas.

20. Ibid.

21. R. D. Holt, "The Introduction of Barbed Wire into Texas and the Fence Cutting War," *West Texas Historical Association Yearbook,* June 1930, 75.

22. Alexander, *Rawhide Ranger, Ira Aten,* 112.

23. Holt, "The Introduction of Barbed Wire into Texas and the Fence Cutting War," 76: "The 'Knights of the Knippers' were organized under such names as The Land League, The Owls, The Javelinas and the Blue Devils." Utley, *Lone Star Justice: The First Century of the Texas Rangers,* 233: "The 'Knights of the Knippers' threatened bodily harm to selected fence builders and cut offending fences."

24. Harold D. Jobes, "Fence Cutting and a Ranger Shootout at Green Lake," *Wild West History Association Journal,* October 2009, 40.

25. Henry D. and Frances T. McCallum, *The Wire That Fenced the West, 165:* "The Texas Rangers were called to police areas of danger, by authority of the state."

26. Monthly Return, Company D, Frontier Battalion, January 1884, TSA.

27. Monthly Return, Company D, Frontier Battalion, February 1884, TSA. The MR definitely places the site of the fence cutting arrests at Green Lake, but makes notation that they occurred in Crockett County. In all likelihood this is understandable geographical confusion associated with the area's organizing county governments. For a brief profile of B. D. Lindsey, who would also serve as a U.S. Mounted Customs Inspector, and later, an elected Bexar County sheriff at San Antonio, see, Stephens, *Texas Ranger Sketches,* 83-86. Also, Tise, *Texas County Sheriffs,* 43.

28. Captain Sieker to AG King, February 29, 1884, TSA. This letter clarifies the contemporary geographical error cited in above listed endnote. Clearly Captain Sieker mentions that the offense took place in Edwards County.

29. Captain Sieker to AG King, May 31, 1884, TSA.

30. Wayne Gard, *Frontier Justice,* 108: "Smoldering resentment against fencing was touched into flame by the 1883 drought."

31. Rocksprings Women's Club Historical Committee, *A History of Edwards County,* 347.

32. Jobes, "Fence Cutting and a Ranger Shootout at Green Lake," 45-46.

33. Captain Sieker to AG King, August 8, 1884, TSA.

34. G. B. Greer to Governor Ireland, July 19, 1884, TSA.

35. Monthly Return, Company D, Frontier Battalion, July 1884, TSA; P. C. Baird, "The Fight at Green Lake Waterhole," *Frontier Times,* March 1926, 35.

36. G. B. Greer to Governor Ireland, July 30, 1884, TSA.

37. Corporal P. C. Baird's Report of Scout to Green Lake, August 8, 1884, TSA; Mike Cox, *The Texas Rangers: Wearing the Cinco Peso, 1821-1900,* 34: "But Baird wanted to catch them cutting the fence, a felony," 327.

38. Baird, "The Fight at Green Lake Waterhole."
39. G. B. Greer to Governor Ireland, July 30, 1884, TSA.
40. Corporal P. C. Baird's Report of Scout to Green Lake, August 8, 1884, TSA.
41. G. B. Greer to Governor Ireland, July 30, 1884, TSA.
42. Baird, "The Fight at Green Lake Waterhole," 35.
43. G. B. Greer to Governor Ireland, July 30, 1884, TSA.
44. Baird, "The Fight at Green Lake Waterhole," 34-35: The Rangers were short of ammunition due to naïveté, having wasted plenty on the trip to Green Lake "and began making an invoice of their available supply of ammunition and found their magazines and belts much depleted by reasons of rattlesnake shooting being good the evening before crossing the divide. I [Baird] being the only man having a good supply, hastily divided with the boys; in fact divided until I was short on cartridges myself, having not any to spare for decoy or idle shots."
45. Captain Sieker to Quartermaster Johnson, August 30, 1884. "I have just recd a bill from Burt & Vaughn, M.Ds. who put in a bill for 45$ for a visit w Pvt. W. W. Bakker at Green Lake, Edwards Co. Green Lake is a good 35 miles from Junction City where they reside, and I thought I would rather get you to approve the acct. before paying it. I think it a little steep but Physicians here tell me that one dollar per mile is their regular charge so I suppose he charged 10$ for attentive. . . . Baker is all right and reported to duty yesterday." Letter in TSA. The good doctors were dead set against negotiating with the state's penny-pinching bureaucracy. See, Captain Sieker to Quartermaster Johnson, September 30, 1884, TSA: "Enclosed find letter from Drs. Burt & Vaughn, they would not cut their bill so I paid it as directed, also a bill for Medicine which I enclose." Jobes, "Fence Cutting and a Ranger Shootout at Green Lake," 43.
46. Baird, "The Fight at Green Lake Waterhole," 36.
47. Tom Dragoo (Mrs. Eugene Mays, ed.) "My Early Days In Edwards County" a contribution to *History of Edwards County,* 54-55.
48. Telegram. P. C. Baird to Captain Sieker, August 5, 1884, TSA.
49. G. B. Greer to Governor Ireland, July 30, 1884, TSA.
50. Lieutenant Frank Jones to AG King, September 26, 1884, TSA.
51. Captain Sieker to AG King, September 29, 1884, TSA.
52. Captain Sieker to AG King, September 30, 1884, TSA.
53. Frederick Wilkins, *The Law Comes to Texas: The Texas Rangers, 1870-1901,* 247: "All the Rangers were cleared of any wrongdoing at an inquest [Preliminary Hearing]. . . ."
54. Monthly Return, Company D, Frontier Battalion, August 1884, TSA.
55. Monthly Return, Company D, Frontier Battalion, October 1884, TSA.
56. Jobes, "Fence Cutting and a Ranger Shootout at Green Lake," 46.
57. Alexander, *Rawhide Ranger, Ira Aten,* 53-54.

58. Monthly Return, Company D, Frontier Battalion, September 184, TSA.
59. Alexander, *Rawhide Ranger, Ira Aten,* 54-55.
60. Aten-1941, HML&HC.
61. Monthly Return, Company D, Frontier Battalion, November 1884, TSA.
62. Alexander, *Rawhide Ranger, Ira Aten,* 57-103; Peter R. Rose, *The Reckoning: The Triumph of Order on the Texas Outlaw Frontier.* This finely researched and written work details early day Kimble County criminality. Specific to this citation would be the in custody death of Bill Allison as mentioned on 209, n. 43.
63. Monthly Return, Company D, Frontier Battalion, November 1884, TSA.
64. Harold Preece, *Lone Star Man: Ira Aten, Last of the Old Time Rangers,* 58. The author may be right. However, a note of caution is warranted. The core strength and weakness of this book is that it's "partly" true.
65. Alexander, *Winchester Warriors,* 18-19. For an insightful and exhaustively researched examination of the administrative side of the Frontier Battalion's early days—through the eyes of its first commander—the reader is referred to the exceptional *Texas Ranger John B. Jones and the Frontier Battalion, 1874-1881* by Rick Miller.
66. Genealogical files P. C. Baird, Mason County Historical Commission.
67. The most comprehensive compilation of facts and thoughtful analysis regarding this blood-feud is Johnson's *The Mason County "Hoo Doo" War, 1874-1902.* Relevant details relating to the killing of two soldiers on Mason's courthouse square may be accessed through Chuck Parson's outstanding *The Sutton-Taylor Feud: The Deadliest Blood Feud in Texas,* a historical work pleasantly free from illogical revisionist interpretation and absent a predetermined agenda.
68. Robert K. DeArment, *Deadly Dozen: Forgotten Gunfighters of the Old West,* Vol. 2, 210-212.
69. Tise, *Texas County Sheriffs,* 357.
70. J. Marvin Hunter, "P. C. Baird, the 'Old Sleuth,'" *Frontier Times,* March 1928, 225-228.
71. Ibid.
72. Ibid.
73. Ibid.
74. Deputy Sheriff P. C. Baird, Mason County to AG King, January 4, 1887, TSA.
75. AG King to Captain Jones, January 7, 1887, Letter Press Book, July 28, 1886-May 4, 1887, 262, TSA.
76. Monthly Return, Company D, Frontier Battalion, January 1887, TSA.
77. Tise, *Texas County Sheriffs,* 357.
78. J. Marvin Hunter, "Brief History of the Early Days in Mason County." *Frontier Times,* February 1929, 185.

79. Ibid., 186.

80. Chief Clerk of the Adjutant General's Office Henry Orsay to P. C. Baird, November 27, 1896, TSA; P. C. Baird, Special Ranger, to Adjutant General Mabry, December 31, 1896, TSA. For a biography of John H. Rogers, a Ranger and U.S. Marshal of prominence, see Paul N. Spellman's fine treatment *Captain John H. Rogers, Texas Ranger.*

81. Letterhead stationery The First State Bank of Mason, December 31, 1896, TRHF&M.

82. Typescript, "The Reynolds—Seaquest Mansion" by Nadine Baird Meadows, the youngest daughter of P. C. and Kittie Baird. Courtesy the Mason County Historical Commission.

83. Tise, *Texas County Sheriffs,* 358; Blackburn, *Wanted,* 226.

84. *Fort Worth Record,* May 16, 1914.

85. Ibid.

86. Hunter, "P.C. Baird, the 'Old Sleuth,'" 225.

87. For a brief historical sketch of Mason County's now defunct community of Katemcy see Mike Cox's *Central Texas Tales,* 98-97

88. Undated and unidentified news clip; Typescript, "The True Account of a Murder" by Nadine Baird Meadows, Courtesy the Mason County Historical Commission; J. Marvin Hunter in "Brief History of Early Days in Mason County" identifies the murder victim as Luke Chamberlin and correctly names the murderer as Ernest Kelley.

89. Typescript, "A Prisoner Named Vanderver" by Nadine Baird Meadows, Courtesy Mason County Historical Commission. This anecdotal tale is taken at face value. There has been no effort to corroborate Mrs. Meadows' story with primary sourced documents and, in truth, there need not be—she was there that Sunday afternoon.

90. *Mason County News,* March 15, 1928; J. Marvin Hunter, ed., *Frontier Times,* April 1928, "P. C. Baird is Dead," page 315; Genealogical Files, Mason County Historical Commission.

Chapter 8

1. Earl Zarbin, ed., *Taming the Salt: Salt River Project,* 7: "Wrongly used and poorly presented, history can be pretty deadly stuff. There is nothing—not even the desert—quite so desiccated as the monotonous recitation of names and dates and facts." Penned with tongue in cheek—maybe—Jack D. Rittenhouse writing the Foreword for Mary Jo Walker's delightful *The F. Stanley Story,* did not seem overawed with someone's advanced educational credentials, just because they had them: "Many bank their inner fire when they don their doctoral robes and are content to plod along as routine teachers, living as comfortably as a toad in a puddle of buttermilk, looking upon their diploma as a union card." See page 11.

2. Family lore and oral history is somewhat supported and supplemented: Stephen L. Moore, *Savage Frontier: Rangers, Riflemen, and Indian Wars in Texas,* Vol. 2, 138-139; Walter Lord, *A Time to Stand: A Chronicle of the Valiant Battle at the Alamo,* 130.

3. Roy and Jo Ann Stamps, *The Letters of John Wesley Hardin,* 58.

4. Most all genealogical files—even those that cannot be name specific traced to an author—are in agreement regarding Gus Chenowth's birthday; however, depending on the particular document his place of birth is given as Tennessee or Kentucky, and in one paper, Hardin County, Kentucky.

5. Alden Hayes, *A Portal to Paradise,* 109.

6. Will C. Barnes, *Arizona Place Names,* 238; James E. and Barbara H. Sherman, *Ghost Towns of Arizona,* 90; Philip Varney, *Arizona Ghost Towns and Mining Camps,* 56.

7. Isaac Goldberg [From an Original 1894 Manuscript]. "As Told by the Pioneers," *Arizona Historical Review,* April 1935, 75.

8. John R. Murdock, *Arizona Characters in Silhouette*: "As a prospector Weaver discovered the famous placer mine along the Colorado river where old La Paz later sprang up and became a thriving camp." See page 46.

9. Nell Murbarger, *Ghosts of the Adobe Walls,* 20; Charles Baldwin Genung, Kenneth M. Calhoun, ed., "Yavapai Country Memories, 1863-1894," *The Smoke Signal,* Spring/Fall 1982, page 39: "We stayed at La Paz two days. . . . La Paz at that time [1863] was a town of several hundred inhabitants with several stores, a bakery and feed corral but no post office nor mail service."

10. Joseph Miller, *Arizona: The Grand Canyon State,* 363.

11. Frank Love, *Mining Camps and Ghost Towns: A History of Mining in Arizona and California Along the Lower Colorado,* 34.

12. Melissa Ruffner Weiner, *Prescott Yesteryears: Life In Arizona's First Territorial Capital,* 7.

13. Love, *Mining Camps and Ghost Towns,* 35-36.

14. Jay J. Wagoner, *Early Arizona: Prehistory to Civil War.* 454. Some accounts add Thomas Gainor as one of the soldiers killed at La Paz.

15. Erick Melchiorre, *Gold Atlas of Quartzsite, Arizona, Volume I, Northern Dome Rock Mountains,* 46.

16. Frank C. Lockwood, *Pioneer Days in Arizona,* 343.

17. Goldberg, "As Told by the Pioneers," 75.

18. Florene Parks, Quartzsite Historical Society, Inc. to author December 30, 2012; Dennis Casebier, "Camp Beale's Springs Sojourn at the Colorado River Indian Reserve," *Journal of America's Military Past,* Spring 1997, 17.

19. Richard C. McCormick, *Arizona: Its Resources and Prospects,* Reprint, Introduction by Sydney B. Brinckerhoff, 9.

20. Marshall Trimble, *Arizona: A Panoramic History of a Frontier State,* 218.

21. Roscoe G. Willson, *Pioneer and Well Known Cattlemen of Arizona*, 8.
22. Lockwood, *Pioneer Days In Arizona*, 343; Murbarger, *Ghosts of the Adobe Walls*, 20.
23. John A. "Gus" Chenowth: Predecessor of John Wayne." Handwritten summary of the remembrances of Charles A. Chenowth as told to Mrs. George F. Kitt, 1933, Courtesy Arizona Historical Society, Hayden Files, Tucson, Arizona; Will C. Barnes, *Arizona Place Names*, 128; Martha Summerhayes in *Vanished Arizona: Recollections of My Army Life* notes a stopover at Desert Station: "At night we arrived at Desert Station. There was a good ranch there, kept by Hunt and Dudley, Englishmen, I believe. . . . their ranch was clean and attractive which was more than could be said of the place where we stopped next night, a place called Tyson's Wells." See page 138. Mrs. Summerhayes' travels were subsequent to the time Gus Chenowth divested himself of an interest in Desert Station; Lyola "Ola" Agnes Chenowth, typescript "My Father's Life As I Remember It": "As I have said before, father had the largest freight teams on the road." Typescript courtesy Arizona Historical Society, Tucson, AZ.
24. Murbarger, *Ghosts of the Adobe Walls*, 353.
25. Pauline Sandholdt, "James McMullen and the La Paz Road." Typescript courtesy the Quartzsite Historical Society, Inc. and the Tyson's Well Stage Station Museum, Quartzsite, Arizona.
26. Pauline Sandholdt, "John A. 'Gus' Chenowth: Predecessor of John Wayne," referencing the Yuma County Supervisors Book No. 1, May 8, 1867. Courtesy Quartzsite Historical Society, Inc. and the Tyson's Well Stage Station Museum, Quartzsite, Arizona.
27. Loyola Agnes "Ola" Chenowth, "My Father's Life As I Remember It," 2: "Oxen were too slow for him so he finally built his teams up to consist of all mules." David Nevin, *The Expressmen*, 60: "Mules continued to have their fierce partisans, however, and the choice usually depended on the work to be done. Mules were faster than oxen, taking one or two weeks less than oxen to cover the same distance. . . . Furthermore, mules posed a temptation to thieving Indians, because they could be ridden. . . ."
28. Kitty Jo Parker Nelson, "Prescott: Sketch of a Frontier Capital, 1863-1900," *Arizoniana: The Journal of Arizona History*, Winter 1963, 21.
29. Weiner, *Prescott Yesteryears: Life In Arizona's First Territorial Captial*, 13.
30. Ibid., 13. The author's pricing of a peach or apple in Prescott at $1.00 is believable. Pricing flour at $350.00 per hundred weights seems somewhat overinflated—but then again—merchants will extract what the traffic will bear: Then or now!
31. Patrick Grady, *Out of the Ruins: Pioneer Life in Frontier Phoenix, Arizona Territory 1867-1881*, 24.

32. *Arizona Weekly Miner*, August 22, 1968; *San Bernardino Guardian*, July 11, 1868.
33. Darlis A. Miller, *Soldiers and Settlers: Military Supply in the Southwest, 1861-1886*, 296.
34. Ibid.
35. Weiner, *Prescott Yesteryears: Life In Arizona's First Territorial Captial*, 13: "Freighting wagons were the only means of supplying Prescott with foodstuffs and equipment."
36. Genung, "Yavapai Country Memories, 1863-1894," 37.
37. Ibid: "The handling of the grass knocked the insects off."
38. *San Diego Union*, July 21, 1869.
39. *San Bernardino Guardian*, September 5, 1868; Barnes, *Arizona Place Names*, 81.
40. Pauline Sandholdt, "Before There Was Quartzsite," Typescript, Quartzsite Historical Society; Andrew Wallace, "Fort Whipple in the Days of Empire," *Smoke Signal*, Fall 1972: "By 1867 the Indian problem was serious. . . ." See page 117.
41. Miller, *Soldiers and Settlers*, 298.
42. Chenowth, "My Father's Life As I Remember It."
43. Unidentified historical typescript, "A Sketch" (probably authored by one of Gus Chenowth's children). Courtesy Charles R. Chenowth, Santee, California.
44. Dan L. Thrapp, *Al Sieber, Chief of Scouts*, 54.
45. William Fourr, "Reminiscences of William Fourr," As told to Mrs. George F. Kitt, *Arizona Historical Review*, October 1935, 73. A biographical sketch of William "Uncle Billie" Fourr may be found in Roscoe G. Willson's *Pioneer Cattlemen of Arizona*, 34.
46. Dan L. Thrapp, *The Conquest of Apacheria*, 53.
47. *Arizona Weekly Miner*, October 24, 1868.
48. Ibid.
49. Constance Wynn Altshuler, *Cavalry Yellow and Infantry Blue: Army Officers in Arizona Between 1851-1886*, 268-269.
50. Constance Wynn Altshuler, *Chains of Command: Arizona and the Army 1856-1875*, 149.
51. Ibid., 150; Hayes, *A Portal to Paradise*, 109-110.
52. *Arizona Weekly Miner*, October 24, 1868; Florene Parks, "La Paz Massacre": "Although the perpetrators were never caught or brought to justice their act was largely responsible for the founding of Camp Colorado by the U.S. Army. This encampment was established about five miles south of Parker [Arizona] and continued in existence until 1871 when it was abandoned." Copy in author's possession.
53. Melchiorre, *Gold Atlas of Quartzsite, Arizona*, 64.
54. Chenowth, "My Father's Life As I Remember It."
55. Grady, *Out of the Ruins: Pioneer Life In Frontier Phoenix, Arizona Territory 1867-1881*, 1-32.

56. Ibid., 17; Zarbin, *The Taming of the Salt*, 9.

57. *Arizona Weekly Miner*, July 24, 1869.

58. *The Arizona Republican*, April 13, 1921. An article based on the remembrances of L. E. Williamson.

59. George H. Kelly, *Legislative History of Arizona, 1864-1912*, 45-46.

60. Yuma County, Miscellaneous Book I, La Paz, Arizona Territory.

61. Naomi M. Zunker, "Maricopa: New County In Arizona Territory," *The Smoke Signal*, Fall 1992, 154; Marshall Trimble to author and Jan Devereaux, November 18, 2008.

62. *The Arizona Republican*, April 13, 1921.

63. Zunker, "Maricopa: New County In Arizona Territory," 155-156; Larry D. Ball, *Desert Lawmen: The High Sheriffs of New Mexico and Arizona, 1846-1912*, 66.

64. Jane Eppinga, *Arizona Sheriffs: Badges and Bad Men*, 71,

65. There is considerable confusion as to whether Mary Murray's father's name was William Pinckney Murray or James Pinckney Murray. Most genealogical family trees potted in the modern era from internet sources choose William, but much of the secondary research, citing primary sources—including certification of marriage—identifies the person as James Murray.

66. Certifications of Reverend Franklin McKean and Justice of the Peace Charles Carter, Sacks Collection, Arizona Historical Foundation; Lockwood, *Pioneer Days in Arizona* reports: "Thomas T. Hunter, who came to the valley early in 1868, states that the first child of American parents born in the settlement was John Adams' daughter and also records that an older daughter of this family was married April 1, 1868, to a cowboy, William Johnson." Lockwood goes on to mention: "Mrs. C. H. Gray was the first American woman to enter the valley. . . ." See page 338. Interestingly, C. H. Gray was one of the witnesses at the marriage ceremony of Gus Chenowth and Mary Murray. It is not inconceivable that the Johnson/Adams marriage was the first in the Salt River Valley, and that the Chenowth/Murray ceremony was the first taking place after Phoenix became county seat subsequent to the May 1871 elections.

67. U.S. Census, 1880, Phoenix, Maricopa County, Arizona Territory. Rilla and Eula Murray are enumerated as living in the household of John A. and Mary Chenowth, and further particularized as Gus' "Sisters in Law"; Chenowth, "My Father's Life As I Remember It." Gus' daughter Ola says: "He adopted all her [Mary's] half brothers and sisters and furnished a school for them until the city schools were opened. . . . Not until his two youngest adopted girls finished the course in college. . . . They were the only two with a college degree. Rilla married a man by the name of Osborn, Eula married a rich stockman by the name of Riggs. Both names are familiar to Arizona Citizens."

68. *Arizona Weekly Miner*, December 14, 1877.
69. Ibid., March 3, 1878.
70. Ibid., May 3, 1878.
71. *Salt River Herald*, August 10, 1878.
72. Chenowth Family Tree, a genealogical diagram, courtesy the late Amos and LaDorna Chenowth, McNeal, Arizona, and supporting first-person interviews with Rhetta (Chenowth) Smith, the late Dorthy (Chenowth) Jesse, Charles Randolph Chenowth, as well as Lynn and Amy Chenowth.
73. Grady, *Out of the Ruins*, 34-36.
74. *Salt River Herald*, August 10, 1878.
75. Grady, Out of the Ruins, 34-36.
76. *Weekly Arizona Miner*, December 14, 1877 and March 3, 1878.
77. *Weekly Arizona Miner*, May 3, 1878.
78. James V. "Jim" Parks to J. Evetts Haley and Hervey Chesley, February 27, 1945, Duncan, Arizona: "Old Man Chenoweth [*sic*] was preaching over there. . . ." in HML&HC.
79. Herbert E. Ungnade, *Guide to the New Mexico Mountains*: Peloncillos, "These mountains are a narrow range of low hills rising 1,000—1,500' above the Animas and San Simon Valley on both sides of the New Mexico-Arizona border." See page 168. T. M. Pearce, *New Mexico Place Names: A Geographical Dictionary,* 148.
80. George Hilliard, A *Hundred Years of Horse Tracks: The Story of the Gray Ranch*, 8: "the Bootheel's isolation encouraged the commerce in stolen cattle that took place across the border in both directions. Outlaws, cattle rustlers, smugglers, and Indians all made New Mexico's Bootheel a wild and dangerous place. . . ."
81. Doris French, ed., Mary McLaughlin, contributor, "Amos Chenowth's Story": He [Gus Chenowth] had a big adobe corral with walls about eight feet tall where they kept the cattle and horses safe from the Indians. This corral was about two acres in size." *Arizona National Ranch Histories of Living Pioneer Stockman* 18, 1998, Courtesy Rhetta Smith, Parker, Arizona; Hayes, *A Portal to Paradise*, 137.
82. *Grant County Herald and Southwest*, January 29, 1881. Absent acquisition of the actual newspaper edition, a listing of Silver City's contributors to the "Scalp Fund" and the amounts they individually pledged may be easily retrieved from Bob Alexander's *Six-Guns and Single Jacks: A History of Silver City and Southwestern New Mexico*, 286, n. 618.
83. Ibid.; for an excellent treatment of a specific raid inflaming the passions of Grant County residents the reader is referred to Daniel D. Aranda's "Apache Depredations in Doña Ana County: An Incident in Victorio's War," *Southern New Mexico Historical Review*, January 1996.
84. Bob Boze Bell, "Curly Bill's New Bronco," *True West*, August 2013, 65.

85. Charles Augustus Chenowth, "John Augustus Chenowth," Typescript, Hayden Files, Arizona Historical Society, Tucson, Arizona.

86. Hayes, *A Portal to Paradise,* 111.

87. Grant County Deed Book 6, Silver City, New Mexico, pages 193-194, a land notice filed December 26, 1880, signed by J. I. [Joseph Isaac] Clanton and John Ringo.

88. *Tombstone Epitaph: National Edition,* August 1985, Byline Carson Morrow.

89. Ted Raynor, *Old Timers Talk in Southwestern New Mexico,* 66-67; Hayes, *A Portal to Paradise,* 114-115; Alexander, *Lawmen, Outlaws, and S.O.Bs,* 278.

90. Hayes, *A Portal to Paradise,* 114-115. There are, as would be expected, several versions of this event. One asserts during the attempted robbery Gus pulled his six-shooter from beneath his oil-cloth slicker, the other has him slyly removing a .50 caliber Sharps carbine from his saddle scabbard, and poking the muzzle underneath his horse's belly, thus getting the drop on Cherokee Jack Rogers. Reconciling these differences is impossible and irrelevant. The gist of the story remains unchanged: Gus was not robbed, and Cherokee Jack was told to vamoose.

91. John Sinclair, "The Sugarloaf Mountains: The Magical Peloncillos," *New Mexico Magazine,* July 1979, 49; Peter Aleshire, "Tumultuous Chiricahuas," *Arizona Highways,* November 2002, 35: "said sermons over the people he [Gus Chenowth] killed. . . ." Hayes, *A Portal to Paradise,* 115; Sandholdt, "James McMullen and the LaPaz Road" absent supporting clarification refers to Gus Chenowth as "a hot-headed teamster."

92. Pesonal interviews with the late Amos and LaDorna Chenowth, and their daughter Rhetta Smith, a wellspring of Chenowth family data and an indispensable contributor for this chapter.

93. Personal interviews as cited.

94. A sampling of the recorded business transactions of Gus and Mary Chenowth may be accessed at Silver City, New Mexico of Grant County Deed Books #17 page 552, #17 page 593, #24 page 57, #24 page 168, #24 page 313, #24 page 659, #28 page 6, #37 page 387, #41, page 4, #54 page 358, and #54 page 360.

95. Thrapp, *Conquest of Apacheria,* 334.

96. Alexander, *Six-Guns and Single-Jacks: A History of Silver City and Southwestern New Mexico,* 220.

97. *Southwest Sentinel,* November 17, 1885.

98. Daniel D. Aranda, "Josanie—Apache Warrior," *True West,* May-June 1976, 39.

99. Don Worcester, *The Apaches: Eagles of the Southwest,* 295; Thrapp, *Conquest of Apacheria* adds "although twice dismounted and several times near capture, he escaped into Mexico with the loss of but one man." See page 339.

100. Arnold Dyre, "Commentary by Arnold Dyre." The author, a great-grandson of Gus and Mary Chenowth, reports: ". . . .Gus Chenowth was crossing Whitetail Flats, returning from Turkey Creek with a load of lumber salvaged from Galeyville's empty shacks. As he passed the point of Blue Mountain, a party of Apache approached him on horse-back. Gus raised his rifle in warning and the Indians veered off to Turkey Creek." Internet clip courtesy Rhetta Smith, Parker, AZ.

101. Although Apaches did not take scalps with the vigor of Plains Indians, it was, nevertheless, an accepted practice and not an isolated anomaly that an Apache would unsheathe the scalping knife. June 30, 2013, interview with Daniel Aranda, author and research authority on Apache warfare in southern and southwestern New Mexico.

102. Aranda, "Josanie—Apache Warrior," 64: "Josanie rejoined his brother's warriors in Old Mexico. . . ."

103. Peter Aleshire, *The Fox and the Whirlwind: General George Crook and Geronimo—A Paired Biography,* 149; Edwin R. Sweeney, *From Cochise to Geronimo: The Chiricahua Apaches, 1874-1886,* 557: "His [Loco's] men disliked Geronimo, whom they blamed for the tragedy on Alisos Creek." And, "Years later, one man, who had been a boy at this time, blamed their problems on Geronimo—a sentiment held by many of the peaceful Chiricahuas and their descendants into the twentieth century." See page 570.

104. Hayes, *A Portal to Paradise,* 167; Bill Cavalier, "The Settlers of Skeleton Canyon," *Bootheel Magazine,* Spring 2005, 16: "Skelton Canyon winds its way through the Peloncillo Mountains for approxi-mately eight miles, roughly half in Hidalgo County, NM and half in Cochise County, AZ. The first recorded settler is the Clanton family in the early 1880's, who had two dugouts near the east mouth of the canyon (located near the present-day Blair well.)"

105. Chenowth, "My Father's Life As I Remember It." Gus Chenowth's daughter, Ola, although but a child at the time, personally remembers Geronimo's and the Apaches' stopover at the Cienega Ranch subse-quent to the Indians' September 1886 surrender.

106. Ibid.: "He [General Miles] refused to pay for the watermelons, however."

107. McLaughlin, "Amos Chenowth's Story."

108. Various interviews with the descendants of Gus and Mary Chenowth. Certainly with an eye cast toward quantifiable history detailing the final surrender of Geronimo the reader is referred to the excellent treatment by Sweeney, *From Cochise to Geronimo,* particularly Chapter 25, "All Chiricahuas Are Created Equal," 552-575.

109. Alexander, *Desert Desperadoes,* citations throughout. Interestingly and commendably, even Wyatt Earp's accomplished biographer, Casey Tefertiller, in *Wyatt Earp: The Life Behind the Legend,* divulges that Murder and Mr. Earp were bedfellows: "By Wyatt Earp's own admission, he shot a man begging for his life." See page 227.

110. Kim Allen Scott, "The Most Contemptible Character I Ever Saw," *True West*, August 2013.

111. Karen Holliday Tanner and John D. Tanner, Jr., *Last of the Old-Time Outlaws: The George West Musgrave Story*, 5; also, Karen Holliday Tanner and John D. Tanner, Jr., *The Bronco Bill Gang*, 79.

112. Jeffrey Burton, *The Deadliest Outlaws: The Ketchum Gang and the Wild Bunch*.

113. Sinclair, "The Magical Peloncillos," 49.

114. Howard Bryan, *Robbers, Rogues, and Ruffians: True Tales of the Wild West*, 232-233; Jeff Burton, *Black Jack Christian: Outlaw*, 19; Alexander, *Desert Desperadoes*, 236-237; Tanner and Tanner, *Last of the Old-Time Outlaws*, 84. Credibly, Lieutenant Doug Dukes, Austin Police Department, an accomplished Old West researcher and writer, with but the slightest touch of humor gently reminds: "Friendly fire really isn't too friendly!"

115. Hilliard, *A Hundred Years of Horse Tracks*, citations throughout.

116. *Silver City Independent*, August 30, 1904; Pioneer Foundation Interviews, Robert Bell to Lou Blachley, Tape 21, page 6. Courtesy Terry Humble, Bayard, New Mexico.

117. Hilliard, *A Hundred Years of Horse Tracks*, 90.

118. *Territory of New Mexico vs. Howard Chenowth*, Case 1111, New Mexico Supreme Court Records [1906], Recorded Testimony of Pat Nunn, New Mexico Records Center and State Archives, Santa Fe, New Mexico.

119. *Silver City Enterprise*, September 2, 1904. By one account Pat Nunn had purchased the timepiece as a gift for his wife, see, Alton Turner, "New Mexico Shoot-Out," *Frontier Times*, March 1969, 36.

120. *Territory of New Mexico vs. Howard Chenowth*, Case 1111, New Mexico Supreme Court Records, Testimony of Pat Nunn. "Kennedy made a remark several times, 'Don't give up your gun [and] kill the sons-of-bitches.'"

121. Don Bullis, *New Mexico's Finest: Peace Officers Killed in the Line of Duty, 1847-2010*, 249; Alexander, *Lawmen, Outlaws, and S.O.Bs*, 282-283.

122. *Silver City Independent*, August 30, 1904; *Silver City Enterprise*, September 2, 1904

123. Ellen Cline, "The Story of a Cowboy," *Cochise County Historical Journal*, Fall/Winter 1997, 40.

124. *Silver City Enterprise*, September 2, 1904.

125. *Silver City Independent*, August 30, 1904; Bullis, *New Mexico's Finest*, 166.

126. Interviews with the late Amos (son of Howard Chenowth) and the late LaDorna Chenowth, McNeal, Arizona.

127. *Silver City Enterprise*, December 29, 1905; Hayes, *Portal to Paradise*, 232: "He removed bales from the middle of the pile to make a small bay that could be quickly closed off with a bale of hay. Howard lived there for months, until he quit the country."

128. Alexander, *Lawmen, Outlaws, and S.O.Bs,* 284-285.
129. That Howard Chenowth was employed on Brazilian cattle ranches is undisputed. Family lore asserts that he was a foreman on the famed King Ranch in Brazil, which is not consistent with King Ranch history, however. Lisa A. Neely, King Ranch Archivist, to author, November 20, 2002: "In reply to your request for verification of the material on Carl Martin [Howard Chenowth] and his empoloyment with the Brazilian property of King Ranch, I'm afraid there has been a lot of misinformation. King Ranch did not begin its ranching operation in Brazil until 1953."
130. *Certificate of Marriage, Estado de Matto Grosso,* September 1918, Courtesy Amos and LaDorna Chenowth.
131. Alexander, *Lawmen, Outlaws, and S.O.Bs,* 285.
132. Last Will and Testament of John A. Chenowth, April 2, 1913, Grant County Courthouse, Silver City, New Mexico.
133. *Silver City Enterprise,* May 2, 1913.
134. Certificate of Death, Arizona Department of Health, Divison of Vital Statistics, Mary M. Chenowth.

Chapter 9

1. Martha Gilliland Long, ed., *Llano County Family Album: A History,* 108; Death Certificate, James Dallas Dunaway, Texas State Board of Health, Bureau of Vital Statistics, Austin, Texas.
2. Ibid.; for details regarding Llano County's jails, see, Blackburn, *Wanted: Historic County Jails of Texas,* 216-217, and Joan Upton Hall, *Just Visitin' Old Texas Jails,* 129-131.
3. Caldwell and DeLord, *Texas Lawmen,* 159-160.
4. Warrant of Authority and Descriptive List, J. D. Dunaway, TSA; *San Antonio Daily Express,* April 27, 1907; Harris, Harris, and Sadler, *Texas Ranger Biographies,* 94.
5. Allan R. Townsend, *Meanest Kid in Town: Memories of Llano, Texas 1890-1904,* 109-111. The author, at age 78, was writing of his childhood and states that "Toots" Dunaway was a constable rather than the city marshal of Llano, which conflicts with Dunaway's primary source statements. For this part of the narrative, the discrepancy is not critical. Excerpts from *Meanest Kid in Town* are courtesy Karylon A. Russell.
6. Long, *Llano County Family Album,* 108; Harris, Harris, and Sadler, *Texas Ranger Biographies,* 94.
7. Warrant of Authority and Descriptive List, J. D. Dunaway, TSA.
8. Monthly Return, Company B, Ranger Force, July 1903, TSA.
9. Monthly Return, Company B, Ranger Force, August 1903, TSA.
10. Monthly Returns, Company B, Ranger Force, September, October, November 1903, TSA.

11. Monthly Return, Company B, Ranger Force, December 1903, TSA.

12. Monthly Return, Company B, Ranger Force, January 1904, TSA.

13. Albert Bigelow Paine quoting McDonald in *Captain Bill McDonald, Texas Ranger*, 266.

14. Ben Pyle, ed., *Trinity County: A Legend of Its Own*, 225.

15. John Leffler and Christopher Long, conts., *The New Handbook of Texas,* Vol. 6, p. 566: "The Trinity County area also became a haven for Confederate deserters and criminals during the war, and public order broke down. . . . Though the vigilantes resorted to summary justice and lynched a number of men, the county was still in turmoil when the war ended. . . . Meanwhile, local citizens were also harassed by outlaws such as John Wesley Hardin, who grew up in Trinity County"; Marohn, *The Last Gunfighter: John Wesley Hardin*, 48-52; Metz, *John Wesely Hardin: Dark Angel of Texas*, 5-6.

16. Caldwell and DeLord, *Texas Lawemn: More of the Good and the Bad*, 353-354.

17. Thad Sitton, *The Texas Sheriff: Lord of the County Line*, 57 and 65.

18. Monthly Return, Company B, Ranger Force, February 1904, TSA.

19. Weiss, *Yours to Command*, 220-221.

20. Monthly Return, Company B, February 1904, TSA; Paine, *Captain Bill McDonald*, Appendix C, "Report of Captain W. J. McDonald, Commanding Company B, Ranger Force," 409-416.

21. Monthly Return, Company B, Ranger Force, March 1904, TSA; Paine, *Captain Bill McDonald*, 414.

22. Ibid.

23. Monthly Return, Company B, Ranger Force, April 1904, TSA.

24. Monthly Return, Company B, Ranger Force, September 1904, TSA; Tise, *Texas County Sheriffs*, 253.

25. Ibid.

26. Weiss, *Yours to Command*, 221; Paine, *Captain Bill McDonald*, 270-271.

27. Monthly Returns, Company B, Ranger Force, October and November 1904, TSA.

28. Monthly Return, Company B, Ranger Force, December 1904, TSA; AG Hulen to Captain McDonald, January 3 and 4, 1905, TSA.

29. Ibid.

30. *Shiner Gazette*, May 2, 1907. "J. D. Dunaway is stationed at Trinity where his family is living. . . . ."

31. Monthly Return, Company B, Ranger Force, January 1905, TSA.

32. Monthly Return, Company B, Ranger Force, February 1905, TSA; Roy R. Barkley & Mark F. Odintz, eds., *The Portable Handbook of Texas,* Contibutor C. L. Sonnichsen, "Feuds," 322: "In 1905 two flareups over prohibition, one at Groveton and the other at Hempstead brought feud motives into play."

33. Captain McDonald to AG Hulen, March 21, 1905, TSA; Monthly Return, Company B, Ranger Force, March 1905, TSA; Captain McDonald to AG Hulen, September 20, 1905, TSA.
34. Monthly Return, Company B, Ranger Force, April 1905, TSA.
35. Captain McDonald to AG Hulen, June 5,1905, TSA; AG Hulen to Ranger J.D. Dunaway, June 5, 1906, TSA.
36. Captain McDonald to AG Hulen, June 30, 1905, TSA.
37. Weiss, *Yours to Command,* 226; Monthly Return, Company B, Ranger Force, July 1905, TSA.
38. Monthly Return, Company B, Ranger Force, October 1905, TSA.
39. Captain McDonald to AG Hulen, November 6, 1905, TSA; Monthly Return, Company B, Ranger Force, November 1905, TSA; Tise, *Texas County Sheriffs,* 321.
40. Private J.D. Dunaway to Adjutant General John A. Hulen, February 7, 1906, TSA.
41. Monthly Returns, Company B, Ranger Force, February 1906, and Company A, Ranger Force, April and May 1906, TSA.
42. J. H. Schlittler to AG Hulen, June 23, 1906, TSA: "the Sheriff (Gene Graham) resigned & Gee McMeans was made Sheriff. . . ." In his letter to the AG, Schlittler alleges that the dispute between Dunaway and McMeans revolved around the former accusing the latter of "having a hand" in the misappropriation of a quantity of blankets, "$300 worth," stolen from a train wreck. The letter writer further asserted, after the appointment of McMeans, "we now have a gang here who runs things to suit themselves. It is impossible to convict any of them at present." Tise, *Texas County Sheriffs* does not list the interim appointment of McMeans. See page 167.
43. Spellman, *Captain J. A. Brooks, Texas Ranger* quoting the *Ector County Democrat,* Juine 18, 1906, 174.
44. Telegram, Ector County Judge Branch Isbell to Governor Lanham, June 18, 1906, TSA.
45. Telegram, Ranger Private N. P. Thomas to AG Hulen, June 18, 1906, TSA.
46. Two Telegrams: AG Hulen to Sergeant Dunaway, June 18, 1906, TSA.
47. W. T. Malone to AG Hulen, June 17, 1906, TSA. The date of the letter is in error. It had to been written on or after June 18, 1906.
48. Resolution: Praising actions of Ranger Thomas, Signed, Branch Isbell, County Judge, June 19, 1906, TSA.
49. Captain Brooks to AG Hulen, June 24, 1906, TSA.
50. Spellman, *Captain J.A. Brooks, Texas Ranger,* 174; Monthly Returns, Company A, Ranger Force, for June and July 1906 reflect Sergeant Dunaway's leave of absence, TSA. For more on the life and career of Gee McMeans the reader is referred to the exceptional work of Bill O'Neal in *The Johnson-Sims Feud: Romeo and Juliet, West Texas Style.* Citations thoughout.

51. Sergeant Dunaway to AG Hulen, June 28, 1906. In this letter Dunaway is pleading for an audience with AG Hulen, because "Captain said something about reducing me in ranks & I have been misrepresented to you and him by one Mr. Thomas who is a private in Co. A. and will ask you to hold the Charges up and let me come to Austin to make a true report. . . ." Letter found in TSA.

52. Captain John R. Hughes to Adjutant General J. O. Newton, January 21, 1909, TSA: "they got to be enemies while at Odessa when they were both in Capt. Brooks Company." For details concerning the death of Texas Ranger N. P. Thomas, see, Caldwell and DeLord, *Texas Lawmen: More of the Good and the Bad,* 395-396.

53. Monthly Return, Company A, Ranger Force, October 1906, TSA; Tise, *Texas County Sheriffs,* 303.

54. Spellman, *Captain J. A. Brooks: Texas Ranger,* 175-176; Partial List of Texas Ranger Company and Unit Commanders, compiled by Christina Stopka, Director, TRHF&M Research Center; Darren L. Ivey, *The Texas Rangers: A Registry and History,* 185; Harris, Harris, and Sadler, *Texas Ranger Biographies,* 292.

55. Sergeant H. A. Carnes, Company D, Ranger Force to AG Newton, May 18, 1907, TSA.

56. Ibid. Sometimes, primarily in secondary source documents, Kenley's name is spelled "Kinley" and occasionally "Kenly." Presumably the best source is Kenley's letterhead stationery and his signature, "R. O. Kenley."

57. Trinity County Attorney H. L. Robb to Captain McDonald, September 9, 1905, TSA.

58. Sergeant Carnes to AG Newton, May 18, 1907, TSA. As early as 1905 Captain McDonald was noting troubling behavior on the part of the sheriff: "but am not surprised that Stanley [*sic*] would turn him loose for his gang can't afford to have him caught for he will give the whole bunch away." Captain McDonald to AG Hulen, September 13, 1905, TSA.

59. F. W. Meyer to Governor Lanham, October 25, 1906, TSA: "I will write you about the Groveton trouble. I am the Father of Detective F.R. Meyer, who got murdered at Groveton." Monthly Return, Company D, Ranger Force, October 1906, TSA; Cora G. Bowles, *A History of Trinity County Texas,* 94.

60. Carnes to AG Newton, May 18, 1907, TSA.

61. Ibid.; Sergeant Carnes to Assistant Adjutant General E.M. Phelps, November 12, 1906, TSA; Tise, *Texas County Sheriffs,* 496.

62. W. S. Randolph to Governor Lanham, November 25, 1906, TSA.

63. Carnes to AG Newton, May 18, 1907, TSA; Carnes to AAG Phelps, November 17, 1906, TSA: "after the State had introduced all its witnesses and rested the defense withdrew the case of H.O. Park and Virgil Winslow without putting any witnesses on stand. Judge Boone

dismissed the other three cases and ordered H.O. Park and Virgil Winslow to be placed in Palestine Jail without bail, there will be no further disposition of the case until the last week of January. . . ." Monthly Return, Company D, Ranger Force, October 1906, TSA; Bowles, *A History of Trinity County Texas* brings the legal battle over Meyers' murderers to an end: "These were tried for the crime, but a jury at Palestine, Texas, found them not guilty." See page 94.

64. Telegram: W. G. VanVleck to Adjutant General Hulen, December 24, 1906, TSA: "We fear serious trouble at Glidden at the hands of strikers or their sympathizers. Sheriff Colorado county advises unable to afford any protection whatever and suggest requesting that three or four rangers be sent there at once. Please advise quick what action you can take." Telegram: Sheriff W. E. Bridges to Governor Lanham, December 24, 1906, TSA: "Please send four or five rangers to Glidden. Trouble expected on account of strike and I have no suitable men to furnish protection." Monthly Returns, Company D, Ranger Force, December 1906 and January 1907, TSA.

65. Sergeant J. D. Dunaway, Company A, Ranger Force to AG Hulen, December 26, 1906, TSA.

66. Monthly Return, Company D, Ranger Force, February 1907, TSA; Fred Tarpley, *1001 Texas Place Names,* 24; Monthly Return, Company B, Ranger Force, February 1907, TSA.

67. Sergeant J. D. Dunaway, Company B, Ranger Force to AG J. O. Newton, March 23, 1907, TSA; Monthly Return, Company D, Ranger Force, March 1907, TSA.

68. *San Antonio Daily Express,* April 27, 1907.

69. William Warren Sterling, *Trails and Trials of a Texas Ranger,* 360.

70. R.O. Kenley to Governor T.M. Campbell, April 15, 1907, TSA; AG Newton to W.E. Pope, District Attorney, Madisonville, Texas, April 13, 1907: "By the direction of the Governor, I would invite your attention to the enclosed copy of a letter from Mr. R.O. Kenley of Groveton, Texas, in which he makes specific charges of gross ill treatment in violation of law, by attack made on him by Sergt. J.D. Dunaway of the Ranger Force, on the afternoon of April 9th. . . . Therefore, you are requested to at once institute an investigation, to be conducted as secretly as possible, and at the same time expeditiously, in order that the true facts in regard to this attack on Mr. Kenley may be brought to light, and the guilty party punished. . . ." TSA.

71. Monthly Return, Company D, Ranger Force, April 1907, TSA; *The San Antonio Light,* April 27, 1907.

72. *San Antonio Gazette,* April 27, 1907; *Fort Worth Star Telegram,* April 27, 1907.

73. *Dallas Monrning News,* April 27, 1907.

74. AG Newton to Captain Frank Johnson, Company A, Ranger Force, April 29, 1907: ". . . . till Captain Hughes and his men have completed

the investigation into the attempted assassination of Sergt. Dunaway and former County Attorney Robb of Trinity County. Have just learned that Robb died from his wounds. Sergt. Dunaway is now at Trinity, and from our last report it would seem he will recover, although he is serious wounded having been shot in six places." TSA; *The Shiner Gazette* of May 2, 1907 particularized Dunaway's wounds: "He is hit six times, once in the left shoulder, through the left part of the chin, once in the abdomen, once in the throat, and in both legs below the knee."; From the *Fort Worth Star Telegram* of April 27, 1907: "Attorney Robb is said to be still unconscious."; That Robb was never expected to recover is reflected in two April 28, 1907 letters from Captain Hughes to AG Newton. ". . . . we all think Robb will die". . . ."Dunaway is doing very well but we expect that Mr. Robb will die. He had fever and was very restless yesterday evening—he is shot in the brain." TSA.

75. Sterling, *Trails and Trials of a Texas Ranger,* 360; As repeated in the newspaper, Ranger Sergeant Dunaway's telegraphic message read: "Send Rangers at once. Waylaid and shot all to pieces. Not serious." *The San Antonio Daily Express,* April 27, 1907; Mike Cox, *Texas Ranger Tales: Storeis That Needed Telling* opts for the afore cited version, 284, but in Cox's *Time of the Rangers,* the author words Dunaway's telegraphic message as "I am shot all to pieces, Everything quiet." 41; In a letter to Captain Frank Johnson on April 26, 1907, AG Newton advised: "Have received a telegram from Ranger Dunaway in which he states that he was shot all to pieces, but does not think his wounds serious." TSA; Regardless exactness, the meaning remains unachanged.

76. Monthly Return, Company D, Ranger Force, April 1907, TSA; Captain Hughes to AG Newton, April 27, 1907. "We arrived here [Groveton] about 1P.M. today." TSA.

77. *Shiner Gazette,* May 2, 1907.

78. AG Newton to Captain Johnson, April 27, 1907, TSA.

79. *Dallas Mornting News,* May 3, 1907.

80. Monthly Return, Company D, Ranger Force, April 1907, TSA; Newspaper coverage in the *Jefferson Jimplecute,* May 3, 1907, enumerates R.E. Mintona rather than Minton as listed in the MR. The *Dallas Morning News* of April 27, 1907 enumerates Mintona as being one of the arrested parties. In either event, this is the brother-in-law referred to by the adjutant general. For the *Dallas Morning News* story of May 3, 1907, Minton is mentioned.

81. Sergeant J.D. Dunaway to AG Newton, May 24, 1907, TSA.

82. *Bisbee Daily Review,* April 27, 1907.

83. Dr. F. L. Barnes to AG Newton, May 3, 1907, TSA.

84. A. H. Dunaway to AG Newton, May 4, 1907, TSA; Phyllis Whitt Almond and Sarah Oatman Franklin, *Cobwebs & Cornerstones,* 38-53. Excerpts courtesy Karolyn Russell.

85. Telegram: AAG Phelps to A.H. Dunaway, May 6, 1907, TSA; AG Newton to Colonel Leroy Trice, V.P., I & C. N. Ry., May 10, 1907, TSA; AG Newton to G. Radetzki, General Superintendent, H. & T. C. Ry., May 10, 1907, TSA; AG Newton to Sergeant Carnes: May 11, 1907: "Keep the information concerning this movement a profound secret from everyone except those directly interested, as it is absolutely necessary that all precaution be taken in order to avoid another attempt at assassination." TSA; AG Newton to Captain Hughes, May 11, 1907, TSA.

86. S.E. Barnes to Governor T.M. Campbell, May 8, 1907, TSA.

87. *Fort Worth Star Telegram*, June 11, 1908: "Hundred Pistols Taken from Crowd Entering Court House"; *Belleville News Democrat*, June 13, 1908: "A count of the artillery later disclosed an even hundred guns"; Tise, *Texas County Sheriffs*, 243.

88. *Palestine Daily Herald*, June 16 and 18, 1908; *Dallas Morning News*, June 17, 1908.

89. Sterling, *Trails and Trials of a Texas Ranger*, 360.

90. Monthly Returns, Company B, Ranger Force, February, May, June, July, August, September, October, November, and December 1907, TSA.

91. AAG Phelps to Captain Ross, July 3, 1908, TSA; AAG Phelps to W.G. VanVelk, Vice President, G.H. & S.A. Ry. Co., July 3, 1908, in TSA: "I would highly appreciate annual passes over your road for Rangers J. D. Dunaway and Sam McKenzie for the remainder of 1908. Sergeant Dunaway and McKenzie are now stationed at Alice, but have been ordered to report to Captain Hughes at Comstock for duty on that frontier. "

92. At this juncture although formally detailed to Company D, Dunaway's and McKenzie's activities are reported in the Company B Monthly Returns. For this citation, the MR for July 1908, TSA.

93. This incident—somewhat atypically—was enumerated in both the Company B and Company D Monthly Returns. The November 1908 MR for Company B places the date of arrest as October 29, and the name of the arrested suspect as S. A. Knight. The November 1908 MR for Company D gives the date of arrest as October 29 but identifies the prisoner as S. A. Wright. Obviously the confusion is phonetically attributable. The quotation is taken from the Company D MR, TSA.

94. Monthly Return, Company D, Ranger Force, March 1909, TSA.

95. Charles C. Hartley, Sheriff, Val Verde County, to Captain Hughes, Ranger Force, April 8, 1909, TSA; Tise, *Texas County Sheriffs*, 505.

96. Captain Hughes to AG Newton, April 11, 1909, TSA.

97. Captain Hughes to AG Newton, April 11, 1909. Second letter, TSA.

98. AG Newton to Captain Hughes, April 16, 1909, TSA; In all fairness to Dunaway it seems that the Val Verde County sheriff, after learning

of the Ranger's dismissal, had second thoughts—for one reason or another. See, Sheriff Charles C. Hartley to AG Newton, May 9, 1909, TSA:

> I wrote Capt. John R. Hughes, a letter sometime past in regard to Sergeant J.D. Dunniway [*sic*], asking him to move Mr. Dunniway from Del Rio, if he could use him elsewhere, as I didn't think we could get along together satisfactory as two brother officers should; therefore thought it best for Capt. Hughes to move in time, as I have above stated. I understand since I wrote the letter to Capt. Hughes that Dunniway is likely to be discharged from the Ranger service on account of my letter, I did not ask for him to be removed from the service, nor did I want him removed from the service; I also understand that it was reported to you that Dunniway and I, did not speak which is not true, we had no hard words while he was here, nor did we have any trouble; except as stated in my letter to Capt. Hughes, and will ask you not to discharge him on my account from the Ranger Service, I only waned him removed from Del Rio, believing it best for both him and I.

99. Monthly Return, Company B, Ranger Force, May 1909, TSA.
100. Harris and Sadler, *Texas Rangers and the Mexican Revolution,* 198.
101. Sheriff L.A. Clark, Edwards County, to Governor James E. Ferguson, March 15, 1915, TSA; Tise, *Texas County Sheriffs* for the youngest sheriff in the history of Edwards County. 169.
102. Charles H. Harris III and Louis R. Sadler, *Plan de San Diego: Tejano Rebellion, Mexican Intrigue* is the most comprehensive examination of the Plan of San Diego to date. For particular emphasis on the Texas Rangers during this timeframe the seminal work is Harris and Sadler, *The Texas Rangers and the Mexican Revolution: The Bloodiest Decade, 1910-1920.* Not surprisingly Utley's assessment in *Lone Star Lawmen* is on target, dead center: "During the summer of 1915, panic swept through both Anglo and Mexican populations. The Plan of San Diego uprising gave genuine cause for panic." 35.
103. Petition from the undersigned signatories of Llano County in support of J.D. Dunaway, February 24, 1915. Twenty signatures, TSA.
104. Telegram: Sheriff L.A. Clark, Edwards County to Governor James E. Ferguson, March 15, 1915, TSA.
105. Adjutant General Henry Hutchings to Captain J. J. Sanders, Company A, Ranger Force, March 13, 1915, TSA.
106. Captain Sanders to AG Hutchings, March 15, 1915, TSA.
107. Enlistment, Oath of Office and Description Ranger Force, J. D. Dunaway, March 29, 1915, TSA: Warrant of Authority and Descriptive List, J.D. Dunaway, Company C, Ranger Force, March 29, 1915, TSA; AG Hutchings to Captain J. J. Sanders, April 6, 1915: "His Excellency, the Governor, directed the enlistment in the Ranger Force of J.D.

Dunaway, F. [Francis] A. [Augustus] Hamer, W. F. Bates, E. [Eugene]
B. Hulen and B.B. Paris [Byron B. Parrish], and in order that these men
might not be forced on a Company Commander, they were assigned to
Company C." TSA.

108. AG Hutchings to Hon. [Sheriff] J. W. Almond, April 2, 1915, TSA.
That the Rangers were directly answerable to a county sheriff is made
perfectly clear in the Scout Report of W. L. Barler for April 1915:
"Enlisted in Company "C' Ranger Force April 9th in El Paso, Texas.
Left El Paso by orders from Sheriff John W. Almonds [*sic*] of Val
Verde Co. April 19th and arrived at Del Rio on April 30th. On same day
left Del Rio with Sheriff Almonds for Bill Hutto ranch . . . . and on
April 21st from Bill Hutton ranch with Sheriff Almonds and Ranger
Dunaway . . . . to report to sheriff. . . . Stayed in Del Rio by orders of
sheriff . . . . Sheriff 26th ordered [me] to join Ranger J.D. Dunaway
at Geo Mire ranch. . . ." The assertion that Rangers were under direct
control of a county sheriff is further reinforced in Private Barler's
Scouting Report for May 1915: "[May] 7-8-910 ordered by Sheriff
Almonds to stay in Del Rio." Both reports are in TSA.

109. Harris and Sadler, *Texas Rangers and the Mexican Revolution,* 200.

110. Company C Scout Reports for April 1915, J. D. Dunaway, W. L. Barler,
and F. A. Hamer. Hamer's arrest report for the month is for Fletcher
Gardner, Theft of Hogs and Willis Cross, Theft of Goats, TSA.

111. Scout Report, Nat B. Jones, May 1915, TSA; Harris and Sadler, *Texas
Rangers and the Mexican Revolution,* 200.

112. Scout Report, Nat B. Jones, June 1915, TSA.

113. AG Hutchings to J.D. Dunaway, Rocksprings, Texas, April 2, 1915
and AG Hutchings to J. D. Dunaway, Rocksprings, Texas, April 4,
1915, as well as an April 6 follow-up letter, TSA.

114. Harris and Sadler, *Texas Rangers and the Mexican Revolution,* 189-190;
Monthly Return, Company B, June 1915, TSA.

115. For details on the deaths of Rangers Hulen and Burdett see Alexander's
*Riding Lucifer's Line: Ranger Deaths Along the Texas Mexico
Border,* Chapter 16 for Hulen, Chapter 17 for Burdett; additionally,
an exceptional source for same, in an abbreviated format, would be
Caldwell and DeLord, *Texas Lawmen: More of the Good and the
Bad,* 399-400. For the death of Pascual Orozco see Bob Alexander,
Fearless Dave Allison: Border Lawman, 184-204. Not surprisingly,
when trying to paint with a broad brush and implicate Texas Rangers in the death of nearly every Mexican or *Tejano* killed during
1915, in some treatments Rangers are credited or discredited with
the killing of Orozco. There were no Texas Rangers present at the
time of his death, although both William Davis Allison and Herff
Alexander Carnes, who were there, had previously held Ranger
commissions.

116. Harris and Sadler, *Plan de San Diego: Tejano Rebellion, Mexican Intrigue.* Citations throughout.

117. Allen Gerlach, "Conditions Along The Border—1915 The Plan De San Diego," *New Mexico Historical Review* 43, no. 3 (1968): 195-213.

118. Harris and Sadler, *Texas Rangers in the Mexican Revolution,* 248.

119. Charles H. Harris III and Louis Ray Sadler, *The Plan De San Diego: Tejano Rebellion, Mexican Intrigue,* 257.

120. Ibid. The authors furnish a table—scorecard—for *Plan de San Diego's* victories and defeats, concluding that the *sediciosos'* "principal military accomplishment was wrecking a train," 261.

121. James N. Leiker, *Racial Borders: Black Soldiers Along the Rio Grande,* 14: "Aware of these dangers, army commanders attempted when possible to station blacks far from 'Anglo' settlements, thus mostly along the Rio Grande. This practice, however, also failed to reduce racial turmoil. While black soldiers and Hispanic residents mixed peacefully on occasion, mistrust and violence characterized their relationships." John D. Weaver, *The Brownsville Raid: The Story of America's "Black Dreyfus Affair,"* 21: "Captain Edger remembered a conversation with Dr. Frederick J. Combe, the town's mayor, who had once served with black cavalryman as a medical officer. 'These people will not stand for colored troops; they do not like them,' the Mayor had said. 'These Mexican people do not want them here.'" Milo Kearney and Anthony Knopp, *Boom and Bust: The Historical Cycles of Matamoros and Brownsville,* 197-198.

122. Monthly Return, Company B, Ranger Force, September 1915, TSA; Tise,*Texas County Sheriffs,* 173.

123. Thomas J. Martin to Governor James E. Ferguson, October 7, 1915, TSA.

124. Ibid.; Harris and Sadler, *Texas Rangers and the Mexican Revolution,* 198.

125. Governror Ferguson to AG Hutchings, October 9, 1915, TSA.

126. AG Hutchings to Thomas J. Martin, October 28, 1915 and Thomas J. Martin to AG Hutchings, October 30, 1915, TSA: "I am this morning in receipt of your favor advising me of the removal of Ranger Dunaway. I take this means of thanking you for your prompt attention to this matter." Gillespie County Case #909 reduced to Simple Assault.

127. Captain J. M. Fox to AG Hutchings, November 18, 1915, TSA; Case #909 transferred to JP Court.

128. Adjutant General James A. Harley to J. D. Dunaway, Feburary 15, 1918, TSA.

129. Long, *Llano County Family Album: A History,* 108.

130. Certificate of Death, James Dallas Dunaway, February 21, 1923, TSA.

Chapter 10

1. David Johnson, *John Ringo*. Quoting a letter from Chuck Parsons to Johnson, June 28, 1994. 163.

2. David Johnson, *John Ringo, King of the Cowboys: His Life and Times From the Hoo Doo War to Tombstone* (rev. 2nd ed., Denton: University of North Texas Press), 198.

3. Bob Boze Bell, "Ambush at Guadalupe Pass," *True West*, March 2004, 47; Isenberg, *Wyatt Earp: A Vigilante Life*, presents a refreshing treatment with a comprehensive and nonpartisan examination of Wyatt Earp's continual and purposeful reinventions as a pop culture hero, despite his thoroughly identifiable criminal record and self-puffed past: "In southern Arizona in the early 1880s, however, Wyatt was not the stalwart defender of law and order that Lake, Flood, Hooker, and Wyatt himself made him out to be; nor were the cowboys an organized-crime syndicate," 115. And, "If Newman Clanton was not the Robin Hood of southern Arizona, neither was he its Al Capone. Popular culture remembers Clanton as a frontier crime boss for much the same reason that Wyatt Earp is usually remembered as a duty-bound law-man: the action-detective genre demands that a sharp distinction be drawn between the criminal and the crime-solving hero. Forrestine Hooker, John Flood, and Stuart Lake each made that distinction clear. Yet as a poor, rural migrant who ventured into crime, Clanton was not so different from the bootlegger Nicholas Earp or Nicholas's son Wyatt, the onetime horse thief and brothel enforcer," 125.

4. The interested reader is referred to Chuck Parsons' *The Sutton-Taylor Feud: The Deadliest Blood Feud in Texas* and James M. Smallwood's *The Feud That Wasn't: The Taylor Ring, Bill Sutton, John Wesley Hardin, and Violence in Texas*. Though but this writer's viewpoint, the feud thesis carries more weight than the fanciful conspiracy spin.

5. John E. Conklin, *Criminology*, 387-388; Robert M. Bohm and Keith N. Haley, *Introduction to Criminal Justice*, 37: "Unlawful acts of members of highly organized and disciplined associations engaged in supplying illegal goods and services . . ."; Bruce L. Berg and John J. Horgan, *Criminal Investigations*, 462: "For our purposes we will define organized crime as a highly structured, disciplined, self perpetuation association of people, usually bound by ethnic ties, who consprie to commit crimes for profit and use fear and corruption to protect their activities from criminal prosecution."

6. Frederick Nolan, "'Boss Rustler' The Life and Crimes of John Kinney," Part I, *True West*, September 1996, 14-15.

7. Ibid.; Margaret G. Kinney to Lewis A. Ketring, Jr., February 27, 1973: "the family came west to Illinois."

8. Robert W. Lull, *James M. Williams: Civil War General and Indian Fighter*, 184. Additional descriptive data regarding Fort Selden and

everyday life at the post may be found in this recently released and most excellent treatment of military life in the frontier west.

9. Ibid., 180.
10. Timonthy Cohrs and Thomas J. Caperton, *Fort Selden, New Mexico: Fort Selden State Monument*, 18.
11. Miller, *Soldiers and Settlers*, 336.
12. Lull, *James M. Williams: Civil War General and Inidan Fighter*, 188.
13. Paxton P. Price, *Pioneers of the Mesilla Valley*, 158; Dale F. Giese, *Forts of New Mexico*, 48.
14. Jan Devereaux and Bob Alexander, "Trumpeting Elephants and Kicking Asses: Republicans vs. Democrats, New Mexico Style," *True West*, January/February 2010, 26-31.
15. Robert N. Mullin, "Here Lies John Kinney," *Journal of Arizona History*, Autumn 1973, 226; Philip J. Rasch, "John Kinney 'King of Rustlers' Was for Law, Too," *The Southwesterner*, October 1962, 16.
16. Nolan, "'Boss Rustler' The Life and Crimes of John Kinney," Part 1, 15.
17. For Jessie Evans see Grady E. McCright and James H. Powell, *Jessie Evans: Lincoln County Badman*; For Jimmy McDaniels see Bob Alexander, *Lawmen, Outlaws, and S.O.Bs*, Chapter Two, "Adrenaline, Alcohol, and Attitude." Also see *Revenge! And Other Tales of the Old West*. Eds. Mark Boardman and Sharon Cunningham. Chapter Two, "The Many Lives and Suggested Death of Jim McDaniels" by Paul Cool. For Charles Ray see Philip J. Rasch *Desperadoes of Arizona Territory*, Robert K. DeArment, ed., Chapter Six, "Ray, Alias Deal." Also, Peter Brand, "Sherman W. McMaster(s), The El Paso Salt War, Texas Rangers and Tombstone," *Western Outlaw-Lawman History Association Journal*, Winter 1999.
18. Nolan, "'Boss Rustler' The Life and Crimes of John Kinney," Part 1, 15-16.
19. Mullin, "Here Lies John Kinney" quoting the *Mesilla Independent*, July 21, 1877, 226.
20. Santa Fe *Daily New Mexican* May [?] 1883, quoted in *Frontier Times*, October 1936, 11.
21. Rasch, "John Kinney: King of the Rustlers," 10; Shortly, Sheriff Mariano Barela killed a drunken Leandro Urieta.
22. *Mesilla Valley Independent*, November 2, 1877.
23. *Mesilla Valley Independent*, November 10, 1877.
24. On November 16 and 17, 1877 the Doña Ana County Grand Jury returned felony indictments against John Kinney for Assault and Assault to Murder. The indictment for murder would be filed the following year on the 24th day of June. See notes of historian Robert N. Mullin, archived at the Haley Memorial Library in Midland, Texas. Also, William A. Keleher *Violence in Lincoln County, 1869-1881: The New Mexico Feud That Became a Frontier War*, 160-161. Also, edifying interviews with Lewis Ketring, Tucson, AZ, a longtime authority on the Lincoln County War.

25. Frederick Nolan, *The West of Billy the Kid,* 21; Bob Alexander, "Guns, Girls and Gamblers: Silver City's Wilder Side," *Western Outlaw-Lawman History Association Journal,* Winter. 2005, 12-20.

26. John Kinney's relationships with these two New Mexico Territory lawmen may be further explored by accessing Bob Alexander's *Sheriff Harvey Whitehill: Silver City Stalwart* and *Dangerous Dan Tucker: New Mexico's Deadly Lawman.* Numerous citations to John Kinney throughout both volumes. For article-length profiles of Dan Tucker the reader is referred to Robert K. DeArment's *Deadly Dozen: Twelve Forgotten Gunfighters of the Old West,* Chapter Five, "Of Shy and Retiring Disposition—Dan Tucker" and "Deadly Deputy" as published in the November 1991 edition of *True West*; Kinney to Ketring, February 27, 1973: John Kinney "was a miner by trade. . . ."

27. Leon Claire Metz, *The Shooters,* 217.

28. Charles Francis Ward, "The Salt War of San Elizaro (1877)," Master of Arts Thesis, Uniiversity of Texas, Austin, Texas 1932.

29. Utley, *Lone Star Justice: The First Century of the Texas Rangers,* 188-189.

30. Bob Alexander, "Tucker X Texas = Trouble!" *Wild West History Association Journal,* June 2008. 7.

31. C.L. Sonnichsen, *The El Paso Salt War,* 5.

32. U.S. House of Representatives, Executive Document No. 93, 45th Congress, 2nd Session, 1878, titled *El Paso Troubles in Texas* [HR-ED 93]. For this particular quotation, HR-ED 93—Statement of Ward B. Blanchard, February 11, 1878, 70.

33. Ward, "The Salt War of San Elizaro (1877)," 8.

34. HR-ED 93—Statement of Sheriff Charles Kerber, February 2, 1878; Paul Cool, *Salt Warriors: Insurgency on the Rio Grande,* 49-50.

35. Ibid.; Also, J. Morgan Broaddus, *The Legal Heritage of El Paso,* 153: "We find the justices-of-peace at Ysleta, Concordia, Caudrilla, and Socorro incompetent and their dockets are found in unsatisfactory condition. In most cases, we find them kept in the Spanish language, and not in proper form, as required by Law. The constables in most precincts do not speak English." Recognizing lower courts' closeness to the people, the Texas Congress enacted legislation permitting the use of Spanish in justice-of-the-peace courts west of the Guadalupe River, 57. For additional details regarding Sheriff Kerber the reader is referred to the skillfully researched and written "Salt War Sheriff: El Paso's Charles Kerber" by Paul Cool, NOLA *Quarterly,* January-March 2003, 19-34.

36. C. L. Sonnichsen, *Pass of the North: Four Centuries on the Rio Grande,* Vol. 1, 186-210.

37. Sonnichsen, *The El Paso Salt War,* 27; Jack Shipman, "The Salt War of San Elizario," *Voice of the Mexican Border,* December 1933, 157-164 and January 1934, 198-215.

38. Charles M. Robinson III, *The Men Who Wear the Star: The Story of the Texas Rangers,* 226.

39. Alexander, *Riding Lucifer's Line: Ranger Deaths along the Texas-Mexico Border,* 52-68.

40. Report of the Adjutant General, State of Texas, 1878, TSA; HR-ED 93, Statements of Juan N. Garcia, 96; Benjamin S. Dowell, 54; and Wesley Owens, 59; Alexander, *Desert Desperadoes: The Banditti of Southwestern New Mexico Territory,* 100-101; Eugene Cunningham, "Salt," *Frontier Times,* January 1930, 156: "By the standard of the day and place, Cardis got no more than his just deserts, 'what was coming to him' as the oldtimers would phrase it. He had incited this trouble with the aid of Borajo [*sic*] across the River in Guadalupe. He had opened a feud with Howard and for him it was to obey the ancient Arkansan maxim of 'let every man kill his own snakes.' He must have misread Howard's character gravely, not to have been alert for just this action." M. L. Crimmins, "The Salt War of San Elizario, Texas," *Frontier Times,* April 1931, 298.

41. Oath, Enlistment Roll, Recruits for Co. C. Detachment, Frontier Battalion, TSA; Frances T. Ingmire, *Texas Ranger Service Records, 1847-1900,* Vol. 4, 41.

42. Utley, *Lone Star Justice,* 205. Elaborating further in this award-winning book Utley unhesitatingly concludes: "Late in 1877, bracketing triumphs over feudists and outlaws, Major Jones confronted the severest challenge to his leadership. It thwarted him and ended in the most humiliating failure in the annals of the Texas Rangers," 188. Not surprisingly Rick Miller in his award-winning biography *John B. Jones, Texas Ranger* is much more charitable about the matter of Jones' personal handling of the El Paso Troubles, 179-180. Likewise, Paul Cool in his award-winning treatment *Salt Warriors* is quite benevolent—and factually accurate—as to the biographic profile and subsequent actions of Lieutenant John B. Tays, Texas Ranger, 142-143. For a chapter dealing with these contentious El Paso County events, Alexander in his award-winning *Desert Desperadoes* focuses the spotlight on both Major Jones' perceptible successes and failures or, more specifically, the author's personal analysis of those successes and failures, 102-103. There is a salient thrust: Nonfiction researchers and writers are permitted—encouraged—to put their interpretative spin on the facts—but are professionally prohibited from changing or misrepresenting those facts. Interested readers may judge the real merits of their arguments, accepting or rejecting their positions. Provoking meaningful thought is a wholesome and worthwhile exercise.

43. Owen P. White, *Lead and Likker,* 36; Leon C. Metz, *Turning Points in El Paso, Texas,* 46.

44. Utley, *Lone Star Justice*: "Under Charles Howard's provocation, the movement cascaded into a revolt that Cardis could not contain and that Borajo did not wish to contain," 206.

45. Cool, *Salt Warriors*, 196: "All three corpses were mutilated and dumped into a well." Sonnichsen, *The El Paso Salt War* asserts on page 50: "When night came a wave of mobsmen stormed Ellis's place and killed Captain Garcia's son Miguel." Cool resourcefully corrects: "Miguel [Garcia] was apparently so seriously wounded that virtually all accounts misidentified him as one of the dead," 182. A review of the Muster Roll, Detachment of Company C, Frontier Battalion, archived at TSA is precise, revealing that Garcia "Discharged January 8, 1878" which clearly is subsequent to his reported demise as carried in the December 21, 1877 editon of the *Mesilla Valley Independent*. Unquestionably, there is possibility that wounds he suffered could have somehow later contributed to his death, but he would not have been a Tay's Ranger at that time. Correspondingly, Miguel Garcia is not—as far as this author can determine—listed on memorials particularizing law enforcers and/or Texas Rangers killed in the line of duty. Paul Cool also adroitly reports: "The Texas Rangers and their companions reportedly killed between five and fifteen Paseños and wounded as many as forty to fifty more. They themselves had lost two dead (Sergeants Mortimer and McBride) and at least five wounded (Price Cooper, John Eldridge, Miguel Garcia, the last probably seriously, Corporal Mathews, slightly, and Captain Garcia)," 197.

46. Robert J. Casey, *The Texas Border: And Some Borderliners*, 149-150: "Other 'foreigners,' which is to say Americans, were driven out of town and their homes looted. . . . the looters carted $30,000 worth of property of Americans and other foreigners across the river [Rio Grande] in forty-eight hours." Utley, *Lone Star Justice*, 197: "In fact, sensing not only a chance for revenge on the hated gringo [Howard] but for plunder as well, Mexicans had converged on San Elizario from both sides of the border, swelling the throng to more than five hundred." Cool, *Salt Warriors*, 169: "Those who sought adventure, plunder, or a chance to redress grievances against Americans now saw their opportunity in San Elizario." And, "The new recruits included outsiders set on plundering. . . . . Would looters leave anything behind?" 179. Also, "Meanwhile, chaos reigned in San Elizario. Some insurgents or hangers-on degenerated into a looting mob," 199.

47. Utley, *Lone Star Justice,* 197: "Except for the passions generated by the war furor, they came mainly for loot." Frederick Wilkins, *the Law Comes to Texas: The Texas Rangers, 1870—1901*, 142: "The mob was looting Atkinson's store and house even before the bodies had been dragged away. They took everything, clothing, jewelry, furniture, bedding." Mike Cox, *The Texas Rangers: Wearing the Cinco Peso, 1821-1900*: "Some saw it as time to avenge the murder of Cardis and reassert their right to the salt. Others simply took it as an opportunity for looting. The crowd soon grew murderous." See page 286. Cool, *Salt Warriors*, somewhat unproductively it may be argued, seems to be

awarding a free pass for clear-cut criminality, based solely on ethnicity: "In the days after Howard's execution, 'wagon load after wagon load of plunder was hauled away from town to the opposite side of the river [Rio Grande],'" 205. And, "Neither the insurgent soldiers nor their leaders can be blamed for the looting of the Anglo stores," 209. Without a doubt, were one an Anglo storeowner or homeowner at the times, one might wish to argue any political correctness of outright stealing—no matter the lameness of excuses. And, again, it's relevant to remind the reader that the vast, vast majority of *Mexicanos* voluntarily and smartly and honorably chose not to participate in any acts of thievery and murder—whatsoever!

48. *Galveston Daily News*, January 6, 1878.
49. Sonnichsen, *The El Paso Salt War*, 42.
50. Cool, *Salt Warriors*, 191: "Whatever the passion for their cause, ordinary Paseños cannot all have viewed the pillaging in their towns as a good thing. They understood that victory would be followed by more looting. Their leaders could promise victory but could not guarantee order."
51. Metz, *The Shooters*, 230. "It is a story of well-intentioned men on all sides who gave way to misguided prejudice." Andrés Tijerina in his contribution, "Foreigners in Their Native Land: The Violent Struggle between Anglos and Tejanos for Land Titles in South Texas during Reconstruction," as published in *Still the Arena of Civil War: Violence and Turmoil in Reconstruction Texas, 1865-1874*, Kenneth W. Howell, ed., impotently posits the 1877-1878 turmoil at El Paso (post Reconstruction) had evil premeditated ethnocentric ambitions: "Moreover, the Salt War appears to have all the markers of the ethnic cleansing seen in the other major raids of the 1870s—the raids, mass murders, systematic rape, and the same callous dehumanization of Tejanos." See page 322. If one were to actually subscribe to a theory of ethnic cleansing in this case, taking into consideration the totally lopsided *Mexicano* population numbers in El Paso County, the laying siege to legitimate Texas Rangers and others, the admitted duplicity of the mob's spokesmen, the extralegal executions and bloody mutilations, coupled with the acknowledged looting of stores and homes and rioting, it would seem most logical to ask: "Just who was trying to ethnically cleanse who?" Paul Cool, author of the most comprehensive and scholarly treatment of the subject thus far, *Salt Warriors*, is not at all vague: "Others were more bloody-minded. For them, Howard's death was but a step along the path to cleansing the county of *gringos*." See page 168. Utley, *Lone Star Justice*, 200: "Unsated by the executions, the crowd cried for death to all the gringos, which meant the Rangers." Perhaps, C. L. "Doc" Sonnichsen in the little tome about this truly irrational conflict hits closer to home, bringing readers back to real world reality: "The Salt War, like all wars, was

wasteful and unnecessary, unless to prove to a pessimist that men can die bravely in a bad cause." See page 61.

52. Alexander, "Tucker X Texas = Trouble!" 5-16. The hard fact that Dan Tucker was nominally in command—not a big plus in one's résumé—of the Silver City Rangers is drawn from a multitude of primary sources. One would be the newspaper article in Silver City's *Grant County Herald* of Saturday, January 5, 1878: "D. Tucker has been chosen captain of the Silver City Company now in El Paso county." A second relevant citation would be John Kinney's actual discharge paper from the New Mexico Territory posse ostensibly carrying the color of Texas law. The document is quoted and displayed in its entirety in Nolan's "'Boss Rustler' The Lives and Crime of John Kinney," Part I. "This is to certify that John Kinney, a private of Lt. Tucker's Company of Volunteers of State forces is hereby honorably discharged from the service of the State . . . . [Signed Sheriff Charles Kerber, dated February 10, 1878.]" Page 15.

53. Sonnichsen, *The El Paso Salt War*, 48.

54. Ward, "The Salt War of San Elizaro (1877)," 122; Cool, *Salt Warriors*, in writing on page 214 of New Mexicans answering Sheriff Kerber's plea for help, pens: "At this writing, no roster has come to light, though evidence indicates one existed." Although he does not explicitly identify the "evidence" by source or type, clearly the author is referencing the undeniably scandalous crowd from the Silver City area, fellows like Dan Tucker and John Kinney. However, not all of the volunteers opting to lend a hand were dubious characters and, perhaps, Keleher in *Violence In Lincoln County* is alluding to the mysterious roster: "Anxious to get into the fight, the Grant County Light Brigade was mobilized in Silver City, hurried to Mesilla and El Paso, but failed to reach San Elizario before the fighting had subsided. The brigade, made up of officers, included Brig. Gen. Dan Corcoran, Col. Americus Hall, Lt. Col. Alex Mitchell, Major Daniel Keho, Capt. Edward Deadwater, First Lt. Paul W. Keaton, Second Lt. George Cassidy, First Sgt. Frank Mullins, and Master of Transportation, J. M. Williams," 157. ¿Quién sabe?

55. *Galveston Daily News*, December 26, 1877.

56. *Grant County Herald*, January 26, 1878.

57. Rasch, "John Kinney 'King of Rustlers' Was for Law, Too," 16; Cool, in "Salt War Sherriff: El Paso's Charles Kerber" confirms that post the frenzied rioting and subsequent run amok retaliation: "Among other Lincoln and Dona Ana County bad men to hang about El Paso was John Kinney, who opened up a saloon in Franklin, the Oriental." See page 30. For *Salt Warriors*, which Cool published subsequent to the article, he identifies Kinney's saloon as the Exchange, a location the author characterizes as "a social and business center for the criminals . . ." 264.

58. Thrapp, *Encyclopedia of Frontier Biography,* Vol. 2, 786.

59. *El Paso Times,* June 25, 1916.

60. Rasch, "John Kinney 'King of Rustlers' Was for Law, Too," 16; Cool, "Salt War Sheriff: El Paso's Charles Kerber" reports the last name of Kinney's six-shooting adversary as Haytema. See page 30; nearly all accounts are in agreement: the fellow was nicknamed "Buckskin Joe."

61. Cool, *Salt Warriors,* 288.

62. Alexander, *Desert Despradoes,* 124-125; Paul Cool, "Bob Martin: Rustler in Paradise." *Western Outlaw-Lawman History Association Journal,* Winter 2003 and Paul Cool, "El Paso's First Real Lawan, Texas Ranger Mark Ludwick," *National Outlaw/Lawman History Association Quarterly,* July-September 2001.

63. Lieutenant J. A. Tays to Major J. B. Jones, November 6, 1878, TSA: "I sent a strong detachment to Franklin as I had a report that an attempt would be made by a party headed by Kenny [*sic*] to run the Election there own way and when Sgt. Ludwick arrived in town they made demonstration against him & his men but on finding him firm they cooled down."

64. Of course, as thus far presented and as will be yet reported, there is no dearth of material highlighting the criminal career of John Kinney, however, for the short timeframe that the rascal spent in El Paso post the so-called Salt War mess, the most comprehensive coverage may be found in Paul Cool's *Salt Warriors,* citations throughout. Unfortunately, because it leaves a thoroughly false impression that John Kinney actually had the overwhelming support of El Paso County's Anglo electorate, Andrés Tijerina for his contribution in *Still the Arena of Civil War,* Kenneth W. Howell, ed., profess but cannot entirely sustain: "After the so-called Salt War was over, the Tejano villages were left 'deserted' and their crops and ranches abandoned. Kinney, on the other hand, became saloonkeeper and later sheriff of El Paso, reportedly allowing his men to continue raids and use his saloon as an exchange house for stolen property." See page 322. Lieutenant James A. Tays in a letter to Major John B. Jones in TSA, dated 16 November 1878, is more than empathically clear, although overlooking his observations may be convenient within agenda-driven regurgitations: "This may be the case and if so the case is no worse than it has been for the last six months as the retiring Sheriff [Kerber] has not made the least attempt at arrest since Electioneering began[.] This is the reason the Americans have not supported him in this Contest." Also, Bryan Callaghan notified Major John B. Jones in a letter dated December 9, 1878: "Mr. Kerber is a good man but his acts of late have made him very unpopular—the Mexican people are unanimously against him and he is very much disliked by great many of the Americans. Kerber committed grievous blunders in the discharge of his official duties. . . ." Letter in TSA. John Kinney was

never sheriff of El Paso County and, in fact, his ally Sheriff Charles Kerber lost his next election to a *Mexicano*. Also, Tise, *Texas County Sheriffs*, 172-173. And, too, it must not be understated—nor overstated—at least a partial "desertion" of villages and "abandonment" of agricultural pursuits was because not just a few *Mexicanos* jumped to the other side of the border, sneakily avoiding the very real possibilities of criminal indictments and/or legal extradition for their participation in the earlier illicit rampage. Judge Allen Blacker messaged Major Jones on 5 September 1878 that much of the "Mexican population fled from the towns of San Elizario, and most of them left Socorro and Ysleta. These were in no wise, that is Known, connected with the mob. It is said, by those who ought to Know, they left through fear." Letter in TSA. Alas—and it's probably a blend of both—that "fear" was induced in the minds of those *Mexicanos* that chose not to participate in the rampage, as retribution from the rioters and looters who had on the one hand. On the other, they no doubt were in "fear" of wrought-up Texas Rangers and "Americans" seeking their own brand of revenge.

65. Philip J. Rasch, *Warriors of Lincoln County*, Robert K. DeArment, ed., 160-161. Also see, Frederick Nolan, *The Lincoln County War: A Documentary History*, 478-479; Nolan, in "'Boss Rustler' The Life and Crimes of John Kinney" reproduces a copy of John Kinney's deputation by Sheriff Peppin: "This is to certify that I have summoned John Kinney, as one of my Posse to assist in quelling the Riots in Lincoln Co." See page 18.

66. Susan E. [McSween] Barber to J. Evetts Haley, 16 August 1927 at White Oaks, New Mexico, HML&HC.

67. Frank Coe to J. Evetts Haley, 20 March 1827, San Patricio, New Mexico, HML&HC.

68. Yginio Salizar to J. Evetts Haley, 17 August 1927, Lincoln, New Mexico. HML&HC; Bob Boze Bell "Left For Dead: Yginio Salazar vs Peppin's Thugs." *True West*. July 2013. 46-47; Also see George W. Coe *Frontier Fighter*, 125-128.

69. Numerous are the secondary sources reflecting John Kinney's theatrics on the Lincoln County stage during the Five-Days Battle. The reader may wish to brush up with Nolan's *The Lincoln County War: A Documentary History*; John P. Wilson's *Merchants, Guns and Money: The Story of Lincoln County and Its Wars*; T. Dudley Cramer, *The Pecos Ranchers in the Lincoln County War*; Joel Jacobsen, *Such Men as Billy the Kid: The Lincoln County War Reconsidered*; Maurice G. Fulton, *History of the Lincoln County War: A Classic Account of Billy the Kid;* Robert N. Mullin, ed; Mark Lee Gardner, *To Hell on a Fast Horse: Billy the Kid, Pat Garrett, and the Epic Chase to Justice in the Old West*; Robert M. Utley, *Billy the Kid: A Short and Violent Life*; Kathleen P. Chamberlain *In the Shadow of Billy the Kid: Susan*

McSween and the Lincoln County War; Keleher, *Violence in Lincoln County*; and Rash, *Warriors of Lincoln County*.

70. Lieutenant J. A. Tays to Major J. B. Jones, September 16, 1878, TSA.

71. Lieutenant J. A. Tays to Major J. B. Jones, September 30, 1878, TSA.

72. Monthly Return, Company C, El Paso Detachment, September 1878, TSA.

73. Lieutenant J. A. Tays to Major John B. Jones, October 17, 1878, TSA; Monthly Return, Company C, El Paso Detachment, October 1878, TSA: "H. Crist Killed by Accidental discharge of a Pistol, Oct. 13th 1878." Regrettably on the author's part, the death of Texas Ranger Henry Crist was not mentioned in *Riding Lucifer's Line: Deaths along the Texas-Mexico Border*. The omission was not due to excluding the death because it didn't meet preprogrammed criteria for inclusion—it may not have—but in candor the author was completely unawares of this terrible tragedy, an oversight—pure and simple—no whining, no excuses. Likewise, Texas Ranger Private Crist's name is not listed in any of the books and other published sources—there are not just a few—in possession of this writer which particularly identify peace officers killed in the line of duty, purposefully or accidentally. Ranger Crist, at the bare minimum, deserves honorable mention: He was a full-fledged Texas Ranger, on duty, where he was supposed to be and doing what he was supposed to be doing. His sacrifice should not be overlooked, devalued, or disregarded.

74. Rasch, "John Kinney: King of the Rustlers," 11.

75. Alexander, *Lawmen, Outlaws, and S.O.Bs*, Vol. 2, 214-215.

76. Nolan, *The Lincoln County War: A Documentary History*, 415.

77. From time to time it's written that John Kinney was present at the time of Kid Antrim's death in Pete Maxwell's house at Fort Sumner, New Mexico Territory. In part the confusion may be credited to spur-of-the-moment guesswork, rushed research and, unfortunately, an ambiguous early day newspaper citation. The Prescott *Weekly Journal Miner* [August 29, 1919] somewhat confusingly reported, in part: "His [John Kinney's] exploits in bandit fields are best known and shown by the five bullet wounds in his body, and his sagacity in running down Billy the Kid closed a criminal wave in New Mexico of death and destruction without parallel in border lawlessness." Moreover phonetic confusion, too, sometimes raises its ugly head. The three New Mexico Territory lawmen at Fort Sumner when Billy the Kid was killed were Patrick Floyd "Pat" Garrett, John William Poe, and Thomas Christopher "Kip" McKinney—not John Kinney. Adding to the muddle Keleher in *Violence in Lincoln County* identifies the third deputy as "T.L. 'Tip' McKinney" but, either way, it was not the subject of this vignette, mobster John Kinney.

78. Alexander, *Desert Desperadoes*, 198.

79. Ibid. 210; His greed is echoed in Kinney to Ketring, April 3, 1973: "always telegraphing home for money."
80. Alexander, *Sheriff Harvey Whitehill,* 159.
81. Philip J. Rasch, "The Rustler War" *New Mexico Historical Review,* October 1964, 259.
82. Gordon R. Owen, *The Two Alberts: Fountain and Fall,* 129; Nolan, "The Life and Crimes of John Kinney," 20-21.
83. Rasch, "John Kinney: King of the Rustlers," 11.
84. Susan E. [McSween] Barber to J. Evetts Haley, 16 August 1927. Although bragging of killing fourteen men, there is yet no reasonably sourced evidence to support such an assertion: That John Kinney would lie is not far-fetched.
85. *Rio Grande Republican,* February 17, 1883, as reported by A. M. Gibson, *The Life and Death of Colonel Albert Jennings Fountain,* 114; Bill Reynolds, *Trouble in New Mexico,* Vol. 3, 255.
86. Rasch, "John Kinney: King of the Rustlers," 11.
87. Emma M. Muir, "The First Milita," *New Mexico Magazine,* October 1952, 45.
88. Larry D. Ball, "Militia Posses: The Territorial Militia in Civil Law Enforcement in New Mexico Territory, 1877-1883," *New Mexico Historical Review,* January 1980, 54.
89. Frederick Nolan, "The Life and Crimes of John Kinney," Part 2, *True West,* October 1996, 13.
90. Santa Fe *Daily New Mexican,* February 17, 1883.
91. Rasch, "The Rustler War," 260.
92. *Silver City Enterprise,* October 1, 1886; Alexander, *Sheriff Harvey Whitehill,* 162.
93. Ball, "Militia Posses: The Territorial Militia in Civil Law Enforcement in New Mexico Territory, 1877-1883," 55.
94. Mullin, "Here Lies John Kinney," 235.
95. Gibson, *The Life and Death of Colonel Albert Jennings Fountain,* 116; F. Stanley, *The Lake Valley Story,* 10-12; Larry D. Ball, *Desert Lawmen: The High Sheriffs of New Mexico and Arizona, 1845-1912,* 357.
96. Alexander, *Desert Desperadoes,* 202-203.
97. Ibid.
98. George Wythe Baylor, Jerry D. Thompson, ed., *Into the Far Wild Country: True Tales of the Old Southwest,* 26.
99. Nolan, "The Life and Crimes of John Kinney," Part 2, 14.
100. Ibid.
101. Alexander, *Desert Desperadoes,* 204.
102. *Silver City Enterprise,* March 15, 1883.
103. Ibid., March 22, 1883. This was atypical—maybe? See, Kinney to Ketring, April 3, 1973: "He was unpredictable."
104. Santa Fe *Daily New Mexican,* May [?] 1883; Alexander, *Desert Desperadoes,* 205.

105. John Kinney's prison records courtesy Lewis A. Ketring Jr., via Kansas State Historical Society; Karen Holliday Tanner and John D. Tanner, Jr., *Directory of Inmates: New Mexico Territorial Penitentiary, 1884-1912*: "The [Prison] board formally accepted the completed [New Mexico Territorial] prison on August 17 [1885]. . . .Four days later, Governor Edmund G. Ross proclaimed the penitentiary open. . . ." viii.

106. El Paso *Lone Star*, April 25, 1883; Records reveal Kinney told prison officials his trade was that of a "butcher."

107. Owen, *The Two Alberts*, 135-139; Robert K. DeArment, *Jim Courtright of Fort Worth: His Life and Legend*, 125: "In response to the complaints that the actions of his militia had been cold-blooded and cruel. . . ."

108. Prison Records as cited from Lewis A. Kentring, Jr.; Nolan, "The Life and Crimes of John Kinney," Part 2, 16-17.

109. Ibid., 18-19; Philip J. Rasch, "Kinney, King of the Rustlers Loses Crown When Caught at Lake Valley," *The Southwesterner*, November 1962, 17; Mullins, "Here Lies John Kinney," 240.

Chapter 11

1. Gregory Michno, *The Settlers War: The Struggle for the Texas Frontier in the 1860s*, "The winter of 1868 was one of the worst seasons of raiding in Texas history," 346.

2. Putman, *Navarro County History*, 180-181. The Hanks are listed as one of the families of "prominence."

3. Clark C. Spence, "The Livery Stable in the American West." *Montana Magazine*, Spring 1986. 36-49.

4. Biographical and genealogical information courtesy Navarro County Sheriff Leslie Cotten.

5. Ibid.; U.S. Census, 1900 and 1910, Navarro County, Texas.

6. Ibid.

7. The seminal work on Jesse Rascoe is found in Robert K. DeArment's *Deadly Dozen: Forgotten Gunfighters of the Old West*. Vol. II. 127-140; Tise, *Texas County Sheriffs*, 389.

8. Ibid.; Cecil Bonney, *Looking Over My Shoulder: Seventy-five Years in the Pecos Valley*, 24: "Another Roswell law officer whom I well remember was J. J. Rascoe . . . . he always rode a very fine sorrel horse. He had scabbards strapped to either side of his saddle. In one he carried a sawed-off double barreled 12-gauge shotgun; in the other he had a Winchester .30-30 repeating rifle. . . . Around his waist he wore a cartridge belt, always completely filled. On his left hip, because his right arm was missing, he wore a regulation double-action Colt .45."

9. Ronald G. DeLord to Sheriff Leslie Cotten, January 31, 2005.

10. *Corsicana Observer*, December 10, 1870.

11. *Corsicana Observer*, July 29, 1871.

12. Caldwell and DeLord, *Texas Lawmen: The Good and the Bad*, 67.

13. Caldwell and DeLord, *Texas Lawmen: More of the Good and the Bad*, 89-90.

14. *San Antonio Daily Light*, September 10, 1891; For a most interesting piece detailing the life and six-shooting adventures of Rufus Highnote, see E. E. Freeman, "A Mania for Killing." *Wild West History Association Journal*, October 2010, 34-42.

15. Navarro County Indictment #3627: *State of Texas vs. B.H. Davis, Murder*, Courtesy Sheriff Leslie Cotten.

16. Convict Record Ledger Data Transcription Form No. 34118: Boyd White, TSA.

17. Biographical and genealogical files courtesy Sheriff Cotten; U.S. Census, 1910, Navarro County, Texas.

18. Photographs of Hanks' non-lethal law enforcement paraphernalia courtesy Robert Haltom.

19. Caldwell and DeLord, *Texas Lawmen: More of the Good and the Bad*, 282.

20. *Corsicana Democrat and Truth*, June 27, 1912.

21. Written Murder Confession of Boyd White, June 29, 1912. Courtesy Sheriff Cotten.

22. *Dallas Morning News*, June 27, 1912.

23. Interview with Robert Haltom by author, January 30, 2013.

24. Murder Confession of Boyd White, June 29, 1912.

25. Indictment. Navarro County Criminal Case #8188. Boyd Whtie: Murder.

26. Capias Warrant: Cause #8188, Boyd White: Murder.

27. Instructions to the Jury, Navarro County Criminal Case #8188. Boyd White: Murder.

28. Return of Verdict. Navarro County Criminal Case #8188. Boyd White: Murder.

29. Conduct Register Transcription Form. Boyd White, Inmate #34118, TSA.

30. Ibid.

31. Ibid. By act of the Board of Prison Commisioners Boyd White had his "lost time" due to behavioral problems restored on July 21, 1924, and a letter to that effect "filed with papers."

32. Proclamation of Pardon, Boyd White, January 17, 1927, TSA.

Chapter 12

1. Alexander, *Rawhide Ranger, Ira Aten*, 13.

2. Unpublished typescript of Virginia [Kimmons] Abbott, dated April 1, 1961 and titled "My Autobiography," 1. Courtesy Betty Aten, Austin, Texas and enlightening interviews with descendant Bruce Archer, Dallas, Texas.

3. Stephens, *Texas Ranger Sketches*, 16-18.

4. Austin Ira Aten to Calvin Grant Aten, June 28,1890; Alexander, *Rawhide Ranger, Ira Aten,* 238.
5. Castro County Historical Commission, *Castro County, Texas, 1891-1981,* Vol. 1, 32.
6. Stephens, *Texas Ranger Sketches.* "It soon became apparent to all that life on the family farm was neither to his liking nor suited to his temperament. Because of what has been called a 'wild streak'. . . ." 18.
7. The possibility—and likelihood—that this alleged shooting incident was transposed to a bona fide gunplay of Eddie Aten's though recitations of oral history is discussed in Alexander' *Rawhide Ranger, Ira Aten* 399 n. 61.
8. Particular details of this gunfight may be gleaned from several sources, including but not limited to Alexander's *Rawhide Ranger, Ira Aten* 243-257; Mark Boardman's "Ira Nails the McClellands," *True West,* July 2009. 52-53; Castro County Historical Commission, *History of Castro County, 1889-1989,* Vol. 1, 29; and the first person account of Ira Aten as contained in the 1928 interview of Ira Aten by J. Evetts Haley. Hereafter Aten-1928. HML&HC.
9. Gournay, *Texas Boundaries,* 108.; Monthly Return, Company D, Frontier Battalion, TSA: ". . . . Left Camp Cleveland, Buchel Co. under orders. . . ."
10. Alexander, *Winchester Warriors,* 259.
11. Monthly Return, Company D, Frontier Battalion, September 1892, TSA.
12. Telegram. Sergeant D. L. Musgrave, Company F, Frontier Battalion, to AG Mabry, July 22, 1893, TSA.
13. DuCoin, *Lawmen on the Texas Frontier: Ranges and Sheriffs,* 124.
14. Ibid.
15. George W. Baylor to AG Mabry, February 15, 1893, TSA.
16. Sheriff Frank B. Simmons to AG Mabry, February 1, 1893, TSA; Petition of El Paso County Grand Jury, January 31, 1893, TSA.
17. Captain Jones to AG Mabry, January 25, 1893, TSA.
18. Monthly Return, Company D, Frontier Battalion, June 1893, TSA.
19. George Wythe Baylor, *Into the Far, Wild Country: True Tales of the Old Southwest,* 30.
20. George Baylor to AG Mabry, July 9, 1893, TSA; Chuck Parsons, *Captain John R. Hughes: Lone Star Ranger,* 82.
21. Captain John R. Hughes to AG Mabry, September 4, 1893, TSA.
22. Captain Hughes to AG Mabry, September 6, 1893, TSA.
23. Ibid. "Assault was made on R. E. Bryant who was at that time a deputy sheriff of El Paso county and was performing his duty by trying to arrest Severo Olguin for theft of Cattle. Docket No. of said cause is No. 1463," TSA. Also, George Baylor to AG Mabry, July 9, 1893, TSA.
24. Captain Hughes to AG Mabry, September 4, 1893, TSA.
25. Parsons, *Captain John R. Hughes,* 82.

26. Monthly Return, Company D, Frontier Battalion, June 1893, TSA; Captain John R. Hughes to AG Mabry, March 13, 1895, TSA: "In regard to R.E. Bryant being a Deputy Sheriff. . . . . He was a Deputy when I took the company. Holding the Deputy commission does not interfere with his duties as a ranger and is a great help to the Sheriff as there is not another man outside of the ranger company that is fitted to do the civil work in this valley. It was always my understanding that there was no objection to a Ranger holding a Deputy Sheriff or Dept. U.S. Marshal com. but was only objected to on account of collecting double fees from the state."

27. Ibid.

28. Parsons, *Captain John R. Hughes,* 82.

29. Captain Hughes to AG Mabry, September 6, 1893, TSA.

30. George Baylor to AG Mabry, July 9, 1893, TSA.

31. Ibid.; *San Antonio Daily Express*, July 1, 1893.

32. Monthly Return, Company D, Frontier Battalion, June 1893, TSA. The quotation of Captain Jones is taken directly from the MR.

33. Corporal Carl Kirchner to AG Mabry, July 2, 1893, TSA.

34. El Paso County Sheriff Frank B. Simmons to Texas Governor J. S. Hogg, July 7, 1893, TSA.

35. Governor Hogg to AG Mabry, August 22, 1893, TSA.

36. Captain Hughes to AG Mabry, September 6, 1893, TSA.

37. Special Ranger Ernest St. Leon to AG Mabry, July 1, 1893, TSA.

38. Alexander, *Winchester Warriors,* 266-269; Alexander, *Riding Lucifer's Line: Ranger Deaths Along the Texas-Mexico Border.*

39. Captain Hughes to AG Mabry, August 25, 1893, TSA; Alexander, *Winchester Warriors,* 269-270; Monthly Return, Company D, Frontier Battalion, August 1893, TSA; For an all-embracing look at lawman Scarborough the reader is referred to the brilliant treatment by Robert K. DeArment, *George Scarborough: The Life and Death of a Lawman on the Closing Frontier.*

40. Captain Hughes to AG Mabry, February 8, 1895, TSA.

41. Monthly Return, Company D, Frontier Battalion, October 1893, TSA.

42. Captain Hughes to AG Mabry, December 1, 9, and 31, 1893, TSA; Alexander, *Winchester Warriors,* 271; Monthly Return, Company D, Frontier Battalion, December 1893, TSA.

43. Alexander, *Riding Lucifer's Line,* 139-145; Stephens, *Bullets and Buckshot in Texas*, 45.

44. Monthly Return, Company D, Frontier Battalion, June 30, 1894, TSA.

45. Ibid.

46. Monthly Return, Company D, Frontier Battalion, July 1894, TSA.

47. Spellman, *Captain J. A. Brooks: Texas Ranger,* 83; Alexander, *Winchester Warriors,* 277-278; Monthly Return, Company D, Frontier Battalion, July 1894, TSA: "Corpl. Aten and three men started to Temple on account of strike on rail road. . . ."

48. Monthly Return, Company D, Frontier Battalion, July 1894, TSA.
49. Stephens, *Texas Ranger Sketches,* 19.
50. Monthly Return, Company D, Frontier Battalion, August 1894, TSA.
51. Lucy Miller Jacobson and Mildred Bloys Nored, *Jeff Davis County, Texas,* 162-163.
52. Alexander, *Lawmen, Outlaws, and S.O.Bs,* 178; Monthly Return, Company D, Frontier Battalion, March and April 1895, TSA.
53. Captain Hughes to AG Mabry, July 25, 1895, TSA; Monthly Return, Company D, Frontier Battalion, July 1895, TSA.
54. Harold Weiss, Jr., "The Texas Rangers Revisited: Old Themes and New Viewpoints." *Southwestern Historical Quarterly,* April 1994, 640.
55. Jack Skiles, *Judge Roy Bean Country,* 31.
56. Leo N. Miletich, *Dan Stuart's Fistic Carnival,* 59.
57. Captain Hughes to AG Mabry, January 21, 1896, TSA; Weiss, *Yours to Command,* 118.
58. Robert K. DeArment, *Broadway Bat: Gunfighter in Gotham, The New York City Years of Bat Masterson,* 26: "A force of Mexican Rurales patrolled the south side of the Rio Grande to see that Stuart did not stage this fight in Juarez. To block the promoter from moving the affair over the line into New Mexico Territory, Congress rushed through a measure prohibiting prizefighting in any United States territory, and deputy U.S. marshals poured into El Paso to enforce the law."
59. Captain Hughes to AG Mabry, January 22, 1896, TSA.
60. Weiss, *Yours to Command,* 114; AG Mabry would later remark in a report to Lieutenant Governor George T. Jester, "I had a close and constant espionage placed, not only on the principals, but also on the passenger depot and the cars loaded with paraphernalia of the ring, with instructions to follow the latter to wherever hauled." See, Albert Bigelow Paine's *Captain Bill McDonald: Texas Ranger: A Story of Frontier Reform,* Appendix A, 400.
61. Captain Hughes to AG Mabry, January 12, 1896, TSA.
62. Telegram, Governor C. A. Culberson, Austin, to AG Mabry, El Paso, February 12, 1896, TSA.
63. C. L. Sonnichsen *The Story of Roy Bean: Law West of the Pecos,* 186.
64. Miletich, *Dan Stuart's Fistic Carnival,* 173; Robert Julyan, *The Place Names of New Mexico,* 343; Robinson, *The Men Who Wear The Star: The Story of the Texas Rangers,* 260.
65. Monthly Return, Company D, Frontier Battalion, February 1896, TSA: "Sergt. Aten made Scout from El Paso to Langtry to investigate arrangements made by Prizefighters—out 3 days, travelled 600 miles."
66. Miletich, *Dan Stuart's Fistic Carnival,* 171; Sonnichsen, *The Story of Roy Bean,* 186.
67. DeArment, *Broadway Bat: Gunfighter in Gotham.*20; Skiles, *Judge Roy Bean Country,* 32.
68. Miletich, *Dan Stuart's Fistic Carnival,* 186,

69. Ibid. 173; David Haynes, *Catching Shadows: A Directory of 19th Century Texas Photographers,* 18.
70. Alexander, *Winchester Warriors,* 289.
71. Weiss, *Yours to Command,* 118.
72. Captain Hughes to AG Mabry, March 15 and March [?], 1896. The incompletely dated letter says in part: "I will send Sergt. Aten with detachment from Alpine to Pecos. They will arrive at Pecos about March 20th. I have given Sergt. Aten full instructions. . . ." Letter found in TSA.
73. Captain Hughes to AG Mabry, July 27, 1896 and August 12, 1896, TSA.
74. Clayton W. Williams, ed., *Texas' Last Frontier: Fort Stockton and the Trans-Pecos, 1861-1895,* 396-397; Ellis Lindsey and Gene Riggs, *Barney K. Riggs: The Yuma and Pecos Avenger,* 176-182.
75. Monthly Return, Company D, Frontier Battalion, October 1896, TSA; Bill C. James, *Barney Riggs: A West Texas Gunman.* On pages 14-15, the author states Barney Riggs came clear of the killings after a jury returned a not guilty verdict.
76. Monthly Return, Company D, Frontier Battalion, November 1896, TSA.
77. Captain Hughes to AG Mabry, December 21, 1896, TSA.
78. Captain Hughes to Quartermaster W. H. Owen, January 17, 1897, TSA.
79. Captain Hughes to P. S. Elkins, January 17, 1897, TSA.
80. Captain Hughes to Quartermaster Owen, January 20, 1897, TSA. For an interesting and seldom cited account of one of Jim Miller's foiled murder attempts, see *Land of the High Sky: Stories Along the Rio Pecos* by John H. Wilson, as told to Sue Wilson, pages 6-7.
81. Captain Hughes to Quartermaster Owen, February 10, 1897, TSA; Monthly Return, Company D, Frontier Battalion. February 1897, TSA.
82. Monthly Return, Company D, Frontier Battalion, March 1897, TSA.
83. Ibid.
84. Stephens, *Texas Ranger Sketches,* 19.
85. Monthly Returns, Company D, Frontier Battalion, June, July, August, September, and October 1897, TSA.
86. Captain Hughes to AG Mabry, February 28, 1898, TSA; Monthly Return, Company D, Frontier Battalion, March 1898, TSA; Captain Hughes to Adjutant General A. P. Wozencraft, September 9, 1898, TSA.
87. Monthly Return, Company D, Frontier Battalion, May 1898, TSA.
88. Monthly Return, Company D, Frontier Battalion, July 1898, TSA.
89. Captain Hughes to AG Wozencraft, July 11, 1898, TSA.
90. Stephens, *Texas Ranger Sketches,* 19.
91. Clifford Alan Perkins, an old-time border patrolman confirmed in *Border Patrol: With the U.S. Immigration Service on the Mexican Boundary, 1910-1954,* 42: "If a smuggler was killed at night and fell in the river, we forgot about the body unless it showed up downstream on the American side."

92. Captain Hughes to Adjutant General Thomas Scurry, April 13, 1901, TSA: "I expect to enlist E. D. Aten to fill one of the places. Aten is an old Ranger of Co. D." Hughes to Scurry, April 17, 1901: "I have enlisted E.D. Aten and enclose you his oath of office," TSA; Monthly Return, Company D, Frontier Battalion, April 1901, TSA.

93. Captain Hughes to AG Scurry, May 4, 1898, TSA.

94. Description and Valuation of Horses of Co. "D" Rangers, July 11, 1901, TSA.

95. Monthly Return, Company D, Frontier Battalion, June 1901, TSA.

96. For an abridgement explaining demise of the Frontier Battalion and creation of its replacement, see Alexander's Part II Introduction "The Ranger Force Era, 1901-1935" as spelled out in *Riding Lucifer's Line*. Also, Weiss, *Yours to Command*, 199-211.

97. Monthly Return, Company D, Ranger Force, November 1901, TSA.

98. Stephens, *Texas Ranger Sketches,* 20. During an October 3, 2012, interview by author with Mr. Stephens he reported that in the early 1970s during the research phase for *Texas Ranger Sketches* he had the pleasure of exchanging written correspondence and conducting telephone interviews with Eddie Aten's widow, Gertrude Backus Aten. The spelling "Bacus" in *Sketches* is typographical error. Mr. Stephens also reported that Eddie Aten's rifle of choice was an 1886 Winchester and his six-shooter was a Colt's .45 caliber.

99. Stephens, *Texas Ranger Sketches*, 19.

100. Ibid., 20.

101. Bruce A. Glasrud and Harold J. Weiss, Jr., eds. *Tracking the Texas Rangers: The Nineteenth Century*, James M. Day, "Rangers of the Last Frontier of Texas," 278-279; Parsons, *Captain John R. Hughes*, 240.

102. Donald M. Yena, "Texas Authority in Metal: Badges, History and Related Artifacts," *The Texas Gun Collector*, Spring 2008, 5; also, interview by author with Mr. Yena on October 4, 2012.

103. The 1936 trip to Texas is primary sourced through a delightful series of letters Ira penned while on the trip, as well as period photographs. Frank Jones' pocket watch is now a part of the Donald M. and Louise Yena collection, San Antonio, Texas. As of this writing (August 2013) the watch, along with Frank Jones' Winchester and Frontier Battalion era gold badge, are on extended display at the Texas Ranger Hall of Fame and Museum, Waco, Texas, courtesy Donald and Louise Yena.

104. Stephens, *Texas Ranger Sketches,* 20; unidentified Round Rock, Texas, newspaper clip February 5, 1953.

Bibliography

Non-published sources—manuscripts, typescripts, theses, dissertations, tape recordings, official documents, courthouse records, tax rolls, petitions, correspondence, prison records, census records, licensing records, interviews, etc.—are cited with specificity in chapter endnotes.

Books

Aleshire, Peter. *The Fox and the Whirlwind: General George Crook and Geronimo—A Paired Biography*. New York, NY: John Wiley and Sons, 2000.

Alexander, Bob. *Riding Lucifer's Line: Ranger Deaths Along the Texas-Mexico Border*. Denton: University of North Texas Press, 2013.

———. *Rawhide Ranger, Ira Aten: Enforcing Law on the Texas Frontier*. Denton: University of North Texas Press, 2011.

———. *Winchester Warriors: Texas Rangers of Company D, 1874-1901*. Denton: University of North Texas Press, 2009.

———. *Lawmen, Outlaws, and S.O.Bs*. Silver City, NM: High-Lonesome Books, 2004.

———. *Lawmen, Outlaws, and S.O.Bs*. Volume II. Silver City, NM: High-Lonesome Books, 2007.

———. *Desert Desperadoes: The Banditti of Southwestern New Mexico*. Silver City, NM: Gila Books, 2006.

———. *Sheriff Harvey Whitehill: Silver City Stalwart*. Silver City, NM: High-Lonesome Books, 2005.

———. *Dangerous Dan Tucker: New Mexico's Deadly Lawman*. Silver City, NM: High-Lonesome Books, 2001.

———. *Six-Guns and Single-Jacks: A History of Silver City and Southwestern New Mexico*. Silver City, NM: Gila Books, 2005.

Almond, Phyllis Whitt, and Sarah Oatman Franklin. *Cobwebs and Cornerstones*. Kerrville, TX: A Bi-Centennial Project of the Junior Women's Culture Club, 1976.

Altshuler, Constance Wynn. *Cavalry Yellow and Infantry Blue: Army Officers in Arizona Between 1851 and 1886*. Tucson, AZ: The Arizona Historical Society, 1991.

————. *Chains of Command: Arizona and the Army, 1856-1875*. Tucson: Arizona Historical Society, 1981.

Anson, Richard H. and Gerald D. Robin. *Introduction to the Criminal Justice System*. New York: Harper and Row Publishers, 1990.

Awbrey, Betty Dooley, and Claude Dooley. *Why Stop? A Guide to Texas Historical Roadside Markers*. Houston, TX: Lone Star Books, 1978.

Ball, Larry D. *Desert Lawmen: The High Sheriffs of New Mexico and Arizona, 1846-1912*. Albuquerque: University of New Mexico Press, 1992.

Barkley, Roy R., and Mark F. Odintz, eds. *The Portable Handbook of Texas*. Austin: Texas State Historical Association, 2000.

Barnes, Will C. *Arizona Place Names*. Tucson: University of Arizona Press, 1988.

Barry, James Buckner (James K. Greer, ed.) *Buck Barry: Texas Ranger and Frontiersman*. Lincoln: University of Nebraska Press, 1978.

Baylor, George Wythe (Jerry D. Thompson, ed.) *Into the Far, Wild Country: True Tales of the Old Southwest*. El Paso, TX: Texas Western Press, 1996.

Berg, Bruce L., and John J. Horgan. *Criminal Investigations*. New York: McGraw-Hill, 1974.

Blackburn, Ed Jr. *Wanted: Historic County Jails of Texas*. College Station: Texas A&M University Press, 2006.

Bohm, Robert M. and Keith N. Haley. *Introduction to Criminal Justice*. New York: McGraw-Hill, 2002.

Bonney, Cecil. *Looking Over My Shoulder: Seventy-five Years in the Pecos Valley*. Roswell, NM: Hall-Poorbaugh Press, Inc., 1971.

Bounds, Virginia J. and Imogene C. Barham. *Limestone County Texas Cemetery Survey*. Vol. 1. n.d. n.p.

Bowles, Flora G. *A History of Trinity County Texas, 1827 to 1928*. Groveton, TX: Trinity County Historical Commission, 2008.

Brisbin, James S. *The Beef Bonanza: or, How to Get Rich on the Plains*. Norman: University of Oklahoma, 1959.

Brice, Donaly, and Barry Crouch. *The Governor's Hounds: The Texas State Police, 1870-1873*. Austin: University of Texas Press, 2011.

————. *The Great Comanche Raid: Boldest Indian Attack of the Texas Republic*. Austin, TX: Eakin Press, 1987.

Broaddus, J. Morgan. *The Legal Heritage of El Paso*. El Paso, TX: Texas Western Press, 1963.

Brundidge, Glenna Fourman, ed. *Brazos County History: Rich Past, Bright Future*. Bryan, TX: Family History Foundation, 1986.

Bryan, Howard. *Robbers, Rogues and Ruffians: True Tales of the Wild West*. Santa Fe, NM: Clear Light Publishers, 1991.

Bullis, Don. *New Mexico's Finest: Police Officers Killed in the Line of Duty, 1847-2010*. Los Ranchos, NM: Rio Grande Books, 2010.

———. *Ellos Pasaron Por Aqui—99 New Mexicans . . . . And a Few Other Folks*. Chesterfield, MO: Science and Humanities Press, 2005.

———. *New Mexico Historical Biographies*. Los Ranchos, NM: Rio Grande Books, 2011.

Burns, Rollie (W.C. Holden, ed.) *Rollie Burns: Or, An Account of the Ranching Industry on the South Plains*. College Station: Texas A&M University Press, 1986.

Burroughs, Jean M., ed. *Roosevelt County History and Heritage*. Portales, NM: Bishop Printing Company, 1975.

Burrows, William E. *Vigilante!—The Story of Americans . . . . Then And Now . . . Guarding Each Other*. New York: Harcourt Brace Jovanovich, 1976.

Burton, Jeffrey. *Black Jack Christian: Outlaw*. Santa Fe, NM: Press of the Territorian, 1967.

———. *The Deadliest Outlaws: The Ketchum Gang and the Wild Bunch*. Denton,: The University of North Texas Press, 2009.

Cabeza de Baca, Fabiola. *We Fed Them Cactus*. Albuquerque: University of New Mexico Press, 1954.

Caldwell, Clifford R. and Ron DeLord. *Texas Lawmen: The Good and the Bad, 1835-1899*. Charleston, SC: The History Press, 2011.

———. and DeLord. *Texas Lawmen: More of the Good and the Bad, 1900-1940*. Charleston, SC: The History Press, 2012.

———. *An Anthology of Old West Tales: Selected Works of Clifford R. Caldwell*. Mountain Home, TX: Self published, 2012.

———. *Dead Right: The Lincoln County War*. Mountain Home, TX: Self published, 2008.

———. *Robert Kelsey Wylie: Forgotten Cattle King of Texas*. Mountain Home, TX: Self published, 2013.

Caperton, Thomas J. and Timothy Cohrs. *Fort Selden*. Santa Fe: Museum of New Mexico Press, 1993.

Carlson, Chip. *Tom Horn—Blood on the Moon: Dark History of the Murderous Cattle Detective*. Meeteese, WY: High Plains Press, 2001,

———. *Joe Lefors—"I slickered Tom Horn. . . ."* Cheyenne, WY: Beartooth Corral LLC, 1995.

———. *Tom Horn, "Killing Men is My Specialty."* Cheyenne, WY: Beartooth Corral LLC, 1991.

Carlson, Paul H. and Tom Crum. *Myth, Memory and Massacre: The Pease River Capture of Cynthia Ann Parker*. Lubbock: Texas Tech University Press, 2010.

Casey, Robert J. *The Texas Border: And Some Borderliners*. Indianapolis, IN: The Bobbs-Merrill Company, 1950.

Cashion, Ty. *A Texas Frontier: The Clear Fork Country and Fort Griffin, 1849-1887*. Norman: University of Oklahoma Press, 1996.

Castro County Historical Commission. *Castro County, Texas, 1891-1981*. Dallas, TX: Taylor Publishing, 1991.

Chamberlain, Kathleen P. *In The Shadow of Billy the Kid: Susan McSween and the Lincoln County War*. Albuquerque: Univesity of New Mexico Press, 2013.

Chaput, Don. *The Earp Papers: In a Brother's Image*. Encampment, WY: Affiliated Writers of America, 1994.

Chrisman, Harry E. *Lost Trails of the Cimarron*. Denver, CO: Sage Books, 1961.

Clayton, Lawrence, and Joan Halford Farmer, eds. *Tracks Along the Clear Fork: Stories From Shackelford and Throckmorton Counties*. Abilene, TX: McWhiney Foundation Press, 2000.

Coe, George W. *Frontier Fighter: The Autobiography of George W. Coe, Who Fought and Rode with Billy the Kid*. Albuquerque: University of New Mexico Press, 1951.

Conklin, John E. *Criminology*. Boston, MA: Allyn and Bacon, 1998.

Cool, Paul. *Salt Warriors: Insurgency on the Rio Grande*. College Station: Texas A&M University Press, 2008.

Cox, Mike. *The Texas Rangers: Wearing the Cinco Peso, 1821-1900*. New York, NY: Forge Books, 2008.

———. *Central Texas Tales*. Charleston, SC: History Press, 2012.

———. *Time of the Rangers: Texas Rangers From 1900 to the Present*. New York: Forge Books, 2009.

———. *Texas Ranger Tales: Stories That Need Telling*. Plano, TX: Republic of Texas Press, 1997.

Cox, Sr., Ross J. *The Texas Rangers and The San Saba Mob*. San Saba, TX: Self published, 2005.

Cramer, T. Dudley. *The Pecos Ranchers in the Lincoln County War*. Orinda, CA: Branding Iron Press, 1996.

Cunningham, Sharon and Mark Boardman, eds. *Revenge: And Other Tales of the Old West*. Lafayette, IN: Scarlet Mask Enterprises, 2004.

DeArment, Robert K. *Bravo of the Brazos: John Larn of Fort Griffin, Texas*. Norman: University of Oklahoma, 2002.

———. *Alias Frank Canton*. Norman: University of Oklahoma Press, 1996.

———. *Deadly Dozen: Forgotten Gunfighters of the Old West*. Norman: University of Oklahoma Press, 2003.

———. *George Scarborough: The Life and Death of a Lawman on the Closing Frontier*. Norman: University of Oklahoma Press, 1992.

———. *Broadway Bat: Gunfighter in Gotham, The New York City Years of Bat Masterson*. Honolulu, HI: Talei Publishers, Inc., 2005.

———. *Jim Courtright of Fort Worth: His Life and Legend*. Fort Worth, TX: Texas Christian University Press, 2004.

DeLord, Ronald G., ed. *The Ultimate Sacrifice: Trials and Triumphs of the Texas Peace Officer*. Austin, TX: Police Officers Memorial Fund, 2000.

Devereaux, Jan. *Pistols, Petticoats, and Poker: The Real Lottie Deno, No Lies or Alibis*. Silver City, NM: High-Lonesome Books, 2009.

Dobie, J. Frank. *Cow People*. Boston, MA: Little Brown and Company, 1964.

DuCoin, Candice. *Lawmen on the Texas Frontier: Rangers and Sheriffs*. Round Rock, TX: Riata Books, 2007.

Emmett, Chris. *Fort Union and the Winning of the Southwest*. Norman: University of Oklahoma Press, 1965.

Eppinga, Jane. *Arizona Sheriffs: Badges and Bad Men*. Tucson, AZ: Rio Nuevo Publishers, 2006.

Evans, Cindy and Pauline Hochhalter, eds. *The Genealogy and History of Brown County Sheriffs*. Brownwood, TX: Brown County Historical Society, 2008.

Exley, Jo Ella Powell. *Frontier Blood: The Saga of the Parker Family*. College Station: Texas A&M University Press, 2001.

Farmer, David ed. *History of The Cattlemen of Texas*. Austin, TX: Texas State Historical Association, 1991.

Farmer, Randolph W. *"Curly Bill"—Horse Thief, Cattle Dealer, Murderer, Lawman: 1858-1909*. Tucson, AZ: Westernlore Press, 2012.

Fehrehbach, T. R. *Comanches, The Destruction of a People*. New York: Alfred A. Knopf, 1979.

Fulton Maurice G. (Robert N. Mullin, ed.) *History of the Lincoln County War: A Classic Account of Billy the Kid*. Tucson: University of Arizona Press, 1968.

Galbreath, Lester W. *Fort Griffin and the Clear Fork Country*. Albany, TX: Self published, 1997.

Gibson, A. M. *The Life and Death of Colonel Albert Jennings Fountain*. Norman: University of Oklahoma Press, 1965.

Giese, Dale F. *Forts of New Mexico*. Silver City, NM: Phelps Dodge Corporation, 1995.

Gilbert, Miles with Leo Remiger and Sharon Cunningham. *Encyclopedia of Buffalo Hunters and Skinners*. Union City, TN: Pioneer Press, 2003.

Gillett, James B. *Fugitives From Justice: The Notebook of Texas Ranger James B. Gillette*. New Haven, CT: Yale University Press, 1925.

Glasrud, Bruce A. and Harold J. Weiss, Jr., eds. *Tracking the Texas Rangers: The Nineteenth Century*. Denton: University of North Texas Press, 2012.

Gober, Jim (James R. Gober and Byron Price, eds.). *Cowboy Justice: Tale of a Texas Lawman*. Lubbock: Texas Tech University Press, 1997.

Gournay, Luke. *Texas Boundaries: Evolution of the State's Counties*. College Station: Texas A&M University Press, 1995.

Grady, Patrick. *Out of the Ruins: Pioneer Life in Frontier Phoenix, Arizona Territory, 1867-1881*. Cave Creek, AZ: Arizona Pioneer Press, 2012.

Gregg, Josiah (Max L. Moorhead, ed.). *The Commerce of the Prairies*. Norman: University of Oklahoma Press, 1954.

Gwynne, S. C. *Empire of the Summer Moon: Quanah Parker and the Rise and Fall of the Comanches, the Most Powerful Indian Tribe in American History*. New York: Scribner, 2010.

Haley, J. Evetts. *The XIT Ranch of Texas, And the Early Days of the Llano Estacado.* Norman: University of Oklahoma Press, 1967.

———. *Charles Goodnight: Cowman and Plainsman.* Norman: University of Oklahoma Press, 1977.

———. *George W. Littlefield, Texan.* Norman: University of Oklahoma, 1943.

Hall, Joan Upton. *Just Visitin' Old Texas Jails.* Abilene, TX: State House Press, 2007.

Hardin, John Wesley. *The Life of John Wesley Hardin as Written by Himself.* Norman: University of Oklahoma Press, 1977.

Harris III, Charles H. with Frances E. Harris and Louis R. Sadler. *Texas Ranger Biographies: Those Who Served 1910-1921.* Albuquerque: University of New Mexico Press, 2009.

——— and Louis R. Sadler. *The Texas Rangers and the Mexican Revolution: The Bloodiest Decade, 1910-1920.* Albuquerque: University of New Mexico Press, 2004.

——— and Louis R. Sadler *The Plan De San Diego: Tejano Rebellion, Mexican Intrigue.* Lincoln: University of Nebraska Press, 2013.

Havins, T. R. *Something About Brown: A History of Brown County, Texas.* Brownwood, TX: Banner Printing, 1958.

Hayes, Alden. *A Portal to Paradise.* Tucson: University of Arizona Press, 1999.

Haynes, David. *Catching Shadows: A Directory of 19th Century Texas Photographers.* Austin: Texas State Historical Association, 1993.

Hilliard, George. *A Hundred Years of Horse Tracks: The Story of the Gray Ranch.* Silver City, NM: High-Lonesome Books, 1996.

Hinkle, James F. *Early Days of a Cowboy on the Pecos.* Roswell, NM: First National Bank, n.d.

Holden, Frances Mayhugh *Lambshead Before Interwoven: A Texas Range Chronicle, 1848-1878.* College Station, TX: Texas A&M University Press, 1982.

Hopping, Richard C. *A Sheriff-Ranger in Chuckwagon Days.* New York: Pageant Press, 1952.

Howell, Jr., H. Grady. *For Dixie Land I'll Take My Stand: A Muster Listing of All Known Mississippi Confederate Soldiers, Sailors, and Marines.* Ocean Springs, MS: Chickasaw Bayou Press. 1991.

Howell, Kenneth W. ed. *Still the Arena of Civil War: Violence and Turmoil in Reconstruction Texas, 1865-1874.* Denton: University of North Texas Press, 2012.

Hudson, Weldon I. *Navarro County, Texas Marriage Records, 1847-1881.* Corsicana, TX: Self published, n.d.

Ingmire, Frances T. *Texas Ranger Service Records, 1847-1900.* Vol. 4. St. Louis, MO: Ingmire Publications, 1982.

Isenberg, Andrew C. *Wyatt Earp: A Vigilante Life.* New York: Hill and Wang, 2013.

Ivey, Darren L. *The Texas Rangers: A Registry and History*. Jefferson, NC: McFarland & Company, 2010.

Jacobsen, Joel. *Such Men as Billy the Kid: The Lincoln County War Revisited*. Lincoln: University of Nebraska Press, 1994.

Jacobson, Lucy Miller, and Mildred Bloys Nored. *Jeff Davis County, Texas*. Fort Davis, TX: Fort Davis Historical Society, 1993.

James, Bill C. *Barney Riggs: A West Texas Gunman*. Carrolton, TX: Self published, 1983.

John, Elizabeth A. H. *Storms Brewed in Other Men's Worlds: The Confrontation of Indians, Spanish, and French in the Southwest, 1540-1795*. College Station: Texas A&M University Press, 1975.

Johnson, David. *The Mason County "Hoo Doo" War, 1874-1902*. Denton: University of North Texas Press, 2006.

———. *John Ringo, King of the Cowboys: His Life and Times From the Hoo Doo War to Tombstone*. Rev. 2nd ed. Denton: University of North Texas Press, 2008.

———. *John Ringo*. Stillwater, OK: Barbed Wire Press, 1996.

Juylan, Robert. *The Place Names of New Mexico*. Albuquerque: University of New Mexico Press, 1998.

Kearney, Milo, and Anthony Knopp. *Boom and Bust: The Historical Cycles of Matamoros and Brownsville*. Austin, TX: Eakin Press, 1991.

Keleher, William A. *Violence in Lincoln County, 1869-1881: The New Mexico Feud That Became a Frontier War*. Albuquerque: University of New Mexico Press, 1957.

Kelly, George H. *Legislative History of Arizona, 1864-1912*. Phoenix, AZ: Manufacturing Stationers, Inc., 1926.

Kenner, Charles L. *The Comanchero Frontier: A History of New Mexican-Plains Indian Relations*. Norman: University of Oklahoma Press, 1994.

Leiker, James N. *Racial Borders: Black Soldiers Along the Rio Grande*. College Station: Texas A&M University Press, 2002.

Leonard, Lawrence. *Clayton Family History*. San Angelo, TX: Self published, n.d.

Lindsey, Ellis and Gene Riggs. *Barney K. Riggs: The Yuma and Pecos Avenger*. Xlibris Corp., 2002.

Liu, Joanne S. *Barbed Wire: The Fence That Changed the West*. Missoula, MT: Mountain Press Publishing, 2009.

Long, Martha G. *Llano County Family Album: A History*. Llano, TX: Llano County Historical Society. 1989.

Lord, Walter. *A Time to Stand: A Chronicle of the Valiant Battle at the Alamo*. New York: Bonanza Books, 1987.

Love, Frank. *Mining Camps and Ghost Towns: A History of Mining in Arizona and California Along the Lower Colorado*. Los Angeles, CA: Westernlore Press, 1974.

McAlavy, Don, and Harold Kilmer. *High Plains History of East-Central New Mexico*. Clovis, NM: High-Plains Historical Press, 1980.

McCallum, Henry D., and Frances T. McCallum. *The Wire That Fenced The West*. Norman: University of Oklahoma Press, 1965.

McCoy, Joseph G. (Ralph P. Bieber, ed.) *Historic Sketches of the Cattle Trade of the West and Southwest*. Lincoln: University of Nebraska Press, 1985.

McDonald David R., and Timothy M. Matovina, eds. *Defending Mexican Valor in Texas: José Antonio Navarro's Historical Writings*. Austin, TX: State House Press, 1995.

Maddux, Vernon R. *John Hittson, Cattle King on the Texas and Colorado Frontier*. Niwot, CO: University of Colorado Press, 1994.

Marohn, Richard C. *The Last Gunfighter: John Wesley Hardin*. College Station, TX: Creative Publishing, 1995.

Melchiorre, Erik. *Gold Atlas of Quartzsite, Arizona, Volume I, Northern Dome Rock Mountains*. Qurtasiter, AZ: Roc Doc Publications, 2011.

Metz, Leon Claire. *John Selman: Texas Gunfighter*. New York: Hastings House, 1966.

———. *Encyclopedia of Lawmen, Outlaws, and Gunfighters*. New York, NY: Checkmark Books, 2003.

———. *John Wesley Hardin: Dark Angle of Texas*. El Paso, TX: Mangan Books, 1996.

———. *The Shooters*. El Paso, TX: Mangan Books, 1976.

———. *Turning Points in El Paso, Texas*. El Paso, TX: Mangan Books, 1985.

Michno, Gregory, and Susan Michno. *A Fate Worse Than Death: Indian Captivities in the West, 1830-1835*. Caldwell, ID: Caxton Press, 2007.

———. *The Settlers' War: The Struggle for the Texas Frontier in the 1860s*. Caldwell, ID: Caxton Press. 2011.

Miletich, Leo N. *Dan Stuart's Fistic Carnival*. College Station: Texas A&M University Press, 1994.

Millard, F. S. *A Cowpuncher of the Pecos*. Bandera, TX: J. Marvin Hunter—*Frontier Times*, n.d.

Miller, Darlis A. *Soldiers and Settlers: Military Supply in the Southwest, 1861-1885*. Albuquerque: University of New Mexico Press, 1989.

Miller, Joseph. *Arizona: The Grand Canyon State*. New York: Hastings House. 1966.

Miller, Rick. *Texas Ranger John B. Jones and the Frontier Battalion, 1874-1881*. Denton: University of North Texas Press, 2012.

———. *Sam Bass and Gang*. Austin, TX: State House Press, 1999.

———. *Bounty Hunter*. College Station, TX: Creative Publishing, 1988.

Mishkin, Bernard. *Rank and Warfare Among the Plains Indians*. Lincoln: University of Nebraska Press, 1940.

Moneyhon, Carl H. *Texas After the Civil War: The Struggle of Reconstruction*. College Station: Texas A&M University Press, 2004.

———. *Edmund J. Davis: Civil War General, Republican Leader, Reconstruction Governor*. Fort Worth: Texas Christian University Press, 2010.

Moore, Stephen L. *Savage Frontier: Rangers, Riflemen, and Indian Wars in Texas*. Volume 2. Denton: University of North Texas Press, 2006.

Morgan, Tabitha Landsaw, and Frank Duane Jenkins. *Two Texas Pioneers Called Hugh Martin Childress*. Ballinger, TX: Self published, 1978.

Mosley, May Price (Martha Downer Ellis, ed.) *"Little Texas" Beginnings in Southeastern New Mexico*. Roswell, NM: Hall-Poorbaugh Press, Inc., 1973.

Murbarger, Nell. *Ghosts of the Adobe Walls*. Los Angeles, CA: Westernlore Press, 1964.

Murdock, John R. *Arizona Characters in Silhouette*. Fray Marcos De Niza Edition. Arizona. A self-published reprint by Mrs. John R. Murdock of the serialized articles of 1933-1939.

Navarro County Historical Society (Nancy Marcus Land, ed.) *Navarro County History: Public Buildings, Historical Events, and Early Businesses*. Corsicana, TX: n.d.

Nevin, David. *The Expressmen*. New York: Time-Life Books, Inc., 1974.

Nolan, Frederick. *The Wild West: History, Myth and the Making of America*. Edison, NJ: Chartwell Books, 2000.

———. *Bad Blood: The Life and Times of the Horrell Brothers*. Stillwater, OK: Barbed Wire Press, 1994.

———. *The West of Billy the Kid*. Norman: University of Oklahoma Press, 1998.

Nordyke, Lewis. *John Wesley Hardin, Texas Gunman: The Complete and Fabulous Story of One of the Old West's Most Notorious Outlaws*. Edison, NJ: Castle Books, 1957.

Oden, Alonzo Van (Ann Jensen, ed.) *Texas Ranger's Diary and Scrapbook*. Dallas, TX: Kaleidograph Press, 1936.

O'Neal, Bill. *The Johnson-Sims Feud: Romeo and Juliet, West Texas Style*. Denton: University of North Texas Press, 2010.

Otero, Miguel. *My Life on the Frontier 1864-1882*. New York: The Press of the Pioneers, 1935.

Owen, Gordon R. *The Two Alberts: Fountain and Fall*. Las Cruces, NM: Yucca Tree Press, 1996.

———. *Las Cruces, New Mexico: Multicultural Crossroads*. Las Cruces, NM: Red Sky Publishing, Inc., 1999.

Paine, Albert Bigelow. *Captain Bill McDonald: Texas Ranger: A Story of Frontier Reform*. Austin, TX: State House Press, 1986.

Parsons, Chuck. *Captain John R. Hughes: Lone Star Ranger*. Denton: University of North Texas Press, 2011.

———. *Clay Allison: Portrait of a Shootist*. Seagraves, TX: Pioneer Book Publishers, 1983.

———. *The Sutton-Taylor Feud: The Deadliest Blood Feud in Texas*. Denton: University of North Texas Press, 2009.

——— and Donaly E. Brice. *Texas Ranger N.O. Reynolds: The Intrepid*. Honolulu, HI: Talei Publishers, 2005.

———— and Norman Wayne Brown. *A Lawless Breed: John Wesley Hardin, Texas Reconstruction and Violence in the Wild West.* Denton: Univeristy of North Texas Press, 2013.

Pearce, T. M. *New Mexico Place Names: A Geographical Dictionary.* Albuquerque: University of New Mexico Press, 1965.

Perkins, Clifford Alan. *Border Patrol: With the U.S. Immigration Service on the Mexican Boundary, 1910-1954.* El Paso, TX: Texas Western Press, 1978.

Poldervaart, Arie W. *Black-Robed Justice.* Santa Fe: Historical Society of New Mexico, 1948.

Price, Paxton P. *Pioneers of the Mesilla Valley.* Las Cruces, NM: Yucca Tree Press, 1995.

Preece, Harold. *Lone Star Man: Ira Aten, Last of the Old Time Rangers.* New York: Hastings House, 1960.

Putman, Wyvonne, ed. *Navarro County History.* Quanah, TX: Nortex Press, 1975.

Pyle, Ben, ed. *Trinity County: A Legend of Its Own.* Groveton, TX: Trinity County Historical Commission, 2006.

Rasch, Philip J. (Robert K. DeArment, ed.) *Desperadoes of Arizona Territory.* Laramie, WY: National Association for Outlaw and Lawman History, 1999.

————. *Warriors of Lincoln County.* Laramie, WY: National Association For Outlaw and Lawman History, 1998.

Rathbun, Daniel C. B., and David V. Alexander. *New Mexico Frontier Military Place Names.* Las Cruces, NM: Yucca Tree Publishing, 2003.

Raynor, Ted. *Old Timers Talk in Southwestern New Mexico.* El Paso, TX: Texas Western Press, 1960.

Reynolds, Bill. *Trouble in New Mexico: The Outlaws, Gunmen, Desperados, Murderers, and Lawmen for Fifty Turbulent Years.* 3 vols. Bakersfield, CA: Self published, n.d.

Richardson, Rupert Norval. *Comanche Barrier to South Plains Settlement.* Austin, TX: Eakin Press, 1996.

Robinson III, Charles. *The Frontier World of Fort Griffin: The Life and Death of a Western Town.* Spokane, WA: Arthur H. Clark Company, 1992.

————. *The Men Who Wear the Star: The Story of the Texas Rangers.* New York: Random House, 2000.

Rocksprings Women's Club Historical Committee. *A History of Edwards County.* San Angelo, TX: Anchor Publishing, Company, 1984.

Roe, Frank Gilbert. *The Indian and the Horse.* Norman: University of Oklahoma Press, 1955.

Rose, Peter R. *The Reckoning: The Triumph of Order on the Texas Outlaw Frontier.* Lubbock: Texas Tech University Press, 2012.

Rynning, Thomas. *Gun Notches: A Saga of a Frontier Lawman Captain Thomas H. Rynning as Told to Al Cohn and Joe Chisholm.* San Diego, CA: Frontier Heritage Press, 1971.

Sáenz, Andrés (Andrés Tijerina, ed.) *Early Tejano Ranching*. College Station: Texas A&M University Press, 1999.

Secoy, Frank Raymond. *Changing Military Patterns of the Great Plains Indians*. Lincoln: University of Nebraska, 1953.

Sherman, James E., and Barbara H. Sherman. *Ghost Towns of Arizona*. Norman: University of Oklahoma Press, 1969.

Shillingberg, William B. *Tombstone, A.T., A History of Early Mining, Milling, and Mayhem*. Spokane, WA: Arthur H. Clark Company, 1999.

Sinise, Jerry. *George Washington Arrington: Civil War Spy, Texas Ranger, Sheriff and Rancher*. Burnet, TX: Eakin Press, 1979.

Sitton, Thad. *The Texas Sheriff: Lord of the County Line*. Norman: University of Oklahoma Press, 2000.

Skiles, Jack. *Judge Roy Bean Country*. Lubbock: Texas Tech University Press, 1996.

Smallwood, James M. *The Feud That Wasn't: The Taylor Ring, Bill Sutton, John Wesley Hardin, and Violence in Texas*. College Station: Texas A&M University Press, 2008.

Smith, David Paul. *Frontier Defense in the Civil War: Texas' Rangers and Rebels*. College Station: Texas A&M University Press, 1992.

Smith, Tevis Clyde. *Frontier's Generation: The Pioneer History of Brown County, With Sidelights on the Surrounding Territory*. Brownwood, TX: Self published, 1980.

Sonnichsen, C. L. *I'll Die Before I'll Run: The Story of the Great Feuds of Texas*. New York: The Devin-Adair Company, 1962.

———. *The Story of Judge Roy Bean: Law West of the Pecos*. New York: The Devin-Adair Company, 1958.

———. *Tularosa: Last of the Frontier West*. New York, NY: The Devin-Adair Company, 1960.

——— *Pass of the North: Four Centuries on the Rio Grande*. Vol. I. El Paso, TX: Texas Western Press, 1968.

Spellman, Paul N. *Captain John Rogers: Texas Ranger*. Denton: University of North Texas Press, 2003.

———. *Captain J. A. Brooks: Texas Ranger*. Denton: University of North Texas Press, 2007.

Spence, Ruth Griffin. *The Nice and Nasty in Brown County: A Collection of Stories*. Brownwood, TX: Banner Printing Company, 1988.

Stamps, Roy, and Jo Ann Stamps. *The Letters of John Wesley Hardin*. Austin, TX: Eakin Press, 2001.

Stanley, F. *The Milnesand New Mexico Story*. Pep, TX: Self published, 1968.

———. *The Rogers New Mexico Story*. Pep, TX: Self published, 1967.

———. *The Lake Valley Story*. Pep, TX: Self published, 1964.

———. *The Loma Parda Story*. Nazareth, TX: Self published, 1969.

———. *The Liberty Story*. Nazareth, TX: Self published, 1972.

Stephens, Robert W. *Texas Ranger Sketches*. Dallas, TX: Self published, 1972.

———. *Bullets and Buckshot in Texas*. Dallas, TX: Self published, 2002.

———. *Walter Durbin: Texas Ranger and Sheriff.* Dallas, TX: Self published, 1970.

———. *Mannen Clements—Texas Gunfighter.* Dallas, TX. Self published, 1996.

Stokes, Katy. *Paisano: The Story of a Cowboy and Camp Meeting.* Waco, TX: Texian Press, 1980.

Stratton, Porter A. *The Territorial Press of New Mexico, 1834-1912.* Albuquerque: University of New Mexico Press, 1969.

Summerhayes, Martha. *Vanished Arizona: Recollections of My Army Life.* Philadelphia: J. B. Lippincott Co., 1908.

Sweeney, Edwin R. *From Cochise to Geronimo: The Chiricahua Apaches, 1874-1886.* Norman: University of Oklahoma, 2010.

Tanner, Karen Holliday, and John D. Tanner, Jr. *Directory of Inmates: New Mexico Territorial Penitentiary, 1884-1912.* Fallbrook, CA: Runnin' Iron Press, 2006.

———. *Last of the Old-Time Outlaws: The George West Musgrave Story.* Norman: University of Oklahoma Press, 2002.

———. *The Bronco Bill Gang.* Norman: Univeristy of Oklahoma Press, 2011,

Tarpley, Fred. *1001 Texas Place Names.* Austin: University of Texas Press, 1980.

Tefertiller, Casey. *Wyatt Earp: The Life Behind the Legend.* New York: John Wiley & Sons, 1997.

Tise, Sammy. *Texas County Sheriffs.* Hallettsville, TX: Tise Genealogical Research, 1989.

Theobald, John, and Lillian Theobald. *Wells Fargo in Arizona Territory.* Tempe: Arizona Historical Foundation, 1978.

Thrapp, Dan L. *Encyclopedia of Frontier Biography.* 3 vols. Lincoln: University of Nebraska Press, 1988.

———. *The Conquest of Apacheria.* Norman: University of Oklahoma Press, 1967.

Towsend, Allan R. *The Meanest Kid in Town: Memories of Llano, Texas 1890-1904.* Kerrville, TX: Llano County Historical Society, 1968.

Trafzer, Clifford E. *The Yuma Crossing: A Short History.* Yuma, AZ: Yuma County Historical Society, 1974.

Trimble, Marshall. *Arizona: A Panoramic Hisotry of a Frontier State.* New York: Doubleday & Co., 1977.

Ungnade, Herbert E. *Guide to the New Mexico Mountains.* Albuquerque: University of New Mexico Press, 1995.

Urbanek, Mae. *Wyoming Place Names.* Missoula, MT: Mountain Press Publishing Company, 1988.

Utley, Robert M. *Lone Star Justice: The First Century of the Texas Rangers.* New York: Oxford University Press, 2002.

Varney, Philip. *Arizona Ghost Towns and Mining Camps.* Phoenix: Arizona Highways Books, 1995.

Wagoner, Jay J. *Early Arizona: Prehistory to Civil War.* Tucson: University of Arizona Press, 1975.

Walker, Ed, with Helen Wilkerson and Marilyn Read. *Guilty . . . . But Not as Charged.* Denton, TX: Zone Press, 2009.

Walker, Mary Jo. *The F. Stanley Story.* Santa Fe, NM: Co-publication of New Mexico Book League, Albuquerque, and The Lightning Tree—Jene Lyon, Publisher, 1985.

Watts, Peter. *A Dictionary of the Old West.* New York, NY: Promontory Press, 1977.

Weaver, John D. *The Brownsville Raid: The Story of America's "Black Dreyfus Affair."* New York: W.W. Norton & Company, Inc., 1970.

Weedon, Pattie Lee Cross. *Early Communities of Lake Brownwood.* Brownwood, TX: Self published, 1980.

Weiner, Melissa Ruffner. *Prescott Yesteryears: Life in Arizona's First Territorial Capital.* Prescott, AZ: Primrose Press, 1976.

Weiss Jr., Harold J. *Yours to Command: The Life and Legend of Texas Ranger Captain Bill McDonald.* Denton: University of North Texas Press, 2009.

White, James C. *The Promised Land: A History of Brown County, Texas.* Brownwood, TX: Brownwood Banner, 1941.

White, Owen P. *Lead and Likker.* New York: Minton, Balch & Company, 1932.

Wilkins, Frederick. *The Law Comes to Texas: The Texas Rangers, 1870-1901.* Austin, TX: State House Press, 1999.

Williams, Clayton W., ed. *Texas' Last Frontier: Fort Stockton and the Trans Pecos, 1861-1895.* College Station: Texas A&M University Press, 1982.

Williams, J. W. *The Big Ranch Country.* Austin, TX: Nortex Press, 1971.

Willson, Roscoe G. *Pioneer Cattlemen of Arizona.* Phoenix, AZ: The Valley National Bank, 1951.

———. *Pioneer and Well Known Cattlemen of Arizona.* Phoenix, AZ: The Valley National Bank, 1956.

Wilson, John H. as told to Sue Wilson. *Land of the High Sky: Stories Along the Rio Pecos.* El Paso, TX: Self published, 2006.

Wilson, John P. *Merchants, Guns and Money: The Story of Lincoln County and Its Wars.* Santa Fe: Museum of New Mexico, 1987.

Wilson, R. L. *Colt—An American Legend.* New York: Abbeville Publishing Group, 1985.

Worcester, Don. *The Apaches: Eagles of the Southwest.* Norman: University of Oklahoma Press, 1979.

Yelderman, Pauline. *The Jay Birds of Fort Bend County.* Waco, TX: Texian Press, 1979.

Young, Elliott. *Catarino Garza's Revolution on the Texas-Mexico Border.* Durham, NC: Duke University Press, 2004.

Zarbin, Earl. *Taming the Salt.* Phoenix, AZ: Communications and Public Affairs, The Salt River Project, n.d.

Zesch, Scott. *The Captured.* New York: St. Martin's Press, 2004.

Periodicals

Aleshire, Peter. "Tumultuous Chiricahuas." *Arizona Highways*. November 2002.

Alexander, Bob. "Square Deals and Real McCoys." *Wild West History Association Journal*. June 2011.

———. "Tucker X Texas = Trouble." *Wild West History Association Journal*. June 2008.

———. "Guns, Girls and Gamblers: Silver City's Wilder Side." *Western Outlaw-Lawman History Association Journal*. Winter 2005.

Aranda, Daniel D. "Josanie—Apache Warrior." *True West*. May-June 1976.

———. "Apache Depredations in Doña Ana County: An Incident in Victorio's War." *Southern New Mexico Historical Review*. January 1996.

Baird, P. C. "The Fight at Green Lake Waterhole." *Frontier Times*. March 1926.

Ball, Larry D. "Militia Posses: The Territorial Militia In Civil Law Enforcement in New Mexico Territory, 1877-1883." *New Mexico Historical Review*. January 1980.

Beeler, Sylvia. "Reminiscences of Early Day Pioneers." *The Snake River Press*. October 16, 1980.

Bell, Bob Boze. "Left for Dead: Yginio Salazar vs. Peppin's Thugs." *True West*. July 2013.

———. "Ambush at Guadalupe Pass." *True West*. March 2004.

Boardman, Mark. "Ira Nails the McClellands." *True West*. July 2009.

Brand, Peter. "Sherman W. McMaster(s), The El Paso Salt War, Texas Rangers and Tombstone." *Western Outlaw-Lawman History Association Journal*. Winter 1999.

Brown, Larry K. "The Art of Murder—Robert D. Meldrum: Lawman, Killer, Artist." *Casper Star-Tribune*. March 30, 1997.

Carson, John. "Wyoming's Mysterious Badman." *Frontier Times*. Winter 1961.

———. "The Middle Years of Bob Meldrum." *Old West*. Spring 1970.

Casebier, Dennis. "Camp Beale's Springs: Sojourn at the Colorado River Indian Reserve." *Journal of America's Military Past*. Spring 1997.

Cavaliere, Bill. "The Mountain Ranges of Hidalgo County." *Bootheel Magazine*. Fall 2005.

———. "The Settlers of Skeleton Canyon." *Bootheel Magazine*. July 2005.

Cline, Ellen. "The Story of a Cowboy." *Cochise County Historical Journal*. Fall/Winter 1997.

Cool, Paul. "Salt War Sheriff: Charles Kerber." *National Outlaw/Lawman History Association Quarterly*. January-March 2003.

———. "Bob Martin: Rustler in Paradise." *Western Outlaw-Lawman History Association Journal*. Winter. 2003.

———. "El Paso's First Real Lawman: Texas Ranger Mark Luidwick." *National Outlaw/Lawman History Association Quarterly*. July-September 2001.

Crimmins, M. L. "The Salt War of San Elizario, Texas." *Frontier Times*. April 1931.

Cunningham, Eugene. "Salt." *Frontier Times*. January 1930.

Cunningham, Sharon. "The Allison Clan—A Visit." *Western Outlaw-Lawman History Association Journal*. Winter 2003.

———. "Clay Allison: 'Good-Natured Holy Terror.'" *Wild West*. October 2013.

Day, James M. "El Paso's Texas Rangers." *Password*. Winter 1979.

Devereaux, Jan and Bob Alexander. "Trumpeting Elephants and Kicking Asses: Republicans vs. Democrats, New Mexico Style." *True West*. January/February 2010.

Fourr, William, as told to Mrs. George F. Kitt, "Reminiscences of William Fourr." *Arizona Historical Review*. October 1935.

Freeman, E. E. "A Mania for Killing." *Wild West History Association Journal*. October 2010.

French, Doris, ed. "Amos Chenowth." *Arizona National Ranch Histories of Living Pioneer Stockmen*. Volume 18. 1998.

Gard, Wayne. "The Fence Cutters." *The Southwestern Historical Quarterly*. July 1947.

Genung, Charles Baldwin, Kenneth M. Calhoun, ed. "Yavapai Country Memories, 1863-1894." *The Smoke Signal*. Spring/Fall. 1982.

Gerlach, Allen. "Conditions Along The Border—1915 The Plan De San Diego." *New Mexico Historical Review*. 43: 3. 1968.

Goldberg, Isaac. "As Told By The Pioneers." *Arizona Historical Review*. April 1935.

Haley, J. Evetts. "The Comanchero Trade." *The Southwestern Historical Quarterly*. January 1935.

Havin, R. R. "Activities of Company E, Frontier Battalion, Texas Rangers, 1874-1880." *West Texas Historical Association Yearbook*. 1935.

Holt, R. D. "The Introduction of Barbed Wire into Texas and the Fence Cutting War." *West Texas Historical Association Yearbook*. 1930.

Hunter, J. Marvin. "Callahan County Pioneer Passes Away." *Frontier Times*. July 1947.

———. "Brief History of the Early Days in Mason County." *Frontier Times*. February 1929.

———. "P. C. Baird, the Old Sleuth." *Frontier Times*. March 1928.

———. "P. C. Baird is Dead." *Frontier Times*. April 1928.

Jobes, Harold D. "Fence Cutting and a Ranger Shootout at Green Lake." *Wild West History Association Journal*. October 2009.

Johnson, M. L. "Trailing West." *Frontier Times*. January 1969.

———. "Battle With Indians in Runnels County." *Frontier Times*. January 1946.

Jordon, Philip D. "The Town Marshal: Local Arm of the Law." *Arizona and the West*. 16.

Kenner, Charles. "A Texas Rancher in Colorado: The Last Years of John Hittson." *West Texas Historical Association Yearbook*. October 1966.

————. "The Great New Mexico Cattle Raid—1872." *New Mexico Historical Review*. October 1962.

————. "Guardians in Blue: The Untied States Cavalry and the Growth of the Texas Range Cattle Industry." *Journal of the West*. 1995.

McMechen, Edgar C. "John Hittson: Cattle King." *The Colorado Magazine*. September 1934.

Martin, Andrew. "I Knew Bob Meldrum." *Old West*. Spring 1970.

Muir, Emma M. "The First Militia." *New Mexico Magazine*. October 1952.

Mullin, Robert N. "Here Lies John Kinney." *The Journal of Arizona History*. Autumn. 1973.

Nelson, Kitty Jo Parker. "Prescott: Sketch Of A Frontier Capital, 1863-1900." *Arizoniana: The Journal of Arizona History*. Winter 1963.

Nelson, Morgan. "First Among the First—James Patterson, 1833-1892." *Wild West History Association Journal*. October 2009.

Nolan, Fredrick. "'Boss Rustler' The Life and Crimes of John Kinney." Part I. *True West*. September 1996.

————. "The Life and Crimes of John Kinney." Part II. *True West*. October 1996.

————. "A Sidelight on the Tunstall Murder." *New Mexico Historical Review*. July 1956.

Peters, J. S. "Riders for the Grant." *Western Outlaw-Lawman Association Journal*. Summer 2002.

Polk, Cal, (Chuck Parsons, ed.) "Life of Cal Polk." *Plum Creek Almanac*. Fall 2011.

Rasch, Philip J. "The Hittson Raid." *New York Posse of the Westerners Brand Book*. 1963.

————. "The Rustler War." *New Mexico Historical Review*. October 1964.

————. "John Kinney 'King of the Rustlers' Was For Law Too." *The Southwesterner*. October 1962.

————. "John Kinney: King of the Rustlers." *The English Westerners' Brand Book*. October 1961.

Rister, Carl Coke. "Harmful Practices of Indian Traders of the Southwest." *New Mexico Historical Review*. July 1931.

Scott, Kim Allen. "The Most Contemptible Character I Ever Saw." *True West*. August 2013.

Sinclair, John. "The Sugarloaf Mountains: The Magical Peloncillos." *New Mexico Magazine*. July 1979.

Smith, Glen. "Some Early Runnels County History, 1858-1885." *West Texas Historical Association Yearbook*. 1966.

Spence, Clark C. "The Livery Stable in the American West." *Montana Magazine*. Spring 1986.

Stanley, Samuel. "The Fence Cutter's War." *Real West*. August 1985.

Sullivan, Jerry. "Devils in Sombreros—The Comancheros." *True West*. October 1970.

Turner, Alton. "New Mexico Shoot-Out." *Frontier Times*. March 1969.

Utley, Robert M. "Billy the Kid and the Lincoln County War." *New Mexico Historical Review*. April 1986.

Wallace, Andrew. "Fort Whipple in the Days of the Empire. *The Smoke Signal*. Fall 1972.

Wallace, Ernest. "Colonel Ranald S. Mackenzie's Expedition of 1872 Across the South Plains." *The West Texas Historical Association Yearbook*. October 1965.

Wallis, George. "Cattle Kings." *New Mexico Magazine*. June 1936.

Whitehead, Ruth. "The Bloody Fence Cutting War." *The West*. December 1969.

Williams, Clayton W. "That Topographical Ghost—Horsehead Crossing." *Old West*. Winter 1974.

Yena, Donald M. "Texas Authority in Metal: Badges, History and Related Artifacts." *The Texas Gun Collector*. Spring 2008.

Zunker, Naomi M. "Maricopa: New County in Arizona Territory." *The Smoke Signal*. Fall 1992.

Newspapers

Laredo Times
Galveston Daily News
El Paso Times
El Paso Lone Star
Clarendon News
Colorado Chieftain
Rocky Mountain News
Santa Fe New Mexican
New York Evening Post
The Bryan Eagle
West Kerr Current
Cleburne Chronicle
Corsicana Democrat and Truth
Houston Post
Dallas Morning News
The Examiner
San Antonio Daily Herald
San Antonio Daily Express
Luling Signal
Austin Daily State Journal
Indian Journal
Runnels County Record
Saratoga Semi-Weekly Republican
Rawlins Semi-Weekly Republican
The Snake River Press
Casper Star-Tribune

Ballinger Banner-Leader
San Saba News
Fort Worth Record
Forth Worth Daily Democrat
Mason County News
Palestine Daily Herald
Shiner Gazette
Jefferson Jimplecute
Fort Worth Star Telegram
Bisbee Daily Review
Bellville News Democrat
Mesilla Valley Independent
Grant County Herald
Southwest Sentinel
Silver City Enterprise
Silver City Independent
Salt River Herald
Arizona Weekly Miner
Arizona Republican
San Bernardino Guardian
San Diego Union
Corsicana Observer
Rio Grande Republican

Index